The Literary Atlas ^{of} Cairo

The
Literary
Atlas
of Cairo

One Hundred Years on the Streets of the City

Edited and Introduced by
Samia Mehrez

The American University in Cairo Press
Cairo New York

First published in 2010 by
The American University in Cairo Press
113 Sharia Kasr el Aini, Cairo, Egypt
420 Fifth Avenue, New York, NY 10018
www.aucpress.com

Dar el Kutub No. 13994/09
ISBN 978 977 416 347 0

Dar el Kutub Cataloging-in-Publication Data

Mehrez, Samia
        The Literary Atlas of Cairo: One Hundred Years on the Streets of the City / Samia
    Mehrez.—Cairo: The American University in Cairo Press, 2010
        p. cm.
        ISBN 977 416 347 0
        1. Egypt—Description and travel.   2. Cairo (Egypt)—Description and travel.
        916.261

1 2 3 4 5 6   15 14 13 12 11 10

Designed by Fatiha Bouzidi
Printed in Egypt

For Cairo and her authors

Contents

Acknowledgments

When I first started the research on this project, I never imagined I would find such a staggering amount of literary material on Cairo which, even after considerable editing, still dictated the decision to publish two volumes instead of one: *The Literary Atlas of Cairo* and *The Literary Life of Cairo* (forthcoming). I am therefore first and foremost utterly grateful to Cairo's authors who, in this context, are *the authors of Cairo*, the city that readers will encounter and experience through this collective atlas. Without these authors' inspiring works and their willingness to be part of this literary map, *The Literary Atlas of Cairo* would have simply not existed.

To complete this project within a year as I had envisioned, I requested and was granted leave without pay from the American University in Cairo. I have been supported throughout the year by several grants that allowed me to dedicate all my time to researching, compiling, translating, editing, and producing this work. I am indebted to the Ford Foundation Egypt and the Netherlands Cultural Fund in Egypt for their instant interest in and support of *The Literary Atlas of Cairo* proposal. I am equally grateful to the Arab Fund for Arts and Culture for their generous funding of this project. Mark Linz, Director of the AUC Press, and Ibrahim El Moallem, President of Dar al-Shorouk, both made an immediate commitment to support and publish this work based on my initial proposal. I wish to thank them both for their insight and confidence and sincerely hope that the end product lives up to their expectations.

My concentrated and rather lonely year of work on this project could have only been sustained through endless conversations with friends and colleagues who listened tirelessly over and over again to how the manuscript was coming along: its structure, its contents, its stories, and its problems. I want to thank Huda Lutfi, Moustapha Hasnaoui, Barbara Harlow, Joseph Massad,

Nashwa Azhari, Mona Prince, Randa Shaath, Sherif Boraie, Iman Ghazallah, Ragui Assaad, Heba El-Kholy, Mona Abaza, Kamal Fahmy, and Neil Hewison for their kind willingness to read, make comments, and provide suggestions of new texts to be included in the *Atlas*. Their enthusiasm and encouragement have meant the world to me as I raced through to finish what an internal university grant committee had deemed an impossible task to complete within the proposed timeframe.

Artist and photographer Amr Khadr has been my main interlocutor with regard to the details of the *Atlas*. He is also my partner in the *Literary Cairo Installation*, a multimedia exhibition that will be based primarily on the literary material amassed in this *Atlas*. Amr's unique visual work on Cairo and his profound interest in literary representations of the city have allowed us to map out a new project that would integrate the literary and the visual in what we believe may be an unprecedented endeavor. I am grateful to him for sharing his visual experiences of Cairo and for providing me with an extensive repertoire of images from which to select an appropriate cover for this first volume.

The challenge to finish this ever-expanding project could not have been met without the enthusiasm, hard work, and motivating feedback throughout from my research assistant Amira Abu Taleb, who made sure at every juncture that I would be on schedule, working ahead of me, and spurring me on to produce more work for her to do on time. As always, her meticulousness, intelligence, and sharp common sense were indispensable for producing this now two-volume work.

I also wish to thank AUC librarians Jayme Spencer and Ola Seif and members of their respective staff who graciously allowed me to use the Main Library and the Rare Books Library when they were practically closed and preparing to move both libraries to the AUC New Cairo campus.

Mr. Samir Khalil was single-handedly responsible for typing both the English and Arabic manuscripts. I am thankful for his patience, thoroughness, and dedication even as the excerpts kept increasing in number beyond his initial expectations of the workload and the time frame required for producing it.

The AUC Press editorial staff has been tremendously supportive. I particularly wish to thank Merryn Johnson and Noha Mohammed, who have been most helpful at various stages of the production of the manuscript. I initially feared and had been warned that the process of seeking permissions from authors, translators, and publishers across the globe would be an absolute nightmare. Indeed, this proved to be the most time-consuming and mind-boggling aspect of the entire project. I am indebted to all the authors, publishers, and translators who granted me permission to reprint material that is included in this volume. Without their cooperation, promptness, and enthusiasm, this work could have never seen the light.

Finally, I want to thank my son, Nadim, whose critical and aesthetic sense was instrumental in helping me rethink the cover for this volume that now throbs with the energy of the Cairo that he so much loves.

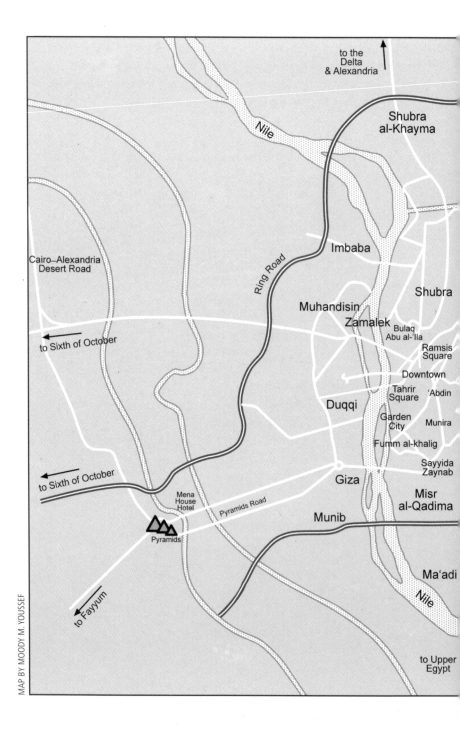

MAP BY MOODY M. YOUSSEF

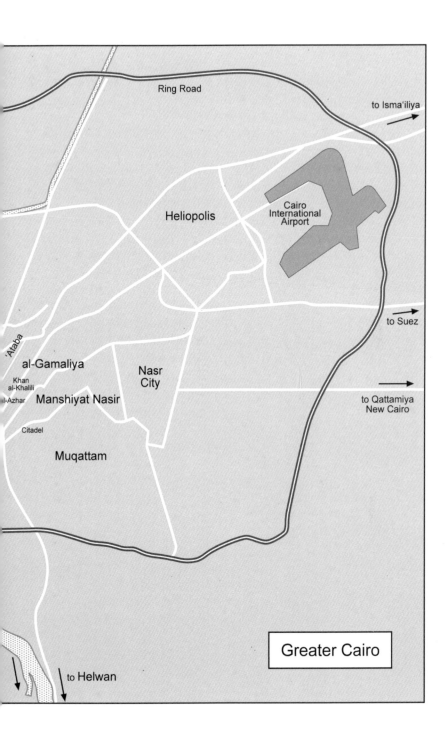

Ring Road

to Isma'iliya

Heliopolis

Cairo
International
Airport

to Suez

'Ataba

al-Gamaliya

Khan
al-Khalili

l-Azhar

Manshiyat Nasir

Nasr
City

to Qattamiya
New Cairo

Citadel

Muqattam

Greater Cairo

to Helwan

Introduction
Cairo, Mother of Cities

Many reasons have come together to motivate *The Literary Atlas of Cairo*, some professional and others personal. Both, however, are thoroughly and intrinsically linked and interconnected since they were being simultaneously shaped during a very particular moment in time. Perhaps the first professional moment in the development of this project was in May 2005, when I was invited by my colleagues Iman Hamdi and Martina Rieker to present a paper at the Cairo Papers Symposium at the American University in Cairo (AUC) titled "Transformations in Middle Eastern Landscapes: From Modernism to Neo-liberalism." I gladly accepted the invitation because, first, as a scholar of Arabic literature, a field routinely marginalized by the dominant social sciences, I was happy to see that the space for interdisciplinary conversation was both possible and welcome. Second, again as a scholar of Arabic literature, I was convinced that many of the issues raised in the social sciences and in urban studies are in fact represented in literary texts that have provided some of the most eloquent and perceptive readings of urban and social reality and its transformation in a form, language, metaphor, and idiom that are part and parcel of such transformations.

The paper I presented at the symposium was entitled "From the *Hara* to the '*Imara*: Emerging Urban Metaphors in the Literary Production on Contemporary Cairo."[1] This paper eventually became the cornerstone for an entire seminar on "Cairo in the Modern Literary Imaginary" that I taught twice at AUC, once in Arabic in 2006 and then again in English in 2007. Both seminars provided magnificent rehearsal grounds for *The Literary Atlas of Cairo* and I remain indebted to the group of students who attended them for their sharp discussions, valuable contributions, and excellent papers, one of which earned a distinguished university award.[2]

But, as I attempt to reconstruct the beginnings of this project through the new and inspiring professional directions it has brought me, I sense that it was equally motivated by a more deep-seated personal anxiety, for it coincided to a great extent with the ever-approaching date of the relocation of the American University in Cairo campus from Cairo's throbbing downtown Tahrir area to its present location in New Cairo. The old campus witnessed my student years at AUC as well as eighteen years of my professional life in the institution.[3] This imminent displacement from the city of my childhood, school years, social life, and professional growth—not to mention emotional attachments and a lifetime of memories—all brought forth a surge of sudden desire to try to capture this ever-expanding space all at once before I was uprooted from it, so to speak. My anxiety was driven home when, as I started working on the *Atlas* immediately after AUC had relocated to New Cairo, I received an e-mail from Faculty Services at the university announcing, for the first time ever, a walking tour of downtown Cairo for members of the AUC community. I must admit that I was horrified at the implications of the idea, since it suddenly transformed bustling downtown Cairo into a museum, a thing of the past, which we could now watch as spectacle when, for most of the twentieth century, AUC had been part of the very making of its modern history. Did these personal anxieties prompt the professional directions that were beginning to take shape and the need I felt for mapping Cairo from the sources I knew best? Perhaps, but the most important thing is that these elements combined lie at the very heart of *The Literary Atlas of Cairo*.

Franco Moretti's *Atlas of the European Novel: 1800–1900* has been a great source of inspiration for *The Literary Atlas of Cairo* as well as my teaching on Cairo in general, since it articulated in very concrete terms precisely what I wanted to do:

> Geography is not an inert container, is not a box where cultural history "happens," but an active force, that pervades the literary field and shapes its depth. Making the connection between geography and literature explicit, then mapping it: because a map is precisely that, a connection made visible— will allow us to see some significant relationships that have so far escaped us.[4]

Despite the differences between Moretti's project and my own, it remains self-evident, to me at least, that we share the conviction that literary geography, as he put it, can "change the way we read novels," and, I would add, can equally change the way we read the space in which these novels came into being. Even though Moretti's *Atlas* encompasses both space in literature (Jane

Austin's England, Balzac's Paris, Dickens's London, and so on) and literature in space (libraries, distribution of literature across space, among others), while *The Literary Atlas of Cairo* confines itself to space in literature only, my project, like his, understands literary geography as a means to pose new questions and look for new answers. Indeed, literary geography provides analytical tools that dissect the text in an unusual way and emphasizes, as Moretti put it, "the only real issue of literary history: society, rhetoric, and their interaction."[5]

The relationship between literature and geography, writers and the space they and their narratives occupy, has been succinctly articulated by Gamal al-Ghitani, one of Egypt's major writers and literary architects of the city, in the following terms:

> Fundamentally, writing is linked to a specific place, the history and past of this place, and the spirit of this place. To be interested in time, and the passage of time, is to be interested in a specific place as well. For space and time are indissolubly tied. Place contains time. That is why remembering a certain event, at a certain date, cannot but evoke the place, the space in which we were at that given moment. . . .
>
> It is for this reason that the relationship between a writer and a place is very important, because place implies time, history, society and human relations.[6]

Even though representations of "real" space in literature are fundamentally an imaginative construction, they will necessarily provide, through narrativity and temporality, a map of real material geopolitics and histories as well as a complex network of human relations across literary topography. In "Semiology and the Urban," Roland Barthes described the city as "a discourse and this discourse is truly language: the city speaks to its inhabitants, we speak our city, the city where we are, simply by living in it, by wandering through it, by looking at it."[7] Not only is the city a "discourse" and a "language," but it also "speaks to its inhabitants"; not only is the city constituted of signs that need to be deciphered and read, but those very signs signify differently for the city dwellers who behold and decode them. Indeed, urban semioticians and planners have moved away from trying to identify universal features of the urban experience and have placed the emphasis on the readers of the city, whose cultural and social positions will determine the very visibility and legibility of the cityscape.[8] The city is not simply a physical presence that writers reproduce; rather, the city is a construct that continues to be reinvented by its inhabitants—in this case, its writers—each according to his or her experiential eye and personal encounter with it. At this level, the city emerges as an actor with real agency that embodies and structures social power as well as political, economic, and symbolic processes. As the writers come to represent the city in literature, they, in turn, become architects of its history whose literary works reconstruct and re-map the city. Even as writers provide us with the familiar landmarks of the city, ultimately these same physical landmarks take on or lose signification for each one of them, depending on the time in which the place and space are written.

Given the dominance of the realist tradition in Arabic literature in general and Egyptian literature in particular, it is no surprise that Cairo, whether it is the historic city or the modern metropolis, should be the main "real" and metaphorical space for much of the literary production during the twentieth century. Urban space, for the writers of the city, has been a major architect of its social, economic, and political fabric. In this literary production, Cairo becomes a protagonist whose existence is indispensable for the existence of the narratives themselves, not to speak of our own reading and decoding of these works. Hence, the city becomes a text that is constantly rewritten, a space that is continuously reconstructed/deconstructed through its ever-shifting, ever-changing signs.

During the twentieth century, specifically since the 1960s, Cairo witnessed an accelerated pattern of physical expansion beyond its historic Islamic neighborhoods and its modern colonial ones. As the renowned historian of the city of Cairo, André Raymond, has noted:

> Cairo's impetuous growth in the past half-century complicates any image one might try to form of it. The traditional city of the late Ottoman era and the two side-by-side cities of the colonial era have been absorbed into a whole so diverse as to prevent any simple conclusions. The faces of the city blur; its centers are many and mobile. But this "fragmented" Cairo can still be reconstituted into more or less coherent wholes, each clearly revealing deep social differences.[9]

Many factors have converged to produce this image of "fragmented" Cairo: the socialist, centrally planned, and public-sector-dominated state economy of the Nasser regime of the 1960s was abandoned for an 'open door' one during the Sadat period (1971–81) that encouraged the private sector and Arab and international investment. This, together with rural–urban migration, led to the appearance of informal and illegal housing during the 1980s, as well as the "ruralization of urban areas," deterioration in living conditions and infrastructure in the old city, and class inequalities and urban problems both social and economic.[10] The state's laissez-faire policies, not only within the economic field, but also in the field of urban planning, have resulted in the uncomfortable coexistence of skyscrapers and multimillion-dollar commercial centers side by side with shantytowns and informal settlements. The mega-city of Cairo has also experienced new patterns of geographic, economic, and social mobility: the influx of an immigrant rural population, the rise of professional and labor migration to the Gulf, new internal migration to factories in satellite cities or coastal tourist developments, the emergence of new patterns of investment and consumption, the disintegration of the "traditional" social fabric, and the emergence of new urban affiliations and solidarities.

The Literary Atlas of Cairo constitutes an unprecedented literary intervention that tries to "re-construct" Cairo from what André Raymond has called its fragments and its many mobile centers. Through a careful selection and juxtaposition of reconstructions and representations of the city of Cairo in Arab literary works throughout the twentieth century, The Literary Atlas of Cairo provides a literary topography of the sociocultural, political, and urban history of the city by bringing together some one hundred works by Egyptian and Arab writers who represent several generations of men and women, Muslims, Copts, and Jews, citizens and lovers of the globalized metropolis, writing in Arabic, English, or French about the city of Cairo. Not travelers, but writers who are city dwellers and residents of Cairo, whose reconstructions of its literary geography and experience with its urban topography can indeed render the cityscape legible, whether that representation is in Arabic, English, or French. As these writers undertake to represent the city in literature, their representations map out many of the changes in the "fragmented" city's geopolitics and its urban fabric, while tracing spatial and social forms of polarization as well as new patterns of inclusion and exclusion within the borderless boundaries of the expanding mega-city. As such, The Literary Atlas of Cairo complements and dialogues with many other existing publications about the city of Cairo in both the humanities and the social sciences, specifically in the fields of history, sociology, anthropology, architecture, urban planning, migration studies, cultural studies, gender studies, and development studies, all of which have explored similar issues, problems, contradictions, and challenges in Cairenes' lives.

Through its thematic chapter organization, The Literary Atlas of Cairo traces, with equal depth, both the developments that have taken place over an entire century in modes of literary production and the unique historical cross-section of the actors within the Cairene literary field. From the premodern prose style that imitates the classical form and structure of the *maqama*,[11] to the elevated neoclassical style of the *début du siècle*, to experimentations with a third language that combines written and spoken Arabic at levels more attuned to the needs of modern narrative texts, all the way to creative uses of the vernacular and the everyday lingo of the street—all these forms of fictional expression, as well as those developed by Anglophone and Francophone Arab writers, are an integral part of the city's literary geography. Likewise, throughout the *Atlas* readers will experience the extent to which class, gender, race, and ethnic background condition and shape these literary reconstructions of the cityscape at both the diachronic and synchronic levels.

On another level, the chapters that constitute this *Atlas* are meant to open up new research questions and new ways of reading Cairo, one of the globe's largest historic, multicultural urban centers, through a century-long literary production by its writers. For example, as I was still working on the *Atlas*, I was asked to participate on a panel during the inaugural festivities for the new AUC campus in New Cairo. I volunteered to present a piece on the representation of AUC in Arab literary works through some of the selections I had collected for this project.[12] It was a surprisingly interesting and rewarding experience, for by tracing AUC's appearance in narratives of the twentieth century, one discovers a fascinating development in the nature of the space accorded to this institution in the national imagery: from being on the margin of Egyptian society to occupying its very center, from being 'other' to becoming an integral part of the writer's and the nation's very identity. Inversely, through these same representations we are able to read the transformations that have occurred in Egyptian society at large during the twentieth century. Indeed, the sheer physical presence of AUC in the heart of downtown Cairo as one of the main axes of the city's throbbing Tahrir Square made it a landmark in narratives whose protagonists' stories, or parts of them, unfold in downtown Cairo. Works by Ihsan Abdel Quddus, Edward Said, Radwa Ashour, Ahdaf Soueif, Ahmed Alaidy, Mahmoud Al-Wardani, Yasser Abdel Latif, Mekkawi Said, May Khaled, and Mourid Barghouti, among others, all map the downtown area with reference to AUC and the history it has participated in making.

And yet all these representations are reconstructions of the "real" space that do not always necessarily coincide with real geography. In trying to map out the coincidences between real and imagined space in Naguib Mahfouz's work, specifically in his *Trilogy* that is set in Gamaliya, the writer's own neighborhood, Gamal al-Ghitani concludes:

Mahfouz consciously mixes the real places with streets that exist solely in his imagination. The city then becomes a cobweb of the real and the imagined. It is an imaginative landscape, constructed of elements so real that we occasionally confuse them with the city itself. Mahfouz gives himself the freedom to merge the real and the imagined, which converge in a city that comes eventually to serve as a representation of his characters' lives.[13]

A literary geography of Cairo then, but which Cairo would this literary atlas represent? And how? These were the difficult choices that had to be made in order for this project to materialize. Given my own area of expertise—modern Arabic literature and, more specifically, narrative literature—it was obvious to me from the start that I would focus on the representation of Cairo in twentieth-century narrative works by Arab writers. But beyond my own field of study there were two crucial determining factors in the choice of material for *The Literary Atlas of Cairo*. First, as Benedict Anderson has argued in *Imagined Communities*, there is an intrinsic relationship between the birth of the imagined community of the modern nation and the new structures, forms, and languages that developed with the novel and the newspaper, for "these forms provided the technical means for 're-presenting' the *kind* of imagined community that is the nation."[14] It is through these new structures of representation that readers came to imagine themselves as a community even if they had never seen and would never see each other. This imagined community is cemented through a "presentation of simultaneity in 'homogenous, empty time,' or a complex gloss upon the word 'meanwhile.'"[15] The novel, then, imitates the nation to a great extent, not only through setting, temporality, character, and event, but also through language. For the purposes of compiling *The Literary Atlas of Cairo* it seemed appropriate to use narrative literature in constructing a literary geography of Cairo precisely because it allows, through its very form and structure, the representation not only of real material geopolitics and histories, but a complex network of human relations across literary topography as well. One could imagine another atlas of Cairo that focuses solely on poetry, for example; however, given the dense, elliptical nature of poetic language, the end product, while no doubt very interesting, would have been substantially different.

The second issue that needed to be resolved was the time frame for the *Atlas*. This was perhaps an easier decision to make, given my choice of the novel as the dominant literary form in the *Atlas*, for not only is the novel related to nationalism and the rise of modern national imaginings, but it is equally related to urbanity and the centrality of the urban experience, both of which have become increasingly dominant in twentieth-century Arab narrative literature. Whether we choose to consider the canonical beginnings of the Arab novel during the first decade of the twentieth century or the more hybrid and cosmopolitan popular fiction from 'below,' there is no denying that the literary geography of the city gradually came to dominate the fictional space—so much so that it prompted Gaber Asfour, one of the Arab world's most prominent literary critics, to label the twentieth century "the time of the novel" *(zaman al-riwaya)*.[16] Naguib Mahfouz was among the first to lead the way during the first half of the twentieth century, with most of his novels set in Old Cairo. Gradually, however, as urban space expanded, and as Old Cairo lost much of its distinctive social and economic fabric through the exodus of its population to the modern metropolis, writers of the city, including Naguib Mahfouz himself, migrated or were displaced to other locations, mapping out many of Cairo's new boundaries and their accompanying social changes and economic developments.

The Literary Atlas of Cairo maps out these migrations and displacements and attempts to reconstruct Cairo as it grows, changes, and expands through its representation in literary works over a century. In collecting, editing, organizing, and translating at least one-third of the material that constitutes this project, I tried to let the city speak, to use Roland Barthes's formulation: I tried to let the city emerge from the literary works, in "fragments," in bits and pieces that, when juxtaposed against each other, would provide a map, would actually "speak to us," as Barthes said. Even though the texts themselves are excerpts from the authors' novels, their juxtaposition and arrangement in the *Atlas* is my own. The act of selection and juxtaposition implicates me at a second degree in the reconstruction of Cairo's literary geography and suggests that the map that is about to unfold before the readers is but one of many possible maps that would ultimately depend on the perspective of the "cartographer" or the city dweller—myself—and how the city "spoke" to me.

The Literary Atlas of Cairo was originally expected to be one volume. However, given the amount of material that has been amassed, it became clear to me and to the publishers that we were actually producing two volumes, even after major cuts had been made in the material that had originally been selected. This, then, is the first of two volumes: *The Literary Atlas of Cairo: One Hundred Years on the Streets of the City*. It begins with a "Prelude" that walks the readers into the city and defines the relationship between the city and the authors of its literary geography as articulated by them in their works. In Chapter I, "Mapping Cairo," readers will see the city expanding and changing, for the material presented here traces the city's accelerated physical growth from its original historic Islamic center at the beginning of the twentieth century to its haphazard, unplanned, informal settlements of the latter part of the same century. This is obviously not a "real" map of Cairo, but rather the map that has emerged from the literature itself. As such, the map says as much about the writers of the city as it does about the city itself: who goes where in the city, whether the different "fragments" of Cairo are connected, where the boundaries are, and who trespasses them. Chapter II is entitled "Public Spaces" and focuses on the representation of some of Cairo's landmarks, from the ancient pyramids to the postmodern malls, as they are reconstructed in the texts. These literary representations render the cityscape more legible, for suddenly such physical landmarks that are part of the built environment take on various levels of historical, cultural, and political signification as they are written by the different authors. Chapter III, "Private Spaces," escorts the readers into the privacy of homes and intimate spaces in the city and provides an inventory of domestic rituals, hierarchies, and relationships. The juxtaposition of these private spaces against each other provides a unique glimpse into the contrasts and contradictions in Cairenes' domestic lives as we move from extended aristocratic abodes to displaced individuals' rundown rooms. "On the Move in Cairo"—Chapter IV in this volume—attempts to map out how the lives of these radically different Cairenes intersect as they move about the city in both private and public transportation that provides the link between the public and the private, the outer and inner spaces of *al-Qahira*, the vanquishing city whose inhabitants constantly have to invent new ways to survive in it. Each of the sections in this volume is prefaced by a brief introduction that serves as a layout of the major axes, patterns, and issues that are raised by the selected literary excerpts.

Volume Two is entitled *The Literary Life of Cairo: One Hundred Years in the Heart of the City*. Unlike Volume One, which focuses on the literary geopolitics of the cityscape, Volume Two immerses the reader in the complex network of socioeconomic and cultural lives in the city across that literary geography. *The Literary Life of Cairo* comprises seven chapters, all of which have emerged out of the preoccupations of the literary texts themselves. The first chapter in Volume Two is "Icons of the City," which introduces readers to representations of some of Cairo's prominent profiles, both political and cultural, and their impact on the city's literary geography, from King Farouk to the popular, leftist, blind singer and composer of the second half of the twentieth century, Sheikh Imam Issa. Chapter II is entitled "Cairo Cosmopolitan" and includes a spectrum of literary reconstructions and readings of the city by its multiethnic, multinational, and multilingual writers across class, gender, and generation.

Cairo's controversial cosmopolitan face is further revealed in Chapter III, "Going to School in Cairo," which includes daunting representations of colonial school experiences as well as startling contrasts of postcolonial educational realities. Chapter IV, "The Street is Ours," maps out representations of Cairenes' numerous moments of political participation and oppression in such detail and quantity that these literary representations become the fictional alternative to constrained political activism on the real street. Chapter V focuses on "Women in the City" and explores the space accorded them within the city's literary geography across history and class, while Chapter VI delves deeper into "Cairo's Underworld" to place the city's marginals on its literary map. Finally, Chapter VII, "Cairo's Drug Culture," foregrounds the century-long representations of the very interesting and well-established relationship between writing and drugs, as well as the history of places, paraphernalia, and products in the drug world across class and time, from the salons of the divas of the early twentieth century, to intellectual consumer dens, all the way to street kids and their drug culture. Like the first volume, each of the chapters in Volume Two has an introductory section that leads the readers into the selections and establishes some of the important connecting points between them.

Together *The Literary Atlas of Cairo* and *The Literary Life of Cairo* produce a literary geography of Cairo that goes beyond the representation of space in literature to reconstruct the complex network of human relationships in that space. Unlike Moretti's actual physical maps of nineteenth-century novels, these two volumes provide mental, imagined maps that can then perhaps be traced physically by the readers themselves. As readers discover the major axes, patterns, and issues that are raised by the selected literary excerpts within each chapter, they will also begin to read across the chapters and will trace new and interesting, as yet unwritten, relationships, thereby producing new maps of the cityscape and becoming themselves active authors of Cairo's literary geography. They are not just Baudelairean *flâneurs* who partake of and observe the city,[17] but motivated and implicated participants in reading and mapping the intricate literary geography, life, and lexicon of the city. Beyond this immediate level, it is important for readers to remember that the literary map of Cairo that unfolds in these two volumes is one that is constructed in translation. The representations of the city in Arabic, English, and French original texts for over one hundred years are here mediated through translation into another language. To be aware of this complex linguistic fact is to realize that embedded within both *The Literary Atlas of Cairo* and *The Literary Life of Cairo* is an equally valuable and unique atlas of literary translation that has yet to be written.

Almost twenty years ago, I wrote an article entitled "Re-writing the City: The Case of Khitat al-Ghitani." It was a modest attempt at reading the changing faces of Cairo and the transformation of the city's signs through the works of Naguib Mahfouz and Gamal al-Ghitani. As I started working on the *Atlas* I was struck by how long the idea of mapping Cairo may have been brewing in my mind. Twenty years ago it was a mere chapter in a book, written by one person. Today it has become a collective work about "The City Victorious" produced by almost one hundred writers over an entire century.

Notes

1   This paper eventually became chapter eight in my book *Egypt's Culture Wars: Politics and Practice* (London: Routledge), 2008, pp. 144–67. It has been republished in *Cairo Contested: Governance, Urban Space, and Global Modernity*, ed. Diane Singerman (Cairo: AUC Press, 2009).

2   Amira Abu Taleb, a graduate student in the department of Arab and Islamic Civilizations, won the Leila Fawwaz Award in Arabic Studies at AUC in Spring 2006 for her excellent paper, "Women in the City: Gender, Class, and Space."

3   New Cairo is a new city that was established by presidential degree in 2000 at the southeastern edge of Greater Cairo. It is part of the newly formed Helwan governorate and is home to several private schools and universities, including the American University in Cairo's New Campus, which was officially inaugurated in February 2009. New Cairo has been a place of escape for Egypt's upper-middle and upper classes from the noise and pollution of Cairo. Many of the residences are luxury villas and condominiums located in housing developments and gated communities.

4   Franco Moretti, *Atlas of the European Novel: 1800–1900* (London and New York: Verso, 1998), p. 3.

5   Moretti, p. 5.

6   Luc Barbulesco and Philippe Cardinal, *L'Islam en questions* (Paris: Grasset, 1986), p. 143.

7   "Semiology and the Urban," in Neil Leach, ed., *Rethinking Architecture: A Reader in Cultural Theory* (London: Routledge, 1997), p. 168.

8   Hana Wirth-Nesher, *City Codes: Reading the Modern Urban Novel* (Cambridge: Cambridge University Press, 1996), p. 7.

9   André Raymond, *Cairo: City of History*, trans. Willard Wood (Cairo: AUC Press, 2001), p. 361.

10 Tarek Abul Atta and Mahmoud Yousry, "The Challenge of Urban Growth in Cairo," in Carole Rakodi, ed., *The Urban Challenge in Africa: Growth and Management of Its Large Cities* (New York: United Nations University Press, 1997), pp. 111–49. See also Raymond, *Cairo: City of History*, pp. 337–77, and Eric Denis, "Urban Planning and Growth in Cairo," in *Middle East Report*, 202 (Winter 1997), http://www.jstor.org/view/08992851/di011543/01p00442/0 (accessed 20 May 2006).

11 The *maqama* is an Arabic literary genre of rhymed prose with intervals of poetry and is characterized by rhetorical extravagance. It centers on a trickster figure or roguish character whose wanderings, experiences, and exploits are conveyed by a narrator.

12 For the full text of the presentation, "The Representation of AUC in the Arab Cultural Imaginary," see AUC Memories, http://www1.aucegypt.edu/ncd/onthemove/aucmemories/contributors.html (accessed 10 October 2009).

13 Gamal al-Ghitani, *The Cairo of Naguib Mahfouz* (Cairo: AUC Press, 1999), p. 14.

14 Benedict Anderson, *Imagined Communities: Reflections on the Origin and Spread of Nationalism* (London: Verso, 1983), p. 30.

15 Anderson, *Imagined Communities*, pp. 30–31.

16 Gaber Asfour, *Zaman al-riwaya* (Cairo: GEBO, 1999).

17 The term *flâneur* means 'stroller,' 'lounger,' or 'loafer,' and was used by the nineteenth-century poet Charles Baudelaire to describe a gentleman stroller of city streets who is at once part of and apart from the cityscape, someone with a key role in understanding and portraying the city. Since Baudelaire the idea of the *flâneur* has accumulated significant meaning as a referent for understanding urban phenomena and modernity.

Prelude
Entering the City Victorious

We enter the city of Cairo in the company of three writers whose work spans the twentieth century. They have been hand-picked for this occasion because, despite the time that separates them, they offer us a crucial understanding of the relationship between the literary producers and the space within which they work. The most striking feature about these selections is the extent to which the three authors of different times and social background and status share a common vision of their position and responsibility as creative writers in the city. The three selections that follow are taken from Muhammad al-Muwailihi's 1907 *A Period of Time: A Study and Translation of Hadith 'Isa ibn Hisham*, Naguib Mahfouz's 1959 *Children of the Alley*, and finally Khairy Shalaby's 1991 *The Time Travels of the Man Who Sold Pickles and Sweets*.

All three narrators in these selections are themselves writers: in al-Muwailihi's selection the narrator identifies himself as "'Isa ibn Hisham, my profession is the art of writing"; Mahfouz's narrator describes himself as the first in the alley to make a career out of writing; while in Shalaby's phantasmagoric selection the modern narrator describes himself as the disciple of the thirteenth-century Muslim scholar Ibn Khallikan, and is called upon by the great sixteenth-century historian al-Maqrizi to dictate to him what information he might know about Cairo so he might add it to his *Topography*.

The selections are equally similar in their representation of the writers themselves: not only are the texts about the status and position of writers within the larger social structure of the city, but they also expose perceptions in the city of the forms of writing with which they are engaged. All three narrators are rogue-like characters whose vocation as writers is either not recognized or looked down upon within their urban context: when 'Isa ibn Hisham identifies himself as a writer, his interlocutor, the Pasha, mistakes him for an office clerk and asks him to produce his "inkwell and notebook." Mahfouz's narrator is equally ridiculed and his pioneering choice of a writer's career only brings him "much contempt and mockery." Shalaby's narrator joins the ranks of the dispossessed writers by describing himself as a "vagabond who wanders through time" and is actually arrested for being an intruder and voyeur in the Fatimid palace.

And yet, this century-long representation of the apparent marginal status of the writer is countered in all three passages by the crucial and conscious role these same writers play as underground historians of the city whose knowledge is indispensable for its past, present, and future. Indeed, all three rogue-like narrators are engaged in, responsible for, and entrusted with formidable tasks that bestow upon them symbolic capital and status. In all three selections the narrators emerge as historians of the city, whose experience and words provide alternative faces and lives of the city with its geography, topography, and sociopolitical structure. Not only is 'Isa ibn Hisham deep in thought about lofty existential problems that are the same as those that preoccupied the great eleventh-century poet al-Ma'arri, but he is also the Pasha's guide in the city, who historicizes the changes that have come over it. Similarly, Mahfouz's narrator is the chosen author of the stories of the "alley" for he is "privy to so many of the people's secrets and sorrows" and entrusted with writing them "carefully." Likewise, Shalaby's Quixote-like narrator is an eyewitness of the establishment of the city of Cairo (al-Qahira) itself and is invited by none other than the caliph al-Mu'izz to the first "fully Cairene Ramadan iftar." Later, he encounters Jawhar al-Siqilli, the caliph's military commander and founder of Fatimid Cairo; he shares the new city's maps with the narrator, who in turn re-maps it from his contemporary experience and point of view.

Not only do the three authors establish a powerful bond between their narrators and the space they occupy, but together they also map out the changing faces of that urban space as it is transformed and expanded throughout history: Cairo itself, from Fustat to the Fatimid settlement, from the alley to the Citadel, and from the medieval city of the Mamluks to twentieth-century modern Cairo.

Finally, the selections with which we enter the city are also examples of the changes that have occurred in the representation of Cairo through literary texts of the twentieth century. The archaic style, diction, idiom, and rhythm of al-Muwailihi's early text, that borrows its form and narrative techniques from the premodern rhymed-prose *maqama*, gives way to the modern symbolic novelistic tradition in Mahfouz's text. In Shalaby's selection this culminates in more daring narrative strategies that draw on the oral tradition as well as popular storytelling strategies, deliberately using everyday spoken dialect and idiom as an integral part of the literary text.

Just as the selections span the history of the relationship between literary producers and the city, as well as the writing of and modes of representation of urban space, the English translations themselves provide an interesting glimpse into the transformations that have occurred in the field of Arabic literary translation and the roles and tasks of the translators of Cairo throughout the twentieth century, from the more literal and heavily annotated translation of al-Muwailihi to increasingly more free-flowing, less alienating renditions of Mahfouz's and Shalaby's texts.

With these three writers whose works span the twentieth century you may now enter al-Qahira (The City Victorious).

Udkhuluha bi salamin aminin (may you enter in the company of peace).

Muhammad al-Muwailihi

from *A Period of Time: A Study and
Translation of Hadith 'Isa ibn Hisham*

IN HIS STORY, 'Isa ibn Hisham told us: "In a dream, I saw myself walking
among the tombs and gravestones in the Imam Shafi'i cemetery.[1] It was a
brilliant moonlit night, bright enough to blot out the stars in the sky; in fact,
so gleaming was the light, one could have threaded a pearl and watched a
speck of dust.

As I stood there amid the graves on top of the tombstones, I was contemplating man's arrogance and conceit, his sense of his own glory, his pride,
his total obsession with his own pretensions, his excessive desires, his ideas
of self-aggrandizement, and the way he chooses to forget about the grave.
In his deluded arrogance he hoists his nose into the air and endeavors to
pierce the very heavens with it. Then he can boast about the things he has
collected and use what he owns to claim some kind of superiority. But Death
always coerces him. Once it has enshrouded his artificial splendor and glory
beneath its slabs of stone, it uses that very same nose to block up a crack in
his tomb.

Deep in thought I continued my walk. I recalled the words of the sage
poet, Abu al-'Ala' al-Ma'arri:

> Tread lightly, for methinks the surface of the earth is made only from these
> bodies.
> It would be bad for us to treat our forefathers and ancestors lightly even if
> they did live long ago.
> Walk slowly abroad, if you are able, and do not strut arrogantly over the
> remains of God's people.[2]

Those decaying bones, remains of mighty kings who considered the
earth too paltry a domain and tried to attain the regions bordering the very
stars; those chests which contained courageous and prudent hearts; those
lips which often uttered orders of war and peace; those fingertips which
used to sharpen quills for writing and trim necks with the sword; those faces
and heads which enslaved bodies and souls and which were described as full
moons at one moment and as suns at another; among the dead, rulers are the

equal of the ruled, nor is there difference or distinction between the lowly
and the mighty.

> He is Death for whom rich and poor is both the same; a man who knows his
> way is just like another who has gone astray.
>> In his judgment, the warrior's shield and the maiden's shift are both alike;
>> an emperor's dwellings are mere spider's webs.
>> Such folk are trodden in the dust, while misfortune rides rampant; among
>> people Fate is still the best rider.
>> The bier is like a ship casting its contents to drown in the sea of death,
>> piling up and up.[3]

In the midst of such sobering notions, I was considering the remarkable
things that happen and marveling at the way in which times change. Deep in
thought about the extraordinary things which Fate brings about, I was trying
to probe the secrets of the resurrection. Suddenly, there was a violent tremor
behind me which almost put an end to my life. In terror I looked behind me.
I discovered that one of the graves had opened, and a man had appeared. He
was tall and imposing, carrying himself with a splendid dignity and majesty.
He displayed all the signs of nobility and high birth. I felt as stunned and terrified as Moses on the day when the mountain was destroyed.[4] Once recovered
from the shock, I took to my heels. I heard the man shouting and noticed
him coming in my direction. In order to avoid him doing me harm, I did as he
ordered and stood where I was.

As you will now see and hear, the following conversation occurred. At
times it was in Turkish and at other times in Arabic:

> Man from the grave, 'Tell me, my good fellow, what's your name? What's your
> profession and what are you doing out here?'[5]
>> This man must have been interrogated recently by the two questioning
>> angels, I told myself; that is why he is using their procedure.[6] I asked God to
>> rescue me from these dire straits and come to my aid so that I could escape
>> the arguments of the Day of Reckoning and be protected from this terrible
>> punishment.[7] Then I turned in his direction and answered, 'My name is 'Isa
>> ibn Hisham, my profession is the art of writing, and I came here to find some
>> inspiration by visiting the tombs.[8] I find it more effective than listening to
>> sermons from pulpits.'
>>> 'Well then, secretary 'Isa, where's your inkwell and notebook?'
>>> 'I'm not a secretary in the Treasury or Secretariat, I'm an author.'

'Never mind! Go then, my good author, and look for my clothes and bring me my horse, Dahman!'

'But I have no idea where your house is, sir!'

Man from the grave (in disgust), 'Tell me, for heaven's sake, which country are you from? You can't be an Egyptian. There's no one in the whole country who doesn't know where my house is. I'm Ahmad Pasha al-Manikali, the Egyptian minister of war!'[9]

'Believe me, Pasha, I'm from pure Egyptian stock. The only reason why I don't know where you live is that houses in Egypt are no longer known by the names of their owners, but by the names of their street, lane, and number. If you would be so kind as to tell me the street, lane, and number of your house, I will go there and bring you the things you've requested.'

Annoyed, the Pasha said, 'It's clear to me that you're out of your mind, my dear author! Since when have houses had numbers to be known by? What are they? Some kind of government legislation or army regulations?[10] Anyway, I think the best plan would be for you to give me your overcoat to wrap myself in and come with me till I reach my house.'

With that, I handed over my overcoat. Usually it is highwaymen who rob passersby, but now this fellow was doing it to me as well—and he a grave-dweller!

The Pasha put on the coat with a reluctant disdain. 'Well, necessity has its own rules![11] But then, I have disguised myself in even shabbier clothes than this while accompanying our late revered master, Ibrahim Pasha, on the nights he used to spend in the city so that he could see for himself how people were faring.[12] But what's to be done? How can we get in?'

'What do you mean?'

Pasha: 'Have you forgotten that we're in the last third of the night? There's no one on duty who'll be able to recognize me in this overcoat, and I haven't got the password with me. How can we get the gates opened?'

'You've just told me, sir, that you don't know anything about houses having numbers. Well, I don't know anything about a "password." I've never even heard of such a thing.'

Laughing contemptuously, the Pasha said, 'Didn't I say you must be a foreigner? Don't you know that the "password" is a word issued each night from the Citadel to the officer of the watch and all the guardhouses and gates? No one is allowed to travel at night unless he has memorized this word and can repeat it to the gatekeeper, whereupon the gate is opened for him. It is given out in secret to the people who ask the government for it so that they can carry on their business at night. It's changed every night. So, one night, it will be "lentils," the next night "greens," the next night "pigeons," the next night "fowl," and so on.'

'It's clear to me that you're the one who's not Egyptian. The only use we have for such words is as food. We've never heard of their being used to convey permission to travel at night. In any case, it's almost dawn, so we'll have no further need of such words or any others.'

'That I'll leave to you.'

So we went on our way. The Pasha began to tell me more about himself. He told me tales of wars and battles which he had either witnessed himself or heard about and then went on to recall any number of exploits of Muhammad 'Ali and the great courage of Ibrahim.[13] We continued in this fashion till we reached Citadel Square, by which time it was daylight. The Pasha halted in humble respect, recited the Fatiha at Muhammad 'Ali's tomb and then addressed the Citadel in eloquent Turkish, 'Hail to you, source of bounties, treadmill of the violent Mamluk tyrants, haven of sovereignty, fortress of royal sway, source of might, birthplace of power, and height of glory. You are the refuge of the pleader for help, protection for him who seeks it, treasure house of people's desires, goal of their aspirations, dwelling place of the valiant hero, and resting place of the gallant king. Citadel of Cairo, how many are the poor wretches who you have released out of generosity, how many people who came to you in search of kindness you have obligated with your charity! Many are the pompous men whom you have coerced, and many are the swords you have drawn. You combined power and generosity, and could decide as alternatives between life and death.

Then the Pasha turned toward me and said, 'Hurry with me to my house so that I can put on my clothes, buckle my sword, and mount my horse. Then I'll return to the Citadel and pay my respects to his exalted highness, the dispenser of bounty.'"[14]

Translated by Roger Allen

Notes

1. The cemetery which surrounded the mausoleum of Imam Shafi' (767–820) and lay outside the city walls at that time. One of al-Muwailihi's ancestors was buried there. See 'Abd al-Latif Hamza, *Adab al-maqala al-sahafiya fi Misr* (Cairo: Dar al-Fikr, 1964) 3: 34.
2. The famous blind poet of Syria whom al-Muwailihi admired greatly and quotes throughout the book. A picture of the poet used to hang in the hall of al-Muwailihi's house. See al-Bishri, *al-Mukhtar* 1: 245. The lines of poetry are taken from the collection *Siqt al-zand*, Cairo: Bulaq, 1869, 1: 209; Cairo, 1948, 974.
3. al-Ma'arri, *al-Luzumiyyat*, Cairo, 1891, 1: 123.

4. The story is described in the Qur'an, Sura 7, vv. 138ff.

5. In the original text, the Pasha is not 'the man from the grave' *(al-dafin)* but 'the ghost' *(al-shabah)*. A short passage has been omitted in which 'Isa is told to approach and expresses his fear at doing so.

6. Munkar and Nakir are two angels who question the dead after burial.

7. Yawm al-Qiyama, al-Hashr, al-Hisab: the Day of Reckoning when all people will be judged by God Himself. The Qur'an is full of references to its various aspects, for example the Antichrist, al-Dajjal, the descent of 'Isa, the gathering *(hashr)* and the reckoning itself *(hisab)*.

8. The newspaper article text of 'Fatra min al-zaman' contained the word *katib* which can mean either 'writer, author' or 'secretary, scribe.' Its presence in the original text makes the Pasha's assumption that 'Isa is a secretary more plausible than the present reading.

9. Ahmad Pasha al-Manikali was the minister of war during part of the reign of Muhammad 'Ali. See 'Abd al-Rahman al-Rafi'i, *'Asr Muhammad 'Ali*, Cairo: Maktabat al-Nahda al-Misriya, 1951, 191 and 308. It is interesting to note that in Gabriel Baer, *A History of Land-ownership in Modern Egypt 1800–1950*, London: Oxford University Press, 1962, 48, al-Manikali and Hasan al-Manastirli (to be mentioned in Chapter 6 of *Hadith 'Isa ibn Hisham*) are both quoted in the same paragraph because of the great wealth of their waqf property. In addition, both of these men had this property in the Qalyubiya province of which al-Muwailihi had been mu'awin.

10. The Pasha still uses the Turkish terminology reflecting the era of Muhammad 'Ali, whose knowledge of Arabic is illustrated by the anecdote in Chapter II describing the appointment of the governor of the Sudan.

11. Ahmad Taymur, *al-Amthal al-'ammiyya*, Cairo: Dar al-Kutub, 1956, 320, elaborates on this proverb: "Necessities legalize things which are otherwise forbidden and force men to do things which are undesirable. But men can only be blamed if they do such things out of pure desire, not if they are under some kind of compulsion."

12. The son of Muhammad 'Ali who led the Egyptian army in victorious campaigns against the Wahhabis in Arabia and the Ottoman forces in Syria. When his father became mentally ill, Ibrahim took over the rule, but he died before his father in 1848.

13. The ninth (Dar al-Qawmiya) edition of *Hadith 'Isa ibn Hisham*, published in Egypt in 1964, sees fit to omit the last part of this sentence extolling Muhammad 'Ali and Ibrahim.

14. These were titles by which Muhammad 'Ali was commonly addressed during his reign. See Jean Deny, *Sommaire des archives turques du Caire*, Cairo: Royal Geographical Society of Egypt, 1930, 562, where a list is given of the honorific titles used by Muhammad 'Ali and attention is drawn to al-Muwailihi's use of *dawari* in this particular passage. The original text ended with, "I was amazed by what he had said and wanted to see his resolve through to the end. The story continues."

Naguib Mahfouz
from *Children of the Alley*

THIS IS THE STORY of our alley—its stories, rather. I have witnessed only the most recent events, those of my own time, but I have recorded all of them the way our storytellers told them. Everyone in our alley tells these stories, just as they heard them in coffeehouses or as they were handed down for generations—these sources are my only basis for what I'm writing. Most of our social occasions call for storytelling.

I have witnessed the recent period in the life of our alley and lived through the events that came about through the coming of Arafa, a dutiful son of our alley. It is thanks to one of Arafa's friends that I am able to record some of the stories of our alley. One day he said to me, "You're one of the few who know how to write, so why don't you write down the stories of our alley? They've never been told in the right order, and even then always at the mercy of the storytellers' whims and prejudices; it would be wonderful if you wrote them carefully, all together so that people could benefit from them, and I'll help you out with what you don't know, with inside information." I acted on his advice, both because it struck me as a good idea and because I loved the person who suggested it. I was the first in our alley to make a career out of writing, though it has brought me much contempt and mockery. It was my job to write the petitions and complaints of the oppressed and needy. Although many wretched people seek me out, I am barely better off than our alley's beggars, though I am privy to so many of the people's secrets and sorrows that I have become a sad and brokenhearted man.

But, I am not writing about myself or my troubles, which amount to nothing compared with those of our alley—our strange alley with its strange stories! How did it happen? What was it all about? And who were the children of our alley?

Translated by Peter Theroux

Khairy Shalaby

from *The Time-Travels of the Man Who
Sold Pickles and Sweets*

THE FATIMID CALIPH MUʻIZZ had sent me a personal invitation to break the Ramadan fast at his table—or his dining carpet, as the invitation put it. The occasion was the first fully Cairene Ramadan: that is, the first celebration of the holy month in the newly built city of Cairo. Before the caliph Muʻizz, there had been no such thing as Cairo. The capital of Egypt was a place called Fustat, with its various extensions, each constructed by a new set of invaders in the hope of avoiding the crowds in the streets and escaping the memories of old regimes. Before long, settlements like Askar and Qataʼiʻ had become towns. Eventually, the towns became one large city. Cairo itself had begun its illustrious career as a Fatimid settlement.

I looked up. To my astonishment, we were standing on a tract of open ground enclosed by a boundary wall. Around us, other walls of solid stone formed squares and rectangles and circles on the ground. I looked around me in dismay.

"My God, where on earth am I?"

A man came forward. He was a Moroccan who looked like a wise old soothsayer. He said, "Son, you're in the same place you were before."

Dazed, I asked, "What are those mountains, then?"

"That's Muqattam."

"What's that town over there?"

"That's Fustat and the settlements around it. And those huts over there are the village of Umm Dunayn."

"If that's Muqattam, where's the Salah Salim freeway? Where's the City of the Dead? Where's Darrasa? The mosque of Husayn? Where *am* I?"

He smiled and patted me kindly on the shoulder. "Come along with me."

I followed him across what in my mind was still an alleyway. A short distance away we passed the foundation of a building, then another and another. We were approaching what looked like a camp. It extended from the slopes of the Muqattam hills down to the area that a short time ago had been occupied by the Azhar mosque. The area now contained an enormous orchard with a foundation trench dug around it. Scattered all around were tents of elegant appearance, with soldiers and officials everywhere. We passed an old man with a long beard. He was carrying a reed pen, a calamus, an inkpot, and a sheaf of papers. Some of the soldiers were arguing with him, but he was standing his ground, smiling gently and pausing from time to time to write something down. I recognized him: it was Maqrizi, author of the *Topography*, which is still famous today. Wanting to show my companion that I knew people in high places, I called out without breaking my stride, "Hey, Maqrizi! How are ya?"

He nodded to me as gently as a shining star. Despite my predicament, I had the effrontery to shout, "If you need anything, just let me know!"

He called back, "Actually, I do."

My knees went weak. What if he needed money? Or someone to take his side in the argument he was having?

But he said only this: "If you have any information about this particular plot of land, dictate it to me. I've kept track of everyone who's set foot here going back as many years as I can count, but it never hurts to double check."

I stood there smiling at him like an imbecile and let the Moroccan soothsayer drag me away.

We walked along a path lined with potted plants and armed soldiers who saluted us as we passed. It led us to a cavernous space that looked as if it were built of marble but was actually made of tent cloth, with carpets on the ground. The Moroccan turned a corner and I followed anxiously behind him. Suddenly we were face to face with the generalissimo himself. No one had to tell us who he was; it was clear without his having to say a word. The Moroccan bowed and then pointed to me.

"On the first of Ramadan 358 AH, this individual was apprehended sneaking into the grounds of the palace."

"Palace?" I squawked. "What palace? I swear to God there was no palace."

The generalissimo laughed, looked over at me, and sat back in his gilded chair. To my enormous relief, he said, "I hereby issue a general amnesty and command my troops to cease and desist from any and all hostile activity, in deference to a request by the women of Egypt, who have come to petition me for mercy. So tell me, you there: what mischief have you gotten yourself into?" He smiled.

"So far so good," I thought to myself. Then out loud, "General Jawhar the Sicilian, am I right?"

He nodded. I knelt before him and said, "I beg you to forgive me if I've done anything wrong! I'm a vagabond who wanders through time, and I come and go as I please."

He beckoned me to get up and then pointed me to a chair so large that I nearly disappeared into it. With a glance he dismissed the Moroccan soothsayer. He passed a hand across his short beard and rubbed his face. It was a big round ruddy face, resolute and proud. "In the name of God!" he pronounced. "There is no power or strength except in God, the High and Mighty One!" He fiddled with his worry beads. Then he seemed to recall my presence.

"Are you fasting?" he asked.

"Happy Ramadan!" I cried.

"If you're not a Muslim, don't be shy: ask for something to eat and drink."

"No, Mr. General," I said, as embarrassed as I could be. "I'm a Muslim and a monotheist."

"God be praised," he said in his awkward foreign accent.

A chamberlain, dragging the train of his best-grade baize gown, came in with several rolls of paper under his arm. He came up to Jawhar and unrolled the papers, which turned out to be plans for palaces, minarets, gates, colonnades, and balconies. The two men promptly forgot all about me. Jawhar the Sicilian looked over the papers, comparing the plans. Finally, he announced with a scowl, "The builders' drawings don't match the plans prepared by our master Mu'izz!"

"The differences are minor," the chamberlain replied. "These are construction plans, and they have to be detailed."

In the pleading voice of someone caught outside of his sphere of professional competence, Jawhar explained that he was committed to following the plans of their master Mu'izz, who had designed this city down to the last period and comma.

"We're committed, too. The only changes we've made are because of the nature of the site. They're only minor changes."

"With God's blessing, then!" said Jawhar, taking the pen from the chamberlain and signing one of the papers. Then he spread it out, giving me a chance to take a closer look. Delighted, I exclaimed, "That's the Azhar mosque! It looks just like it!"

Ignoring me, he rolled it up and unrolled another, signed it, and spread it out. It was a plan for an extremely impressive and elaborate palace. Even more delighted, I cried out, "That must be the Great Eastern Palace!"

Jawhar rolled up the plan and said to the chamberlain, "That will be the seat of the Fatimid caliphate."

Translated by Michael Cooperson

Mapping Cairo

The title of this chapter consciously evokes the Arab historiographical genre of *khitat* that persisted well into the nineteenth century and was especially developed in Egypt. Perhaps two of the most prominent examples of this genre and among the most influential are *Khitat al-Maqrizi* (fifteenth century) and *al-Khitat al-Tawfiqiya* by Ali Mubarak (nineteenth century).

The word *khitat* is the plural form of the word *khitta*. Both derive from the Arabic verbs *khattat* and *yakhuttu* which mean to write, to plan, to lay out, to draw (as in a map). The plural form, *khitat*, came to connote an Islamic genre of historiography, distinguished by its spatial organization; a form of social history and topography of the provinces in the expanding Islamic empire that felt the urgency of keeping records of its newly established towns. From the very start, this genre of historiography was directly linked to the authorities: it originated for administrative purposes and therefore, by definition, had a patron whose interests it served and represented.

Writing history in the form of *khitat* was an encyclopedic project about the place with which the historian dealt. Given the historical framework and administrative constraints of the genre of *khitat*, as well as its focus on a specific place and the changes and transformations of such a place under different authorities, it is not surprising that the *khitat* constantly needed to be rewritten. Indeed, the main reason why Ali Mubarak undertook the writing of *al-Khitat al-Tawfiqiya* during the nineteenth century was because, according to him, the Cairo described by al-Maqrizi during the fifteenth century was hardly recognizable anymore.

The selections in this chapter will reveal that Cairo's twentieth-century writers, like its historians, feel the need and responsibility of mapping out their ever-expanding and changing city. Unlike the historians, however their works are "fictional" and are not written for administrative purposes or a particular authority or patron as was the case with the *khitat*. Indeed, what these selections provide is an alternative map of the city that dismantles the classic and comforting distinction between "history" and "fiction," between the "imagined" and the "real" so that it becomes impossible to draw a line between them.

Like the *khitat*, the selections in this chapter escort readers on a century-long visit to Cairo during which they can map out the growth of the city and its multiple coexisting faces and histories. Change and the nostalgia for more familiar and memorable signs of the city that have been eroded by time as well as the various transformations of urban space, not to mention relationships within it, represent some of the main axes of this chapter. The first selection from Naguib Mahfouz's *Midaq Alley* sets the tone and general mood: the seemingly traditional, timeless alley with its architectural symmetry, social order, and hierarchy gives way to the modern, disruptive mores of the new city; the familiar oral poet and *rababa* player is displaced by the modern radio; and the sense of community that opens the text is threatened by an outside world beyond the traditional alley's own boundaries.

Readers will begin their historical visit in medieval Cairo with its exotic odors, its traditional crafts and stalls, baths, and mosques, and will then venture into cosmopolitan Cairo that was intended to be "a part of Europe," with its colonial-style architecture, its new modern neighborhoods, its spacious tree-lined boulevards, and its luxurious palaces only to find themselves descending into "the dregs of the city" where the ruralization of urban space and the absence of urban planning become the hallmark of the mega-metropolis. We witness the displacement of the center from the old city with its spiritual anchors—al-Hussein, al-Azhar, Sayeda Zaynab—to the new cosmopolitan neighborhoods of Manial, Zamalek, Heliopolis, and Garden City, among others. We move from impersonal Maadi skyscrapers that house the nouveaux riches and new petro-dollar residents, to the "mongrel," illegal settlements and shantytowns whose uncontrollable growth pushes the affluent into gated communities, "utopias" where they seek to protect themselves from all those others who "think they are alive" and where "language breaks down to a jargon of grunts."

Cairo is "the siren" that lures the forgotten and dispossessed. They flock to the city and gradually take over its elegant downtown, which becomes a space for squatters, small peddlers, and unemployed youth with broken dreams and unfulfilled longings for a better life. The urban poor occupy the center and the urban rich are pushed further and further out to the edges of the city and its ever-shifting margins.

Even though the writers who map Cairo have no immediate patron or authority to represent, they remain bound by their class affiliations, prejudices, and interests. Indeed, the selections in this chapter not only provide a map of the city but a map of the writers themselves within the city. Geography is ideology: as each one of the writers records the present and past of a given neighborhood or area, his or her economic, social, political, and aesthetic biases are written into the map they each produce. In Chafika Hamamsy's text *Zamalek,* the once aristocratic island becomes a metaphor for all of Egypt: "a place where ugliness competes successfully with beauty, where attempts to maintain a modicum of aesthetic standards are an uphill battle fought daily by a few valiant souls who believe that good will ultimately prevail." Hamamsy's elitist map is pitted against Abdel-Mourid's powerful, human, and witty representation of *zarayib* (pig farms) in the Zabbalin area in the Muqattam hills—a map that effectively eternalizes the garbage collectors' community by capturing the details of their lives before they are disbanded and disappeared by the Egyptian state, along with their pigs, in the aftermath of the H1N1 virus panic, leaving the city's garbage to pile up behind them.

Not only are Cairo's various neighborhoods invested with their own individual histories that are affixed to the names of alleyways, streets, squares, mosques, and palaces, but more significantly, where this literary atlas is concerned these same neighborhoods are inscribed with their own literary histories through their representation in literary texts. Islamic Cairo evokes specific historical imaginary moments in the city that haunt the protagonist's imagination in Ismail Wali al-Din's *Hammam al-Malatili* through the images of "a ghost with a black helmet," "the sound of approaching hooves and neighing horses," and "the head of a dead Mamluk on a brass plate." The same neighborhood equally evokes the city's literary map in Mahmoud Al-Wardani's *Heads Ripe for Plucking* where, as the characters stroll in Islamic Cairo, they spot "the police station that Naguib Mahfouz described in his *Cairo Trilogy,*" "the location of the protagonist al-Sayyid Ahmad Abd al-Gawad's house, where his wife Amina would stand behind the latticed window screen every night waiting for him to return," and the ruins of the very house "where Naguib Mahfouz was born." What readers are about to encounter then is not simply a historical map of Cairo but more importantly and uniquely perhaps a map within a map: not just a historical *khitat* but a literary one that reconstructs the city in literary terms that have become part of Cairo's collective memory and history. This is not Islamic Cairo but Naguib Mahfouz's Islamic Cairo, not downtown Cairo but Radwa Ashour's downtown Cairo, not Manshiyat Nasser but Hamdi Abu Golayyel's Manshiyat Nasser—alternative literary maps through which an entire city is reconstructed and represented.

Naguib Mahfouz

from *Midaq Alley*

MANY THINGS COMBINE TO show that Midaq Alley is one of the gems of times gone by and that it once shone forth like a flashing star in the history of Cairo. Which Cairo do I mean? That of the Fatimids, the Mamluks, or the Sultans? Only God and the archaeologists know the answer to that, but in any case, the alley is certainly an ancient relic and a precious one. How could it be otherwise with its stone-paved surface leading directly to the historic Sanadiqiya Street. And then there is its café known as Kirsha's. Its walls decorated with multicolored arabesques, now crumbling, give off strong odors from the medicines of olden times, smells which have now become the spices and folk cures of today and tomorrow.

Although Midaq Alley lives in almost complete isolation from all surrounding activity, it clamors with a distinctive and personal life of its own. Fundamentally and basically, its roots connect with life as a whole and yet, at the same time, it retains a number of the secrets of a world now past.

The sun began to set and Midaq Alley was veiled in the brown hues of the glow. The darkness was all the greater because it was enclosed like a trap between three walls. It rose unevenly from Sanadiqiya Street. One of its sides consisted of a shop, a café, and a bakery, the other of another shop and an office. It ends abruptly, just as its ancient glory did, with two adjoining houses, each of three stories.

The noises of daytime life had quieted now and those of the evening began to be heard, a whisper here and a whisper there: "Good evening, everyone," "Come on in; it's time for the evening get-together," "Wake up, Amm Kamil, and close your shop!" "Change the water in the hookah, Sanker!" "Put out the oven, Jadda!" "This hashish hurts my chest," "If we've been suffering terrors of blackouts and air raids for five years, it's only due to our own wickedness!"

Two shops, however, that of Amm Kamil, the sweets seller, to the right of the alley entrance and the barbershop on the left remain open until shortly after sunset. It is Amm Kamil's habit, even his right, to place a chair on the threshold of his shop and drop off to sleep with a fly whisk resting in his lap. He will remain there until customers either call out to him or Abbas, the barber, teasingly wakes him. He is a hulk of a man, his cloak revealing legs like tree trunks and his behind large and rounded like the dome of a mosque, its central portion resting on the chair and the remainder spilling over the sides. He has a belly like a barrel, great projecting breasts, and he seems scarcely to have any neck at all. Between his shoulders lies his rounded face, so puffed and blood-flecked that his breathing makes its furrows disappear. Consequently, scarcely a single line can be seen on the surface and he seems to have neither nose nor eyes. His head topping all this is small, bald, and no different in color from his pale yet florid skin. He is always panting and out of breath, as if he has just run a race, and he can scarcely complete the sale of a sweet before he is overcome by a desire for sleep. People are always telling him he will die suddenly because of the masses of fat pressing around his heart. He always agrees with them. But how will death harm him when his life is merely a prolonged sleep?

The barbershop, although small, is considered in the alley to be rather special. It has a mirror and an armchair, as well as the usual instruments of a barber. The barber is a man of medium height, pallid complexion, and slightly heavy build. His eyes project slightly and his wavy hair is yellowish, despite the brown color of his skin. He wears a suit and never goes without an apron, perhaps in imitation of more fashionable hairdressers.

These two individuals remain in their shops while the large company office next to the barber closes its doors and its employees go home. The last to leave is its owner, Salim Alwan. He struts off, dressed in his flowing robe and cloak, and goes to the carriage waiting for him at the street's entrance. He climbs in sedately and fills the seat with his well-built person, his large Circassian mustaches standing out before him. The driver kicks the bell with his foot and it rings out loudly. The carriage, drawn by one horse, moves off toward Ghuriya on its way to Hilmiya.

The two houses at the end of the street have closed their shutters against the cold, and lantern light shines through their cracks. Midaq Alley would be completely silent now were it not for Kirsha's café, light streaming from its electric lamps, their wires covered with flies.

The café is beginning to fill with customers. It is a square room, somewhat dilapidated. However, in spite of its dinginess, its walls are covered with arabesques. The only things which suggest a past glory are its extreme age and a few couches placed here and there. In the café entrance a workman is setting up a secondhand radio on a wall. A few men are scattered about on the couches smoking and drinking tea.

Not far from the entrance, on a couch, sits a man in his fifties dressed in a cloak with sleeves, wearing a necktie usually worn by those who affect western dress. On his nose perches a pair of expensive-looking gold-rimmed spectacles. He has removed his wooden sandals and left them lying near his feet. He sits as stiffly as a statue, as silent as a corpse. He looks neither to the right nor to the left, as though lost in a world all his own.

A senile old man is now approaching the café. He is so old that the passing of time has left him with not a single sound limb. A boy leads him by his left hand and under his right arm he carries a two-stringed fiddle and a book. The old man greets all those present and makes his way to the couch in the middle of the room. He climbs up with the help of the boy, who sits beside him. He places the instrument and the book between them and looks hard into the faces of the men present, as though searching for their reaction to his coming there. His dull and inflamed eyes, filled with expectation and apprehension, settle on the café's young waiter, Sanker. Having sat patiently waiting for some time and having observed the youth's studied disregard for himself, he breaks his silence, saying thickly, "Coffee, Sanker."

The youth faces slightly toward him and after a slight hesitation turns his back on him again without saying a word, completely disregarding the request. The old man realizes the youth will go on ignoring him and, indeed, he expected nothing more.

Just then help came, as though from the heavens, with the entry of someone who heard the old man's shout and saw the youth ignore him. The newcomer shouted imperiously to the waiter, "Bring the poet's coffee, lad!"

The old poet gazed gratefully at the newcomer and said somewhat sadly, "Thanks be to God, Dr. Booshy."

The "doctor" greeted him and sat down beside him. Dressed incongruously in a cloak, a skullcap, and wooden clogs, he was a dentist who learned his profession from life, having had no medical or any other schooling. Dr. Booshy began his professional life as an assistant to a dentist in the Gamaliya district. He learned by observing the dentist's skill and so became proficient himself. He was well known for the effectiveness of his prescriptions, although he generally preferred extraction as the best cure! His roving dental surgery would no doubt have been considered unbearably painful were it not for the fact that his fees were so low. He charged one piaster for the poor and two for the rich (the rich of Midaq Alley, of course!). If there were serious loss of blood, as frequently happened, he generally considered it the work of God. He relied on God, too, to prevent the blood from flowing! Moreover, he had made a set of gold teeth for Kirsha, the café owner, for only two guineas. In Midaq Alley and the surrounding area, he was addressed as "doctor." He was, perhaps, the very first doctor to receive his title from his patients.

Sanker brought the coffee for the poet, as the "doctor" requested. The old man raised the cup to his lips, blowing into it to cool the drink. He then sipped it and continued to do so until it was finished. He placed the cup to one side and only then recalled the ill-mannered behavior of the waiter. Gazing at the youth with apparent disdain, he muttered indignantly, "Ill-mannered fellow . . . ."

He picked up his instrument and began to pluck its strings, avoiding the angry looks Sanker gave him. He played a few introductory notes just as the café had heard him play every evening for twenty years or more. His frail body swayed in time with the music. Then he cleared his throat, spat, and said, "In the name of God." Crying out in his harsh-sounding voice, he continued: "We are going to begin today by saying a prayer for the Prophet. An Arab Prophet, the chosen son of the people of Adnan. Abu Saada, the Zanaty, says that . . . ."

He was interrupted by someone who entered at that point and said roughly, "Shut up! Don't say a single word more!"

The old man lifted his failing eyes from his instrument and saw the sleepy, gloomy eyes of Kirsha, the tall, thin, dark-faced café owner, looking down at him. He stared at him glumly and hesitated a moment as though unable to believe his ears. Trying to ignore Kirsha's unpleasantness, he began reciting again, "Abu Saada, the Zanaty, says that . . . ."

The café owner shouted in angry exasperation, "Are you going to force your recitations on us? That's the end—the end! Didn't I warn you last week?"

A look of disappointment came into the poet's face and he commented critically, "I can see you have been living fast lately. Can't you take it out on someone else?"

Even more exasperated, Kirsha shouted again, "I know what I said and what I want, you imbecile. Do you think I am going to allow you to perform in my café if you are going to slander me with your vile tongue?"

The old poet sweetened his tone a little as he tried to soothe the angry man and said, "This is my café too. Haven't I been reciting here for the last twenty years?"

The café owner took his usual seat behind the till and replied, "We know all the stories you tell by heart and we don't need to run through them again. People today don't want a poet. They keep asking me for a radio and there's one over there being installed now. So go away and leave us alone and may God provide for you."

The old man's face clouded and he remembered sadly that Kirsha's café was the only one left to him and, indeed, his last source of livelihood and one which had served him well. Only the day before, the Caste Café had sent him away. Old as he was, and now with his living cut off, what was he to do with his life? What was the point of teaching his poor son this profession when it had died like this? What could the future hold for him and how could he provide for his son? A feeling of despair seized him and increased in intensity when he saw the look of regretful determination on Kirsha's face. The old man pleaded, "Slowly, slowly, Mr. Kirsha. Public reciters still have an appeal that won't disappear. The radio will never replace us."

Firmly and decisively, however, the café owner replied, "That is what you say, but it is not what my customers say and you are not going to ruin my business. Everything has changed!"

In despair, the old man insisted, "Haven't people listened to these stories without being bored since the days of the Prophet, peace be upon him?"

Kirsha brought his hand down hard on the till and shouted, "I said everything has changed!"

At this the absentminded and statuesque man wearing the gold-rimmed spectacles and the necktie moved for the first time. He turned his gaze to the café's roof and sighed so deeply that his friends almost expected pieces of flesh to come up with the passage of air. In a dreamy tone, he said, "Yes, everything has changed. Yes, indeed, everything has changed, my lady."

Translated by Trevor Le Gassick

Naguib Mahfouz
from *Khan al-Khalili*

IT WAS HALF PAST two in the afternoon on a September day in 1941, the exact time when civil servants left their government offices. Streams of them came pouring out of the ministry's doors like a raging torrent. Their minds had long since become preoccupied with a combination of hunger and sheer boredom, and now they all scattered in different directions under the burning glare of the sun.

Ahmad Akif, whose job was at the Ministry of Works, was among them. At this time of day he usually made his way back to al-Sakakini, but today was different: for the first time he was heading toward al-Azhar. He had been living in al-Sakakini for a long time, stretching back many years, whole decades in fact. Those many years constituted a veritable storehouse of memories—memories of childhood, youth, adulthood, and then middle age. The incredible thing was that it had only taken the family a few days to make up their minds to pack up and leave. They had all felt completely secure in their old house; they had never imagined leaving. But then during the short interval between one evening and noon the next day everyone had started yelling, "A pox on this awful quarter!" Fear and panic had taken over; there was no longer any point in trying to persuade scared folk to change their minds. The old house had soon become a memory of the past, and the new house in Khan al-Khalili was a reality from today and onward into the future. Well might Ahmad Akif quote the phrase, "Praise be to the One who changes things but who never changes Himself!"

The suddenness of the decision to move had left him in a quandary. His heart kept drawing him back to the beloved old quarter. He bitterly regretted the feeling of being tossed out and thrust into one of the ancient popular quarters of Cairo. But at the same time he could not forget the relief he had felt when he realized that he would now be far away from a kind of hell that threatened imminent destruction. Maybe tonight would turn out to be the first time he managed to get any sleep since that terrible night, the one that had given the people of Cairo such a terrible shock.

It was therefore with mixed emotions—sadness and forbearance—that he paced the sidewalk waiting for the trolley that would take him to Queen Farida Square. Sweat was pouring off his brow, and yet he could still feel a certain frisson of pleasure at the thought of new discoveries and the prospect of change: a new place to live, new environment, new atmosphere, and new neighbors. Maybe luck would turn out differently and good times would return once again. Perhaps the ever-so-subtle intimations he was now feeling would manage to shake off the layers of dust left behind by so much lethargy and inject some new sense of life and energy.

This, then, was the sheer delight of exploration, taking risks, and pursuing dreams; not only that, but also a hidden sense of superiority that grew out of his moving from one quarter to another that was of lower status in both prestige and educational level. He had not even set eyes on the new house as yet because he had been at work in the ministry when he was notified that the furniture had been moved first thing in the morning. Now here he was, on his way to the new house following the directions he had been given.

"It's only temporary," he told himself. "They'll have to put up with it as long as the war lasts. Then things will get better."

Could it have turned out any better? Would it have made more sense to stay in the old quarter, even though it would involve watching and listening to the fearsome noises of death . . . ?

Finally he reached al-Azhar and headed toward Khan al-Khalili, his new destination. He made his way through a narrow alleyway in the direction of the quarter in question. To his left and right were new apartment blocks with countless alleyways and walks interspersed between them. They looked like row upon row of imposing barracks where you could easily lose your way. All around him he spotted cafés teeming with customers and the occasional store, some selling taamiya, others jewelry and trinkets. And there were hordes of people, a never-ending flow, some wearing turbans, others fezzes, and still others skullcaps. The air was filled with shouts, yells, and screams, all of them guaranteed to shatter the nerves of someone like himself. He felt ill at ease and jumpy. He had no idea where he was going, so he went over to a Nubian doorman sitting beside the entrance to a building and said hello.

"Where's the street to building number seven, please?" he asked.

The man stood up courteously. "You must be looking for apartment twelve, where people moved in today," he replied, pointing in the right direction. "See that passageway? Take it to the second alleyway on the right, then go as far as Ibrahim Pasha Street, then the third door on the left will be building number seven."

He thanked the doorman and proceeded down the passageway. "Second alleyway on the right," he kept mumbling to himself. "Okay, so here it is. Now, third building on the left." He paused for a moment and looked at his surroundings. The street was long and narrow, with four square apartment buildings on either side, all of them connected by side passages that intersected with the main street. The sidewalks of these passageways and the main street itself were crowded with various stalls: watch repairer, calligrapher, tea maker, rug maker, clothes mender, trinket seller, and so on. Here and there cafés were scattered around, but they were no larger than the stalls. Doormen stayed close to the building entrances, their faces as black as pitch, their turbans as white as milk, with expressions languid enough to give the impression that the perfumed scents and wafts of incense that floated through the air had sent them into a stupor. The atmosphere of the place was enveloped in a brownish haze, as though the entire quarter never saw the sun's rays. The reason was that in many places the sky was blocked by overhanging balconies. The various craftsmen sat in front of their stalls, patiently and skillfully plying their trade and producing little masterpieces; the ancient quarter still preserved its long-standing reputation as a place where the human hand could make exquisite crafts. It had managed to withstand the influx of modern civilization and to confront the insane pace with its own calming wisdom; its simple skills stood counter to complex technologies, its reverie of imagination to an uncouth realism, and its drowsy ocher hue to the gleaming brilliance of modernity. As he took in the scene with confusion, he wondered to himself whether he would be able to get to know this new quarter the way he had the old one. Would the day ever come when he could make his way through this maze without even thinking about it, following the path wherever his feet took him because his mind was so distracted by other matters?

"In the name of God the Compassionate, the Merciful," he intoned as he approached the door.

He walked up the spiral staircase to the second floor and found apartment 12. When he spotted the number he smiled, almost as though he had known it for some time and was pleased to see it again after a long absence. He rang the bell, and the door opened. His mother was standing at the threshold, smiling in welcome.

"Do you see this wonderful new world of ours?" she said with a laugh as she let him in.

Translated by Raymond Stock

Ismail Wali al-Din
from *Hammam al-Malatili*

AL-AZHAR MOSQUE was quiet.... He removed his shoes and greeted the book vendors near the al-Azhar walls before he entered. It was vast. There were many work quarters and dormitories with strange names: to his right the Maghariba and the Jabartiyya. Several people were asleep on the floor. A dormitory crammed with pots and sleeping people. Should he sleep on the washed tile in a corner and cover himself with what he had in his suitcase...?

He left the mosque and greeted the book vendors once more. One of them was sitting with an old woman and a young man drinking tea. Did they all sleep alongside the books till morning? And how did they relieve themselves? How did they wash?

He strolled through one of Khan al-Khalili's vaulted alleys. The streets were narrow and the eyes of the guards were wide open. A strange smell: a mix of herbs and baked bread. He remembered the Fridays when his mother with her small face and fair complexion would insist on baking at home big wide white loaves of bread that resembled the color of her skin.

His heart had been snatched from him . . . where to? He did not know. A sadness, or rather a kind of rift, split his chest. He wanted to find someone to warm this small part of his chest, that little cage between the ribs, a small part that needed to be filled with tenderness. But can tenderness be had from Cairo, the ogress?

The street was dark and scary as if the ghosts were about to dance for him. A ghost with a black helmet quickly entered a house. Many people were hurrying as if afraid of catastrophe. The shops closed down and the women retreated behind the curtains. The sound of approaching hooves and neighing horses, dagger blades shone in the dark . . . the head of a dead Mamluk on a brass plate emerged from a house followed by flame holders, passersby, and beggars shouting, "Such is the fate of murderers." An old man who had witnessed the entire episode said, without moving from his place, "The tyrant lives on and the wronged one has died."

He beat his chest several times. The street was quiet except for a faint light emanating from one of the hammams. All the mosques were quiet and closed. There was a small kerosene lamp hanging at the door of the ful furnace. He stood feeling lost at the door. There was a mosque to his right and many others with minarets hiding each other behind him. The night was a faded yellow. In his heart a small flame of sadness glowed.

He entered the circle of light. The owner was sitting on a wooden bench. He asked if he could spend the night. The owner pointed to one of the empty rooms filled with wooden benches with very slim mattresses and white sheets. He will undress here. He will sleep here. Did he want to go to the hammam? Did he need something warm to drink? Or should he just give Amm Hasanein all his money, his cheap watch and wallet with his ID and the letter of reference?

I want to sleep, Amm Hasanein. I am a stranger to Cairo. I cannot find one soul who is willing to help me. I have been looking for work for the past ten days. I have a high-school diploma but I am unemployed. Is Cairo a humid, sticky city? My wretched soulmates have told me that you only know each other when you need something from each other. . . . Do you walk in a daze? Have you not seen the ghosts yet?

These humid walls, these slim beds that are placed on the ruins of the palace of the Ayyubid princess, Mu'nisa. Do you not feel guilty or ashamed putting your burners and your water and your urine pots on top of the glory of the armies of this small Fatimid palace?

Amm Hasanein placed the wooden slippers next to the bench on which Ahmad was preparing to sleep and he said with exaggerated tenderness, "If you need something to eat just call me, and I'll be right there. If you need something, just call out my name, Amm Hasanein. If you need to go to the hammam call me so that I can show you the way. You are a stranger and we always welcome strangers."

He smiled slyly, reaching for a cigarette from the pack that protruded from the pocket of his trousers. "I will sleep immediately. I will forget the ghosts. I will go to the hammam at dawn and pray at al-Salih Ayyub Mosque."

The light entered through the small scant openings. Ahmad awoke in his room. Many other people were still sleeping on the benches with the slim mattresses. The light was not bright, somewhat purple rather; the light of dawn.

Ahmad got up and covered his lower body with the cloth mihzim. The owner was still sitting on his bench; Amm Hasanein was asleep, resting his head on his elbow. Many men were asleep on the benches. Ahmad stood confused in the middle of the room with his wooden slippers. Which way should he go? Everyone was sleeping. He was afraid to speak. But the owner of the hammam dashed toward him, saying, "What can I do for you, effendi?"

Amm Hasanein also sat up as if he had not been sleeping. He smiled at him. There was still some movement inside the hammam. There were men asking for soap and towels. The light flooded the place with a beautiful gray cloud. Where was beauty? It lay outside in the alleys and narrow streets filled with monuments. Ahmad walked toward the hammam. Inside, the light looked unnatural. There was a warm pool and many other rooms with showers. He noticed the small round openings covered with colored glass in the ceiling like the columns that had turned yellow from the steam and the passage of time. But they were still beautiful. Even the steps leading into the pool were still beautiful.

Amm Hasanein said, "When the water in the pool is clean and clear before the clients take their baths, you can see a colored jinni and trumpets and soldiers and naked beauties in the bottom of the pool."

Ahmad timidly watched men who were completely naked in the pool and under the showers as if it were a city for the nude. He was afraid to leave his towel. An old effeminate man asked him, "Why is it so crowded inside the hammam?"

Three boys surrounded him and started to laugh aloud. Everyone was laughing. Everyone was making fun of him. Why didn't he understand this city?

Amm Hassanein came to his rescue at the right moment. Ahmad came out of the hot pool into the cold one and then walked out. The owner refused to take his money.

"But why? You have a big sign up with the rates clearly marked for everything: the rooms, the soap, the takiyyis."

"You are a stranger and we like to welcome strangers. Why don't you stay with us for a while? So we can get to know each other . . . have tea and some nice hot fitir."

Tea was served, followed by the hot fitir. The crowd gradually shrank in the hammam as men and children, predominantly poor, began to leave. Ahmad had hardly seen any of them in shirts and slacks. He saw the three boys who had surrounded him inside the hammam with its slippery floor sitting in a circle, eating fitir with happy, smiling faces.

Morning songs could now be heard on the radio. Happy songs. The sun slowly began to spread its rays and the hammam looked splendid inside. The faces of the owner and Amm Hasanein were haggard. Amm Hasanein said, introducing him to the group with whom he was eating fitir with sugar, "This is the owner, Ma'allim Ali al-Tayeb, this is our tea-maker, Amm Dawwi, and the three boys: Kamal, Samir, and Fathi. They never leave the hammam. They are like the master's children and so am I: Hasanein Abita."

The boys smiled when Amm Hasanein uttered his surname that meant 'idiot.' The owner gave them a stern look. But they mischievously kept repeating the name Abita with exaggerated, loud, rough, drawn-out sounds.

Ahmad smoked a cigarette with them and told them the story of his ten days in Cairo and that he did not want to return to his mother and father empty-handed. He did not dare visit his aunt for she now belonged to a different class altogether. Should his mother ever find out that he had gone to see his aunt she would hate him for the rest of her life.

Ma'allim Ali al-Tayeb, the big and rosy-cheeked owner, said, "You came at the right moment. I was looking for someone to do the bookkeeping for me."

Ahmad thought to himself: What bookkeeping, when all the rates were clearly marked on a blackboard with how many clients entered the hammam and how much each paid? Then he heard al-Tayeb's voice, "It is not the hammam that worries me, but the ful furnace next door to the hammam. The men there are robbing me of my money. Sometimes there are fifty pots of ful; sometimes there are only twenty. It's the same fire and the same loss. Sometimes we cook the ful ourselves and sometimes people bring their own ful pots to cook in our furnace until dawn."

"But do you think I would be capable of working for you?"

"Of course! Don't you know how to count? Didn't you tell me you have an important diploma and that you want to go to university? But this is not all. I also own a workshop in al-Darb al-Asfar where we make silver jewelry to sell in Khan al-Khalili. All this business is not mine alone. My brothers are my partners and they are ruthless: they ask to see the books and the accounts."

At first, Ahmad was silent, but then he said, "I really don't know what to say! But I'm ready to accept after all the warmth you have shown me. I feel I am among family. But if I find another job with the man to whom I will deliver my letter of reference, I will have to leave you."

"Even if you find the man, will he hire you immediately? I have a distant relative who graduated from university and has been unemployed for the past two years. Do you really believe you will be hired soon?"

"That's what my father told me. Anyway, I am at your service. I feel very close to you after this short time. And I love the area. It is an everlasting spiritual space and you live in the shadow of its history. I love that."

Ma'allim al-Tayeb smiled as he walked out of the hammam, having put on his expensive gray coat. Amm Hasanein said, "I will go in and clean up after the folks."

Is it not strange that you should come to Cairo to work in a company that occupies a high-rise building with an elevator and uniformed office boys, only to find yourself hurled into a place underground where you take on the responsibility of hot and cold water, a black ful furnace that feeds on garbage, and a small workshop that makes jewelry? Your mother had thought you would become like a little moon that would light her way or a small sun that would warm her heart. Will you write to her and say: I finally found work in a ful furnace after ten days of continuous searching? When you enter it you come out black like a slave. Will you tell her that you sleep in a sticky place covered with water and soap and filled with naked men? That this was all you could find? Only this narrow dead end? That you were hungry and naked; that your underwear is filthy and that your shoes are worn out; that you want a hot meal with a lot of butter, and that you miss your days in Ismailiya; that spring will not return . . . and that you fear the winter?

Ahmad went out through the large wooden door. He passed through a narrow glass door, after which he found himself all alone in a large desolate hall. Amm Hasanein was still scrubbing the floor and changing the water in the pool. Amm Dawwi was sleeping on a high bench in one of the rooms. The three boys were fast asleep on the benches. Their legs were naked and so were their chests. Ahmad covered them with a white sheet before he left.

The neighborhood was now teeming with women and men. The cooking pots were made of brass. This was what first met his eye.

He wanted to visit the mosque he had found the day before. It had small domes surrounding the main large one and a tall, slender minaret without balconies. There were domes only at the very top. He had inquired from the guard about the mosque. . . . He said: "Muhammad Bek Abul-Dahab." But the ceiling had lost all its engravings. They had been washed away with time. It was a new mosque, not like Qalawun or Barquq mosques. O people of our time, why do you neglect your monuments? A time of suffering and bondage!

Translated by Samia Mehrez

Mahmoud Al-Wardani

from *Heads Ripe for Plucking*

THEY SET OUT FROM the hotel. As they got out of the cab at the corner of al-Muizz Street, a whiff of al-Ghuriya's aromas, with all its spice and scent shops, caught Alia in the face. Every time she came to this district she was intoxicated by its sharp fragrant blend that wafted in gusts to reach her even on the outskirts of Gamaliya. She remembered that it was to Fuad al-Shafie that she owed her intimate knowledge of the district and passion for it. For over a year, she had spent hours on end just about every day wandering around with him there. She came to know every inch of the area all the way from Bab al-Khalq—which was a stone's throw away from her father's family house, though she was barely aware of it until she met Fuad—to the bus stop right next to Sidi al-Jaafari Mosque in Darrasa.

Of the aroma of al-Ghuriya, Fuad used to say it mellowed your very bones. He taught her to pick it out at a distance as they walked down from Bab Zuwayla. He would lead her as they sauntered through al-Ghuriya's maze of narrow alleyways as if it were a feast for all the senses.

When she managed to get a grip on herself she pulled her black leather jacket tightly around her and gestured toward the wall and dome to their right.

"Sir, I'll be your guide for the evening," she said. "This here is the Ghuri dome. I expect you've heard about Sultan al-Ghuri?"

"Oh, yes."

"He was the last of the sultans of the Mamluk Dynasty who fought the Ottomans and was defeated by them in the Levant. He is probably the only sultan who was not buried in the mausoleum he built for himself during his reign."

"As I recall, he died beneath the horses' hooves during that last battle."

She drew closer to him. "Actually, my knowledge of history is scanty except for this period, and that on account of my love for this place." He patted her shoulder but she pulled away from him with a bothered look. As he registered her reaction she hastened to match his step, as if apologetically, and pointed to a nearby minaret.

"This is Abul-Dahab Mosque, followed by al-Azhar Mosque, and right behind it is an area called al-Batniya where hashish used to be sold quite openly."

They walked through the dirty underpass amid the beggars who dotted the passage and thronged the entrance. She leaned ever so slightly toward him as they climbed up the last steps heading for the square, as if making up for her brusqueness. It was chilly, now that night had fallen, and Abd al-Wahab, wrapped in a dark woolen coat, looked willowy as he stepped aside every now and then to let Alia lead the way. The alleyways and the houses, he remarked, reminded him of old Basra. "Anyway, I've never been so lucky as to be accompanied by such a beautiful young woman, and so knowledgeable about one of the most renowned and mysterious cities in the world."

She took him in the direction of Khan al-Khalili. Once past the Husayn Hotel passageway and into the Khan proper, Abd al-Wahab surrendered himself to the experience. The alleyways were almost empty, the chill in the air dictating the pedestrians' slow, deliberate pace. He peered through the store windows, drinking in all they held—prayer beads; scarabs; wood carvings; silver and copperware; kohl sticks and jars; Qur'an holders; trays, plates, and waterpipes; statues of gods and pharaohs; divans in the corners and pharaonic- and Mamluk-style chairs; sequined fabrics; chunks of stone; perfumes; mummified animals, tigers, and hawks; the ankh, key of life; pendant lamps; ornaments and gold jewelry. There were stores, side by side to the right and to the left, the passageways between them just wide enough for two people. He barely paused now; try as he might, he was too enchanted to stop. Alia was observing him closely with a hint of a smile on her face. She felt comfortable with Abd al-Wahab, indeed, almost drawn to him. Something about his face, gestures, and sentences that ended as suddenly as they began suggested restraint. He had a manly timidity that Alia liked and that set her at ease to act spontaneously. He moved as if mesmerized between the glass panes and mirrors that refracted the light of hidden lamps until they had finally wound their way back to al-Muizz Street.

Alia was not sure why the memory of Fuad al-Shafie came back to her so insistently just then. Things were different with Fuad, the way we discovered each other, she thought to herself. When we read *Cancer of the Soul* together, I could see why my aunt was loved by everyone, especially by her generation, because she had defended it despite its major sins and successive failures that had overtaken its very dreams. Fuad used to say that what amazed him about Iqbal and her generation was their ability to dream, they who had left everything in ruins for their successors. He's right, Alia thought, I have no dreams, no wishes whatsoever. At most I may have dreamt that my mother and I would be able to beat her cancer, and that Fuad and I should stay friends despite our failure to love each other. She had to admit that she owed Fuad not only her passion for Gammaliya but also her good times with his wacky friends whom she used to meet whenever he took her to the Hurriya Café for a glass of beer or to the Bustan Café where they would sit in the wide passageway that had witnessed so many violent fights between the touts who service tourists over their sleazy customers.

Sensing Abd al-Wahab's eyes on her, she gestured toward a narrow alleyway opposite.

"See this alley here? It's called Alley of the Jews. They used to live there until the 1956 Suez War."

"We too have an Alley of the Jews in Basra. I think they even had a whole quarter to themselves in Baghdad."

"There are hardly any Jews still living here of course. I remember reading a feature article that said there were thirty-three elderly women left who have decided to meet their death here where they were born."

"My dear, don't involve me in talk about the Jews or I'll be charged with anti-Semitism!" he said with a smile. "Well, this Khan is a strange, fascinating place. You have such great artists. Only now does it make sense to me that people call Cairo 'Mother of the World.' Would you believe that I feel familiar with Cairo? I have this strange feeling that I've roamed through its alleyways before."

As he walked alongside her in al-Muizz Street, Alia was thinking that they did not really know each other as she had imagined, despite the dozens of messages they had exchanged over a period of three months. His panic at a mere passing reference to Jews did not seem justified to her. She was aware, of course, that Israel waves the specter of anti-Semitism in face of all and sundry. Still, it was odd that Abd al-Wahab, too, should be susceptible to it.

It was probably past nine in the evening by then and the weather was getting chillier. She drew her jacket tightly around her. There were few pedestrians but the cafés here and there were crowded. When they reached the Mosque of al-Salih Najm al-Din Ayyub she paused.

"See the ruins of that mosque there? Its style is different from all the others in this area because it was built in the Ayyubid Dynasty. It's called the Mosque of al-Salih Najm al-Din Ayyub after one of the Ayyubid sultans who ruled Egypt after the Fatimid Dynasty."

In the quiet of the night Abd al-Wahab contemplated the mosque. Its architectural style did seem unique. The façade closest to them, which was floodlit, supported what looked like the vestiges of a tower.

"You're quite right," he turned to her, "though I still think that the biggest surprise is you."

"As I said, this is the one part I know of Egypt, or of the whole world, for that matter. My father had a passion for history, as you know, and it seems I inherited this from him."

"Yes, of course. Anyone who reads the magnificent scenario he wrote about Urabi cannot fail to notice. By the way, we still haven't spoken of the co-authored book by the late Iqbal and Shaker."

"We'll get around to it," she said as she led him across the street. "But first, I want to show you this hammam. It's a popular public bath that was still functioning until a few months ago. And just past it is the finest and most important collection of monuments that was built by Sultan al-Nasser Muhammad ibn Qalawun."

The floodlights gave the minarets and domes a singular presence. He stood gazing raptly and listening to her.

"This is the oldest intact collection of monuments. Had it not been for conservation work we would have lost an invaluable treasure. You really ought to see it all in broad daylight. Only then will you discover the enchantment of the Qalawun collection—the architectural design and the scrupulously calculated alignment of the domes, columns, minarets, entrances, and doorways."

"But the night brings its own enchantment, too."

"See that sabil water house across the way? It dates back to the Ottoman period. So the street you're walking in is several centuries old."

"What's the name of this street?"

"It's al-Muizz li-Din Allah al-Fatimi Street."

"A single street that bears on either side all these centuries and kings and sultans!"

"Well then, let's keep going. If we walk straight ahead, we'll be crossing into the Ottoman period, heading for the Bab al-Nasr gate, the southernmost perimeter of the old city."

"Alia, dear," he broke in, "aren't you too young to be steeped in all these details?"

"As I was saying, I inherited my father's passion for history. Besides, I have a friend who's besotted with this place. He was the one who opened my eyes to Islamic Cairo. Come this way, I have a surprise in store for you."

They crossed the street, and a few steps down the road he stopped again.

"This is incredible! It's nothing less than a theater," he exclaimed.

For the first time she noticed that it did indeed resemble a theater. There were steps leading up to a slightly elevated expanse beneath the arches and semi-arches of hewn stone.

"You have a point, Abd al-Wahab. I hadn't noticed that it looked like a theater. It's called Bayt al-Qadi, the Judge's House. The judge used to sit inside and adjudicate between the people who gathered out here in what you've called the theater, waiting for their turn to go in. But this isn't the surprise I had in store for you."

"What could be a bigger surprise than this theater?"

"Follow me."

He followed her across the street where she pointed to a one-story building in front of them.

"This is the police station that Naguib Mahfouz described in his *Cairo Trilogy*."

"Now that is a surprise."

"I assume you've read his *Trilogy*," she said, pointing to the opposite side of the street. "You can imagine that this is more or less the location of the protagonist al-Sayyid Ahmad Abd al-Gawad's house, where his wife Amina would stand behind the latticed window screen every night waiting for him to return."

"Amazing. What can I say?"

"And right here where you see this residential building, there was another house that fell into ruins. This is where Naguib Mahfouz was born."

"This is too much for me at one go."

"Then let's sit at this café."

The café overlooked a small square. She picked two chairs on the pavement. Noticing her wrap her black leather jacket around her, Abd al-Wahab said, "It's bitterly cold. Shall we move inside?"

"It's probably best to stay here so we don't catch cold—it's really warm inside the café. Well, what do you think?"

She watched him smilingly as he knit his eyebrows.

"It's incredible. Truly amazing, Alia. It's nothing less than a stage. All it takes is some chairs you'd spread out here in the square, and then you'd have an audience."

A lean, elderly waiter came up to them with a smile.

"How about some tea with mint? You won't find the like of it anywhere else in the world," Alia offered then turned to the waiter. "Tea with mint, and make it special for the guest. . . ."

They had taken another turn and she pointed to a small yellow building nearby.

"This is the government mint. You know what that is, don't you?"

"Yes, just as I can read and write!"

As they burst out laughing their shoulders touched and they remained close as they trod the stones of the alley in semidarkness.

"Listen. We're quite close to the shrine of Umm al-Ghulam, 'The Boy's Mother.' Hers is quite a story. Ready to hear it?"

"Yes, dear."

"It's a very beautiful story. Umm al-Ghulam, a kind Egyptian woman, was sitting at home when into her lap landed the head of al-Husayn, which, after his murder at Karbala, had fled to Cairo, with the caliph's soldiers in pursuit. According to the biographical narrative about Umm al-Ghulam, she slew her son and threw his head to the caliph's soldiers to save al-Husayn's head, which is buried here. Umm al-Ghulam's shrine still exists and to this minute it exudes the scent of musk and amber, yes, to this very minute. I can take you to her shrine right now and you'll be able to smell it for yourself. There's only one little problem—a historical problem that the account overlooked, namely that Cairo hadn't been built yet when al-Husayn was murdered."

Alia was breathless as she narrated the story. She fell silent as the lights from the widening street reached them while they slowly approached al-Husayn Mosque.

Translated by Hala Halim

Yahya Hakki

from *The Lamp of Umm Hashim*

My grandfather, Sheikh Ragab Abdallah, coming to Cairo as a young boy with the men and women of the family to obtain blessings from visiting the family of the Prophet, would be pushed forward as they approached the entrance to the Mosque of Sayyida Zaynab. The instinct to imitate the others made it unnecessary to push the boy; along with them, he would drop down and cover the marble doorstep with kisses, while the feet of those going in and out of the mosque almost knocked against his head. If their action was witnessed by one of the self-righteous men of religion, he would turn his face away in indignation at the times and would invoke God's aid against idolatry, ignorance, and such heresies. As for most people, they would simply smile at the naivety of these country folk, with the smell of milk, mud, and fenugreek emanating from their clothes. They would understand in their hearts the warmth of these people's longing and veneration for the place they were visiting, people unable to find any other way than this to express their emotions. Deeds, as the saying has it, are by intention.

As a young man, my grandfather moved to Cairo in search of work. It is no surprise that he should choose to live as near as possible to his much-loved mosque. And so it was that he settled in an old house that was a religious endowment, facing the mosque's rear ablution basin in the alley named Ablution Lane. I say 'was' in the past tense because the heavy axe of the town planning department has since demolished it along with other Cairo landmarks. While the axe wrought its will, though, the soul of the square escaped unscathed, for the axe was able to wipe out and destroy only those things that were of brick and stone.

My grandfather later opened a store for grain in the square itself, and thus the family came to live within the precincts of Umm Hashim—Sayyida Zaynab—and under her protection: her holidays became our holidays, her feasts our feasts, and the mosque's muezzin the clock by which we told the time.

My grandfather enjoyed the blessings of Umm Hashim, and his business flourished. No sooner had his eldest son finished his studies at the elementary Qur'anic school than he took him into the business. As for the second son, he went to al-Azhar University, where he spent several unsuccessful years, after which he went back to our village to become its school teacher and the official responsible for performing marriages. There remained the youngest son, the last child—my uncle Ismail—for whom fate, and the improvement in his father's fortunes, made it possible to provide a brighter future. At first, his father was perhaps frightened, having forced his son to learn the Qur'an by heart, to send him to al-Azhar, for he could see the young boys in the square calling after young men with turbans:

Pull off the turban—
Under the turban a monkey you'll find!

But Sheikh Ragab, with a heart full of hope, handed him over to a government school, where he was helped by his religious upbringing and village background, for he quickly excelled by his good manners and his respect for his teachers, together with deportment and much perseverance. Though not elegantly dressed, his clothes were clean. More than that, he was more manly and was capable of expressing himself better than his pampered colleagues, the children of town folk who were disadvantaged by faulty Arabic. It wasn't long before he surpassed his fellows, and he had about him a certain unmistakable bearing that caused the family's hopes to be set on him.

While still a lad he came to be called Mr. Ismail or Ismail Effendi and was treated like a grown man, being given the best of food and fruits.

When he sat down to study, the father, while reciting his prayers, would lower his voice to a whisper that was almost a melting of tremulous devotion, while his mother walked about on tiptoe, and even his orphan cousin Fatima al-Nabawiya learned how to stop her chattering and to sit silently in front of him like a slave girl before her master. She became accustomed to sitting up with him into the night, as though the lesson he was studying were hers, gazing at him with her sore eyes with their inflamed lids, and with her fingers ceaselessly at work on some piece of knitting. Who was there to say to Ismail: Take note of those hands into which has crept a strange life, a delicate touch, an awakened sensitivity? Do you not realize that the sign of the approach of blindness in a seeing person is when his hands begin to acquire sight?

"Get up and go to sleep, Fatima."

"It's still early—I'm not sleepy yet."

From time to time her eye would water and transform him into a blurred shape. Wiping her eye with the end of her sleeve, she would go back to gazing at him. For her, wisdom was to be found in every word he uttered.

Dear God! How was it possible for books to contain all those secrets and enigmas? How was it that the tongue could pronounce all those foreign languages? As he grew in stature in her eyes, the more she shrank and dwindled before him. His gaze might fall on her two pigtails and he would smile musingly. These girls! If only they knew how empty-headed they were!

When he retired to bed, and only then, did the family feel that its day had ended; only then did it begin to think about tomorrow's needs. Its life, its movements were dedicated to his comfort. A generation was annihilating itself so that a single member of its progeny might come into being: it was a love whose strength had attained the force of an animal instinct. The solicitous hen sits on her eggs, paralyzed and meek like a nun at prayer. Are such instincts a bountiful gift, or are they a tribute paid to some despotic tyrant of iron will, with a yoke around every neck, shackles on every leg?

The family clung to this boy with the ardor of those deprived of all liberty and free will. Where in God's name was the beauty in it? The answer to that question lies in my heart. Whenever those past days were depicted to me, I would find my heart beating at the memory of them; there would appear before me the face of my grandfather, Sheikh Ragab, his face surrounded by a halo of pure light. As for my grandmother, the Lady Adeela, with her naive goodness, it would be stupid to think of her as being human, for, if so, then what would angels be like! How hateful and ugly the world would be were it to be devoid of such submission, such faith!

Year after year, Ismail came first in his class. When the results of the examination were announced, glasses of sherbet would be passed around the neighbors, even to the odd passerby. The woman selling taamiya and busara made from beans would make trilling cries of joy and would ask God to keep him safe, and Master Hassan, both barber and doctor for the district, would achieve his usual tip. The Lady Adeela, for her part, would burn incense, thus fulfilling her vows to Umm Hashim. Loaves of bread would be baked and stuffed with sprouting beans, and Umm Muhammad would carry them off in a basket on her head. No sooner did she appear in the square than the loaves would be seized, the basket would disappear, her milaya would be gone, and she would stumble bashfully back home, partly in amused anger at the greed of Sayyida's beggars. Her experience would provide the family with amusement for several days.

Thus, in the protection of God, then in that of Umm Hashim, Ismail grew up. His life did not take him outside the quarter itself and the square; the farthest excursion he ever made was to Manial, where he would walk beside the river or stand on the bridge. With the coming of evening and the waning violence of the sun, when the sharp reflections and straight lines had changed to curves and illusions, the square would come to itself and would be empty of visitors and strangers. If you are of pure heart and conscience and listen carefully, you will be conscious of a deep, secret breathing traversing the square.

Perhaps it is Sidi al-Itris, the mosque's doorkeeper—for is not his name numbered among the Servants?—sitting in his private quarters, shaking the dust of the day's work from his hands and clothing as he breathes a sigh of satisfaction. Were it your good fortune to hear this deep breathing, you might at that instant take a look at the dome and see it engirdled by a radiance of light, fading then growing stronger like the flickerings of a lamp toyed with by the breeze. This is the lamp of Umm Hashim that hangs over the shrine—walls cannot obscure its rays.

Slowly the square fills up again. Exhausted, sallow-faced, and bleary-eyed, each person is dressed in what chance has bestowed upon him, or, if you will, what he has found to hand. The calls of the street vendors make a mournful melody:

"Great green broad beans!"

"Eat something sweet and call down blessings on the Prophet!"

"Tender radishes!"

"Use a miswak for keeping your teeth clean, just as the Prophet did!"

What is the hidden tyranny they complain of! What is the burden that weighs down the breasts of them all! And yet, for all that, their faces show a kind of contentment and serenity. How easily they forget! Many are the hands that take in so few piasters and milliemes. Here there is no law, no standard measure, no fixed price; there is only custom, giving favors, and haggling, allowing the scales to tip freely and giving a fair weight, and sometimes being fraudulent and cheating. It's all free and easy. Rows of people are seated on the ground with their backs to the wall of the mosque; some squat on the pavement: a medley of men, women, and children. You don't know where they have come from nor how they will pass from sight: fruit that has fallen from the tree of life and has become moldy under its canopy.

Here is the school of beggars. One of them, his back weighed down under a sack full of bits of bread, calls out: "A crust of bread for God's sake. O doers of good—I'm hungry."

Then there's the young girl who springs up all of a sudden in the middle of the lane, naked, or almost so: "O you who clothe a woman, O Muslim—may God never bring such a scandal to a woman of yours!"

Her screeching voice attracts faces to the windows. Her bewitching eyes enchant the women who have looked down at her and they shower her with heaps of rags and tattered clothing. In an instant she has melted away, vanished. You don't know: has she flown off or has the earth swallowed her up?

And here is a blind vendor of mixed condiments, who will not sell to you unless you first greet him, when he will recite to you the legal formula for buying and selling. The day draws to a close and the vendor of pickles takes his leave with his barrels, and the feet of the man with the foot-lathe leave their daily work and their tools to take their owner off home. The tram remains a rapacious beast, claiming its daily toll. The evening draws on, freshened by a diffident breeze. Soft laughter mingles with the harsh guffaws of men high on hashish. If you turn off the square into the entrance to Marasina Street you will hear the uproar of drunks in the Anastasi Bar, which the locals have nicknamed the "Have a Good Time" Bar. A drunk emerges from it, raging and staggering and accosting the passersby:

"Show me the toughest guy around here."

"Get lost, you so-and-so."

"Let him be, poor wretch."

"May God forgive him."

The sorrowful, tired specters of the square are now stirred by some sort of delight and merriment. There is no care in the world, and the future is in the hands of God. Faces come close together in affection and the person in pain forgets to complain, and a man will spend the last of his money on a narghile or a game of cards. Let come what may! The sounds of the clashing of the scales of a balance grow less, the handcarts disappear, the candles are being put out inside the baskets. It is now that Ismail's walk around the square comes to an end. He is familiar with every corner, every inch, every stone. No vendor's call is new to him, nor the place from which it comes. The crowds enfold him and he is like a drop of rain that is swallowed up by the ocean. So used to the ever-recurring, ever-similar images, they find not the least response within him; he is neither curious nor bored, knowing neither contentment nor anger. He is not sufficiently detached for his eye to take them in. Who will say to him that all these sounds he hears and of which he is unaware, all these forms his eye alights on and which he does not see, that all these have an extraordinary power to creep into the heart, to penetrate stealthily, to establish themselves in it and to settle down in its very depths so that one day they will become his very substance? As for now, his glance picks out no particular aspect of life—all it has to do is to look.

Translated by Denys Johnson-Davies

Muhammad Galal

from *Mounira Days*

SAMIR ABD AL-KARIM emerged from his neighbor's apartment in Mounira. He made his way to the offices of the magazine to which he had not been back for several years. He preferred to walk. He wanted to forget his lifetime friend, Salah Abd al-Ghani, who was trying to cast his net around Soheir, the woman he loved and wanted to marry.

He saw a woman whose house had fallen into ruins on Mawardi Street, squatting on the pavement of the school building that had once been a palace. She was washing her clothes and hanging them on the iron railing of the palace.

He walked along Ismail Pasha Sirri Street. People still used "Pasha" when they mentioned the name of the street in conversation despite its visible deterioration, as if they were still hanging on to the glamour days of Mounira that their fathers had told them about. Samir remembered when his father took him in his arms when he was still a little boy and said, "I bought you a house in the neighborhood of pashas."

His clothes were soiled by a football that a child playing on the street had kicked. The coffee-shop waiter around the corner dashed to clean his trousers. Some of the young men who were playing backgammon stopped the game and talked to him about his novel that had been turned into a controversial TV serial. He looked at his watch. He was late getting to the office where he was expected to take over as editor-in-chief. He promised the young men that he would resume the conversation at some other time. As he walked on, he saw construction workers demolishing the remains of Ismail Pasha Sirri's palace. He remembered when he was a little boy he would approach the palace only to be reminded by the guard dogs that he had overstepped boundaries, while the Nubian bawwab laughed, sitting on his seat in his black garb embroidered with gold thread like the lion on Qasr al-Nil Bridge.

He smiled to himself and crossed Qasr al-Aini Street to Garden City. The cars rushed past him. He stood contemplating the street. In the past, he used to call it the royal street. This was where he used to watch King Farouk's procession. He remembered when his father once sent him to a bakery that was well known for its excellent bread—his father was used to bringing the family together at the banquet-like breakfast on Fridays. The street was being washed and had lost the tram line that used to cut through it. He imagined that the king was about to pass through. But he knew it would be Queen Farida. He loved the queen. He had many photographs of her. He would not lose this chance. He held the bread in his arms and stood waiting for her procession. Finally her beautiful royal car appeared. She enchanted him with her angelic smile. He applauded her with all his might until he dropped the bread. He picked it up as the procession swept ahead. When he got home, his father had gone to Friday prayer and his big brother gave him a spanking.

He remembered when he went to Farida's painting exhibition in Paris on his last visit. He saw her love for Egypt and the Nile in her paintings. This encouraged him to talk to her. She was quite accessible so he found himself telling her about the spanking. She apologized gracefully. So he said to her, as if defending the queen, "Queen Farida should never apologize."

He suddenly noticed that the dense traffic on Qasr al-Aini Street had stopped. He walked across Garden City to the Nile Corniche as he always did on his way to the office. He found himself in front of the Ibrahimiya School where he had been a student. He felt nostalgic, embracing it with his eyes. He walked toward the iron gate. He heard the school bell ringing. He stopped. He was seized by a desire to become part of them. As they rushed around him he felt transported to his enchanted childhood days. He remembered that at the end of the school day he would rush out of school before the rich students. He would watch them get into their luxury cars. The car attendant used to call on the cars according to protocol: the royal car first, then the cars that belonged to pashas, followed by those that belonged to beys. He, the son of a mere effendi, felt he was better off than them. He walked freely, moving from one pavement to the other; he played football on his way home to Harat Omar when he wanted.

He remembered his relative who used to work in the secretariat of the Cabinet when he announced to Samir's mother that the Pasha had agreed to enroll him in the exclusive Ibrahimiya School just for the relative's sake.

A Mercedes dashed past him. It could have knocked him down had he not taken refuge on the pavement. He heard someone insult the nouveaux riches.

As he walked on the streets of Garden City he felt nostalgic for the past. He was rather surprised at himself. When he was young he had dreamed of a revolution against all those who lived in Garden City. He asked himself: does one change as one gets older and become nostalgic for a place one had hated in the past? He noticed how run down his surroundings were. He was angry. He felt that the revolutionary regime had deliberately neglected Garden City out of revenge against the neighborhood that controlled the fate of the whole country. He stopped in front of Nahhas Pasha's palace. It still looked stately despite the neglect. He remembered when it would be besieged by demonstrators who—himself included—would climb up the palace walls and trees and squat on the ground until Nahhas Pasha would come out to meet them. He was their only hope against the corrupt king whom they used to spot in one of the palaces in Garden City where he came to play cards.

He walked under the shade of a big tree that seemed to be defying neglect. The smell of jasmine intoxicated him. He picked one. His eyes fell on an ugly cement structure. He felt he was suffocating. He hurried toward the Nile, his old love since his Arabic teacher prophesied that he would become a writer. Tayeb Effendi's words had left him sleepless and he had become obsessed with the idea that every writer had a jinni that he must wait for on the shores of the Nile, so that writing would descend upon him. That is why he seized every opportunity to go to the Nile and wait for his jinni. Until one day the flood came, destroying bridges and submerging homes, and he felt a spring of words gushing from within him. His words overflowed on the paper. He couldn't sleep all night. He remained awake in order to guard his words for fear that if he slept, they might all disappear. In the morning, his Arabic teacher asked him to read what he had written to the class. They applauded him. His teacher said, "A writer is born." Then he knew he had found his jinni.

Translated by Samia Mehrez

May al-Telmissany
from *Heliopolis*

IT WAS IN 1925. The baron would die one year later and his body would be buried at the Basilica.

The house was built on the edge of the new oasis. It was surrounded by a spacious courtyard covered with red tile and surrounded by a railing with spear-like tips. The gate opened onto a long alleyway that led up to the only entrance to the house. The farther the buildings were from the center of the neighborhood, the less visible the prominent Islamic style that dominated the al-Bawaki area, and the more pronounced the European colonial one.

Approximately thirty years from this date, the owner of the house built two more levels above the three already existing ones. The ceilings were lower and the floors were covered with mosaic tile. The bathroom walls were half covered with ceramics and the other half was painted shining pistachio green. The family that had migrated from Abbasiya in search of quiet and clean air settled in three floors; the third and fourth were in the traditional style while the fifth was modern. The building overlooked a square and two wide streets; one of them led to Ismailiya Square while the other led to al-Gami' Square, then to the Basilica, and finally to what was once known as Abbas Street.

The three balconies overlooked the square facing the English School and the students' racing track; on the other side one could hear the chirping of birds emanating from a small wild garden. At dawn, Atum-Ra hid behind the trees, and during the early morning hours his arms would descend upon the students' heads at school. If you were on the fifth-floor balcony you would see stretched out before you the buildings around the square on the eastern side and the Heliopolis Courthouse on the western side, as well as the desert that extended to the north beyond the school walls.

The map of the square changed every one or two years. The streets that branched out from it changed their traffic directions: sometimes they were one-way, at others two-way. The cement cubicles, triangles, and cylinders that were used to control the change of traffic flow by their positioning vis-à-vis the square were sometimes used as flowerpots, or could be good for a traffic-control kiosk or a public phone booth that quickly went out of order. The cars that drove across lost their sense of direction amid the triangles and the cylinders: they turned where they were not allowed to and they went forward where they were only allowed to turn right or left. There were many accidents at the far end of the square by the school. The traffic policeman usually stood there (none of them ever died) and seldom did the accidents cause deaths or serious injuries. The tramway sped through the night and did not stop at the stations. It hit a cat or a rat. It only hit people in the morning. The circular square, as is the case with all other squares, had several names: Abu Bakr al-Siddiq, the English School, and for the layman it was known as the beginning of Haroun Street.

Around the year 390 BC Plato was on his way to Egypt carrying a large shipment of oil the sale of which would cover his stay and his studies. He was around thirty-eight. In Egypt he witnessed arts and culture that were based on an old civilization intertwined with modern elements that were brought together with Persian, Greek, Assyrian, and African cultures, which came to be known as the pharaonic civilization. It may have been this civilization, so immersed in its traditions and so desirous of the new, that inspired the form of the republic as he imagined it, where human happiness became possible with stability and where one constitution that governed all the people was enough to provide plenty. Apparently Plato studied under the Ra priests in old Heliopolis before returning to Athens. The road from Memphis to the sacred city of On was decked with statues of the sphinx. Heliopolis is the Greek name for On, capital of the thirteenth province of Lower Egypt. It is Per-Ra, or "the house of the sun," that is the city of worship of Ra the creator, who rises on the earth. It is the eye of the sun in the language of the Arab conquerors. Its priests have a special status in the history of ancient religions, as they were the first to develop a theory of creation and the idea of a unitary god, father of all other gods. In *al-Wisada al-khaliya*, Abd al-Halim Hafez stood amid the ruins of old Heliopolis and sang twice. The temple of Seti I from the Nineteenth Dynasty was found by Schiaparelli in 1903 and had been transported to Turin. The photographs from *al-Wisada al-khaliya* are the only remaining images of the monuments of pharaonic Heliopolis: the sand, the columns, the remains of a temple, and an obelisk.

In 1905 the Belgian industrialist Baron Empain considered building this new city north of Cairo. It is located on a plateau above the Nile level near the ruins of the old city of Ain Shams. It was named after its old Greek name: Heliopolis. Construction began in 1906 and the beautiful Arab designs were made by the Belgian architect Gaspar. It was declared a financially independent area from Kafr al-Shurafa and Kafr Farouk by royal decree in 1936. The baron would spend several months in his palace with his wife and son. He knew that the oasis of Heliopolis was far from the site of the old city, for the ruins were closer to the Nile than to the desert of Ain Shams and the tombs were hidden underground in Matariya. But the baron was an industrialist and an expert in modes of transportation, an old capitalist who loved beauty. Hence the stunning style of his palace that was inspired by Indian architecture, a style not seen in any Egyptian buildings until that time. We also know that when the Heliopolis Company started to reclaim desert land in the area, it planned and constructed several buildings at its own expense that still stand at the entrance to Heliopolis, with their characteristic vaults supported by luxurious granite columns brought from Aswan. The company allowed people to buy land at forty piasters per square meter while it undertook construction according to an agreed-upon design. Both the land and the buildings were paid for in installments over fifteen years at a low interest rate and a symbolic down payment of no more than several pounds. The company attracted people to the new neighborhood by constructing a metro line and a second tram line that came to be known as al-Waziri and al-Metro al-Abyad. The line started from Abbasiya and cut through al-Khalifa al-Ma'mun Street. It also built an attraction park where the Roxy cinema is located today. This was all new, so it attracted people from Cairo and the provinces, who came for outings and discovery.

Translated by Samia Mehrez

Nabil Naoum Gorgy
from *Cairo Is a Small City*

FROM THE BALCONY OF his luxury apartment, architect Adel Salem stood watching some construction workers at a site across the boulevard, at the center of which lay a big garden. The building under construction had foundations already and some protruding supports for the first floor. A young blacksmith with long hair was intent on bending the iron rods of different lengths. Adel noticed how this young man had parked his Jawa motorbike next to a huge crane that was awaiting the future floors of the building. "How the scene has changed!" Adel could still remember the image of the old masters and workers who carried the steel on their shoulders with recently acquired muscle.

The sun was about to set. The steel columns in several new structures looked like dark skeletons against the light in this calm area on the edge of Heliopolis.

As was usual every day, at the same time, a herd of sheep and goats descended upon the central garden, followed by two Bedouin women: one on donkey-back and the other, a younger one, on foot beside her. And as usual, Adel's gaze was focused on the younger one on foot, in a black dress that concealed her beautiful body just as much as it revealed it: she had wrapped her waist with a red band and was wearing green plastic shoes. He wished she would see him on his balcony. But even if she were to see him, Adel thought to himself, these Bedouins have very peculiar manners that are very different from what he was accustomed to, which makes it difficult to communicate with them. And what would make him speak to her? This is what he was thinking as he followed her with his eyes, as she ran after a lamb that had almost been run down by a car or a goat that had lagged behind the herd.

Given his experience with society women, Adel knew that she had captivated his heart. He passed his days on the balcony, sunset after sunset, without her knowing of his existence.

Had it not been for that day when he went to buy some fruit and vegetables from one of the vendors along the metro street, who, upon seeing one of the Bedouin women chasing another herd, called her by name and gave her the remains of the shop after fondling her body—had it not been for that day, Adel would have never been able to concoct this plan on which he was intent, no matter what, for the sake of the woman who had stolen his mind. Since Adel believed that every human being had his own Satan that was better appeased to fend off his wrath, he finally decided to go for the forbidden and the impossible. He knew from forty years of experience in this pact with his own Satan that he had acquired an audacity that set him apart from his friends and allowed him to accede to this social status, through which he was able to buy his apartment, the price of which he dared not mention even to his own parents, who, if not suspicious, would be envious.

So, from his balcony on the second floor in Turmudhi Street, architect Adel Salem yelled at the top of his voice, "Hey, girl!" calling the woman who was following the herd. When she continued to walk unheedingly he called out again, "Hey, sheep seller." Before she was too far away he repeated, "sheep." Adel did not care much for the surprise of the bawwab, who, upon hearing his voice, sprang from his place in front of the entrance to the building, thinking that Adel was calling him. Adel told him calmly that he wanted him to follow the Bedouins and tell them that he had a lot of leftover bread that he wanted to give to the sheep.

From his balcony, Adel heard the bawwab call to the two women with an authoritative Upper Egyptian voice. The one on the donkey stopped and turned around, which allowed Adel to quickly see her face when she looked up toward him with a knowing, perceptive gaze. The girl, however, continued behind the herd. The woman was older, with a full body and an overbearing look that she made no attempt to conceal. She turned around on the donkey and crossed the street that separated the garden and Adel's building, then waited in front of the entrance. Adel collected all the bread he had in the apartment and placed it on a brass tray. He hurried down and did not wince from approaching the old woman while looking at her. She opened a sack near her leg into which he emptied all the bread.

"Thank you!" she said as she turned away without looking at him. He raised his voice so she could hear him saying, "More, tomorrow."

For almost a month, Adel would buy bread that he didn't eat even on days when he was away or out of the house for the whole day. He used to leave a big paper bundle of bread with the bawwab to give to the Bedouin woman on the donkey and the other one whom the architect's heart desired.

Since Adel had a sixth sense for the expected and the probable, after one lunar month had passed he stood in the same spot in front of the building with the brass tray filled with bread, and what he hoped for finally happened: the old woman on the donkey went on her way, while the young one turned her head to the left and to the right before crossing the street and he suddenly found her standing in front of him. Beauty itself! His heart almost stopped. How could this beauty exist without shame that everything else before and after it would be described as ugly? When she stood directly across from him with her kohl-lined eyes he felt the danger of her mere twenty years: her tall body, her slender waistline, her rounded breasts, and the movement of her buttocks when she turned around and walked away with the bread, thanking him. His imagination froze at the memory of her beautiful face even as she was still nearby: her high cheekbones, her delicate nose, and her painted lips; her silver crescent-like earrings and the necklace that adorned her chest. This beauty was overwhelming. Adel could think only of Salma—whose name he found out when her mother asked her to hurry when she lingered behind during these lovers' rendezvous.

Adel no longer minded the whistles of the construction workers who had been mounting one level after the other in the building across the street. He was completely taken by Salma's splendor. Even though it had all started as a daring game that might end in a brief encounter or a greeting, it became an absolute necessity for him to be home before sunset so as not to miss the chance of seeing her. This is how architect Adel Salem fell in love with the beautiful Bedouin girl, Salma.

Since history is written by historians, Adel, whose profession was architecture, decided to historicize this love in the form of a building whose every column would represent one day, and every level, one month. He had noticed that at the end of twenty-eight days, with the full moon, Salma would come to him to take the bread, instead of her mother. He, the architect, started to watch the moon: he would be heartbroken with its eclipse and his soul would brighten with the advent of its fullness until it became whole and heralded the happy encounter between lover and beloved.

In seven months he saw her seven times. Every time she would give him the same look she gave him the very first time he saw her, the look that melted his heart and disarmed him completely, teasing out that fear for which he knew no reason. She had become the only one who could cure him. Suddenly, after the seventh month, Salma spoke to him for a long time. She told him that she lived with her family by a water spring that was an hour's walk north of the airport. It was a salty spring surrounded by a freshwater one. She bathed in the first one and rinsed herself in the second. Both were surrounded by palm trees and pasture. Her father, the owner of the spring and surrounding land, had decided to honor him. "Tomorrow, he will come by to invite you over. For tomorrow we celebrate the shearing of the wool."

Adel could not believe his ears, for it was all beyond what he had ever imagined or expected.

The next day, Adel arrived at the site of a few marvelous tents spread out over a vast expanse of sand underneath palm trees by the edge of a spring it was hard to believe actually existed so close to the city of Cairo. Adel was even more astonished when he saw Salma's father driving a recent-model Peugeot car. He found the beauty of the area surrounding the spring incredible. "This is the land of the future," thought Adel to himself. If he could buy some feddans now he would become a millionaire overnight. This is the Cairo of the future. This is the deal of a lifetime, he said to himself.

On the way, the father asked Adel about his profession and where he had resided before coming to the desert and its people. Adel could feel more than just questions in the father's tone, but he explained that away through Bedouin traditions. Around the spring, a huge herd of camels, sheep, and goats had assembled, a testimony to the father's wealth.

As the car approached the tents, Adel noticed that a group of men had gathered in an open tent. When the father and his guest got out of the car, the men shuffled around, forming a U-shaped gathering that was completed when the father and his guest sat down at one of its extremes. Three men sat in front of them; their intricately wrinkled faces bore the mark of time.

Adel was mesmerized by the scene, to the extent that he failed to notice Salma's presence until she went from one tent to the other in his direction with her gaze fixed on him.

One of the three squatting men spoke. Adel heard him speak about the desert and water and sheep; the roads leading to the oasis, the valley, the cities, and the water springs; Bedouin tribes and blood ties. He spoke about the urgency of protecting these roads and springs and palm trees with their dates, and sheep with their milk that is food for the newborn. He also spoke about how small the valley was when compared to the desert that is infinite.

Just as Adel had built the seven-story building that represented seven months, each with twenty-eight days, in order to see Salma's face every full moon, so did he feel that this tribunal had been set up to try him for the death of the man who had suddenly appeared before him on one of the dirt roads of

Kharga Oasis and Fartoush just after sunset. He still remembered the moment quite vividly: he was with a friend, on their way home from the western plateau to the valley after they had visited the iron mines in the Kharga oasis. Instead of taking the paved road that leads to Asyut, they took a rugged dirt road that descended toward Fartoush near Qena. His friend was supposed to present a report on the possibility of paving this dirt road and extending a railway line to the valley.

As they descended the plateau toward the valley and discerned the greenery at a distance, two armed men appeared before them. Adel remembered amid the fear and surprise, belief and disbelief, and with a speed that felt fatal at the time, he shot a bullet from the pistol that he was using for the first time. One of the men fell in front of him and, as happens in films, the other one ran away. As for him and his friend, they fled in their car, ending the memory of the moment upon their arrival in the valley.

Because Adel had killed a human being, he had the courage to accept Salma's father's invitation.

That day, the man accused him, saying, "You were with a friend in the car. You killed Mubarak ibn Rabie when he appeared in front of you with Ziyad al-Rahib."

This is how the architect Adel Salem was executed in the northwestern desert of the city of Cairo. One of the men grabbed him by the hair and placed his head on a marble-like rock then struck the point of a sharp dagger into his neck between the bones of his clavicle.

Translated by Samia Mehrez

Radwa Ashour

from *A Piece of Europe*

THE ONLOOKER WROTE:
The boy suffered from an eye disease so they sent him to Vienna for a cure.

During this two-year trip, he was not accompanied by his father, who was a very busy man whose responsibilities required him to travel constantly between Egypt, Syria, and the Arabian Peninsula. Despite the boy's tender age, there was no reason to worry about him, not only because of his financial position but also because of the escorts his father had secured for him. In addition, because of his father's status and power, he benefited from the protection and care of the Austrian rulers; he mingled with the country's aristocracy and was the immediate protégé of the Austrian foreign secretary.

The boy lived in Vienna, he cured his eye disease; he saw its streets and its buildings and visited its palaces. He partook of the banquets and parties of its noblemen where men danced with women to captivating waltz music, the men in tailcoats with black tight-fitting trousers that separated the thighs and the women in colorful dresses tight around the bust that flowed amply under the waistline.

Before he turned fifteen a royal decree was issued to send him on an educational mission to France. So the boy moved to Paris to study in its learning institutions. It is certain that the photograph we have in our possession was taken when he was fourteen and still living in Vienna, or immediately after that when he was studying in Paris. In the photograph one sees the face of a child and the body of a thin young man; his taut disposition betrays importance and status, evoking a sternness that is accentuated by the embroidered Albanian military vest that fits tightly around the chest and waist with a high collar surrounding the neck. The boy is wearing a short Turkish tarbush on his head that hides two-thirds of his forehead. The tarbush has a long tassel that resembles the tail of a horse. The boy spent four years in France and then returned to Egypt.

How many times did he visit Paris or Vienna afterward? I do not exactly know and will not seek to find out. I will move on immediately to a particular visit to the French capital which he made seventeen years after his return to Egypt. He was obviously no longer a boy. He had become a robust man with a mustache and beard that covered his cheeks. He wore a long tailcoat decorated with five medals in pure gold, three of which were in the shape of octagonal stars with crescents in the middle; the other two inlaid with precious stones. He spoke French and Turkish fluently as well as Arabic to a lesser degree.

During this particularly interesting visit the French capital was witnessing an architectural revolution led by a man whose name was Haussmann. He planned the new township of Paris, demolishing, changing, and dismantling entire areas for the sake of new, wide, and straight boulevards that intersected at round points decked with public gardens that, even though manmade and groomed, resembled small forests. An architectural revolution whose leader had forgotten nothing, even the sewage, seemed like a baffling construction, to which important visitors of the city were taken on tours.

On this trip, during which he visited Paris, London, Paris again, and then Asitana (Istanbul), the Ottoman sultan bestowed upon him the title of Khedive of Egypt. So he returned to his seat of power carrying a resounding new title and unlimited dreams of demolition and construction. He formed a new government in which he assigned his new minister of public affairs a plan for a new Cairo similar to the one undertaken for Paris. He did not ask his minister to demolish the old city, for he was in a hurry, thinking about the grand celebration he was planning in two years' time. He would settle for a new neighborhood and the modernization of an old one for the time being.

For the sake of accuracy, one has to note that this sudden urbanization plan was not altogether new. His grandfather, who also dreamed of a modern city, was the first to bring foreign teachers to introduce European-style architecture to Egypt, thereby giving the population a preview that would prepare them for the demolition of old monuments to make way for the new boulevard, al-Sikka al-Gadida. I am referring to the scene of bulldozers and cranes as they uprooted homes, mosques, sabils, trees, doors, and mashrabiyas, as well as graves. But, as I said earlier, the grandchild did not have enough time for demolition, or perhaps his minister, who was a brilliant man despite all else, preferred to focus his energy on planning a new city, so he only demolished a limited area and built anew in the neighboring space.

I was born in this new area that is known today as Downtown and that was originally named Ismailiya. Today I sit in a building right next to the one where I was born, and write a century after the death of Ismail—who had ordered the construction of the neighborhood—and the deaths of his minister of public affairs, Ali Mubarak, and his aide, Mahmoud al-Falaki, both of whom supervised the execution of the plans. This new neighborhood, known to many historians as "*Rumi* Cairo," leaves Islamic Cairo behind, well settled in its past, content with it or submerged in it, and looks ahead toward a new world that would draw in the city with its public institutions, its royal palaces, and its commercial centers. The city is literally transported to the geographic— not metaphoric—west, where Ismail's Cairo extends from Abdin Square and Ataba Square to the Nile on their west, and from the Nile to the island on its west. The seat of power was moved from the Citadel and came to be housed in Abdin Palace, with its Italian façade and corrugated iron gates and fence adorned with the royal crown and the first initial of Ismail's name in stylized Latin letters in pure gold. The Citadel with its rugged stone walls remained on top of the plateau, awaiting its turn in the archive of monuments.

The Ismailiya neighborhood was but a part of Ismail's formidable architectural accomplishments: within a few years he had bought four hundred and fifty bridges and one thousand miles of railway rails and telecommunication wires; he built schools, institutions, theaters, a museum, and a national library, as well as palaces and gardens designed by European architects whose many names we can no longer remember, let alone pronounce correctly.

The rise of Egyptian cotton on the world market provided the necessary funds for this renaissance, along with close monitoring of the income of peasants, not to mention the debt. It may be important to mention here, even if this may appear as a digression, that the urban expansion of Cairo during Ismail's reign was matched only by what the city had witnessed five centuries earlier, during the reign of al-Nasser Qalawun, the sole difference being in the fate of both men and the country itself.

Ismail died in exile when he was sixty-five, but in his very last photograph he seems older. He looks aged and broken in his seat: two protruding bones on the upper forehead, two slack eyelids, and a withdrawn face, with a mustache and completely gray beard. He is wearing a heavy winter coat with two shirts underneath and a knitted woolen cloak on top, plus a piece of sheepskin wrapped around his waist and legs.

During his long illness, Ismail wanted to return to Egypt to die there but he was not allowed. Later, his body was brought back and he was buried next to his mother. He was not buried in the area that he had founded, but rather to its east in Rifai. Ismailiya continued to expand the way he had wanted, with designs by Austrian, French, Italian, and Swiss architects, but with a minor change in the plan of the area on the edge of the square that was named after him: Qasr al-Nil (the Nile Palace), north of the square, became the barracks of the occupying army, and Qasr al-Dubara (Dubara Palace), to the south, became the actual seat of power of Evelyn Baring, otherwise known as Lord Cromer.

The story of the boy whose eyesight was cured in Vienna, who was enchanted by its buildings, and who became Egypt's royal sovereign, after which he was carried by the yacht al-Mahrusa to exile in Italy is an old story. It began and ended half a century before my birth. I was born at the same time as his grandchild Farouk, "the beloved prince of the nation." All shows at the cinema, whether in Arabic or in a foreign language, ended with the royal anthem, for which we stood. When I was fifteen years old there no longer was a royal anthem, because "the beloved prince" had been exiled from the country on the same al-Mahrusa that had carried his grandfather to his place of exile in Italy.

We were in Cairo, living in a four-story building on Qasr al-Nil Street, when Farouk boarded al-Mahrusa in Alexandria in July 1952. The building is still there. I sometimes walk past it. I raise my head to look at its balconies: the small, crescent-like balconies that look like jewels surrounding the tall French windows, and the long rectangular ones that are more spacious. Each one is adorned with corrugated iron, intricate designs that come together in floral motifs. I cross the street in order to have the necessary distance to view the entire building. I cross again to steal a quick look at one of the entrances. I recall myself alone or with my mother or father or siblings on the balcony. Baehlar Passage is across the street with its arches. To our right extends Qasr al-Nil Street toward Mustafa Kamel Square. To our left is Sulayman Pasha Square; we can see part of it, with the bronze statue in the center, and two out of four intersections, and the Groppi building, and the entrance to the shop with a sign that reads "Groppi 1924," and another sign written in Latin letters followed by "Confiserie de la maison royale."

Translated by Samia Mehrez

Midhat Gazalé
from *Pyramids Road*

WE LIVED ON MARIETTE Pasha Street, which owed its name to a French Egyptologist born in 1821 of modest parents in Boulogne-sur-Mer. He discovered the fabulous treasures of Saqqara, west of the Giza pyramids, which my brother and I never failed to admire from our balcony against the setting sun's ball of fire.

Mariette pillaged Egyptian antiques, shipping thousands of pieces to France, among them The Seated Scribe, one of the Louvre's most valuable possessions. Upon being elevated to the dignity of bey, then pasha, by Viceroy Said, he went from looter to staunch defender of Egypt's millenary heritage. The museum he created in 1863 received so many new pieces over the years that it had to be moved to its present location in 1902, across the street from our apartment.

Following his death in 1881, he was succeeded by Maspero, another Frenchman, who interred his illustrious predecessor in a sarcophagus underneath a small pharaonic mausoleum facing the museum's entrance. On hot summer evenings, my brother and I often sat on the balcony to do our homework. Two or three stories below, one of our neighbors, obviously very fond of oriental music, turned on his radio every night with his windows wide open, affording our studious pair a delightfully mellow musical background. It was as though the music rose from within the museum, and we loved to fantasize that the palace musicians and dancers were performing for the pharaoh.

"We live in the heart of French archaeology!" proudly exclaimed my father, for Mariette Pasha Street was perpendicular to Maspero, Champollion, and Antikkhana streets, the latter word meaning 'antiquities museum' in Turkish.

Midan Sulayman Pasha, the focus of Cairo's cosmopolitan life, was only five minutes away. Built in 1924, the celebrated Groppi's tearoom adorned one of its corners with its beautiful arched entrance and art deco mosaics. Every afternoon, having emerged from their naps and abundantly dabbed their faces with lavender cologne, idle French-speaking Cairenes met for tea and pastry to the music of a skimpy European chamber orchestra, unless they crossed the street to Café Riche, the rendezvous of intellectuals, political activists, and artists. Sulayman Pasha's statue stood in the middle of the square, facing the street that bore his name. Converging on the roundabout, Sulayman Pasha and Qasr al-Nil streets were the most Parisian of all.

Sulayman Pasha was none other than Colonel Sève, a French officer who contributed to three of Napoleon's most disastrous defeats, then converted to Islam and changed his name. He was placed by Muhammad Ali at the head of the new Egyptian regiments in 1819, eight years after Bonaparte's defeat at the hands of the British, and later elevated to pasha. We only vaguely knew that his great-granddaughter Nazli had married King Fuad and given birth to King Farouk in 1920. Sulayman was buried in Cairo under a charming cast-iron pavilion, not far from his wife Maryam.

I remember Cinema Miami, Cinema La Potinière with its open-air theater, and the festive opening of Cinema Metro, the only place in town with air-conditioning and wall to wall carpeting, where *Gone with the Wind* was premiered as World War II raged. All three cinemas stood within walking distance of one another on either side of Sulayman Pasha Street. Little did we know that La Potinière, named after the Parisian Théatre de la Potinière, meant 'gossip corner' in French, and that Miami was a faraway American summer resort. The Italian owner of Cinema Miami, Mr. Bianco, who lived on the fourth floor of our building, offered my parents a permanent pass that entitled us to sit in the first-tier box every Saturday afternoon, a major contribution to our vast cinematic culture. I owe my command of English and my hatred of the Nazis to Hollywood's MGM, RKO, 20th Century Fox, Universal Studios, United Artists, etc. We did not discover French films until after the war, without much enthusiasm I must confess, as we felt little kinship with Jean Gabin's scabrous adventures or Maurice Chevalier's Parisian pranks, despite our fluency in French. One of the few exceptions was Jacques Tati's *Jour de fête*.

The luxurious stores bordering Sulayman Pasha Street bore foreign names, written in French. They closed on Sunday and remained open on Friday, the Muslim holiday.

En route to the Lycée, we crossed Ismailiya Square, facing the infamous British barracks, a daily reminder of their colonial presence on our soil. The square owed its name to Khedive Ismail, who was remembered for the lavish festivities that accompanied the Suez Canal opening, eventually dragging Egypt into bankruptcy. At the request of the French and British, Ismail was exiled to Turkey. En route to Emitgan, he paid a visit to King Umberto of Italy at the Favorita Palace. He died in exile in 1879, three years before the bombardment of Alexandria by the British.

From our balconies, we could see "Tommies" from all over the British Commonwealth parading on Empire Day and other similar occasions—Scotsmen in tartan kilts, bearded Sikhs, Aussies wearing Indiana Jones hats. We became familiar with their marches and their nostalgic songs. To this day, I cannot help being stirred by the sound of a bagpipe, poignant, proud, and heroic.

Upon reaching Ismailiya Square, we passed the famous Issaievitch restaurant which served the most legendary ful and falafel sandwiches in town. The place was owned by two brothers, probably Yugoslavian, and had become the rendezvous of the city's patrician *jeunesse dorée*, who relished that poor man's delicacy. One of the bothers sat at the cash register, perched atop a platform near the entrance, from which he kept a suspicious eye on the comings and goings in his establishment. The server ladled the steaming beans out of a large spherical copper kettle into warm, freshly baked Syrian bread and seasoned them with oil, adding a dab of salt that he scooped out of a tin bowl with a scruffy teaspoon. Issaievitch was particularly vigilant when our group of Lycée students was being catered to, because we often slipped the server a minuscule bakshish in exchange for a surreptitiously generous serving, causing the owner to grumble in the server's direction, "Lighter, your hand, lighter!" probably the only Arabic words he knew.

Upon leaving the square, we would pass the barbershop where we had our once-a-month haircuts, then the Astra Milk Bar, where a mixed crowd of Lycée and American University students daily flocked. The milk bar also attracted a group of handsome young Egyptian army officers who idly palavered over a milkshake, and sometimes merrily chatted up the girls in English.

Little did we suspect that the Astra milk bar was precisely the place where a group of young officers, perhaps the very ones we knew, plotted to assassinate finance minister Amir Osman Pasha on January 6, 1946. They were led by an obscure lieutenant named Anwar el-Sadat.

Chafika Hamamsy

from Zamalek

Usta 'Abdu, the family driver, handed the parcel of mughat to Umm Muhammad.

"Here you are! Now that the mughat and nuts are in the house, I hope we shall not wait much longer. It surely must be a boy this time, for three girls in a row is about as much as any man can bear."

"Hold your tongue, old man," answered Umm Muhammad.

"Whatever God sends is welcome. May Sitt Hanim be safely delivered."

It was a beautiful October day, warm still but with a gentle breeze. Fatma Hanim, the object of this concern, shifted her heavy body in the large armchair and mentally reviewed all the little odds and ends that needed to be attended to before the baby's birth. The layette was ready, but more important, so was the house—that Zamalek mansion, sometimes referred to by flatterers as Sarayat al-Zamalek. The house stood at the angle of two main streets on the island of Zamalek. According to uncorroborated sources, Zamalek was man-made, the result of accumulated earth thrown into this very large section of the Nile as canals and waterways were dug up by Muhammad 'Ali and his successors in the process of creating modern Egypt. To most people, it seemed to be a lush, green island of peace miraculously born out of the capricious meandering of the river in its race toward the sea.

Whatever cause lay behind its existence, the island was beautiful with its lovely shaded streets, where acacias and poinciana lent their glorious hues of pink, purple, and red in summer, and promising branches of scattered green leaves in winter.

In the 1920s and early 1930s, it became the fashionable neighborhood of Cairo gradually replacing Hilmiya al-Gadida and Mounira. In fact, the westward movement of the city was sustained all through the nineteenth and early twentieth centuries, sliding down as it were from the Citadel and moving from Abbasiya (in the east), where the upper classes of the nineteenth century had built their residences, to Hilmiya, Mounira, Garden City (also called Qasr al-Dubara), and Zamalek. There were, of course, less elegant neighborhoods that ran along as well, such as Manial, Dokki, and parts of Giza. But Zamalek in the 1930s was the jewel of the capital despite the fact that the British Residence and other embassies were located in Garden City. . . .

The island of Zamalek was linked to the mainland by three bridges, two on the eastern shore, Qasr al-Nil Bridge and Bulaq or Abu al-'Ela Bridge, and one on the western shore, the Badi'a Masabni Bridge (also known at the time as Kubri al-Ingiliz, or Englishmen's Bridge, renamed the Galaa Bridge after the 1952 Revolution). The most beautiful one, Qasr al-Nil Bridge, was built in 1933 by a British company to replace the narrow causeway originally devised in 1872 by Maurice Adolphe Linant de Bellefond, a French Saint Simonian engineer who at one time became chief engineer of the Suez Canal. With increasing traffic to and from the island, a more substantial structure became imperative. The new bridge was elegant, its stiff steel structure decorated by lamp posts which "shimmered over the Nile like a bride on her wedding night." However, its most outstanding feature was the four bronze lions—two guarding the bridge at either end—the work of Alfred Jacquemart, a French sculptor. The lions were originally meant to stand around Muhammad 'Ali's statue in Alexandria, but Linant de Bellefond thought better of it and appropriated them for his bridge, where they have stood ever since. Bulaq Bridge was two decades older, inaugurated in 1912 by Ismail Sirri Pasha, the incumbent minister of public works. It has been variously called Bulaq Bridge, after the neighborhood which it links to the island, Fuad al-Awwal Bridge, after the reigning monarch, and later Abu al-'Ela Bridge after a minor sheikh, Hussein Abu al-'Ela, whose shrine stands nearby. Whatever the name, it dutifully served its purpose well until the end of the twentieth century when it was pensioned off and replaced by the Fifteenth of May Bridge. Traffic over Bulaq Bridge was heavy as it linked Bulaq to the main thoroughfare of the island. This two-way avenue, originally called Fuad al-Awwal Street, renamed after the Revolution Twenty-sixth of July Street, boasted in the early 1920s and up to the early 1950s a tramway that crossed the island from east to west and back. From the 1920s to the 1940s, this avenue functioned as a frontier, a demarcation line that separated the 'good side' of Zamalek in the south from the 'bad side' in the north. On the 'good side' stood the Gezira Club, the Grotto Gardens, the Gezira Palace, lovely houses, and tree-lined avenues.

Most British officials, connected with either the Agency—later known as the Embassy—or the Egyptian government, lived there. Little by little, perceptive Egyptians realized that this was indeed a lovely neighborhood and started acquiring land there as well. The price of the square meter at the time varied from one pound for the 'bad' side to three pounds for the 'good' one.

The best way of describing the 'good' side of the Zamalek of the time is perhaps to compare it to a small village in the English countryside. It exuded the same peaceful atmosphere with the early morning sound of birds chirping in the trees and their dusk riot when settling for the night. There were no stray dogs then, just family pets or hounds guarding villas and gardens. Every person was identifiable, every bawwab recognized each of the children who cycled by, and safety in the street was ensured by an occasional shawish. These were the glorious days of Zamalek.

On the other side of the demarcation line lay the 'bad' side. Actually, there was nothing wrong with it except that it was still untamed, partially covered by marshland or uncultivated plots with a few palatial houses along the Nile facing Bulaq, such as the Tawfik Doss villa or the Aisha Fahmi miniature palace. And yet, maybe because it was where squatters' huts survived longer, that an overall gloomy and derelict atmosphere prevailed. Whatever the reason, in the 1920s, and well into the 1940s the distinction was very clear. The third bridge, the Badi'a Masabni Bridge on the western side of the island, links it to Giza, the first outpost of Upper Egypt. It is a small bridge spanning the narrow branch of the Nile. It owes its early name to the famous belly dancer Badi'a Masabni whose cabaret stood at the end of the bridge on the Giza side. The Casino Badi'a played a prominent role in the sociopolitical scene of the first half of the twentieth century. Important political figures would meet there to discuss issues of the day while watching the graceful, if somewhat opulent, gyrations of Madame Badi'a performing her dance. The rumor that she was a British agent, actively engaged against the Axis forces, as was occasionally asserted, may or may not have been true. It could have been spread by Hitler's admirers in Cairo as a piqued reaction to her lack of enthusiasm for the Fuehrer's cause. Whatever the case, beyond doubt she played a role in launching the careers of famous belly dancers such as Samia Gamal, Tahia Cariocca, and Bebba Ezz al-Din.

Though her casino was not a 'salon' or a political club, it was often said that ministerial cabinets were sometimes formed, or dissolved, during these evenings of oriental merry-making. The idyllic situation in Zamalek eventually deteriorated and its peaceful beauty gradually disappeared. With the advent of the 1952 Revolution and the sudden population explosion of the early 1960s, the 'good' and the 'bad' slowly merged. And, like everything else since then, Zamalek became a microcosm of Egypt, a place where ugliness competes successfully with beauty, where attempts to maintain a modicum of aesthetic standards are an uphill battle fought daily by a few valiant souls who believe that good will ultimately prevail. In the 1930s however it was still a beautiful island, a world all on its own, and right in the heart of it stood Fatma Hanim's home.

Naguib Mahfouz

from *Midaq Alley*

"This is the end of the road."

"But the world doesn't come to an end with Muski Street," he protested. "Why can't we stroll around the square?"

"I don't want to be late, as my mother will be worried."

"If you'd like, we can take a taxi and cover a great distance in a few seconds," he pointed out temptingly.

A taxi! The word rang strangely in her ears. In her whole life she had only ridden in a horse-drawn carriage and the magic of the word "taxi" took time to die away. But how could she possibly ride in a taxi with a strange man? She was overcome by a powerful desire for adventure. She was amazed at her capacity for reckless adventures, and it was difficult to say what most influenced her thoughts at this moment, whether it was the man who so stirred her or the adventure itself. Perhaps the two were really one. She glanced at him looking cunningly in her direction, a trace of that infuriating smile of his on his lips. Her feelings changed abruptly. "I don't want to be late."

Slightly disappointed, he asked, trying to appear sad, "Are you afraid?"

"I'm not afraid of anything," she replied indignantly, her anger increasing.

His face lit up, as though now he understood many things. Gaily he said, "I'll call a taxi."

She made no objection and fixed her gaze on the approaching taxi. It stopped and he opened the door for her. Her heart pounding, and clutching her cloak, she bent down and entered. The man followed her, saying to himself delightedly, "We have saved ourselves two or three days groundwork already."

Hamida heard him say, "Sharif Pasha Street." Sharif Pasha! Not Midaq Alley, or Sanadiqiya, Ghuriya, or even Muski, but Sharif Pasha Street! But why this particular street?

"Where are you going?" she asked.

"We will have a little run around and then go back," he said, his shoulder touching hers.

The taxi started and she tried to forget everything for a while, even the man sitting so close to her. Her eyes were bewildered by the dazzling lights as a splendid, laughing new world appeared through the windows. The movement of the taxi had an effect on both her mind and her body and a delightful feeling of intoxication stole over her. She seemed to be riding in an airplane, high, high above everything. Her eyes shone with delight and her mouth dropped open.

The taxi moved slowly, making its way through the sea of carriages, motorcars, trams, and people. Her thoughts traveled with it. Now her willpower deserted her and her emotions were intoxicated as her heart, her blood, and all her feelings danced within her. She was suddenly aware of his voice whispering in her ear, "Just look at the fine ladies in their superb clothes!" Yes, they were swaying and dancing along like luminous stars . . . how beautiful they were, how wonderful.

Only now did she remember her own old cloak and slippers and her heart sank. She woke from her sweet dream as though at the sting of a scorpion. She bit her lips in annoyance and was overcome by a fighting spirit of rebelliousness. She noticed he had snuggled close to her, and she began to sense the effect of his touch creeping over her. This enraged her, and she pushed him away more forcibly than she intended. He glanced at her to see what was the matter and then took her hand and gently placed it between his own. He was encouraged by her permissiveness and searched for her lips with his mouth. She seemed to resist and drew her head back slightly. However, he did not find this a sufficient restraint and pressed his lips to hers. She trembled violently and felt an insane desire to bite his lips until they bled. The same insane desire, indeed, as whenever she got into a fight. However, he drew away before she could obey her instinct. Rage burned within her, urging her to throw herself at him and dig her nails into his neck, but suddenly she was soothed by his polite voice. "This is Sharif Pasha Street . . . and that's my house a little way ahead. Would you like to see it?"

Her nerves on edge, she looked where he pointed and saw several blocks of skyscraper apartments, and she had no idea which one he meant. He told the driver to stop and said to her, "It's in this building. . . ."

She could see a towering building with an entrance wider than Midaq Alley. Turning away from it in bewilderment, she asked almost inaudibly, "Which floor is it on?"

"The second," he replied, smiling. "You won't suffer any hardship by condescending to visit it."

She shot him a critical, angry look and he went on: "How quickly you get angry! Well, anyway, do let me ask you why it would be wrong. Have I not visited you many times since I first saw you? Why can't you visit me, just once?"

What did the man want? Did he think he had fallen on easy prey? Had the kiss she had permitted given him an appetite for better, more dangerous things? Had his conceit and self-confidence blinded him? And was it love that made her lose her senses? Fury flamed within her, and she gathered all her strength for the challenging battle ahead. She wished she could obey her instinct to go wherever he wished just to show him how mistaken he was and bring him back to his senses. Yes, her rebellious nature told her to plunge straight into the battlefield. Could she possibly make the challenge and then refuse to accept it? What angered her were not the moral issues involved or her shyness; these could never infuriate her. No, what hurt was the slight to her pride and her belief in her own strength and her uncontrollable desire to use insulting language and have a good fight. Indeed, the desire for adventure which had led her to enter the taxi was still with her. The man looked at her closely, saying to himself thoughtfully, 'My darling girl is that dangerous type that explodes when touched. I must be very careful in handling her.'

He spoke again, politely expressing his hope: "I would very much like to offer you a glass of lemonade."

"Just as you wish," she muttered, looking at him in a stern and challenging fashion.

He stepped out of the taxi, very pleased with himself. She followed boldly with apparent indifference and stood examining the building while he paid the driver. Her thoughts recalled the alley she had just left, and she felt amazed at the unexpected adventure that brought her to this massive building. Who would ever believe it? What would Radwan Husseiny say, for example, if he were to see her entering this apartment block? A smile played over her lips, and she had a strange feeling that today was certain to be the happiest one in her whole life.

The man hurried to take her by the arm and they entered the building together. They walked up a wide staircase to the second floor and turned into a long corridor until they stopped at the door of an apartment on the right. The man drew out a key from his pocket and unlocked the door, saying to himself, "I've saved at least another day or two!" He pushed the door open wide for her and she went in, while he followed, locking the door behind them. She found herself in a long hall with rooms leading off on both sides and lit by a strong electric light. The apartment was not empty, for besides the light that was on when they entered, she could hear sounds from behind one of the closed doors; people were talking, shrieking, and singing inside.

Ibahim Farag went to the door opposite the entrance, pushed it open, and asked her to come in. She found herself in a medium-sized room furnished with leather-covered couches somewhere between armchairs and sofas in shape. In the middle was an embroidered rug. Facing the door inside the room was a mirror.

Translated by Trevor Le Gassick

Yusuf Idris
from *"The Siren," in Rings of Burnished Brass*

SHE WAS IN NO sense warped, or morally flawed, and her behavior and way of life were unimpeachable. She was a nice country girl with a superior mind that was capable of some finesse. It was this that had led her to choose Hamid rather than Mustafa, although Mustafa was an official night patrolman with a guaranteed wage, and he also had a tiny patch of land and a small buffalo of his own. Hamid, meanwhile, had not a penny in the world and was at least five years older than Mustafa, and was dark brown, almost black. But she would be doing her mind an injustice if she said that it was responsible for the choice: behind it there was always an obscure hazy finger pointing, which almost spoke to her, insisting, demanding that she should take Hamid rather than Mustafa, because Hamid was working in Cairo.

She had known all along that her life in their village was limited, and that inevitably, in one way or another, she would end up living in the capital. That vast shining place, "The Mother of the World" they called it, that with its splendor and luxury peeled away the deposits left by squalor and abuse and transformed those who lived there into men and women of class. Hadn't her cousin Fatima who'd gone there to work as a maid come back looking like a

European? You could hardly recognize her when she got off the train wearing a dress and carrying a handbag. So what about her, when she wasn't going to be a maid but the wife of the doorman of a block of flats high as the sky?

The voice that whispered to her and convinced her that her place was in Cairo had certainly turned out to be right. As everybody assured her, she was not made to work the hard earth from sunrise to sunset; her white body, pure white, was created for life in the capital and her prettiness was not of the countryside. For, by village standards, Fathiya was pretty, one of the prettiest girls in her village, fair-skinned like a rich man's daughter—and only the rich are fair-skinned. It was true that she was tall and skinny, but that was the diet of oil and maize, and when she started to eat white bread and butter she would grow plumper. Her place was in Cairo, and strangely enough the voice that kept reiterating this notion to her did not come from outside her, but from within.

There she would live, where the streets were broad and sweet and clean and not a speck of dust would cling to you if you lay down to sleep on them. The great spread of shining flashing lights at nighttime changed darkness into broad daylight, or something more wonderful than daylight. The women were beautiful and looked like Europeans, and the men had pink faces and were rich and drove cars and spent pounds without a pang of regret as the money left their pockets. There was food in abundance, kebabs, sweet smells, hotels; and there the Nile, the mighty Nile, had its source.

In this paradise she would find her place; the hidden voice had always assured her of this and so she was not at all surprised when matters settled themselves. Hamid approached her, her family were hesitant, and it was she who was full of enthusiasm and accepted him gladly.

Only a week later she set off and found herself at last, as she had dreamt she would be a thousand times, in the heart of Cairo, in the building whose ten stories she had always tried to picture to herself. It must be said that she did not actually live on any one of the ten floors, but in Hamid's room, which had been hastily constructed for him under the stairs by the owner of the building as an incitement to whoever might marry him, for they hoped that in Hamid's wife, when he married, they would have a maid who would solve the problem of domestic help for them.

But the room was spacious in spite of everything, and it had a bed with a real mattress and a small cupboard and electric light.

It must be said too that Fathiya, beautiful in their village, appeared strange in Cairo. To the inhabitants of the building she looked like a puppet, a bride puppet. She was certainly tall and fair-skinned, and her features were beautiful in a way: she had nice eyes, and a small pretty nose—impossible that it should be the nose of a peasant woman—and a delicate mouth like Solomon's ring, but the trouble was that they appeared quite unsuited to her build and size. It was as if the head had somehow shrunk, and the body stayed the normal size.

But what mattered was that Hamid became light-hearted, changed from the surly, ferocious-looking creature who had snarled and shouted all day to a cheerful human being, busy as a bee, running up and down stairs, jumping up from his seat, greeting people, fetching and carrying, obeying orders. And Fathiya, meanwhile, remained crouched in her place facing the door of the room, observing the broad entrance and the great glass door of the block of flats, watching Cairo, or more exactly that portion of the street outside, that constituted Cairo in her eyes.

She crouched withdrawn, still knowing only what she had seen between the railway station and the block of flats, contemplating the dream become reality. Cairo, much more magnificent than she had imagined or than her cousin had been able to describe, a thousand times grander and more wonderful. Could such crowds of people, such broad streets, such wide squares, really exist? Were people able to live amid that dreadful crush of cars that went so fast that they'd swallow you up if you were off your guard for a moment. The shops and the hoardings and the lights, all colors of the rainbow, flashing on and off, pulsating like single drumbeats through lines of music, the tumult, the uproar, the constant festivities. For it had seemed to her, when, after something of a struggle, Hamid had managed to drag her, terrified, bewildered, half-mad, into the middle of the square before the railway station, that it must be some feast or saint's day or another celebration that she didn't know about to make the people congregate in such vast numbers and make a noise that set her ears jangling. But Hamid had told her, laughing in a knowing way, "It's like that every day."

What a city, where people lived every day as if it were a saint's day or a feast.

Yet as she shrank behind the half-open door of the room, seeing from a distance now and pondering, she began to notice in Cairo, condensed for her in the section of the street facing her, things that she would never for a moment have expected to find in the dream city. Poor people, properly poor, and hungry, and beggars; even in their village itself poverty did not exist in such extremes of ugliness. People lied and swore and were rude to each other, and there were thieves and pickpockets: theft made the existence of her husband and others like him necessary, and provided him with stories of incidents both in the neighborhood and far away that he would relate to her.

The Cairo ladies, whom she had imagined at first to be without exception women of taste, reaching European standards of fashion and beauty, she now realized numbered many ugly ones among them. The majority would have been ugly, had it not been for the red and white paint that they daubed on their faces, and this made them take on color and shine like newly polished shoes and, she concluded eventually, left their owners even more ugly than they would have been without it. The abundance of these ugly women was such that she began to feel a sort of satisfaction with herself. In the beginning she had put her market value no higher than that of a maid to the least of them, but her self-esteem had risen to the point where she reckoned that if she had been dressed like them she would have become the center of attention and been considered a real beauty, as she had been in the village.

Hamid himself seemed to have some sense of his own importance and pride in his job, although she quite failed to understand the nature of his work when they told her about it. She supposed that he had something of the status of official night watchman in the village who carried a gun and commanded respect and fear, but from what she saw of him at work, he looked more like a servant: inclining his head to her, rushing to carry out the orders of Mrs. So-and-So, being bellowed at and scolded by the owner of the building in unfamiliar phrases with words like 'dunce' and 'hypocrite,' quite meaningless to Fathiya, although she presumed that they were perhaps swearwords in Cairo.

Even so, she didn't like the attitude of lofty disdain which he adopted toward the owner of the building the day he tried to insist that Hamid let her work for them: Hamid refused outright, vowing that he himself would stop working for them if they tried to force her. It was a point of view that she couldn't accept when she thought of the pitiful way they lived and their position in the scale of things, so low that it didn't allow them even the equanimity of spirit that comes from having five pounds to your name. This was an opportunity to have enough to live on and to buy a warm dress for winter, and it was more than likely that they would have been given a good meal from time to time. But Hamid refused, rash and capricious, and when she opened her mouth to argue with him he shouted at her as if he owned the building and she was a tenant on the eighth floor.

The truth of the matter was that the economic justification for her desire to work was no more than a pretext, and what she really wanted was to get to know the people of Cairo better, to go into their homes and talk to them. Shut up in the room as she was, her shy introverted nature didn't allow her to do any such thing. Faced with the curious stares of the tenants who stormed the threshold, boring into her for a few moments as they scrutinized her appearance, the way she sat, her clothes, and then smiled or muttered vaguely or merely mocked, she became more closed in on herself and the chains tightened around her. They were chains of her own making; like the tenants of the building, the city around her was always on the move, surging forth, teeming with life, everything in it flowing along and coming together. But she to a certain extent, and her husband Hamid, were not only unable to abandon themselves to the city and its movement, to let it do with them what it did with the others, but were terrified and appalled by it, and recoiled more tightly in upon themselves.

She did, at least, but Hamid—and this dated exactly from the time he had married her and she had come to Cairo—had been able to free himself somewhat, moved about more easily, went to Sayyida Zaynab, to the suburbs, knew where you should change going to al-Husayn. It was not just where he went either, but his attitude of savoir-faire, his air of understanding what went on. He seemed to Fathiya a different person from the dark, silent, shy youth from their village, who would turn his face away if he encountered a procession of women and girls carrying water jars early in the morning. Now he laughed and joked with the men at the garage, collected the rents and reckoned up the money to the last half-penny, and even had friends who were natives of the city, not his relations or men from the same part of the country as him.

It was she alone who remained a prisoner in the room, bound by the narrow crack through which she saw the world of Cairo; and she sensed that the city was not a world but a sea, shoreless and unfathomable. She was going along the brink, but if she once forgot and let her feet carry her on, that would be the end of her. What was frightening was that the sea was not tranquil and still, and did not adopt the same stance in relation to her as she to it; it was oppressive, a heavy sea, and thousands of hands stretched out from it, thousands of smiles beckoned from it, treacherous sirens calling to her, smoothing the way for her to plunge in.

Even the eager call of one of the tenants, with money in his hand and the greengrocer nearby, was a hand reaching out from the sea, paralyzing her with the terror of it and making her freeze where she stood. She withdrew further into herself until it was as if she had seen and heard nothing. She turned away, covering her head, in flight, praying for a miracle to deliver her from the situation. Meanwhile the tenant, giving up, shot her a glance which she did not see, but she felt it, like a bullet in her head, and her ears picked up his muttered comments, correctly interpreting the obscenities contained there.

She was shy, introverted, withdrawn: so be it, but life has its incontrovertible rules from which there is no escaping. With her first pregnancy Fathiya had emerged from the room so that her world extended to include the entrance, and with her second child, which followed the first in a matter of months, it took in the pavement adjoining the building and the one opposite, then the street in both directions up to the square that opened out of it.

And now Fathiya began to answer back, and even to initiate conversation. She ran errands and learnt to distinguish between the car bringing the doctor's son home from school and the one carrying the son of the man who worked for the radio. She knew all the gossip about the tenants from Hamid, and from others, and eventually it reached the point where she became Hamid's source of information about them and their affairs. The story of the midnight visitor who knocked at the flat of the airline employee, especially when he was on night duty at the airport, was only an intimation of what she came to know about the seamy side of life in Cairo, the scandals and intrigues that took place constantly beneath the respectable affluent surface. This is the exclusive province of the concierge, and still more of his wife, with her greater persistence and wiliness in these matters. Despite her narrowness of vision, she sees a lot, especially in the night, and although her mind is small, she can tell the difference between the sister of the man whose wife and children are spending the summer holidays in Alexandria, while he's up to his ears in work, darling, and simply can't get away, and his real sisters who visit the family throughout the year.

Oddly enough, none of this spoilt the dream in Fathiya's head completely: she modified it, but she never lost sight of it. The great city remained great in her eyes, although she could see the bad things everywhere, and this was always her reply to Hamid when every now and then he came back cursing Cairo and everyone in it, having suffered this or that at the hands of one of its inhabitants.

If the ugly slime of evil lay at the bottom then salvation must lie in learning how to float. In this way Fathiya learnt to do what the other thousands and millions of people crowded into Cairo did, floating as they floated in the great terrible surges of movement that rolled through the city.

The only things that ruffled the calm surface of her life sometimes were the tremors set up by the sudden emerging of the apparition which lay in wait for her and ambushed her in the thick of her many duties: the Man, naked, like a dreadful hand stretching out and threatening to pull her down into the mud and filth; and that voice assuring her that the end result of her being in Cairo would be to make her see that she was going to descend to forbidden territory with the Man and there was nothing she could do about it. These occasions left Fathiya exploding with annoyance and irritation and disgust, and determined too that it should never happen, even if she paid with her life. Just you wait and I'll get even with you, Cairo.

Translated by Catherine Cobham

Khairy Shalaby

from *Wedding Thief*

WE DANGLED OUR BODIES off three buses, one after the other, and we found ourselves in the heart of town: Shawarbi Street.

We went into the expensive shoe stores. We claimed that we were returning from Iraq where we worked in the garment industry and that one of our relatives wanted to buy this pair of shoes from us, so how much was it worth in Egypt now so that we are fair to him?

All the shops were clean and filled with effendis and clean girls all smelling of jasmine, but they all looked like double-crossers with their cool faces. Some of them ignored us brusquely and refused to talk to us. Others looked at us with kindness and at the pair of shoes with envy, and then pursed their lips and did not answer. Still others inspected the pair of shoes with disdain and said they were worth ninety pounds. One group said that the pair of shoes was an imitation of an original brand name, while another said that the original brand name was itself imitated on the market. There were also those who threatened to call the police for no reason. But we could see in all their eyes that the pair of shoes was expensive and that they would all love to have them one way or another, even if they had to accuse us of having stolen the shoes from them. So I whispered in my cousin Awad's ear that the shoes were no joke and that they were worth quite a bit of money.

We walked silently down Shawarbi and Qasr al-Nil Streets through a flood of people, all very well dressed, until it became apparent that we were the only poor among them. Anger and despair were stamped on my cousin Awad's face, along with a dreadful frown that made him look like one of those criminal types we see in the movies and the TV serials. Suddenly he pulled me to a halt and pulled me again as we were turning back to Shawarbi Street. I listened to him inquisitively. He said, "I think we can sell this pair of shoes. Since there are those who know what they're worth, why don't we sell them . . . ?

We were in the heart of Shawarbi Street. I found an electricity box fixed to the ground that looked like a cardboard box with two flaps. I placed a newspaper on top of it, I took out the cardboard box from the big bag and opened it, I took out the shoes and placed them at the tip of the cardboard box in an eye-catching position, and I waited. Awad stood close by.

After a while some of the passersby started to stop and look at the pair of shoes, expressing interest as they walked away. Then everybody started to stop and look. Some started inspecting the shoes, looking at once astonished and suspicious in preparation for a long bargaining session. These were the same people who gave hell to the fortune-card vendors in the shacks of Tall Zenhum. I knew that when asked the price, a successful streetwise merchant should utter it only once and quickly, no matter how high. So I would say one word, quick as lightning, when I was asked about the price: two hundred. I would say it with confidence without looking at the face of the inquirer. Surprisingly, no one was astonished. So I became even more confident. When people heard the price they would re-inspect the shoes, then carefully place them back as if they were made of crystal. Then they would go on their way thanking us profusely.

Eventually, the hagglers stopped by. The haggling encouraged others to stop and look, only to find themselves part of the bargaining game. Until a slim young man with a fair complexion, delicate features, and blue eyes stopped in front of us and spoke in a low, anguished voice while turning over the shoes, "Do you have another pair?"

We said, "No."

He replied, smiling softly, "Of course! This pair alone is a treasure!"

He brought his offer to 160 pounds. We upped it. Final word: 180 pounds. He swore he wouldn't raise his offer. So we let him go. After a while, he came back and produced an expensive wallet from his back pocket, and my heart fluttered at the sight. He took out seventeen big red bills and pointed them in my direction, "This is all I have."

My cousin Awad went wild. He pinched my face and said, "Don't let the money go back into his pocket."

So I grabbed the money and stuck it in my pocket, trembling. I felt I was about to fly as I held this sum of money in my hand for the first time in my life, even if it was not mine. I placed the shoes back in the box and then in the bag; I then tried to wrap them professionally in newspaper.

I cannot begin to describe how happy we were as we ran through Ataba Square trying to find the bus. But we were wary of any close contact so we decided to walk. At the foot of the shacks we sat down to count the money again and look at it happily. He would count and hand it over to me, then I would do the same: ten, twenty, thirty, one hundred. Despite this, Awad's face remained hard with disbelief. . . .

The day had come to an end when I left my cousin Awad at his shack and walked on to mine. I found the fortune cards panels packed in the corridor and the table placed upside down waiting for me, and my mother who had not stopped cursing me. I felt that I was stuck with the fortune card table when I had thought I had freed myself of it. I said to it, "I swear I will not carry you on my shoulder anymore." The idea flashed in my head: tomorrow I will start working in Shawarbi Street and I will take my cousin Awad with me to this grand feast. Egypt's streets are bountiful and filled with crazy people who are willing to buy anything at any price.

Translated by Samia Mehrez

Sonallah Ibrahim
from *Sharaf*

DESPITE THE HEAT AND the humidity, or perhaps because of both, the residents of Cairo took to the street and poured into the downtown area—especially Talaat Harb Square—heading toward specific congregation points in front of garment stores, shoe stores, sandwich joints, and drink stalls, not to mention cinemas and theaters. Sharaf was coming from Tahrir Square, having crossed Talaat Harb, with his back to the statue, of course. He was hungry, thirsty, at a loss as to how to spend the evening.

The options available to him were the following: to go to the movies and watch a bloody film, since the other films with 'scenes' were unavailable, thanks to the censor, a respectable and disciplined woman; to buy a pack of Marlboros; to buy a sandwich, a Coke, and two Cleopatra cigarettes that he despised; to go home. The last option was actually two in one: downstairs and upstairs. Downstairs meant on the street around the corner by the cigarette kiosk where he owed a huge debt, or at the mechanic's shop with the rest of the gang and two joints that would give him a headache and nausea on an empty stomach, then tea at the Corniche coffee shop that was strategically located on the border of an old dry canal that had become a garbage dump (and if the mechanic had a car that was working, the group could go to nearby Maadi and join the gang of students and smoke more joints). Upstairs meant the apartment (small, where there was no place to sit or sleep) and confrontation (with the self and others) and the attempt to resolve the impossible dilemma. . . .

Going home, then, given the two available options, was not attractive. Because he couldn't make up his mind he busied himself, only visually, by selecting the suitable accessories for his new outfit.

He looked over the Van Heusen, Silvano, Vestiaco, Pierre Cardin, and Sonneti sport shirts and stopped momentarily in front of a Levi's that he matched with a pair of Wrangler jeans. He then focused on the accessories: a black Swatch watch with a matching wristband (even though the big watches that looked like a compass were more fashionable), a gold neck chain, and a gold bracelet with his name engraved on it. The outfit was not destined to be completed that evening or the one after, for he couldn't find among the sunglasses by Sting or Police or even Ray Ban the round, gold-rimmed glasses with black lenses that Sylvester Stallone had worn during his latest film.

In the meantime, the crowds had increased and the feminine presence had been filtered and the cars that filled the streets crawled slowly. The fever that accompanied the midnight movie shows broke out, so a large group of young men gathered underneath the huge billboard that Laila Elwi occupied voluptuously. Our young man who showed no experience in front of the shoe store proved that he was well trained in something else. With the eye of an expert he followed the cars that had filled the street, disregarding the more popular cars like Fiat and the more classical ones like Mercedes. He concentrated his attention on the Honda Civic and the Toyota Corolla, until finally he was in luck when he spotted a Golf with dark window shades and music playing full blast, driven by a girl whose hair was flying in the air and whose naked arm, resting on the window, promised much more. But a cruising BMW soon hid her from his view and almost came to a halt in front of him. This was how he found himself looking at two beautiful legs that had been laid bare between her dress as she tried to shuffle her feet between the gas pedal and the brakes. He was not interested in the lower part, but rather the upper one, for he had not yet moved beyond the stage of clinging to that place that fed him, to the place that begot him. But the traffic moved on before he could take a second look. The car raced forward and disappeared from view.

He waited for the traffic to slow down; then he crossed the street. He returned to the square, stumbling over the high pavement in front of an optician's, so that he landed in a muddy hole filled with garbage. A couple of steps later, he found himself in front of Wimpy, so he stopped to look at the hamburger eaters and inspected the illuminated price list, even though he knew it by heart. He walked on until he got to a shawerma stand, the smell of which helped him make a decision based on sacrifice: to content himself with a bag of chips and a Coke.

He joined the other nibblers who crowded the pavements and with whom he shared the opportunity of following the blond phenomenon the minute it appeared: two tourists, one of them in a pair of shorts that revealed two plump sunburned legs underneath strong, full buttocks, while the other demonstrated different strong points, for topping the pair of tight jeans sat a colored, sleeveless blouse that revealed her underarm hair and part of her bra. Anyway, the two girls succeeded in what all the Egyptian political parties failed to accomplish.

In no time, Sharaf found himself at the head of a large group that had responded to the firm buttocks of the girl in shorts, which forced him to use his elbows to preserve his place in the lead. This way, he was immediately behind her when she suddenly stopped, so that he almost bumped into her. She misunderstood the situation, for she turned around with a frown on her face as she opened her handbag and produced a one-pound bill that she hurled at him, repeating a word he could not understand.

She took him by surprise, so he did not extend his hand to catch the one-pound bill, and let it fall to the ground as she continued to walk with her friend with the group of followers at their heels. He looked around him and noticed that he was being eyed mockingly. Perhaps that was the reason why he blushed, turned around, stuck his hands in his pockets, and resumed walking without paying further attention to the money that had fallen, thereby approaching the fate that awaited him.

He did not get very far before he was attracted by another crowd, standing beneath a huge billboard displaying not Laila Elwi's abundance of flesh but Arnold Schwarzenegger's. As he looked at the posters from the film on the bulletin board he heard someone addressing him in English.

He turned around to find himself facing a foreign man: tall, well built, with blond hair, eyebrows, and mustache. He was wearing the shirt of his dreams: short sleeves and black. A gold chain hung around his neck. He said to him, "I have an extra ticket. Do you want it?"

Like all the new generation of Egyptians, Sharaf spoke good English, even better than he did Arabic. But his memory failed him, so he stuttered as he tried to answer, until he finally succeeded in saying, "Thank you. . . . I don't need it."

And like all blond foreigners in Egypt, our friend was not used to taking no for an answer. "You should see this film. It's very exciting. I don't think you will find another ticket."

Sharaf's arsenal in the English language gushed forth and he was happy to be able to put it to use. "Actually, I want to. But I don't have enough money."

The foreign man shrugged his shoulders and said nonchalantly, "I am giving it away because I don't need it. If you don't take it, I will throw it out."

A natural reaction from foreigners, which made Sharaf think again. "Are you sure?"

The man held the ticket and stuck it in Sharaf's hand, saying, "Take it. Don't be (Sharaf didn't understand the word). . . . Hurry up. The show is about to begin."

He took it and followed him into the movie theater to two side-by-side seats in the back, which, given the turn-out, were a real prize. The previews had just ended, followed by the usual intermission, so it was time to chat. The blond guy said, "My name is John. And yours?"

"Ashraf . . . Ashraf Abd al-Aziz. Actually, I am honored."

He meant what he said, for meeting blond foreigners is not an everyday affair. But, for some unknown reason, John started laughing. He extended two long legs and relaxed his robust, open arms on the backs of both seats, thereby touching Sharaf's arm, which Sharaf withdrew instantly. John said, "Actually, the ticket was for a young man like you whom I met this morning. He promised to come but he didn't show up."

Before he could ask for an explanation as to why John distributed movie tickets to young guys, Sharaf found him scrutinizing his mouth. He felt proud because his sister always expressed her admiration of his lips and wished that her own children would have the same lips. At that moment, the film started. He became attentive and followed Schwarzenegger's wonders, completely overwhelmed, while making sure to leave a space for his companion so that their arms wouldn't touch.

When the film ended, John made a comment that Sharaf did not understand, but he nodded his head in agreement. When they were out on the street he asked him, "Where are you from?"

"Australia."

"I thought you were American. You speak exactly like them. Do you live here?"

"Temporarily."

"Since when?"

He shrugged, "A couple of months."

"Your first time?"

"In Egypt, yes. And you . . . where do you live?"

He answered immediately, "In Maadi."

He wanted to describe the place, but he could not conjure up the filthy entrance to the metro station that stinks of sewage and is covered with flies;

the alleys filled with bulges and holes in the ground with flies and mosquitoes hovering in the air; the small houses that seem to be sinking into the ground when it is really the level of the ground that is rising continuously; the rooms that house five to ten people; the lack of water; the radio sets and tape recorders at the windows; the coffee shops and the amplifiers in the mosques and during weddings.

English seemed too complicated for all these details. So he contented himself with saying, "Actually, I live in a beautiful place on the edge of Cairo. You must see it. And where do you live?"

"In Zamalek, where else? Come with me so I can show you my home. You must see it. We are friends now."

His English enabled Sharaf to respond fluently, "Okay."

Translated by Samia Mehrez

Yasser Abdel-Latif

from *The Law of Inheritance*

I EMERGED FROM THE metro underground tunnel on the side that led to Cairo's best-known pavement, where the Ali Baba coffee shop, the Zed cafeteria, and the notorious newspaper vendor were located.

Every time I go downtown from Maadi I choose a different exit from the tunnel, a different entrance into the city: one time I take Bustan Street, another time Tahrir Street, or Qasr al-Nil Street, or Champollion Street. Most of the time I exit on Talaat Harb Street, but this time I will take Muhammad Mahmoud Street.

As Henry Miller walked on the street where his childhood home was located when he returned to Brooklyn after many wasted years in Europe, he found that the grocery store in front of which he had been beaten as a child had been transformed into a funerary services shop. Like Henry Miller, coincidences such as this have played an important role in transforming my relationship with places. If you walk toward Muhammad Mahmoud Street, immediately after the American University to your left, there is a domed building with a gate ornamented with an angular archway. This building houses the kindergarten section of the French Lycée that is right next door to where I spent part of my childhood, when we were still living in my grandfather's house in Abdin, before we returned to Maadi and my transfer to the French Lycée in the neighborhood. During my childhood, this domed building was painted pink; it had a small playground with mosaic floors and a garden that overlooked the larger, sand playground of the school and was separated from it by a delicate wooden gate. The classroom doors surrounded the tile playground and were also decked with angular archways. The details of this pink world enveloped my childhood like a dream: the small water fountain with wide-leaved floating lotus flowers on which occasional frogs would crouch, which we would carefully caress with twigs from trees in our hands; the small puppet theater where Madame Georgette used to stage puppet shows in French, which we could not understand at that time, of course, but which we would enjoy tremendously; the black piano that Madame Nabila Habashi used to play with her beautifully painted nails. How I longed for her to invite me to her home so I could see her in her indoor clothes. I don't know why I imagined that when she stayed home she wore rings on her toes. I remember the extended shadows on the pink walls and how I used the growing shadows to time the end of the school day, when one of the custodians would stand in the small garden between the two playgrounds to ring the bell, after which I would find my mother waiting for me at the gate.

One early morning in 1990 I came to this same place after having taken a heavy dose of sleeping pills that still left me sleepless. I had decided to come and visit my dreamy childhood cradle, hoping to find comfort in memory. I tricked the bawwab by saying that I was coming to follow up on my little brother's enrollment papers, so he allowed me in. I found no trace of my memories in the place. So I left and took the train back to Maadi.

I mentioned Miller's story earlier to say that the pink building of my childhood was now gray—not because of time, but because of a clever painter who chose the right color so that I could stand there after twenty years and contemplate my early childhood.

Which child inside the kindergarten now will stand here twenty years down the line and contemplate it? What color will it be painted? Black, perhaps—the most suitable color for the coming days. The windows and doors with their angular arches will be painted red to match the American fast-food joints across the street from the American University.

If you continue along Muhammad Mahmoud Street until the intersection with Nubar Street you will discover that it changes face. First there is a change of name: it becomes Qawala Street. You are no longer in the Bab al-Luq area; you are in the heart of Abdin, a couple of strides away from Abdin Square and the palace.

The architectural style changes and the street becomes somewhat narrower. Qawala Street is where Muhammad Ali, Khedive Ismail's grandfather and the founder of the palace and square, was born.

Before the intersection of Qawala and Muhammad Farid (formerly Emad al-Din) streets, to the left this time, there is a narrow street, more like an alley, but it was given the status of a street because of a passageway inside it that carries the name as an alley. This street/alley, alley/passageway is Balaqsa Street.

On that street there is a shrine of an anonymous Sufi saint known as Sheikh Hamza. My mother used to take me there as a child to buy something from a food vendor across from the shrine. That was during the celebrations of the Sufi saint's mulid. Because it was a rather small celebration, its festive signs were all grouped within the small space of Balaqsa Street: the swings, the fireworks, and the tents.

During this saint's celebration I saw things that I have never seen again in any of the bigger mulids I attended when I was older. Because they are so much bigger—like the mulid of Sayeda Zaynab—some of the essential details were lost in the swarms of people.

The unique thing I witnessed when I was but the height of my mother's knee was a red kiosk where an old man with a big beard stood at the window. He held a sharp instrument like a razor blade, which he was cleaning with a piece of cotton that he held in his other hand.

I clutched my mother's hand and asked her what the man was doing. She answered casually, "He is the metahir who performs circumcisions." Everything I saw from then on was drenched in red: the fireworks, the tents, the lights, and the blood that flowed from my imagination. What scared me the most and made me wonder in my little head was that I saw them take to him not a boy but a little girl with her legs wide open.

Hanna ibn Saad Allah, the kerosene vendor, lived on this same street/alley fifty years ago—a legendary figure whom I never met but have heard a lot about. I heard that Hanna slept with most of the women in the alley. It is not unusual for such a Casanova figure to emerge once in a while in a place like this. Except that the Casanova of Balaqsa Street did not have the virility required for the part. He was short and skinny, with a gaunt face at a time when beauty was measured by extra pounds of flesh, long before French beauty and sexuality standards took over. He wore clothes always smeared with kerosene, since he worked in his father's store. To top it all, he was Christian.

He would sit behind a greasy table like a rat to receive his female clientele of the street. He made no distinction between the wife of a merchant or a sheikh or an éffendi or a civil servant. He had a unique way of seducing them: since he was from the neighborhood and since he knew all its residents, he would begin by asking his prey about her husband. Gradually, he would impersonate that very same husband, exaggerating his role-playing until the said husband became ridiculous, at which point the wife/prey would discover the lie that was her life. In minutes he would destroy the institution ruled over by the husband. And before things cooled down, he would visit the woman the very next morning, having made sure that the husband was away. The visit would then require simple strategies that he knew all too well, which guaranteed him the woman's desecrated bed.

I heard this story from Sitt Safiya, my grandfather's neighbor before he died, our neighbor after our first move to no. 39 Mustafa Kamel Street in Abdin, and a former lover of the blessed Hanna. She was not telling me the story; rather, she was telling it to my father, whom she treated like one of her own, to the extent that she could joke with him in ways she could not with her own children. She also said that for years her husband wondered about the smell of kerosene, which she would spray on the pillow before they made love to conjure up Hanna's memory. I used to listen and watch with the knowledge that I would understand later.

Sitt Safiya had aged: she was over seventy, with kohl-lined eyes, and would sit like Sekhmet the lioness, goddess of war, on her big armchair in the hallway entrance to her apartment, facing its open door near the stairway of the building. She watched the up-and-down commotion in astonishment, for many strangers were now frequenting the building whose young and old she had known so well. She pursed her lips and clapped her hands against each other in a movement characteristic of lower-class women, whispering, "Forms and colors like Samaan's catalog."

Now I know that Samaan was the Jewish millionaire who owned Sednaoui Department Stores, and that the store catalog contained the different colors of cloth he sold, and that three generations of Cairo and its language separated me from Sitt Safiya.

With the end of Qawala Street we arrive at Abdin Square right across from the big palace. It is a white, low building whose gardens are so vast that one cannot discern the neighborhoods that extend behind it. For the onlooker standing in the middle of the square, the palace constitutes a white horizon that unites directly with the blue sky. In winter, as it is now, the place will look flooded with the light of a constant moon, given the glaring sunlight and the vast green space. You can witness this scene if you strip the palace and its surroundings of their political and social significance, in other words, its history. I am not denying my romanticism, but I am trying to constrain it as much as possible.

Alongside the southern walls of the palace there is Sheikh Rihan Street which extends eastward until Port Said (formerly al-Khalig al-Misri) Street that in turn separates the Abdin, Sayeda Zaynab, and al-Darb al-Ahmar neighborhoods. Sheikh Rihan Street continues west toward Tahrir Square. On a small alley that branches off Sheikh Rihan, and only a few steps away from the palace, lived my grandfather with his family when he was young, before they moved to no. 39 Mustafa Kamel Street, which also branches off from Sheikh Rihan.

Not only was my grandfather's move from Genena Alley to no. 39 Mustafa Kamel Street an indication of upward social mobility, but it was also an indication of the transformation of his family life—more accurately, the transformation from being of the working class to belonging to the class of effendis. He had started his life as a barman in a club that belonged to one of the political parties. From that position, behind the bar, he once allowed himself to intervene in a conversation between a pasha and another notable about Ahmad Amin's book *Fajr al-islam* (The Dawn of Islam). The pasha did not heed the barman's conservative oppositional view, nor did he care that it was articulated by a barman. What really interested him was the fact that the Nubian barman was so cultivated that he had read a book like Ahmad Amin's, which had just been published, not to mention that he had formed a solid opinion about it, even if it was conservative. The pasha discovered, when he asked the barman, that he had a high-school diploma, which, at the time, automatically qualified one to obtain the title "effendi." So, not only did he decide to give him an administrative position at the party headquarters, but he also promised to help him continue his education. Perhaps that was not aristocratic philanthropy on the pasha's part toward this cultivated but miserable barman but rather middle-class solidarity, for the pasha was a former teacher and had previously been charged in the assassination case of the British sirdar, Lee Stack.

This change that took place in my grandfather's profile, and because of which he became part of the class of bureaucratic effendis, was accompanied by another, more profound change, since his distance from serving drinks as a barman allowed him to indulge in his religious tendencies which became very visible: he grew a beard and trimmed his mustache, even though he held on to his European attire.

His newfound religiosity was not part of the Egyptian liberal one of the thirties that transformed writers like Taha Hussein and al-Aqqad into Islamists. Rather, it was a means of assimilating into a larger social structure in which he remained a strange face, of strange color.

Translated by Samia Mehrez

May Khaled
from *The Last Seat in Ewart Hall*

WHEN SHE DRIVES THROUGH Tahrir Square, everything is dwarfed when compared to that building, that lofty edifice that inhabits her completely. The Mugama, the gardens of the square, the former Astra Coffee Shop which has been transformed into a number of glittering fast-food restaurants that cater to her building, Qasr al-Aini Street with all the important national institutions. All of these places derive their very being from surrounding her temple—its structure which she still refuses to believe she has not belonged to for the past fifteen years. In fact, the longer her time away from it, the more she clings to it, is proud of it and of her sense of belonging to it. That Islamic architectural style that has towered over the heart of the city since the twenties of the past century and witnessed a series of events that have shaped the modern history of her country. Here it is, boasting the very best of Islamic architecture and the finest of human resources, with the American flag flying alongside her country's flag. She never really noticed this or that flag. Only one phrase continues to enchant her as if it contained the best that was ever produced by poets, artists, and musicians: "The American University in Cairo." It dominated the façade in Arabic and in English, sitting in an ornamented border that is repainted yearly, along with the renovations of the premises, in bright white so it remains forever young and fresh.

Despite the shudder that overtakes her every time she watches an American politician on TV after everything had been exposed, she still refuses to accept that her building belongs to that dictatorial, imperial power.

Have you fallen in love with it because it resembles you? Or because it foretold what you would become? Here you are, with your head wrapped in a veil and wearing long sleeves so that the upper part of your body gives an incontestable Islamic impression. But if the onlooker were to direct his gaze toward the lower part of your body, he would notice your tight trousers or your denim skirt with lace and patches, and would discover the split within you. He may even be able to read those Latin letters that roam in your head, that visit you in your dreams, and overtake you even when you address your God in gratitude and confidence, knowing that He will accept your own spontaneous way.

The American dream was not part of her imagination, for her roots struck deep into this earth. All the music teachers she ever had united in trying to instill Sayed Darwish's music and lyrics in her soul, the way blood flows in her veins. By the time she had obtained her primary-school certificate, she had also obtained an honorary, unwritten degree: Egyptian to the Marrow. She had memorized "Um ya Masri" (Stand Tall, Oh Egyptian) and "Hubb al-watan fard alayya" (The Love of My Country Is My Duty) and "Ya aziz ayni" (My Eye's Delight), and would become raving mad when someone made a mistake in the lyrics or sang out of tune.

Even when she remembers the time of the Naksa, which shattered so many of her country's intellectuals, she still thinks of it as a string of beautiful memories. Here she is at age four not comprehending what was broadcast on the news. She only memorizes the sweet patriotic songs that are aired after the news. She moves around freely with her brother in the neighbors' apartments in her grandmother's building when she moved with the whole family to the Hadayiq al-Qubba area not too far from Heliopolis: the neighborhood that housed the airports and witnessed the first enemy missiles to hit Cairo. She used to love that blue color that dimmed the window panes and would inspect its shades from dark to light blue, comparing her building to those of acquaintances and friends. Even after the war had ended, she continued to monitor the paint as it peeled over six years until it disappeared completely.

Her small family patriotically kept its head up high, for they considered that the Naksa was the logical outcome of Abd al-Nasser's politics, toward which they had not been sympathetic from the start.

Then why does she want to hurl herself into this unknown foreign place? Did her father and uncle contribute to creating that negative impression of national universities?

You like fairness. You nearly faint from the number of phone calls from acquaintances who appear only just before final exams, and you hate those pieces of paper, scattered by the phone, with names of unknown students asking for favors so that they may get the top grades in their oral exams just because they know one of your father's or uncle's acquaintances at the national universities. You put yourself in Nuzha's place, Aida's daughter who has been cleaning homes with her mother since she was seven and has recently enrolled in the Faculty of Science, or the bawwab Ebeid's son, Anwar, who stays up all night, trying to decipher the long mathematical problems in his difficult field. Then you see them at the tail end of the waiting lists with thousands of other unemployed youth because they are not well connected and lack distinction.

Distinction therefore is the magic word and the primary force in your life. Your mother would spank you if you forgot a verse from the poem you were reciting, or if you added two numbers instead of multiplying them. She would scold you if you came in second. You were spanked in order to wear the nicest dress, ruffled to get a trendy haircut, reprimanded because you refused to show off your talents in singing and impersonation in front of guests, and reproached if you dozed off when the house was full of visitors. You were always expected to distinguish yourself, to be like your name, a lighthouse, Manar. You became like a colt expected to race all the time. So you ran and ran until you became addicted to being at the top.

Strangely, Hisham, your brother, was never expected to achieve half of what you were. Perhaps because he decided on his destiny from the very beginning: to play the middle ground. He was never at the top of his class, so he saved himself and others the headache of waiting for his monthly report cards.

"Sister, all these clever guys are abnormal. That's why they put them away, all together in the same class like loonies." That's what Hisham used to teasingly say to her. The only year he came in fifth in his class, her mother had a party and invited the whole family and the neighbors. But Manar never felt discriminated against as a woman. For her father had enrolled her in that co-ed school because he wanted her to be "complex-free." So she gradually came to identify with members of the other sex because they were funnier and more daring in teasing teachers and less sleazy to deal with. Despite Hisham's nuisances at home, there was a kind of solidarity between them at school. Hisham was only one year older, but ever since she was in third grade, she always considered those in fourth grade to be colossal gods. This feeling increased because of the tradition that the teachers maintained of singing the praises of former students the minute they set foot in class. Even though Hisham was older, he would exploit her close relationship with her teachers because of her distinction in work and general popularity, and would introduce himself as Manar Wahbi's older brother or "the one who did the Haggala dance at the party yesterday." When he was caught playing cards in the back of the classroom or when he put on the white coat and pretended to be the school doctor in the first-floor clinic, nothing saved him from being suspended except her intervention on his behalf with the school's deputy principal, begging her to close the case without taking it to their parents.

So you do value yourself. That is why when you grew up to become "complex-free," as your father had wanted, your voice was a bit louder and your speech faster than those of your female relatives. Because you admired the ways and humor of the other sex, you learned to tell jokes like them, and you learned to hate girl gossip and feuds. You loved loud music and you practiced the latest dance steps so that you could show off at your friends' birthday parties. You never felt you were doing something wrong. That is why your mother called you ill-mannered in comparison with the other female relatives and neighbors whose voices were never heard and who never joked around with boys.

She used to constrain her anger, not for the sake of forgiveness as she does now, but because she did not allow herself to expose their secrets which she knew all too well: one went on a date and held hands with the dropout neighbor, the other kissed her brother's friend, the third stole cigarettes from the wooden box in the living room. She always had the same conversation with the most well-behaved among them,

"What do you do with the boys at school?"

"Nothing."

"But we heard that they found a boy and a girl together in the bathroom of your school.

"Of course not. That never happened."

She would then release a deep sigh and say, "You're so lucky you have boys with you."

You felt choked because of these absurd comments, and so you began to lower your voice and your gaze, and then play in the dark, like them. That is why you wanted to be in a place that would not make you feel different, where the "other" was neither scary nor intriguing, where you could speak your mind without being called "ill-mannered."

Did the novel *Ana Hurra* (I Am Free), which was poorly adapted into a film, have an indirect role in determining your choice of the American University?

Perhaps!

Translated by Samia Mehrez

Radwa Ashour

from *A Piece of Europe*

HE STOPPED AT OPERA Square. There was no Opera House anymore. It had gone up in flames. I had seen it burning. What a coincidence! Was it a Thursday or a Friday? I can no longer remember but I do remember that I was taking my daughters out to the Puppet Theater. I had bought them cotton candy as we waited for the beginning of the show. They devoured it, the youngest one completely mesmerized as she held it up with her right arm like a flag. She did not take her eyes off the pink sugar ball wrapped around a stick in her right hand. She took a bite and said, laughing, "It's gone!" She liked the illusive game. I looked at their clothes and their hair and the happiness that was inscribed on their faces. A growing sense of pride welled up inside me. Then I heard the commotion and the fire engines. I stood with my daughters on the pavement across from Azbakiya Gardens, watching the flames as they devoured the building. But, after a quarter of an hour, the girls had had enough of the fire scene and engines: "Father, we'll be late for the show!" We walked through the alley behind the National Theater, a desolate and neglected dirt road with the stench of urine, but it got us to the Puppet Theater. We went in. I seated my youngest to my right, the middle one to my left, and the eldest next to the youngest. The girls watched the operetta; they laughed, clapping their hands and singing along with the chorus:

This is the Great Night, O brother,
And the crowds are many;
They fill the tents, my friend,
From villages and towns.

The youngest one swayed her body to the music as I watched her with delight. I followed the movement of her head, shoulders, and bust. She swayed gently to the rhythm of the music and the lyrics:

I saw the great saint in my dreams,
A dove fluttering over his shrine.
The moment they woke me up

I dashed over—
Allah Hayy . . . Allah Hayy.

My thoughts wandered back to the fire. Then I was taken back to the show but my thoughts wandered again. The girls laughed at the wooden puppet and the exaggerated movements of her buttocks. I watched, still distracted by the Opera and its woeful past: Verdi's Rigoletto on the inaugural night, Ismail elated in his khedival compartment, with the empress, for whom he built a palace on the occasion of her visit to Cairo, seated beside him, next to her husband, Napoleon III, and Franz Joseph, the emperor of Austria. The French director was seated somewhere in the front. The forced laborers who built the Opera House were asleep in their villages. Verdi was two years late for the inauguration date. And finally *Aïda* was performed for the first time at the Opera House in 1871. Verdi composed *Aïda* in Villa Santa Agata near Pasito in Italy. The conductor, the singers, the actors, and the members of the orchestra were all brought from Europe. The costumes were designed and made in Paris. The Egyptians were given secondary roles and played the percussion. Khedive Ismail sent a telegram to Verdi saying, "Your choice, great Maestro, to compose an opera that is set in my country has fulfilled my dream of creating a national cultural production. This may become the everlasting stamp of my reign."

A lost little girl this small,
On her left foot
An anklet like my own.

This is the Great Night, O brother,
And the crowds are many;
They fill the tents, my friend,
From villages and towns.

The onlooker stood in the middle of the square. The Opera House was here, a whole piece of Europe. It was designed by the architects Avoscani and Rossi in the style of La Scala in Milan. The Opera House was located in the heart of the square. To the left still stood the Caisse de la Dette building. He looked across the square. Over there stood the Shepheard Hotel, a small piece of England, as if it were the British consulate. The demonstrators burned it down in January 1952, along with Thomas Cook travel agency, which occupied part of the hotel premises. Thomas Cook organized tours to Upper Egypt for

British travelers. His cruisers were also a piece of Europe, floating on the Nile in the name of God: the kind of food, the level of service, the language of communication. John Mason Cook, Thomas Cook's son, was tall and robust. I imagined him as big as Rothschild Balfour, except that Rothschild liked collecting butterflies and loved natural history, while John Mason was stern and authoritative, holding the Nile itself, along with the lives of his workers, in his iron fist. It was said that he grabbed a translator who addressed him inappropriately and threw him into the river. Cook was the most important personality in Cairo. This was what *Vanity Fair* magazine reported in 1889. The magazine was right, since the travelers who arrived from overseas relied on Cook's travel agency to organize the details of their trips to Cairo. Then they were transported on Cook's cruisers to Upper Egypt to visit the monuments. On board these God-protected cruisers, travelers would make entries in their diaries at the end of each day. When they returned home they would edit what they had written and send it to be published.

The onlooker gazed at the new building that had been erected in lieu of the Opera House. A big sign read: "Cairo Governorate: Commercial Center and Opera Parking"—a massive eight-story cement structure with dark glass paneling, immediately behind which stood the four-story parking garage, with dim passageways that spiral upward from one level to another where people park their cars for an hourly fee. When I go to the National Theater with one of my daughters, she parks her car in this parking lot. We take a narrow dark stairway that leads us to Ataba Square near the National Theater. I leave the suffocating space of the stairwell and emerge into the open space of the street. And I forget. I always forget that what I imagine as an open space will assault me with a complex stench that may or may not include urine. We slow down to secure our way between the stench and the clamor of the passersby, cars, and the stalls of merchandise that occupy the pavement.

He wanted to cross over to Bosta Street but found it quite difficult to do so. The cars dash toward the flyover on al-Azhar Street and the tunnel. He circled the statue of Ibrahim Pasha before crossing to the west side of the square. They had renovated the place: they added marble tiles that were surrounded by a well-groomed lawn, in the middle of which stood the bronze statue on a new base. Was it new or had it been polished? It looked new. He left the statue behind and crossed the street. He crossed again and returned to the eastern side of the square where the Opera Mall stood: another massive commercial cement structure that occupied the space of the old cinema and casino, Badia's Casino. He bore to the right and stopped at the crossroads. Which of these was Bosta Street? He noticed a lush but dilapidated building to his left, a Victorian-style building that stood across from a small three-story structure painted in green with a minaret at its far end, which he noticed because of the sound of the muezzin's sudden call for prayer through an amplifier. He raised his gaze. The balconies of the building, the minaret, and the amplifier were all thoroughly haphazard and unplanned. He bore to the left, making his way to Sunduq al-Dein (Caisse de la Dette) Street—a three-story building now painted white. They had renovated it. He couldn't see the whole building. The side across from the post office building was hidden from view by small kiosks that sold electrical accessories: wiring, joints, and lamps. So was the other side of the building, even though the merchandise was different: colored postcards, cheap papyrus paintings, prints of Qur'anic verses in cheap golden frames. The postcards and the prints were on display on wooden stands inside the kiosks, while the paintings were spread out on the pavement, partaking of the clamor, the dust, the digging, and the flyover that divided the street and rose slightly above it, transforming it into a narrow suffocating alleyway. He walked cautiously so as not to bump into the passersby or trip over one of the paintings or one of the dug-up holes or the puddles of water that might be the remains of the shopkeepers' routine sprinkling to settle the dust or a leak from a corner where one of the passersby had relieved himself standing with his back to the street. *La ilaha illa Allah.*

He turned and walked home.

Translated by Samia Mehrez

Ibrahim Farghali

from *The Smiles of the Saints*

SHE SIPPED HER COFFEE as she moved toward the balcony. Suddenly she stopped and turned back to the bedroom to fetch a long, creamy-white satin dressing gown from the suitcase. When she went out onto the balcony, where the movement on the quiet street had increased a little, she was shocked by the changes that had taken place.

She noticed the new building that towered opposite her, where the empty lot had been. Abutting it on its left was a building of more modern design, painted in a range of browns and grays. The little row of shops had disappeared. She struggled to bring them to mind while my own memories resurfaced: Amm Muhammad the ironing man, and the roastery for pips and peanuts with its shop opposite that Amm Sanad used to shuttle between, now long closed and turned into a ful and taamiya restaurant. There had also been a little kiosk behind the shops, where Umm Hamdi used to serve up her tea and coffee to passersby and to shopkeepers on the square, like Amm Bakr the grocer, who was separated from Amm Muhammad's grocery by two other shops of identical trade—Amm Fawzi who tailored men's shirts and Amm Higazi who specialized in women's garments. Then there was Amm Abdu the barber and finally Amm Farouq, the shoe mender, at the foot of the building.

She remembered the high-pitched hissing of the gas burner that emitted from the ful and taamiya shop opposite the back entrance of Farid al-Masri Mosque. And the vendor of the sweet luqmat al-qadi whose cry could be heard at seven o'clock, always on time with his shrill, monotonous, "Loka midis!" followed by a phrase she had never understood—"Lokma di Lokma!" His piercing call used to cut across the morning *Asharq al-Awsat* program that broadcast from a huge radio on a wooden shelf above Amm Muhammad the ironing man, as his heavy iron slammed down on garments that were covered by a protective sheet, changing its color from white to a range of dark browns in a pattern of random markings.

Then the coarse cry of the gas seller would suddenly burst out through the square: "Kerosene! Pure kerosene!"

And there would be the owner of the voice, an old man with a snow-white beard, seated at the front of his cart, leaning against a bright yellow cylindrical tank.

She smiled when she remembered the sight of the rubbish bin, a rectangular cabinet of rusty iron, the nightly refuge for cats and a morning source of food for the street dogs that were the target of the dog-catchers' guns, when she would start in her bed at their terrible anguished cries.

Sitting on this balcony long ago as a child she had always been able to look out over the empty lot at the old building spotted with faded yellow. A huge advertisement for Belmont cigarettes on its side wall stretched from the second to the fifth floor, with a tall window in the center where an old woman used to sit all day long without the slightest movement, reminding her of Mary Mounib in the play *Five To*, but absolutely silent as if dumb, and perhaps blind too.

On the right, the balcony had looked over the only square in the old quarter of Turil where, on the opposite side, Farid al-Màsri Mosque occupied the length of the square, with Talaat Harb Street extending as far as the old railway crossing at the edge of the Gadila quarter.

Now she could see only the balconies of the imposing building opposite, enclosed with their aluminum windows, no sign of life in any of them.

She left the balcony to make more coffee and breakfast in the kitchen. On her way she glanced at the hands of the antique wooden clock hanging near the living room, which showed 8:30. She was surprised that two whole hours had passed since she had woken up, then remembered that her mobile was still set to French time. There was only half an hour until her aunt was due.

Translated by Andy Smart and Nadia Fouda-Smart

Naim Sabri

from *District Seven*

RAMI WAS ON HIS way back to Nasr City from downtown, feeling choked because of the draining August heat and the numbing humidity. Driving a car at midday was the ultimate torture. Images of safe arrival and salvation hovered in his imagination: a nice air-conditioned space after a cold shower and an ice-cold beer, then a quiet nap.

Today's meetings were productive. My discussion with the general manager of the company where Magdi works clarified many issues about the export industry in Egypt: the problems of exchange rates, opening accounts, and bank loans. Business was difficult in Egypt. But their company had diversified: they dealt in refrigerators, washing machines, stoves, electrical appliances, not to mention wall-to-wall carpeting, wallpaper, gifts . . . dozens of items that they imported and distributed all over the country. The interesting thing was that they hired Magdi as sales manager. He was good at sales and distribution. Today, Magdi explained their pricing system. He said that pricing had to be in line with the mandates of the Ministry of Supplies and that those who did not comply were penalized. Lots of details. The meeting with the general manager was also very fruitful. It's been a month since I started work but the picture remains unclear. I can't feel my way yet. I agreed with Hagg Abdallah on a feasibility study over six months before beginning the project so we could make the right decisions. If only he would tell me what kind of budget he had in mind. What was the sum he intended to invest? He leaves everything open and it just makes it all the more difficult for me. It is impossible not to set limits or indicators to orient oneself. Was he thinking of investing one hundred thousand dollars, or a million, for example? The size of the investment is determined by the value of the available capital and he doesn't want to commit a specific amount. He keeps all doors open. He doesn't want to miss out on any opportunity. But this open-endedness is a headache for me. He wants me to consider a million ideas. And now I feel lost. It is like being in a labyrinth with no sense of direction. I have to go out to Port Said to understand the Free Zone. I also have to drop by the Investment Organization. I want to inquire about the conditions for setting up investment companies and the governing laws and regulations. It is all very complicated. Here we are, finally arrived! I'll park the car in the shade so that it's not sizzling hot when I take it out this afternoon. I'm hungry. He called out as he opened the apartment door:

"Nano, Alaa. Anybody home?"

Is this possible? It's past two o'clock. Let me take a quick shower before they come. I'm starved. The cold water is very refreshing after this damn weather. I can no longer wait to eat. They're still not home. Maybe I'll find something in the fridge. What?! Nothing there to eat! No solution but to go down and have lunch with mother and Salah Pasha.

He went down to eat with his mother, Ihsan Hanim, who lived on the second floor in Salah Pasha's building below Rami's apartment. Rami said, as Ihsan Hanim opened the door, "I came to have lunch with you and Grandfather."

"Your grandfather has lunch at one o'clock. Have you forgotten his routine?"

Salah Pasha emerged when he heard Rami's voice.

"Hello, Rami. Come on in. Prepare his lunch, Ihsan. I'm already done but I'll sit with you to keep you company. I cannot eat alone. Your mother always has to eat with me."

Alaa came running out when he heard his father's voice. Rami exclaimed, "Alaa is here?! So where's Nano?"

Ihsan Hanim replied, "She left him with me because one of her friends is having an open day, so she went to buy some stuff."

"What is this 'open day' thing?"

Ihsan Hanim replied, "Women who go abroad and buy women's outfits and then sell it in their homes. They call each other up and word gets around. Imported outfits."

Salah Pasha said sarcastically, "Smuggling, in simple language."

"That's news to me, Salah Pasha!"

"There are many things that are new in the country in the past few years. We are in the post-infitah era!"

After a moment's silence, Rami said, "An infitah with the doors wide open, Salah Pasha!"

Salah Pasha replied with exasperation, "Imported goods are all over the place. It's like a fever that has hit the country and very few people are thinking about industry as an option. Most find it easier to do business. We import but we do not export. We consume but we do not produce. And the country is suffering from a national deficit and the rise of exchange rates. The future looks pretty grim. Things are out of control."

Ihsan Hanim called, "Rami, lunch is ready."

Translated by Samia Mehrez

M.M. Tawfik

from *Murder in the Tower of Happiness*

WHEN THE FIRST ARMCHAIR smashed into the asphalt, Sergeant Ashmouni was at his usual spot in the middle of the Nile Corniche, trapped by the road's twin currents turbulently flowing forth to Maadi and back to Old Cairo. He was wiping the sweat away from his eyes with the worn-out sleeve of his white traffic-police uniform—adding a new stain in the process—when surprise from the thunderous impact catapulted him into the fast lane of the riverside road.

The shocked policeman landed in front of a speeding cab whose driver managed, in intoxicated spontaneity, to avoid him, but at the cost of losing control over his loose-braked Fiat 128, which henceforth became liberated from mankind's hysterical rule. The cab's fate had been taken over by the complex laws of aerodynamics, which caused it to spark a chain reaction that, in a split second, had engulfed a public transport bus, a van taking a shift of workers to the steel plant, five private cars, three taxis, a tricycle, and a handcart carrying a pile of lupine beans.

Thus, without prior warning, Ashmouni found himself at the center of an animated carnival that had sprung up in an instant and quickly spread to the other side of the road. This was the side of the road nearest to the towers that have proliferated along the Nile's bank, the side on which the armchair had fallen in the first place.

The incident lasted no more than a few seconds, yet to the policeman, it seemed like an eternity. An open-ended interval during which, in a succession of confused leaps, he tackled buses, passenger cars, and cabs, narrowly avoiding the vehicles hurtling in every direction. Then he achieved that moment of silence he had always longed for. A moment of security—of the sort that, for years, he had scarcely enjoyed. Ashmouni suddenly found himself washed up on an island of calm and serenity amid Cairo's loud, aggressive ocean. He realized he was lying on his back on the ragged grass in the middle of the broad sidewalk along the Nile.

At that moment—at precisely 2:15 p.m. on the second of August 1999—as the sergeant lay on the grass catching his breath and trying to collect the fragments of the past few moments, as his fingertips gingerly checked his chest and bare head to make sure he was unhurt, the plates and glasses, the forks and knives, started to pour like rain. He instinctively rolled his body and wrapped his arms around his head, preparing himself for the impact of the incoming projectiles.

A few seconds later, when the axe had spared his neck, he opened his eyes and cautiously looked upward, just in time to observe the cushions and tablecloths fluttering coquettishly down. So he asked himself the delayed questions:

"What's happening? Has doomsday erupted? Have people gone even crazier than they already were?" Gradually, he regained his composure, and started to contemplate the falling books and drifting sheets of paper. Then he raised his head while supporting his body on his elbows, and started to curse those spoiled brats and their parents who thought that money could compensate for bad behavior. But no sooner had the piano's edge emerged from one of the balconies near the top of the building, than the swearing froze in his throat.

Like an angry cloud, the piano's blackness blocked the disc of the sun. It was a fancy piano. He was familiar with its likes from watching Abd al-Halim and Farid al-Atrash movies. But from his current perspective, the piano lacked any poetic or musical allure. It was menacing, ghost-like, as it floated out of the balcony held by a firm but invisible hand. Its straight, wide edge appeared first, then its silhouette narrowed and ended in the shape of the tip of a roasted sweet potato.

After it had completely cleared the balcony, the piano remained for a few seconds suspended in midair. Then, suddenly, it plunged. The invisible hand had abandoned it to its fate, rendered it to the force of gravity that makes no exemptions. So, like a bomb, it dropped on the unsuspecting Nile Corniche.

The sergeant followed the piano's fall to the ground as if he were watching a movie in slow motion. A movie that remained silent, only to regain sound the moment the piano crashed into a Mercedes parked at the foot of the tower. The sound-bomb was followed by a series of musical groans: materials of diverse densities colliding, springs tinkling, echoes reverberating—in short, the groans of a dying piano. Then there was silence: a tense alert silence.

When an eternity had passed and nothing else fell, the voices started to come in waves. Intermittent whispers at first, then shrill calls: the shouts of those who suddenly remembered a child who had strayed out of sight or a spouse lost in the commotion. Then, like long-range artillery, came the honks of cars kept away from the center of events, expressing a temporary displeasure at this unexplained delay and a more profound anger at being left out of the limelight.

At a glance, Ashmouni grasped that it was Shaker Pasha's new car the piano had flattened and turned into mincemeat. A luxurious silver Mercedes of the model nicknamed "powder" as only drug dealers can afford one. The millionaire would be angry today and buy a new one tomorrow. These people have mountains of cash from which they shovel without counting. As the famous belly dancer says: if she were to pile her money up and stand on top of it, she'd see as far as Timbuktu.

As if Ashmouni's troubles were not enough, just then the officer arrived on his official motorbike with the shiny nickel parts. His expression revealed it had been no small feat to negotiate passage through the impregnable flesh-and-metal wall of interlocked vehicles and people rushing about in confusion. The officer doled out blame to drivers and passengers alike. Nothing was spared the curse of his frigid eyes: buses turned over on their sides, cars that had crashed into lampposts and tree trunks, the 128 taxi that had ended up on top of the lupine bean handcart on the sidewalk next to the Nile.

The officer found Ashmouni shuffling from where the remains of the piano lay squarely atop the squashed roof of the Mercedes to the location of a the broken armchair on the asphalt. The sergeant looked helplessly about him and kept picking up torn books and tattered cushions whose feathers were dispersed on the ground. He had lost all touch with reality as the distinguished officer knew it.

The sergeant's anxiety started to ease when he reassured himself he'd survived the ordeal unhurt, and, even more so, when he understood from the exchanged calls between bus drivers and garage attendants that, due to divine intervention, no one was hurt. The incident had ensnared all these unsuspecting victims in its nets then left them alone as if nothing had happened. So, when Ashmouni at last noticed the officer, he saluted the man as if a simple accident had occurred or a commonplace quarrel had erupted between two drivers.

The officer took his helmet off, held it under his arm, and looked around him in disbelief. Then he came back to the sergeant, eyes bursting with accusation, and muttered through clenched teeth:

"Damn you, Ashmouni."

Translated by M.M. Tawfik

Mustafa Zikri

from *What Amin Did Not Know*

NINNA, ADEL RITA, AND Busi stood on the pavement of the Japanese Garden watching Amin with a quiet, grave smile. Amin walked toward them with a similar smile on his face: very well-mannered and respectful. Amin extended his arm in midair to greet them. In his right hand he held his dinner in a plastic bag that was swinging violently. The sight of Amin's arm held up in midair made Ninna, Adel Rita, and Busi laugh quietly as they came off the pavement to meet Amin. He welcomed them warmly enough to keep them on their best behavior, at least while greeting him. They exchanged kisses and Amin shook their hands warmly. Ninna smiled. At the upper front of his mouth he had three fake teeth made of cheap white metal that was turning gray.

"Hey, man, walkin' through without saying hello. Won't do. What's up?"

From his unique, elevated position, the owner of the small supermarket could see Amin, Ninna, Adel Rita, and Busi through the window moving away from the fence of the Japanese Garden in the opposite direction from Amin's apartment. Farid, the owner of the supermarket, turned toward the small TV screen and zapped from the *Raya wi Sakina* play he had been watching to the foreign film, *The Misfits*. He turned up the volume. After a little while he saw Marilyn Monroe and Clark Gable on the screen.

The entrance to the Japanese Garden was gloomy and dark. A dim phosphoric reddish-yellow light emanated from a pole close to the entrance. Ninna grabbed Amin's neck while Adel Rita and Busi walked ahead. In an attempt to win his sympathy, Amin said to Ninna, "Yes, Ninna, but I don't want to miss the film."

"What film, man?! We don't ever get to see you. Why don't you just join us for a while? A couple of jokes, a couple of stories, you know what I mean. Okay, Amin, baby?"

Amin smiled as he produced his red Marlboro pack and offered a cigarette to Ninna, saying, "You're right!"

Ninna produced a pack of Marlboro Lights and said as he took one, "Thanks. I smoke mild ones. . . ."

The phosphoric light from the pole outside the garden was reflected on the huge Buddha statue. At the foot of the Buddha were his disciples: small, cross-legged statuettes with quiet smiles. They resembled the ones Amin had in his apartment inside a glass niche. There were forty of them surrounding a salty lake with deep green water. Amin sat on one of the disciples' legs with his right hand on his cheek and his left hand across him, hugging his right underarm, with his plastic dinner bag placed in front of him. Ninna raised his arms high up in the air and pressed his white artificial teeth against his lower lip. Adel Rita blocked his ears with a farcical movement while Busi blew air mildly near Amin's extended left arm. Ninna descended upon Amin's hand with a hard, nasty blow that tipped him over so that he almost fell into the lake. His feet landed inside his plastic dinner bag. Ninna, Adel Rita, and Busi cracked up, laughing quietly and viciously with a morbid tone. Amin turned to face them, repositioning himself as he pushed back his eyeglasses and tidied up his dinner bag.

Ninna, Adel Rita, and Busi raised their fingers in midair directly in front of Amin's eyes as they supported each other, swaying back and forth on unsteady legs. Amin said, feigning a smile—or at least it seemed feigned compared to their real laughter:

"Ninn. . . ."

Before Amin could finish saying the name they yelled together:

"Wrong!"

Once again a wave of vicious, morbid laughter rose after the negative answers and once again Ninna's, Adel Rita's, and Busi's legs swayed as they exchanged heavy violent blows directed toward each other's shoulders and jaws. Amin returned to his earlier position and they started fighting over their positions of attack. Adel Rita won and descended upon Amin with a hard blow that shook his body and paralyzed his legs that stood at the tip of the rim of the lake with the plastic bag between them. Amin turned to face them. Their fingers were pointed at his face, and before he could open his mouth Busi said, "It wasn't one of us who hit you, so that you don't go looking."

Adel Rita hit Busi's chest hard with his palm, laughing, and said in a loud voice that scared Amin, "Don't listen to him, Amin, baby. Who was it, Amin, baby? Come on, say."

Adel Rita repeated, "Say it, say it," with the second time louder than the first, shaking his finger and extending it toward Amin, who gradually pulled back his neck and said in a petrified voice, "Adel?"

"Wrong, Amin, baby!"

Amin returned to his earlier position, stiffening his features, body, and legs in preparation for more blows and the most extreme degrees of violence.

Translated by Samia Mehrez

Yusuf Idris
from *"The Dregs of the City"*

ABDALLAH WAS ELATED AS he started off on his quest for Shohrat. It was a novel and thrilling adventure not only because he was certain to recover his stolen watch but because it was going to prove his perspicacity. He looked forward to tracking Shohrat down, to catching her redhanded, to watching her reaction, observing her fear, her denial. New complications would surely crop up but he would know how to handle them. He could already see himself later, telling his friends how adroitly he had handled the whole affair. For the moment he refused to consider adverse possibilities even though they crowded his mind. He was weary of thinking and debating and making new plans every time he discovered a leak, and from that moment he decided to shut off his mind to everything but the scene unfolding before him.

He felt himself melting into the landscape as he rolled along. He could not remember the exact moment when it happened or any specific incident that relegated Shohrat to the back of his mind. He could only recall the dim beginning from al-Gabalaya Street. The long, clean, shaded street; the open spaces and the tall stylish buildings. The peace and the quiet, except for the noiseless flow of elegant cars and a few pedestrians. The air was serene and the Nile flowed gently, and the car glided along as though on a carpet of silk. And Sharaf beside him smoking in silence, smiling with amusement when he remembered his part. Farghali was in the back, holding on to the front seat, the car reeking with his smell, spluttering into Abdallah's right ear every time he spoke.

At the bridgehead they are joined by streams of cars pouring from Zamalek, Gezira, Dokki, and Giza. Bright, colorful, shining, like flocks of birds. In the whirlpool of Qasr al-Nil Square their ranks are swelled by shabby cars and taxi-cabs before they diverge to other streets where movement never stops; narrower, with closer buildings; noisier, with more pedestrians. At Ataba it becomes one great merry-go-round. Automobiles and buses and tram cars and pedestrians and horse-drawn carts mill around in utter chaos. It reaches a peak when they turn into al-Azhar Street. Here, it is a madhouse of pedestrians and automobiles, screeching wheels, howling claxons, the whistles of bus conductors, and roaring motors. Policemen blow their whistles, and hawkers yell in the blistering heat. The roads and pavements are a moving mass of flesh. Everything is wholesale. Riding a vehicle, trading, and even accidents come wholesale. From time to time a warning to be careful rises above the din like the last cry of a drowning corpse.

Driving becomes an agony under volleys of abuse from pedestrians and the eloquent retaliations of Farghali, and Abdallah's determination to get even with Shohrat and avenge his wounded pride. He would strangle her willingly. Get his fingers round her neck and press, tighter and tighter. He is pressing the claxon which lets out a hoot that falls noiselessly on the enormous crowds. Traffic goes at a crawling pace, exasperating, maddening. The mosque of al-Azhar rises indomitable on the skyline, behind a haze of dust. It has stood for generations, watching the deadly struggle while it has remained constant, insusceptible to change. Then they turn to the right.

Acting on Farghali's advice, they park the car and do the last leg on foot. A few paces and Abdallah begins to feel hollow as though he has been left alone in an ancient deserted place. The noise dies down; the quiet is almost tangible. He is Egyptian through and through. His father came from Mounira and his mother from Abbasiya. He has poor relations in Upper Egypt. He has traveled a good deal, gone to many places, and seen the extremes of poverty. Yet here is Cairo, and this place where he finds himself is part of it. The incredible scenes unfolding before his eyes amaze him beyond belief as he delves further in, as though he were sinking in a bottomless pit.

The streets are long and broad at first, carrying illustrious names. They are macadamed and they have a pavement. There are crowded dwellings on both sides, but they have numbers and terraces and decorated gates and the windows have panes and shutters. The shops have owners and tools and assistants and elegantly written signs. The people are clean-shaven and healthy looking. Their clothes are neat and colorful and well cut. Language is polite. The smell of burning fuel and fabrics and perfume fills the air.

The deeper inside, the narrower the streets. The houses shrink and shed their numbers. Windows have no shutters. Shops give way to stalls where the proprietor is himself the assistant and his bare hands his tools. Faces are paler and darker. Clothes are old and faded. Language degenerates into abuse, and the air carries the smell of spices and leather and glue and sawdust.

Still they continue, and the streets grow narrower until they become mere lanes with names that jar on the ear. Rough blocks of stone take the place of macadam and there is no pavement. Eons of time separate the dilapidated dwellings from modern times, the windows are narrow slits with iron bars. There is less movement, stalls are few and far between. Features are coarse, faces are darker, and beards begin to sprout. There is less clothing. No shirts with the trousers, no underpants with the gallabiya. Language breaks down to a jargon of grunts, and kitchen smells ride on the air. Still they continue and the winding lanes lead to alleys paved with dirt, covered with filth and water and slime. There are no stalls; goods are displayed on push carts or a showcase nailed to the wall. The houses have shed their coating of paint and the iron bars on the windows. Children and flies swarm in abundance. Features are coarse and swollen as though bitten by wasps. Clothes are threadbare; some are unclothed: language is loud and shrill, and the smell of slime and decay falls like a pall on the dismal scene.

As they keep on toward their destination the winding lanes and alleys lead to a place without substance where everything melts into everything else. The raised ground compounded of years of accumulated dirt welds with the dilapidated buildings groaning with age. The slimy ground is the same color as the dusty walls. The smell of the earth mingles with the smell of humanity, and the low broken murmurs mix with the barking of dogs and the creaking of old gates, and the dead slow movement of inanimate creatures. The low grimy dwellings are a continuation of the graveyard, stretching forward as far as the eye can see. And the obsequious Farghali leads the way, a grave expression on his face, befitting the grave situation. People greet him and he answers curtly.

They all know him and ask how he is getting on. They treat him with defer-ence, him, the mean janitor, while back in al-Gabalaya Street nobody knows the all-powerful judge.

They walk on through the crumbling buildings propped, like the people, against one another for support. The old lean on the young, the children lead the blind, and the walls support the sick. All are strung together like the beads of a rosary. One spirit inhabiting many bodies. Time does not exist. The child suckling at its mother's breast is the same one who crawls on the garbage heaps and the same one girded with talismans against the evil eye. He is the child who died and the child who escaped death. He is the apprentice at the workshop, the one who fools around imitating actors and calling out abuse. He is the youth in overalls drawing on the stub of a cigarette. The one with a job or out of work. He is that one near the wall, crazed with opium and Seconal and unemploy-ment. He is the old man who prays all day, calling benedictions on the children, lamenting the past as he paints himself a glowing picture of the world to come.

And the betrothed bride. She is the children's mother with the colored head-covering or the black veil. She is the beating mother and the beaten wife. She is that one rummaging for food to feed the hungry brood.

Farghali's voice comes dimly to Abdallah. He is pointing at the only upright building in the lane, saying proudly it is his house, insisting they go in, not forgetting to curse Shohrat who is the cause of his disgrace. Abdallah asks where the blind alley is and whether Shohrat's house is still far. Farghali replies that they have almost reached it. They walk on, followed by inquisitive looks. And behind every suspicious look the word 'stranger' forms, implying danger and distrust.

The women on their doorsteps are weaving conversation out of their idle-ness. They lean their heads together as they watch the strange procession. The whisper travels from doorstep to doorstep. "Police," some say in a hoarse whisper. "Health authorities," hope the optimistic. Then they recognize Farghali, and their whispers die down.

And children. Scores upon scores gather in front and behind and on either side, their eyes bleary with ophthalmia and trachoma, and misery looks out of their haggard faces. Swarms of flies come in their wake. One child shouts as he hurls a stone at Farghali, who reproves him mildly. Soon it is a game. The children gather round Farghali, who chases after them and they scamper away with the flies behind them. Soon they come back and resume their game as the flies resume their buzzing.

Farghali is not sure which is Shohrat's house. He asks one of the women sitting at their doors who points to a house not far off. The name is carried from mouth to mouth, collecting conjecture as it travels. The women leave their places to join the procession of children. Their black veils and the dirt ground and the shouting of the children and the low mumble of adults are all one. The earth boils under the hot sunshine and the stench from its bowels escapes to the sky.

Farghali and Sharaf, surrounded by the curious crowd, wait at the door while Abdallah goes up alone. The house is dark. The interior is like the mouth of a toothless hag. Matches won't light and they drop to the slimy floor. Shohrat is on the second floor, at least that's what they said. The first floor is pitch black and the stink is foul; an army of rats seems to have gnawed at the decaying walls streaked with traces of brine and leakage. Dank, moldy, as if just emerging from a flood. A woman washing at the door of a room in the entrance, one bare white leg exposed, stares at him with suspicion. Her hands stiffen; she can neither let go of the washing nor cover her bare leg. The stairs are worn and shaky, the wooden steps rotten and missing in places. His shoe creaks, and he is panicky with the danger of falling. For the hundredth time the light from the match is blown out by a dank breeze blowing from an invisible source. A cool, dank breeze that chills his marrow, while outside the sun burns hot. The second floor can hardly be called a floor. A bare framework like the ribs of a skeleton forms the roof. Old, tottering, sloping walls, and a door on the landing. It is made of old rough unpolished wood, grayish blue, smudged with the remains of dried-up dough, the excreta of birds and animals, and the bloody imprint of a human palm, flanked by the drawing of a face like a witch's, chalked by some child.

He stretches a hesitant hand to knock on the door.

"I want a word with you," he says to the face that appears in the doorway.

She pales beneath the look he pours on her like a searchlight. Apprehension and fear look out of her eyes. It's Shohrat. She greets him in a broken voice and opens the door wider to let him in. She is wearing a man's old gallabiya slit down the front. Her paleness has traveled to her feet, making her toenails white. He is embarrassed. This trembling woman stole his watch. He was out for her blood when he started on her trail, but now he wavers. He stands debating whether to go on or to turn back. Having come this far, he must go on.

"I want a word with you," he says as he had planned. But his tone is not as he had planned. She lets him in, pale and apprehensive. She tries to hide her embarrassment behind a wan smile. He plans his retreat as he enters. Anything might happen. She might scream for help; he might be assaulted and robbed or killed. Three children emerge from somewhere. A girl, ten years old, tall, dark, skinny, with beady eyes and an expressionless face. Her hair is black and shiny, exuding an odor of petrol, one plait undone and a wooden comb planted at the crown of her head. Two other children, a boy and a girl, or possibly two girls or two boys. They cling to their mother's skirt. Out of the dark, penetrating the smell of petrol, four pairs of eyes are fixed on him with mistrust. He swallows.

"I want a word with you," he repeats mechanically. Shohrat comes too abruptly as though in response to a stimulant.

She sends the children away and shuts the door, but they linger behind it, their eyes shining through the cracks like glow worms. His head is spinning. The room is close and narrow. A faint light filters through a window high in the wall. A decrepit four-poster, rusted all over, with a grubby mattress. A coarse, moth-eaten sack full of something is propped against the wall. A rabbit is sitting on it. At the other end is another grubby mattress, and empty tin cans and chips of wood and a miscellany of junk lie scattered about. There is a picture of Imam Ali on the wall. He is shown smiting an infidel with his sword, but the infidel is still sitting upright in his saddle, his feet firmly in the stirrups, in spite of the gash in his head. Something stirs on the mattress: a man, tall and dark and bald as the water cooler standing beside him. He is stretched out with a scowl on his face, his belt unbuckled, with filthy underwear showing through his open trousers.

"I want a word with you," for the third time.

"Yes?" faintly with a tremor.

"Where is the watch?"

She stiffens and beats her breast with indignation. She denies with the fluttering of her eyelids and the increasing paleness of her face. He repeats his question. She repeats her denial. Intuition assures him she is the thief and he returns more vehemently to the attack. She tries to reply and the words die on her lips. He shouts and she cowers, holding on desperately to her pride. The screams of the children rise above theirs. The eldest tries to take them away as she hears what is being said to her mother. Scenting danger they refuse to go and leave her alone.

His anger grows and he threatens her with the police. He is at the door. She appears not to believe him so he goes to the door. It creaks open. Then he takes her to the window and they both lean out. "All right, Officer," he calls, and Sharaf replies with a wink. Abdallah's face remains frozen and he pulls Shohrat back inside. "Hand it over or you get a year in jail."

Translated by Wadida Wassef

Ibrahim Aslan

from *The Heron*

KIT KAT AND ITS giant stone entrance, the writing on the lofty arch: "The battle of the Pyramids took place here on the 21st of July, 1798." Abdallah brought
his coffee, lingered for a while, then walked off. Amir recalled the day he'd
cried on account of Kit Kat. He knew that the contractor had purchased the
rubble of the Kit Kat club. When he returned from work, he saw the massive,
shiny stones split into pieces, strewn along the empty plot of land behind it
at the entrance to the city of Imbaba. He had stood in a corner of the square,
looking at the square tables draped with white cloth that hung down to the
deep green grass. And the bushes with candles hidden inside, giving off light
like so many small moons. And how so often at night he'd climb the camphor
tree with his playmates. Here was the royal winter hall. On its roof, supported
by marble columns topped with capitals, was another wooden roof around
which hung intricately designed eaves. This was where the king would go during the summer. He looked and saw the king's private entrance with its heavy
brass knocker.

Amir remembered how during the war, they had stood there watching
the Allied soldiers stationed in Kit Kat, near the guava orchards, and on the
houseboats. The black soldiers gazed back at them from the top of the winter
hall, from the tall stone entrance, from behind the barbed wire around the
orchards. They called out, "We're Muslims too!" and threw chocolate bars and
heavy pocketknives with rough, black handles which the kids would exchange
for a few piasters and spend the money on soft drinks. . . .

Muhammad Atiya bought a tire from them and purchased knives from the
kids. Hamama would come with his brother and brother-in-law Salama and
they'd stand under the winter hall yelling, "Giff me won sigaret, Mr. Khawaga!"
The Great Haram hid his drugs under a tree in the guava orchard. And they
walked past the seller of clay drinking jars and pots, and along the long trail
made by feet walking between the nightshade bushes, which sparkled with
tiny blueberries, toward Sidi Hasan Abu Tartour cemetery with its mudbrick
masonry and the graves they climbed to reach the berry bushes.

They'd eat the berries and fill their pockets with them, and at home, he'd
get beaten because the pockets of his gallabiya would be stained with berry
juice. Those tall berry bushes were filled with white and red syrup. There

was Sayyid, the bald-headed boy, and the small yellow rooms on the far side, where the Ministry of Religious Endowments buildings are now, which they say Napoleon built as prisons and which Baron Meyer made into stables for the thoroughbreds he raised and raced. And the floods: the water running, overflowing, churning the red silt, rising until the entrances of the house-boats were level with the road and the gangplanks rose upward to reach the boats. The lotus plants, the ferries, the decorated boats, the whole world on the riverbank. And his father taking his hand and watching the sluggish whirlpools that roiled and collected the flotsam and spun it around, sucking it into their angry vacuums. Amir thought about how the whirlpools cleaned the surface of the water.

He began to become aware that something strange was happening, then after a moment pinpointed the cause: what he was hearing over the loud-speaker wasn't the Qur'an at all. Sheikh Hamada al-Abiad must have finished his recitations, as what he heard was a voice mumbling, "You're talking bullshit." A short period of silence passed, then the voice returned and said that they probably didn't know who the Baron Henri Meyer was: he used to own Imbaba back when it was all just cantaloupe fields. Amir heard the sound of something heavy being dragged along the ground and a loud scraping noise. All the while, the voice went on about how in the past anybody could just stretch out his hand, grab a cantaloupe, and eat it without anyone noticing. But, the voice said, he never did that because those who ate Imbaba's canta-loupes would invariably get the runs. This was a well-known fact. It was even established in history books that when the French army came from Umm Dinar to set up camp nearby and do battle with Murad Pasha of Murad Street fame, they ate the local cantaloupe. And it's written somewhere that when Napoleon saw his army afflicted with diarrhea, he ordered them not to eat the local melons. They could eat cantaloupe from anywhere but Imbaba. And the savants of the French Expedition proclaimed that whoever wanted to eat Imbaban cantaloupe had to boil it in water first. They weren't allowed to eat it without taking that precaution.

Right then, Amir recognized the voice on the loudspeaker. It was Amm Omran. Amir turned to look at those who were sitting in front of the café. He saw that many of them had become aware of what was going on. He smiled and his eyes met those of Faruq and Shawqi. Amm Omran's tired voice came blaring over the loudspeaker hung on the front edge of the building, and Amir heard him saying that one day, way back when, Hagg Awadullah arrived from his distant village while we were in the market. He was short and skinny and didn't resemble any of his children. Amir sort of looks like him, if you look at him really closely. The Hagg worked for the Baron, collecting money from the peasants who rented land and grew cantaloupe on it. And the Hagg would give the money to the Baron. Sometime afterward, the Baron built Kit Kat, which you know of, and leased it to Khawaga Kaloumirous. A young child cried, and Amir heard Umm Abdu patting the child's back with her hand while saying, "Hoooooo." But then two other crying voices exploded. Amm Omran said that when the khawagas brought the materials to build Kit Kat, Hagg Muhammad Musa, Sheikh Hosni's father, got some men together and began to steal wood, bricks, and limestone. Everyday, they'd steal just a little so that the Baron and the khawagas wouldn't notice. Hagg Awadullah knew what was going on, but didn't say anything. We saw Kit Kat grow and grow, and that building was growing right with it that ancient little structure that Maallim Sobhi bought. That building, which you've never liked, which no one's ever liked, was built with bricks and mortar of the highest quality. The roof supports were oak; the banisters, the doors, the windows made from precious wood that smelled like musk; the stairs, the floors of the reception hall, the impressive oak chairs, the authentic white marble, the stained-glass windows. You could say that the building and the Kit Kat Club were made from the same mold, although this is a small building. Yet when you walk by it, it smells exactly like an open vial of sweet ambergris. And this is Kit Kat with its "dancing and drumming and kings and ministers and singing." Hagg Muhammad Musa said that this house belonged to him even though he'd stolen the materials for building it. When they confronted him, he said that he hadn't really stolen them, but had just appropriated them. He wasn't afraid of anybody and would talk about how those who'd built Kit Kat were the real thieves. He was simply taking his fair share and wouldn't prevent anyone from doing the same. Especially since the materials were going to build a huge nightclub that served alcohol.

Hagg Awadullah didn't tell the Baron. Instead, he opened a small grocery store in the building. Hagg Muhammad Musa never collected rent from him. But the grocery store didn't do so well, and he transformed it into Awadullah's Café. The Nubians used to love to sit there. They worked in Kit Kat, then they'd come to the café and drink tea with milk. Nubians love tea with milk better than anything else. And Hagg Awadullah became the chief sheikh in the area.

Amir realized that everyone sitting at the café had turned to look at him, at the place which had become so silent. Not a word. Not a domino clacking or die being thrown. In the middle of the road, between the café and the mosque, Abdallah was standing, his hands in the pockets of his tattered apron, his head bending backward looking toward the blaring loudspeaker. Galal, the juice vendor, was frozen in front of his shop, a machete in his right hand, a desiccated piece of sugar cane in his left. Maallim Husayn, the fish seller, his hair dyed brown, his face serious, was leaning on the countertop in his shop next to the entrance to the Imbaba Cinema. The group of beer-drinking young men had fallen silent at the kiosk of the khawaga who leaned out from the illuminated opening of the shack. Qasim Effendi who'd returned to his place behind the kiosk, crossed his legs.

Over the loudspeaker Usta Qadri English said something unintelligible and Amm Omran disagreed, telling him that what he said could not have taken place because Amm Omran had gone off to war with Abd al-Salam at the time. "God have mercy on your soul, Abd al-Salam. He died when the Turks began to hit us with their artillery, and when I last saw him, they were putting him in a coffin. When I returned, the Army began their blessed revolution. Then they closed the Kit Kat Club, but people broke in and began to open up shops inside the place. There was Hagg Muhammad Musa al-Shami's place; Ahmad Hasan and his partner Muhammad Atiya opened their café there." Usta Qadri English threw in that a sleazy bar was opened too. Amm Omran added, "And the roaster oven where they sold seeds and nuts." It was there till the very end. Until the contractor came and tore it all down, leaving the winter hall for last so he could salvage the wood and marble. People started to pray there on Fridays. Then it was inhabited by Rabie and his children, who made fishing nets. But when the contractor tore that down too, where the Kit Kat Club had once been became a huge vacant lot. Muhammad Atiya couldn't find a space to open a café. So when Hagg Awadullah happened to die that same week, Muhammad Atiya began to rent the café because Awadullah's sons had become effendis. They were educated now and didn't want to work in a café. Some time after this, an article appeared in the papers about how they'd found Kaloumirous murdered in his room at the National Hotel on Sulayman Pasha Street.

The papers said that his throat had been slashed, and that he was wearing a woman's dress. This was all true because Kaloumirous was in fact a khawaga and into khawaga perversions.

In those days, Sobhi was just a wandering chicken vendor, but then God blessed him with a winning lottery ticket and he purchased the building. Usta Qadri mumbled a few words, saying it was Sheikh Hosni who bought it. And Amm Omran said that this was indeed what happened, that the deeds of purchase fell into the lap of the blind Sheikh Hosni. But because he was so indebted to Haram, the hashish dealer, it was Haram who profited, "Yes, sir. Sheikh Hosni's hash and opium habits cost him the house." Usta Qadri said,

"God damn you, Sheikh Hosni!" and slapped his hands together to underscore what he had said. Qadri continued, "Yes sir. Maallim Sobhi made a deal with Haram against that hash head Sheikh Hosni. Together they used his hash debts to make him sell the building." And they were going to make payments on the remainder in the form of a daily fifty piaster piece of hashish for a period of six months. "Oh yes. Haram would play a trick like that on anybody. Why, only today he tricked the police and escaped punishment. He's sitting right now with Fathiya. He stashes his drugs and his money in her house every day, you know. You know, Fathiya. She lives over in Tawakkul Alley."

Amm Omran refused to believe the tale of how Amm Migahid had died. "No. These guys are full of shit," he said. "I'm the one who found Amm Migahid. I'm the one who left my house alone in the middle of the night and went to the shop. I saw him sitting. And he wasn't asleep. I know because when he sleeps, he sleeps on his side. The alleyway was completely empty. I was standing in the cold, saying to him, 'Greetings.' But he didn't reply at all. I was taken aback, because I still didn't know. And I walked into the shop and put my hand on his shoulder saying, 'Why don't you answer me, Migahid?' But he fell from my hand onto his side while looking directly at me. I tried to make him sit up, like he was before, but I couldn't. That's when I knew he was dead. You were asleep. I called out to you, but you didn't answer me. You hadn't turned on the light for me.

"I went to the baker's and began to knock on the window. His wife answered, asking who it was knocking on their window this late at night. I told her that it was me. She asked me, 'Do you need something this late, Amm Omran?' And I said, 'Yes I do. I want you to wake up the baker because Migahid has died.' She woke up the baker, and when he came out, we carried Migahid's body and put it on the wooden ful cart. The baker grabbed one side of the cart and I rolled up my pajama sleeves and grabbed my side. And we went like that through the rain and night to where his family lives. When we got there, we saw them. And when we saw them, we gave them his body. The baker went home after that. As for me, I went home alone without anyone seeing me."

Suddenly, coming over the loudspeaker, there was the loud sound of someone rapping on the door. And the voice of someone asking them to turn the loudspeaker off, because, in case they didn't know it, it was still on. And because he'd heard their conversation while coming over on a ferry across the Nile from Zamalek "where there was a bunch of gunfire." Usta Qadri English cried out, "Oh my gosh!" All at once, everyone burst out laughing and the spirit of Kit Kat Square returned.

Translated by Elliott Colla

Hani Abdel-Mourid

from *Kyrie Eleison*

YOU ALMOST GO CRAZY trying to explain to yourself why you are alone, even though, logically speaking, your aloneness is much better than living where you were before, in Zarayib, when you always felt embarrassed just pronouncing its name in front of strangers. At times you pretended you were from Muqattam, at others, that you were from the Qal'a neighborhood.

The truth is you belong to Manshiyat Nasser, more specifically Zarayib, which strangers unjustly call the Zabbalin area. It is true that Cairo garbage is collected and sorted in the area and that many recycling projects exist there, but there are also civil servants and artisans in various professions whom God has condemned to living in Zarayib.

You once heard your uncle describe your house to one of your relatives, "As you are coming from Helwan on the Autostrade, turn right as if you were heading for Muqattam. Suddenly God descends with his anger upon you, so you make a left and find an uphill route. Take it until you find yourself in front of an area in the enclave of the mountain. Once you get there, you are surely damned."

If you hear these words and then go to Zarayib, you will definitely remember them, and they will resound within you as you make your way uphill. You try to catch your breath and resist the gravity until the ground flattens in front of you. Gradually, your heartbeats slow down, and you find the al-Batal al-Rumani watch repair shop: a small, rundown place where Amm Mantawi sits behind a desk surrounded by glass windows, gazing at an open watch in his hand with a monocle.

Most probably, his son would be standing, well dressed, in front of the shop, greeting passersby and admiring the beauty of the women. Since Julia was the loveliest, she was well deserving of his prolonged scrutiny and sweet eyes. He finally couldn't resist her lure and the swaying of her body. So he married her despite his father's disapproval. For how could William, Amm Mantawi's son, marry one of the girls who sorted the garbage, whose bodies were covered with dirt?

It is true that Julia washed every day after work and scrubbed her feet and arms well and put almond oil in her hair and then went out in her black cloak, parading two white clean arms. She swore to her mother that she would not rest until she had seduced one of the factory owners, who would save her from poverty. Otherwise, she would return to the village where she had worked as a cattle fodder feeder.

She cast her net and only got William, whom she kissed without hesitation, even though all he had was the shop he would inherit after a long time. But his impressive height, his clean hands, and his eyeglasses that made him look like a doctor were enough to convince her. And she remembered Mona, who was ready to elope with him, sacrificing her family and her religious affiliation. He was like a star. The girls who sorted the garbage would look at him from a distance; they would dream of him at night, and during the day he would become material for many tales and sighs. . . .

There are rich people in Zarayib who build their homes on large plots of land. The top floor is for comfortable living. The ground floor has no walls and is used as a space for sorting garbage.

The garbage that is sorted is not just dirty paper and does not resemble what one sees in office bins. It contains potato skins, bird entrails, glass, pieces of gold jewelry, menstrual blood. . . . Azir's elation as he stuffed the dirty bag full of dollars into his clothes, Mariam's soreness from the AIDS-contaminated syringe needle that pricked her.

Worlds fuse and produce rotten dirt that women and children stand in, their legs submerged up to their knees. They search with their hands to collect material for plumbing. Only piles without value remain, awaiting the pig farms.

In one corner the rats fight; in another stands a wooden cart behind which Abdu hides with his bare feet and his anticipating eyes, awaiting the right moment to seize the big bundle of brass wire that he had noticed the night before while he was selling the sorted garbage he had collected during the day. He waited for lunch break and then sneaked in. Only he was there.

She sings for the owner of the khan, for hard times, she sings and her boots—that she was given by one of the NGOs, along with gloves that she never used—sink into the garbage heap. When she first started working she would hold the pieces of meat and fruit and wonder: if this is what gets thrown out, then what gets eaten? And why do they not give all this to the poor? She wonders, and curses the times that have made someone like her, who had been bathing in plenty and butter, leave her village in the footsteps of her mother, who convinced her that human garbage was better than cattle dung and that she would live in a holy place, near Samaan al-Kharraz monastery.

Now, it's all the same. Sometimes she dreams: if only God were to save her by giving her one or two bags like Azir's, who now drives a car and has left Zarayib forever.

He sat in the courtyard with the shisha between his legs. He smokes and swears that she gave in easily, as if she craved it. It's just women's ways that made her refuse in the beginning. But soon she was enjoying it and asking for more. The coal glows, burning the hashish. The story glows, burning the heart with desire for her body that he described all night.

Everyone believes him. Who would not believe Akrash, the thug of Zarayib, who would not hesitate, when cross with you, to cut your face with his sharp pocketknife in the shape of gazelle horns that he shows off, opening and closing it to instill fear.

Abdu, the apprentice who is but twelve years old, is of a different opinion. True, he never articulated it in front of Akrash because they were never in the same milieu. Akrash tells these stories to his acquaintances: the owners of the pig farms, the blacksmiths, the workshop owners, and all those who keep him company in fear for their interests, which he guards and protects.

Abdu sits with the garbage collectors who spend all day carrying a sack collecting plastic and wire. They collect everything to sell by the kilo at the end of the day. In the evening, when they are worn out, they sit by the wall to smoke and sniff colla.

Abdu swore that when she saw evil in Akrash's eyes she threatened to scream. When he held his pocketknife to her side and twisted her left arm behind her back, drove her to one of the corners against her will as she was begging him and crying, when he ripped her clothes, she swore she had her period but Akrash would not listen as she resisted, until she passed out.

When he was done, he collected his clothes, spat on her before leaving, and didn't forget to slit her thigh with his pocketknife.

At this point, Abdu came out of his hiding place. The sight was disgusting, unlike what he had imagined. He lustfully squeezed her breasts, placed the bundle of wire in his sack, and left confidently.

Weeks later, Akrash was overtaken by desire for her body. He stopped her on the street. He softly whispered his yearning in her ear. To everyone's astonishment she spat in his face. He was shocked as well. When he recovered, after she had walked past, he repeated aloud, "Maalesh, I am to blame. Had I slit your face instead of your thigh you couldn't have done this."

Every time she passed by he would hold his thigh mockingly, feigning pain to embarrass her and make her falter on her way.

"Yes, I know that Akrash slept with my wife but what can I do?! She's a dirty bitch." He would say it every time he got into a fight. He would start by trying to defend his wife, by saying that she was honorable and that he fulfilled all her needs. But when the fight got tight, and the sarcastic laughter rose, he would say it, he would say it in front of her, he would say it to her face when she angered him, "Okay, you Akrash slut."

In the beginning she used to swear that she hadn't wanted it, and that she did not give in, and that he was an animal who did it with a dead body after her head had hit the ground. When he continued to insult her and failed to take a stand even though he knew what had happened, she regretted having protected his honor. She has to sleep with all the men in Zarayib to get even with him. She cries, even though she knows that what happened is his fault, "If Akrash respected you as a man, he would never have dared lay hands on me."

She says it to see him cower and mumble some inaudible words. He goes out all night. He returns. He sleeps without uttering a word.

Translated by Samia Mehrez

Hamdi Abu Golayyel

from *Thieves in Retirement*

THE LEADER—GAMAL ABD AL-NASSER—paid a surprise visit to one of the factories his Revolution had established in Helwan. He found that an enormous number of its workers were spending all night in the factory. Delighted with their extraordinary self-sacrifice in the cause of labor, he went up to one of them and pumped his hand with obvious enthusiasm. "Good going, keep it up, hero!"

The man tried to plant a kiss on his palm. "God protect you, Pasha. . . . Abd al-Halim Abd al-Halim here."

"So you're working two shifts, then?"

Trying to respond as he thought the Leader would want, the man said, "God's truth, Pasha, just one shift. Your honor."

"Then why aren't you going home?"

"Where'm I gonna go, Pasha?"—addling the Leader, who had supposed the workers were sleeping in the factory because they were so keen to keep on working, night and day. Surely not because they couldn't find a place to live. For the sake of safeguarding his Revolution, the Leader waved toward a vacant stretch of land that happened to be within eyesight.

"Let them live there!" And the workers rushed forward in a perfect likeness of Revolutionary zeal, toward the empty zone. It was a mere matter of days before Manshiyat Gamal Abd al-Nasser—Nasser's Newtown—entered the world.

On its eastern rim, the Leader's Newtown is hemmed in by high-tension wires that stretch all the way up the Nile to Aswan, three hundred miles to the south. To the west, Manshiyat Nasser's boundary is determined by the filtration area into which all of Cairo's sewage lines pour. To the north is the major thoroughfare of Umar ibn Abd al-Aziz, and immediately to the south sits the sacred space on which Gamal Abd al-Nasser stood when he made his historic gesture. It is basically one modest street, the greatest significance of which is that it is the battlefield for a permanent war between the sewage administration and the bureau of roadworks.

From it branch little side streets bearing nonconsecutive numbers (it isn't clear why). At the beginning of the street you are met by the Star of Helwan Café. There are cafés all up and down the street, but they are frequented by outsiders. The reigning belief in the neighborhood is that respectable workers don't spend their time sitting in cafés.

The Newtown. It's a mongrel place, part village and part unplanned city fringe, destination of squatters and incomers, although, thanks to the wave of Gamal Abd al-Nasser's hand, it has a definite class identity. And perhaps by virtue of that very same gesture, the Manshiyat's residents are well placed to look down their noses at the populace of adjacent neighborhoods. Although they have rebelled against the tin shacks they threw up immediately after the historic hand flick—rebelled and moved into real houses—they remain loyal to their villages, those faraway farming villages that they never, ever visit, yet the memories of which give them a sense of security and protect them from the betrayals of time and the bosses at the factory. If you ask a resident where he lives, he will respond proudly with the name of a tiny village in some governorate, and if you have any inclination to listen he will favor you with a detailed telling of the dramatic circumstances that forced him to leave it. And so they are always on watch for the day in which they will leave the Newtown behind and return to their villages, like the soldier impatiently anticipating his next leave or the emigrant longing permanently for his own people.

Translated by Marilyn Booth

Gamal al-Ghitani

from *"The Guardian of the Shrine"*

I BEGIN WITH THE story of the guardian of the monument.

He is Ashour ibn Mahdi al-Nu'mani, the guardian of Qalawun dome. Since time immemorial, they have called him Amm Ashour, even those older than he. . . .

With the advent of the year 1976 he had spent a lifetime and completed service. He had done his time. He had to leave his place for someone else to replace him. Except that the employees in the Council of Antiquities tried to extend his tenure and wrote to those in power until they were able to extract a decision to extend his service after sixty, for no one knew the dome and its history, no one could protect it like him. It was like his dwelling place; he had no other place to go. Since the forties, the renowned scholar Hasan Abd al-Wahab had arranged for him to live in an old nearby house that had belonged to the Council of Antiquities since the thirties, when it was still known as the Committee for the Preservation of Arab Antiquities. The house was across from the dome to the left as one headed toward Bayt al-Qadi Square. It was known as the house of Mohi al-Din, the last owner before it was classified as a protected monument. It had a beautifully delicate façade and was divided into several rooms and halls. He only used one room but did not neglect the others: he cleaned the ornate corners and the entrances; he removed the cobwebs and the birds' dung off the mashrabiya windows. He swept it all daily. On Fridays he washed the floors. In the middle of his room there was a stone mastaba with a mattress and covers. His clothes were folded in an old, faded basket. It was the same basket his father had carried with him the first time he came to Cairo. He refused to hammer nails into the walls to hang his gallabiya and coat so as not to ruin the monument. He was very attached to the basket. It had the scent of his father. It was all that he had left him. . . .

One day, a man in traditional dress came by. He had a long face and bushy eyebrows. This was what Amm Ashour remembered years later. He greeted Amm Ashour and sat down beside him, not bothered by the dust. He said he had heard about Ashour but that he went further by watching him carefully from afar and quite closely, so that he came to know a lot of things about him. The man smiled but Amm Ashour took no heed of him. So the man said he would enter directly into the subject.

Without further ado, he offered to give Amm Ashour a one-hundred-pound bill that he would pay him as soon as he gave his consent. In short, what he wanted was a piece of colored marble that was fifty square centimeters. That piece was in the dark northern corner of the dome. Not at all noticeable; no one would discover that it was missing. But still, an imitation would be installed to replace it with the same design, the same marble. It would be impossible to see the difference. All that was required of him was to allow two men to enter after sunset. They would do their work quickly and silently in no time. They were experts in dismantling marble. No one would feel their presence, no one would find out. So, what do you say? This happened during the forties one winter. Amm Ashour's face looked angry in the gray light without giving him away as he listened. But as soon as the man finished he said, "One hundred pounds? One hundred pounds?"

The man repeated, "Yes. And I have it in my pocket right now."

Amm Ashour turned around slowly. His dark complexion glowed in the shadow of the dome. He raised his hand. His demeanor did not give him away. He fell upon the man's neck with his two hands. He stood up so as to be in control. His features were transformed: they tightened; he looked cruel and unpredictable, different from his usual self, as if inhabited by someone else. He yelled, "You pigs! You pigs!"

The man's eyes protruded from their sockets. His tongue dangled and went dry. His features loosened. Had it not been for three merchants from Khurunfish and a subia vendor who were passing by, he would have died. They surrounded Ashour. They entreated him to calm down, to remember God. They tried their utmost. Even when they begged him they still failed. But when one of them said, "For your own father's sake, man!"

Only then did he turn toward them looking worn out, disarmed, and disgusted. No one knew how the man ran away. He simply disappeared as if he had been gulped up by the earth.

Later, Amm Ashour said that he was really puzzled that they would know the impact of the mention of his father even though he had not spoken to any of them, had not visited their shops. He hesitated . . . should he call the police? But he did not know the man. He told Hasan effendi Abd al-Wahab what had happened. He commended Amm Ashour and asked him to be vigilant. It all meant that the dome was being eyed, that it was being watched. But he also advised him to be more careful in the future. If he had killed the man, it would have been his end. He did not ever want to see him in prison.

He nodded repeatedly. Whatever Hasan effendi said was not open for discussion.

But this was not the only time he had completely lost his temper. Years after this incident, toward the end of the fifties, the passersby and the residents of the neighborhood, which had become increasingly crowded and had witnessed the rise of a new apartment building at the entrance to Khurunfish, heard, just before sunset, a loud, angry voice coming from the passageway that led to the dome and the mosque. It was accompanied by the screams of a woman. They were surprised to see Amm Ashour pushing a foreign man in front of him, dragging him by his left hand, having twisted his arm behind his back so high that it was very close to his neck. As for his right hand, it was busy slapping the naked back of the man's neck. People were stunned at the sight of the foreign man without his trousers, completely naked so that they noticed he was not circumcised. A woman ran behind them screaming in an unknown language as her hands tried to button up her open blouse.

The story was that they had come, like many other foreigners, to visit the dome. Ashour accompanied them inside. When they finished their tour, they expressed interest in going up to the minaret. Ashour agreed grudgingly. He accompanied them to the back yard where the stairway that led up to the dome began. Here the foot of the minaret began, with the narrow winding stairway that led up to the first floor. Amm Ashour had grown old. He was slower and he had grayed. Climbing up the stairs was a real ordeal for him. He said he would wait for them at the bottom of the stairway and he explained to them how to get inside the minaret. Apparently that was exactly what the foreigner wanted, for he nodded several times in gratitude and hurried on before his companion, after having produced fifty piasters that he quickly stuck in Amm Ashour's hand. They disappeared, but he remained suspicious of the impatience he noticed in the foreigner, the money he produced. Amm Ashour was always composed, even in his reactions, but when he recalled the last look in the woman's eyes toward the man, the blood started boiling in his veins. He ran up the stairs, and when he arrived at the top of the dome where it overlooked the city, he was breathless but he didn't care. He approached the first circular balcony of the minaret and saw them: the man was bent over getting ready as the woman lay between his skinny naked legs getting ready to suck him.

"In the minaret, you sons of bitches!"

This is what he kept repeating as he pushed the man forward on the street leading to Bayt al-Qadi Square. This is what shopkeepers and Abdu the hairdresser and the firemen and various passersby heard. He only stopped when they had arrived at the police station.

Other than these two incidents, Amm Ashour never lost his temper, never insulted anyone, never got into a fight. . . .

Many years had passed since that strange man had come to see him with an offer of a one-hundred-pound bribe at a time when the pound was still of value. Many years separated that incident from the arrival of the young man one early morning. He was somewhat plump, dressed in a shirt and a pair of trousers. He was smoking a cigarette. He introduced himself as Muhammad Halawa, the son of Halawa the lentil vendor.

"I knew your father, God bless his soul. His lentils are unforgettable. I've never had anything like them."

The young man looked happy even though they had warned him about Ashour. He pointed to the pavement across from them toward Sabil Khusraw and said, "I used to stand beside him and wash the dishes in the bucket."

Amm Ashour looked in the direction to which he was pointing. He ran his fingers through his beard, nodding his head silently as if he had forgotten the young man's presence. But the young man was oblivious to his daydreaming and continued talking as if they were still on the same wavelength. He said he was bringing bounty and good money, a gift from heaven that would cost him no effort. He stopped to see the reaction. When Amm Ashour remained silent, he continued. There were many foreign visitors who came to the dome; some of them needed to change dollars or sterling pounds. All he had to do was take what they had in exchange for Egyptian pounds. A simple transaction and he would get a cut every evening, of course. The quiet, distant dome was an ideal place, away from people's eyes.

The young man stopped. He focused his eyes on Amm Ashour's hands as if preparing himself. Perhaps someone had warned him. But the hands remained motionless. He picked up the conversation, saying that he would start the next day; he would bring him five hundred pounds to begin with. He would supply the rates every morning and afternoon. If unexpected fluctuations occurred he would quickly come to him; the market was unpredictable. He said he was close by in Khan al-Khalili, at the entrance of the bazaar toward the jewelers' quarters in al-Sagha. If he ever got a big sum he could always come to him in a minute. The important thing was to be able to tell fake bills from the start, especially the one-hundred-dollar bill.

He turned around slowly. The young man got ready to go. The old man was strange. They had warned him: his long stay alone inside the dome that was nothing but a huge grave; his knowledge of the jinn. But his features remained composed and his hands relaxed. Much as the young man felt comforted, he also felt a desire to laugh when Ashour finally asked, "What about the police?"

Why?

Why did Amm Ashour agree to slowly approach foreigners, whose numbers had increased in recent years, whispering in English, "Change dollars?"

This really puzzled me, especially since the man was about to retire after a long life marked by the discipline that was at the origin of all the stories, that seemed at times unrealistic.

Was he in need?

Not at all!

I am confident when I say this. He does not pay a penny for his house. His salary is more than what he needs. Has he been influenced by the changes that have occurred in general? But how, when he seems so cut off from it all? He would listen to the most disastrous stories and not comment. He would overhear his neighbors' stories about the most atrocious accidents and not be moved. Why does he approach foreigners with this sheepish look when he would have never accepted this in the past? He pretends not to see the women and men who come: he does not follow them; he is no longer concerned when they stay inside for long. When he does follow them, he barely walks them to the entrance in order to ask them if they want to change money.

This all puzzled me. Had I not seen him with my own eyes, I would not have believed it. I am not exaggerating in my account. Everything I have said is based on eyewitness accounts. What I have not witnessed myself, I have relayed through reliable sources, editing some of it for brevity.

But. . . .

Translated by Samia Mehrez

Salwa Bakr

from *"Thiry-one Beautiful Green Trees"*

BEFORE TELLING THE STORY let me say, right at the start, why it is I decided to write it and set in down precisely as it happened to me, just as I have lived it and felt it moment by moment until they brought me to this terrible place. So isolated am I from the world that I have become wholly convinced there is no hope of ever being released, unless it be to go to the world of the dead. Thus it was that I said to myself: write it, my girl. Kareema Fahmi, write your story in detail and hide it away in some safe place, perhaps in the mattress, having scooped out a little hole in one of its sides, so that maybe one day someone will find the pages you've written and will feel pity for you, realizing how wretched you were when, wrongly and by force, they put you in this place merely because you preferred silence, everlasting silence, that day when you decided to cut off your little tongue, that simple lump of flesh with which you were always giving vent to words and thoughts.

I shan't speak of this hellish place in which I am now living; I shan't describe my feelings about the filthy gray walls that keep me from sleeping, keep me staring up at the ceiling the whole night through, frightened they'll close in so tightly on me that they'll fall on to my body and shut off my breathing. I go on watching them drawing nearer and nearer, craftily stealing up on me until they are right close by me, at which I scream with all my strength, and then they move away from me and return again to their original positions. I shan't talk about that, nor about the fat lady with ugly little hairs scattered about under a chin rounded like the small egg of a serpent, as she bears down upon me and plunges her horrible injection in my backside, which, despite all the pain and the hatred, makes me laugh and guffaw so much that I make her enraged by having triumphed over her. I shan't speak of the filthy, poisoned food they put before me every day and against which I have no right to protest. Once I wept long and bitterly when I saw a sparrow slip through the window and eat a few crumbs of it; I ran toward it to frighten it away but it had already picked up a small piece in its beak before flying away, a small piece of the poisoned food I eat. This made me weep bitterly for the whole day as I thought about the kind of miserable end that unfortunate sparrow would meet.

I shan't speak about all that, nor about many other things I have seen in this place, because thinking about such things makes me feel as though I have been tied to some enormous bomb that is about to blow up or, to be more exact, that is about to blow me up and scatter my brains and body in endlessly small fragments. I shall therefore confine myself to writing about what happened to me before I was forced into living in this place, when, one day some years ago, I began to feel there were things that were changing around me, had also in fact changed within myself, forever since I graduated from the university and was appointed as an employee at the Water Company, a few drops from the flood had already made their appearance on the horizon, affecting both people and things, and even animals and plants.

This was the food that came and which I saw sweeping over everything, everything of beauty in my beautiful city, so that on the very day they brought me to live in this frightful place, I was smiling tenderly and looking at the tall buildings scattered here and there, with the van passing through the streets at a crazy speed. I was smiling and saying: farewell, farewell, my beautiful city, the flood has once again swept you away.

I first noticed signs of the flood in the street which I used to walk along on my daily journey from home to my job at the Water Company, that street I loved so much, was so proud of, and about which I felt so strongly because of being an inhabitant of the city in which it lay. Even at this moment as I sit down to write, a feeling of joy flashes through me and my heart is filled with yearning as I imagine the pictures made by the bright, laughing colors of the shop awnings, bright orange and sparkling blue, and that marvellous awning I used to gaze at so long while the vendor handed me the paper cone of monkey nuts, the awning of the Freedom Star shop that sold chickpeas and all types of salted melon seeds and other things to munch and chew.

When the advance of the flood started, the street I had been familiar with since childhood, and along which I had walked so many times, began to change and little by little started to lose its landmarks. The glass of the clean bright shop windows in which, so brilliantly did they shine, one could of a morning see one's face, had begun to lose their luster and grow dull, and the well-laid pavement damp with water during the hot hours of summer had come to be pitted with holes in which dirty water had collected, and I would notice that these holes were becoming larger day by day till they formed what looked like stagnant pools spread around the pavement. Making my way along the street daily, coming and going to work on foot, I would generally amuse myself by gazing at the street's beautiful little trees, and I would count them. I would know that after the blue gum tree there would be the casuarinas, then the Indian fig, and some ten yards before arriving at the door of the Water Company there would be a beautiful tree whose name I never got to know, a tree with spreading branches almost all of whose leaves would fall at the coming of spring when it would be resplendent with a vast quantity of large purple flowers; it would look magnificent, a unique spectacle among the other trees. I knew by heart the number of trees along the way; thirty-one green-leafed trees adorning the street and bringing joy to my heart whenever I looked at them.

Then one day I counted them and found there were thirty. I was amazed and imagined I had miscounted because of being preoccupied with something else as I had been walking. But when I counted them again on my return from the Water Company at midday, I discovered that one of the nine Indian fig trees had disappeared from its place, it had been uprooted and thrown down on the pavement amid the rubble from the old building they were pulling down. It looked to me like the dead body of some harmless bird that had been treacherously done to death without having committed any crime. I found myself weeping bitterly, for nothing but trees was of any use. Terrible lumps stuck in my throat that made me feel I was about to be throttled. From that moment I began to sense changes taking place inside me: there were slight pains in my insides and I would constantly have frightful headaches. To begin with I didn't give the matter much thought, but things continued like this for days and weeks, and after a while the headaches changed into ghastly pains in my head, crazy pains that accompanied every breath I took.

It was then that I went to the doctor, who began giving me sedatives and tranquillizers, though these had no effect. Eventually they diagnosed my condition as being a chronic inflammation of the large intestine brought about by nervous tension. When there were only three trees along the whole of the road, a mere three trees out of the thirty-one, I didn't know exactly what had come over me, nor what calamity had befallen my city or the people in it. All I remember about that period is that my weight went up enormously so that I was regarded as being obese, and that I had lost the capacity to be cheerful. No longer did I have any desire to go to the cinema or to converse with my women friends on any of the topics I used to talk about. I even made up my mind not to think about marriage at all, despite my getting on in years — though I might say that I was by no means ugly. Even after putting on weight as mentioned, I was still regarded by some people as possessing a certain beauty, maybe because of my good complexion, large eyes, and soft hair. The truth was that during this period I was always thinking about one thing: how could I one day get married and bear children who would live in this city? What misery they would experience when they looked around them and found nothing but a vast jungle planted with concrete and colors of gray and brown! Also, I won't conceal the fact that I was even more afraid for my grandchildren, when I thought about what it would be like for them when they came out into the world and lived in this city, without seeing a flower or knowing the meaning of the word.

Translated by Denys Johnson-Davies

Shehata al-Erian

from *The Women of Others*

THE TEN-PIASTER BILL has become something incomprehensible. . . . There was a rumor that it had been canceled, but the government vehemently denied it, which led people to believe that it had actually been canceled. This is how the ten-piaster bill became hated and suspicious for all.

You, yourself, have taken contradictory positions toward it depending on the situation. When you have one or more of these bills on you, you become concerned about the possibility of using them and you tell yourself that it is a legal matter when, at the end of the day, they're just ten piasters with which you can buy nothing.

But my concern is not with its value, but rather with how to get rid of it. Once I gave two or three of these bills to a beggar, and he looked at me disapprovingly despite the sign that is posted by every metro ticket booth confirming that the ten- and five-piaster bills are still in circulation, just like the silver and brass coins. I had amassed quite a number of these bills so I decided to buy a ticket with what I had, just to test the matter. The employee at the ticket booth accepted them, but he looked at me angrily and asked about my destination in a harsh tone.

The problem is I always get this bill as change for anything I pay. And of course, I take it with some hesitation, to save myself a headache but also as a matter of principle, since I really do believe that it is official currency, even though Egyptians do not like this and you will never be able to understand why!

So, I accept it as fate and place it at the top of the pile of bills in preparation to get rid of it as part of any payment, while always ready to exchange it without discussion if asked. For I discovered that those who ask to exchange it are specifically those who enjoy stupid, disturbing discussions that you, as a sane person, should avoid.

Once in the microbus a passenger who was just handing over my fare to the driver was pissed off that I had said nothing, but I changed it immediately when he asked. He was silent for a moment, then he said, "It's been canceled, you know."

So I didn't comment.

He was silent for a bit longer this time and then he said, "Since you know that it's been canceled, why are you giving it to me?"

I didn't pay attention.

He was forced to be silent again, and then said, "I mean, you know that it's been canceled."

"Yes, of course."

"So, forgive me for asking, but if you know that it's been canceled, why do you agree to accept it?"

"To avoid the headache."

And I looked straight into his eyes, smiling. He could not help but smile back, hesitantly at first, and then we cracked up laughing together, and I was finally able to satisfy him and shut him up. You could say that people are sane, after all.

Once I was on the microbus from Sayeda Aisha to al-Malik al-Salih after having attended a concert with friends at the Citadel. The images of the place and the lights were still hovering before me, and I felt at once elated and saddened by the music, and willing to avoid anything to continue to daydream as I looked out of the window onto the Sayeda Nafisa shrine that we were passing by. . . .

A strange cloudy day . . . the beginning of autumn. . . . I noticed that the walls surrounding the shrine were higher and were blocking the view.

The music returned, recalling other melodies as the car crossed Ain al-Sira and approached Abu al-Saoud with the smell of tanneries and the memory of beloved places that have become painfully alienating because of the changes that have befallen them.

"The time has come for you, my heart, to take a stance on life . . . ," as the poet Salah Jahin once said. I repeated that at the Citadel, laughing, as Magid commented on Sabri's graying hair.

The car was approaching al-Gayyara. My memory of the place was dimmed by the twenty years that had elapsed. Thirty-nine is a difficult number. You tell yourself that you've been around a long time in this world. The days just went by . . . the cycle of being has repeated itself thirty-nine summers and winters. Time passed, along with scattered people and stones in the folds of this difficult life beyond belief. You traversed a whole pile of songs, events, friends, and your time was spread among theirs without mercy. Each went on his way . . . perhaps to his destiny . . . you see each other as if for the first time . . . simple, smiling, calm, and in love with Umm Kulthum.

This is a strange day. . . . I feel the old way of being thinning in a fundamental way. Parts of what had been real until recently have been eroded, leaving yet another empty part to be added to the other emptiness in my soul.

The car stopped by the wall of Mibarrat Muhammad Ali: the terminal. I walked alongside the wall toward the metro station. If it had been a bit early, I would have stopped at Abu al-Saoud Square and would have walked back to Hasan al-Anwar Street to eat chez Imam. I would have had tea and a mi'assil . . . but the last metro leaves at 12:05 and it is now midnight.

Perhaps just some tea chez Hammad: what you might call a coffee shop toward the end of the Mibarra wall near the corner of al-Sirga Street as it intersects with Abu Safeen Street. It was at the end of the railway when the Helwan train still existed before the metro.

The man looked the same. His head and shoulders were tilted to the right toward his arm, which he usually held at a right angle that extended to the hand, in which he always carried something: a platter, a chair for a client, the mi'assil, or a shisha, or even empty but always extended like that by habit.

The place is just a wooden kiosk by the wall, against which grew a vine that did not flower, in the shade of a big tree that kept it cool during the day; a part of the wall, enough for two benches without backs and a few old wicker chairs that were now hard to find in coffee shops, three or four round, short, rusty tin tables. The platters and glasses were visibly clean and shining; always the same kind of glasses: yasin, soft and small, the same size for water, coffee, and tea; a number of brass gozas with a reed and a round bottom so that the smoker had to carry it in his hand. Some sat directly on the pavement without a chair, Upper Egyptians who work in construction.

When there used to be a train and the railway was without railings, so that people could cross over to the other side without a problem, Hammad's joint faced a short street that ended at the Nile Corniche. If you sat with your back to the wall of the Mibarra you could see the reflection of the sun on the water of the Nile. Now the joint faced a metro station that blocked everything from view. In place of the station there were trees under which there were the chairs of Mimmih's ghurza for hashish smokers. Also, on the other side of al-Sirga Street there was another old coffee shop . . . and an Indian fig tree whose vertical branch-like roots tried desperately to reach the ground, with some success despite everything. There was a clay water container that dampened the shade of the tree on hot days, where I drank exquisite tea at sunset throughout my bygone youth.

The tree was still there even though it had shrunk a little. The coffee shop had closed down, and in lieu of its doors there were only openings that had been blocked with stones in preparation for the demolition of the whole building.

Hammad was a quiet guy. You seldom heard his voice. He never asked you what you wanted. You could sit for a whole hour and he would pass in front of you several times without any expectations. If you did not mumble your order he would place it in front of you after a while.

Did he recognize me? Perhaps, or at least what he could see of me. His tilted head and his protruding eyes gave you the impression that he couldn't see. When you remembered that the metro might arrive at any minute, you paid the bill, and without paying attention you gave him the ten-piaster bill with the money.

Hammad opened it close to his face, bringing it closer to his eyes. So you noticed.

"Here's another one."

"Don't worry. Not a big deal."

You had brought out some more change while Hammad waved the bill before his eyes, "What a world."

It came out heated, so you shuddered as if it had touched one of your nerves. I don't know how Hammad sensed this. He looked intently at my face and rolled his eyes, mumbling, "You remember the days when we could see the Corniche from here?"

I looked at the huge building of the metro station that blocked the river and I saw the metro coming. I stood up quickly to escape the pain that his dark voice imposed.

I then realized why he was so silent.

Translated by Samia Mehrez

Hamdy al-Gazzar

from *Black Magic*

SHE WAS THE ONLY one who'd stayed with me the whole time. She'd been my companion since I was a kid bounding with energy; always in front of me, she'd be slung from her black leather strap around my neck and left to dangle on my chest as I went out into the street, full of a boyish pride and joy in myself that provoked my peers, not one of whom owned a Japanese Yashica camera. Every month my father gave me four whole pounds—a huge sum, a fortune, for a fourteen-year-old boy—but I'd spend every penny of it: three pounds on 36-exposure Kodak film, and the rest on developing and printing. Amm Chico, the aged photographer who was the proprietor of the Beautiful View studio, would give me a discount of five piasters on printing because I was, as he always used to say, rubbing his bald, sweaty head, a clever little bugger of a colleague and a good customer.

At the beginning I'd photograph anything and everything my eyes fell on. I'd wake at five in the morning and leave our house on Kheirat Street, empty in the calm before dawn. I'd look at the sky and watch the silvery light as it slowly spread. I loved the scene of the sun rising over the minarets, domes, houses, and streets, which would be nearly deserted up to the sudden incursion of school children.

These would emerge from the narrow side streets in small groups wearing their brown smocks of coarse cotton, the little braids of the prettiest and cleverest girls swinging on their chests, on which the breasts had yet to sprout. They'd chatter and leap about hitting one another and cursing and going to buy bean and felafel sandwiches from al-Gahsh on Marsina Street. I'd snap pictures of them and they'd laugh and put their hands on their waists or show off their little bodies in poses imitating their favorite actresses—Sharihan, Yusra, or Laila Elwi.

They used to swarm around me uproariously, hanging onto my shirt sleeve and my pants, the more daring ones asking for the picture and when I'd give it to them. It was difficult to get free of them and only the bell of the elementary school at the end of Marsina Street, with its high walls and green metal gates, would save me. I've forgotten the name of the school now but my memory still retains the faces of some of those girls. They're here, in my old photo album and in the drawers of my desk. I was a copying machine with a quick turnaround production line on the side streets and alleys of Sayyida Zaynab. I took hundreds of pictures of the mosque, dome, and square, of Sidi Atris, of the people clinging to the metal grill around the tomb, of the people who brought tokens of their vows from the depths of Upper Egypt and the Delta and who slept on the thresholds of the mosque, of the people praying and of the dervishes, thieves, vendors, and beggars, of the singers of praise to the Prophet and of the godless, even of the cars driving along Port Said Street, among which I loved the big white ones that passed over the ground like clouds. There was nothing that the eye might possibly see that I wouldn't try to possess through my camera.

I'd cross the square and roam around al-Khudeiri Street, inventorying the crumbling ancient drinking fountains and petty mosques. The colored marble of the drinking fountain of Umm Abbas seduced me into photographing it as I stood between the Southern and the Northern mosques of Sheikhoun.

And when I grew tired of walking and of standing for long periods in front of what I was photographing, I'd sit on the steps at the entrance to Ibn Tulun mosque to be reinvigorated by the cool breezes of morning striking my face, the sky open over my head and close enough to touch if I should stretch out my hand—a sky as pure and naive as myself.

My father would look at my pictures after I'd had them developed and printed at Amm Chico's. He'd gaze at them a long time and look searchingly into my face as though I was hiding another face beneath it, one that was a stranger to him, that he did not know. He'd say, "This is nice," or "This is bad," but in any case he'd always pat me on the shoulder and seem pleased with what I'd done.

That good old Yashica, the first camera I owned, is still in its leather case on the wooden desk in my bedroom. Its projecting magic lens looks out at me; it sees me and encompasses me and watches over me. It follows me as I move in the small space between the desk and the bed, opening drawers, pulling out of them the orange, blue, and transparent gelatin slides and the lenses for different distances and putting them in my small leather bag, which I hang over my shoulder, leaving the Yashica where it is.

I haven't used it for many years. I clean it, polish it, and caress its black body as though I were dealing with a woman with delicate skin whose breasts might be scratched by the coarse touch of fingers or anything else, but I've lost my enthusiasm for using it; it's an ancient memento as distant from me as my childhood.

I decided to go to work and leave Nu'man sleeping. I finished the wash and hung out the clothes, got dressed, put the bag over my shoulder, and left. I had an assignment. Another trivial job to add to my normal jobs. I don't know what impelled me to sit down next to Rihan. He was staring at the cloth and the long needle was burying itself easily in the woven material; then he would tug on it hard, only to bury it again in another spot, his whole body shaking with that regular movement known to skilled tailors. He worked vigorously and expertly, his hand never trembling like an old person's. I sat down on the bench next to him. Long minutes passed during which he continued with his sewing without giving any sign that he was aware of my presence a few centimeters from his thin body. I went on looking at him, envying him his amazing absorption in what he was doing, as though the world beyond the cloth and the bench had ceased to exist for him. Without looking up from the cloth he suddenly said, in a low, affectionate voice, "Welcome, sir. Your presence is an honor."

I was going to say something, but he went on. "I know you're busy, may God be your helper! Television work is exhausting. And you're all alone, with no one to look after you and make sure you eat and have clean clothes. And you such a fine young fellow, God protect you!"

This warm concern, unlike anything I'd experienced for years, took me by surprise.

"You should get married, my son. Marriage is a decent covering for a man just as it is for a woman."

He looked in the direction of the shop and waved to his apprentice.

"Tea and a waterpipe for Mr. Nasser."

"You have a bride for me or what, Amm Rihan?"

"Is that all you need? I'll pick one for you myself. But will she please you?"

"Have you been living here long?"

"Years and years! From before King Farouk ascended the throne of Egypt."

He fell silent, just repeating every now and then, "Welcome, welcome."

I drank the tea and smoked two bowls of molasses tobacco and tried to get Rihan to talk more, but he measured out his words with studied economy. He knew much more about me than I'd expected. I was relieved, because he didn't hold anything against me, even though his reference to my relationship with Fatin was neither innocent nor vulgar. I felt that he knew, understood, and made allowances, though he might be a bit surprised at my situation.

Translated by Humphrey Davies

Omar Taher

from *Looks Like It's Busted*

HOW DO YOU KNOW that you are walking on one of the streets in Cairo?

I have visited many countries and walked their streets, but Cairo streets remain the most dynamic and warm—at least for me—with all the comic relief they offer, starting with the logic of 'steal it' or 'run with it,' all the way to pedestrians who cross the street with their gaze directed upward (reading the bus-line numbers).

- When you take a look around you and find that everyone looks cross and instinctively ready to get into a fight (just say when).

- When you read the handwritten signs on the microbuses and taxis that represent the cream of human experience and wisdom, such as:
  "If only people would stop talking."
  "Don't count my days. I have orphans to feed."
  "The beautiful one is always beautiful even when he just wakes up."
  "Double-crossers."
  "God help the envious."
  "Oh, my beloved."
  "May your prayers be answered, mother."
  "God protect me."
  "If your power allows you to be unjust to people, remember God's power."
  "To each his mind."
  "The unhappy ones bear to the right."
  "No one understands a damn thing."
  "The generous one will not be harmed."
  "I'm not showing off; it is all God-given."
  "For sale, bumpers."
  "The evil eye got me but God in His kingdom has saved me."
- When a person asks you about something in a religious tone, like, "What time is it?" or "How do I get to Talaat Harb Street?" and another answers "straight ahead, insha'allah (God willing)."
- When you see someone crossing the street amid the speeding cars with the skill of a circus acrobat until suddenly, midway, he is almost run over by a fast car that he tries to circumvent by returning to his initial point of departure with even greater skill . . . then he tries again (these tricky acrobatics are, at times, collective).
- When you stop at a traffic light in your car next to a microbus and you find that all the passengers are eyeing you at the same time, meaninglessly.
- When you see someone on the street making a phone call from a Menatel phone booth while someone else stands over his shoulder with a phone card in his hand, awaiting his turn and whiling away the time by eavesdropping on the caller. Upon overhearing the conversation, you may even see him requesting forgiveness from God as he moves backward and taps one palm of his hand into the other: Astaghfir Allah al-Azim (May God grant us forgiveness).
- When groups of fast iftar meal givers invade the street at the sunset call to prayer to provide fasting strangers with bags of dates, with one enthusiastic young man standing in the middle of the street, ready to be run over just for the sake of your iftar.

- When you see a man with an imposing body facing the wall under a bridge . . . relieving himself.
- When the parking attendant yells confidently for you to back up your car, saying, "Come, come, come," as he eyes another car whose driver is looking for a place to park. He abandons you midway and runs in the other direction. The outcome is well known, of course: craaash. Stop!
- When you try to find the source of the pollution, waste, and unruly smog that has aged the face of the capital before its time and you discover that it is all emitted from cars owned by the state: public buses, Central Security trucks, prison trucks, collective employee transportation (like the Agricultural Credit and Development Bank, Military Factory 54, the Ministry of the Environment employee bus), which basically means that the state owes most of the asthma patients an apology and a bouquet of flowers.
- When you find that it is always the men who stop in front of lingerie shop windows (the red flower lingerie).
- When your car is "clutched" because it is double-parked. This basically means that it is blocking two other cars that are legally parked. This way, one clutch blocks three cars in one go (please bring back the tow truck).
- When the traffic light turns red and the speeding cars suddenly stop, while the drivers tug on their seat belts with one hand and throw down the cell phones with the other, avoiding the eyes of the traffic policeman.
- When you find a billboard on the street with an actress or a model with bare shoulders that have been painted over in black by somebody.
- When you find an ordinary citizen making a speed bump on the street. The problem is not that he is making a speed bump where he wants, but rather that he doesn't know how to make it.
- When you find the garbage sweeper throughout the year standing at the congested flyover exit, smiling at every driver who passes by and waving his hand to wish them a prosperous year. He then sweeps a little around the car as he awaits the one-pound note.
- When you see white flags fluttering from a car window despite the repeated defeats of the Zamalek football team. Then you understand that one of the passengers is on his way to Cairo Airport to fly out to Saudi Arabia for the pilgrimage.
- More beautiful is the sight of elderly women (like grandmothers) dressed in white, looking like angels, mounting a tourist bus parked on one side of Gami'a Street on its way to Nuweiba harbor and then to the Kaaba.
- When you see the light poles turned on in broad daylight, with their yellowish bulbs like Isis organic chamomile.

- When you see the very same light poles turned off at night.
- When you see the garbage truck zooming through the street with all the garbage it has collected falling out left and right.
- When you see the picture and name of a respectable man on a billboard side by side with the words "The Symbol of the Wheel."
- When you see the names of streets and you don't know who these people are: Lazughli Square, Nawal Street, Ibn al-Wizz Awwam Street.
- When you find the police patrol car almost always parked.
- When you discover that the responsibility for managing the Cairo street traffic is that of simple policemen who have never lived for one day in Cairo. Each one of them arrived from his village straight to the training center and on to the Qasr al-Nil traffic light.
- When you discover that it is the traffic policeman who is obstructing traffic.
- When you see a young couple sitting quietly and romantically on a seat below the Corniche railing that hides the Nile view, their backs turned to the street. Even though you cannot see their faces, you get the impression that the girl is pulling a long face.
- When the ful cart occupies a space several times its size with tables and chairs that are spread out around it for ful meals: the fresh baladi bread sprawled on the pavement, the water buckets for washing the dishes, and another spread of green onions; in the corner a spot for drinking hot tea and a space to throw up.
- When celebrating the Ahli football team victories becomes a mandate, especially if you are passing through in your car where its supporters are congregating.
- When, from your car window, you spot a newlywed couple posing in their wedding clothes for a souvenir photo in front of the Cairo University fountain, or on Warraq Bridge, or Sixth of October Bridge, or Qasr al-Nil Bridge (you will seldom see the same sight on Fifteenth of May Bridge or al-Galaa Bridge).
- When you see a car backing up on Sixth of October Bridge because the driver missed the Ghamra exit.
- When you see the sign "Pedestrian Walkway" across one of the highways and you realize that, over the years, hundreds of people have been killed in this spot before the state understood that the residents of the area really needed a pedestrian walkway. The funny thing is that the residents have gotten used to crossing the highway underneath the pedestrian walkway.

Translated by Samia Mehrez

Ahmed Khaled Tawfik

from *Utopia*

THERE IS NOTHING NEW in Utopia that arouses your curiosity or enthusiasm. Nothing changes . . . sometimes I imagine that we are detained and that the ones outside are free. It all reminds one of Nazi concentration camps that you see in films about the war.

Utopia . . . the isolated colony that the wealthy have established on the North Coast to protect themselves from the angry sea of poverty outside and that has come to contain everything they need.

You can take a look at its main features with me: the giant gates, the electric fences, the security shifts that are undertaken by the Savco company, which predominantly employs former marines. Sometimes one of the poor tries to slip in without a permit, but he is immediately spotted by a helicopter that pursues and kills him, just like the scene imprinted on my imagination.

Then there is the green area, the school area that is especially conceived to convince parents that they are still performing their role, the faith area that houses a mosque, a church, and a synagogue. Some of the people here still insist on addressing a divine being they cannot see, but the younger generation has done away with that. I think that the older generation's obsession with faith has to do with their fear that they may suddenly lose everything; that they might lose the privilege; that they might find themselves outside. They still do not feel they have earned what they have, whereas their children came into the world believing that they have a right to everything. The old have stopped advising the young to follow in their footsteps.

I also think that the older generation loves to combine wealth and faith. The duo of wealth and faith has been engraved in Egyptian parents' minds for millennia. The image of Hagg Abd al-Sami' as he descends from an airplane returning from al-Hijaz with an expensive, loose cloak around his shoulders, distributing money left and right with an admirable smile glowing on his face, his expensive perfume floating in the air, and his golden rosary in hand— this image seems to be engraved in our parents' minds. I have read a little in religious literature, and in my mind the idea of faith is related to asceticism. Forget that we know each other . . . all this show of faith will not convince me that they don't drink and rape women and men of the Aghyar all the time. They have amassed their wealth from the flesh, dreams, hopes, and health of the Aghyar. That is why I feel that what they are doing is really strange, but then, that's their business.

The mall area . . . here you can buy Phlogestine under the table from some of the security guards to get high. Then you get to the palaces: Elwi Bek's palace (the king of the steel industry), Adnan Bek's palace (the king of meat), my father's palace (the king of pharmaceuticals).

Then there is the private airport, of course, so that you never have to go outside. In the past my people were obsessed with the idea of fleeing to the airport should the ones outside rebel. The trip to the airport would be tough, frightening, and dangerous. The Aghyar would intercept the cars and massacre those inside. I know this because I read a lot. There are many such stories, starting with the French Revolution, when the commoners roamed the streets parading Princess de Lamballe's breasts on two spears, all the way to the Iranian Revolution during the seventies of the twentieth century, when the director of SAVAK, I think, found himself carried on people's shoulders in his car. He found no solution but to stick his gun inside his mouth and pull the trigger. God! Even as I write these words I shudder with excitement. A gun inside your mouth . . . cold metal and one shot and it's all over!

The fear of the trip to the airport convinced my people that they should build their own private airports inside their compound. With time, there was no more fear of a revolution, but the airports remained in place as a show of luxury.

When you go beyond the limits of prudence, you feel that prudence extends to encompass new boundaries that are dominated by habit, boredom, and routine. Even the act of emptying your bladder in the kitchen sink becomes prudent and boring.

The council . . . the smoke from the tobacco . . . the giant office in the administrative building and the look of wisdom in the old generation's eyes . . . the sound of the clock . . . words . . . words . . . I heard them so often that they have lost their meaning: "We are one family, etc. We are not like the Aghyar, etc." I heard it all a thousand times. . . .

Now we are entering Aghyar land. This is the other world we left a long time ago, the day we hid behind the walls of Utopia.

Shubra. That's what they call it. Shubra, which I have only ever seen in films. The name has a strange, rough ring in my ear. It must sound like Sierra Madre or Rio Grande to the Americans. The bus stops in the middle of the crowds and the passengers alight. So I gesture to Germinal to come down with me. Not a bad beginning.

Where did that woman go? I don't know. That's how faces without a name melt away in the dark and the crowds.

An astonishing mix of odors, voices, scenes. . . . The most dominant smell is that of sweat, with which the smell of food and dirt and human waste, even blood, are mixed.

There are many overloaded food carts . . . many kinds of food: there is a heap of rice and a heap of kuskusi; there are oranges and tangerines and hot drinks the names of which I do not know . . . for some time now there have been alcohol vendors, but what kind of alcohol is this? A bottle the size of your palm costs fifty pounds despite the inflation! If it were urine it would have cost more! Old perfume bottles filled with unidentifiable liquids. I think that red alcohol is a common element in all these liquids. Murad said that selling alcohol on the street was inconceivable twenty years ago, but morals erode like metal that is subjected to running water. The strange thing is that these methylene-based drinks do not cause these people blindness as they do all over the world. If their stomachs are of rock, their livers are of steel, and their optic nerve is an electrical cable.

The sandwiches are another problem . . . a heap of sandwiches . . . one filled with what they claim is liver and sells for twenty pounds each! If this were rat liver they would not be able to sell it at this price.

After some time in this world, I came to the conclusion that these people are pretending that they are alive. They pretend that they are eating meat and they pretend that they are drinking wine, and of course they pretend that they are drunk and that they have forgotten their problems. They pretend that they have the right to sin, they pretend that they are human beings.

Only now do I understand why we isolated ourselves in Utopia. Nothing remains in this world except poverty and the gaunt faces with hungry, savage eyes. Thirty years ago, these people had some rights, but today they are completely forgotten. Even electricity and water have become a problem for each one of them. Those who can obtain a generator or dig a well are in heaven; otherwise, they have to endure.

The strange thing is that their numbers have increased with unbelievable speed. The fertility rate in Utopia is almost down to zero, whereas theirs is constantly on the rise. A man has ten children, five of whom die because he cannot get any medical services. But they still increase in number despite everything. It seems that they depend completely on herbs and popular medicine. My father has a monopoly over medical supplies in the market, and the prices are astronomical, but there is always a buyer. The riddle of this country is that there is always a buyer at any price. This proves that Marx was most probably stupid when he imagined that the balance will be reached when the poor have purchasing power.

Some of these people are religious because religion is their only hope in a better life after death. It is not possible that one be tortured throughout his lifetime and then die and be transformed into carbon without reward and punishment. In Utopia we have many religious people. The flights that go to pilgrimage are never-ending, but the reason, I think, is that Utopia's masters are afraid they might suddenly lose everything; that they might wake up to find themselves in the midst of these crowds buying liver sandwiches and drinking red alcohol. The matter requires a substantial number of pilgrimages and prayers so that they can evade this gloomy fate. At the end of the day, it is difficult to find a truly religious person.

The Egyptian pilgrims continued their collective and organized disappearance on Saudi territory. The employees in one of the hotels in Mecca and those of the company organizing the trip discovered that all the pilgrims residing in the hotel (seventy-two of them) have run away during the night without anyone so much as feeling or seeing them as they left with their belongings. Usama al-Ashri, deputy to the Minister of Tourism, said, "The strange thing about the second incident is that the pilgrims left their passports and their tickets, contrary to the first incident, during which the pilgrims attacked the bus driver and the representative of the organizing company in order to obtain their passports." (Masrawy website, 26 August, 2007)

We walk among the crowds completely dazed. We must not attract attention to ourselves. But I feel the weight of the adventure into which we have hurled ourselves.

Germinal tugs at my hand nervously, so I look in the direction she's indicating. There is a wooden cage with piles of disgusting chicken skin. The real disaster is that people actually buy these things. I try to gulp down the nausea . . . she will give us away with her hysterical attitude . . . if one of them were to look closely at our faces he would see that we have never known hunger.

The vendor calls us, "Come, brother . . . since when have you not cooked your food with fowl? This skin does the job."

He raises a piece of skin and shows it around to attract buyers.

It seems that chicken feet are also in demand . . . the heads . . . the wings . . . but where is the chicken itself? Even their chicken has been transformed, it seems, into bones covered with skin only. No muscle and no entrails.

A wandering boy picks up something from a stall and runs off, followed by curses and slippers hurled through the air.

Heaps of old dirty used clothes are sold at one hundred pounds a piece. Some say that the pound was higher than the dollar in the past. I cannot believe that, when the dollar is now worth thirty pounds. This is a frightening model for inflation because the price of a shirt will not exceed twenty-five cents. That is why things cost in the hundreds of pounds. I think they prefer bartering anyway, since it is closer to the truth.

Now we come out of the market area and proceed into an area full of tin or bamboo shacks . . . the floor is wet and your feet are submerged in water: a mixture of mud, dirty wash water, and sewage. I walk cautiously because any faltering in this area would mean suicide.

At the doors of the shacks the women stand: dirty and ugly, laughing at me seductively. I think that the youngest must be way over thirty-five. She does this job not because she is late getting married but for money.

As far as I know, there is no law that allows prostitution, but it has become a real phenomenon, more powerful than law, more powerful than convention.

I know that the upper age of marriage is forty for women and there is no limit on the age of men. Then one of those economic coups took place, so the conditions of marriage became more lax. It is enough for you to find someone who would accept you; then you don't have to worry about a home and an income. Each one will look after himself and the children will find their own bread somehow. This is how the marriage age dropped again.

This was all uglier than necessary; more horrific than necessary; more realistic than necessary.

Translated by Samia Mehrez

Ibrahim Issa

from *Nationalist Ghosts*

THE STATE PAVED THIS new highway during the past summer months. It took off from the main desert road, first in several winding turns, and then it became a two-way, four-lane highway with a divider. Paving this highway cost tens of millions of pounds, for which they scrambled around in the general budget. It was a very vital highway since it saved an hour's drive between Cairo and the North Coast, especially that luxury compound that was built by a busy construction company owned by a powerful tycoon. The highway was still virgin, unfinished, and had not been officially inaugurated by the president, as is the celebrated tradition with all of Egypt's contractors' bridges, sewage systems, and roads, the openings of which he has attended in person over the years. The inauguration of a bridge came to be considered a political event, the opening of a new road a presidential celebration.

The highway was not finished yet, but many impatient youngsters and tired old wigs had decided to take the new shortcut, especially during summer when the days were longer. It had no rest houses and was quite dangerous because there were no gas stations. It became the Egyptian summer adventure, and proof of the courage of the North Coast compounds' youth and a sign of the older generation's folly. But the rich and famous used it, protected by processions of security cars and emergency cars with tinted windows that blocked others' prying eyes and the dust. Cell phone companies hastily erected rickety power poles that collapsed with the first winter winds to hit the desert road. But now it was almost January: the darkness had thickened, the days were shorter, the cold was nipping and damp, and the storms were violent. So Galal and Azza had a row with the gang and took the new highway to shorten their trip and begin two nights of celebrating Wael's acquittal.

During that twilight zone between light and darkness, as Galal was driving the Cherokee, he pulled a white hair from his sideburns and held it up to inspect it. He held the steering wheel with the tips of his fingers and looked at Wael's and Karim's faces. Karim retorted with a strange question, "Why are your eyes so red, Galal?"

Wael zealously explained, "Galal's eyes are always red."

Karim understood the undertones of the question and smiled. There was Wael, with his well-built body and his impressive chest muscles, anxious to protect Galal from any criticism or insult. Galal built a throne around himself when he sat at the steering wheel of the Cherokee: his sense of power swelled, as if he were sticking his foot in the face of the world when he stepped on the gas. He became aloof and more conceited. When he turned the steering wheel, it was as if he were turning the entire world with a remote control, the whole of the universe at tip of his car.

Karim said, as he threw a beer can from his seat at Wael's face in the back seat, "Have you not noticed, Galal, all the cars that take this road are Grand Cherokees?"

His comment was intended to boost Galal's pride, for he was the founder of the Society of 4 x 4 Lovers: a group of friends from school and university days who had accumulated years and amassed power but still held on to their childish adoration of the Cherokee. They alone, apart from all other people, celebrated the birth of the Jeep on July 23 every year. . . .

The yearly ritual for the Society of 4 x 4 Lovers was that on every July 23 they took their Jeeps at night to the desert by the pyramids. They would put one of their cars in the middle of a circle of similar cars and would turn on their headlights after placing a cake on top of the Jeep in the middle. Galal would climb onto the top (he continued to do so until he felt he had grown too old for it and handed over the responsibility to someone else) and light a huge candle in the middle of the cake. Music would then go off from all the cars, followed by popping beer cans open and splashing them on the sides of the car amid dancing girls and boys from the Society of 4 x 4 Lovers. Later, the back seats of the cars would witness what normally follows from such celebrations. The only year the group did not celebrate was when the media made noise about Satan worshipers and other such ridiculous stories. So they canceled the party out of fear.

It was a newly paved, wide highway for those traveling to the luxury North Coast compounds that are colonized by the country's tycoons. One could spot Mercedes-Benzes and Chevrolets and BMWs on the way to and from the coast, but only the Cherokee became the official car for the wealthy children's weekend trips to their palaces and villas.

The strange thing was that the more the Cherokee was mentioned, the more the gang felt close to each other and warmer inside; bound by something like an umbilical cord, an invisible bond that enveloped their arms and hearts around this car, of which every one of them owned one or two models. Karim Daoud was the first to introduce them to the Jeep Cherokee, when they were still children and it was brand new in Egypt. His grandfather owned one of the twelve thousand cars that were produced in Egypt between 1978 and 1986, when production of the Cherokee XJ started. In 1992 it was offered to Galal as a present from his father, Fahim al-Nahhas. As for Wael, his father, Mustafa al-Ghazali, had made the Egypt Chrysler Company contract come true. Production increased from four thousand cars a year to sixteen thousand, of which one car went to each member of the gang. They also began to make friends at the club and at dance parties and private discotheques. As they left these places they would find that their Jeeps, parked together, looked like a TV commercial about a certain class. Galal's ex-wife always said that he loved his Jeep more than he loved her. Once when Galal hit her during a fight, he said, completely out of context, "It is no coincidence that the Jeep Cherokee is the American army vehicle."

Today, they took Galal's car and Azza drove Wael's car, since Wael was not allowed to drive it. They were celebrating his acquittal for having run over an entire family with the very same car. Galal tilted his head backward as he drove and looked at Wael. "Where's the damn joint you said you fixed?"

Wael did not reply, but his eyes bulged out of their sockets and he started shaking and yelling, so that Galal instinctively hit the brakes. Karim banged his head against the front window and Galal strained his neck, while Wael screamed even louder as his teeth hit the gear box, "My car! Azza has had an accident!"

Galal got out of his car and ran toward the other one which was mired in the sand. He felt that a whole drama was about to come to a close. He ran, and so did Wael and Karim behind him. Horrified, they crossed to the other side of the highway, where the car was turned over in the opposite direction with pieces of broken glass and metal shrapnel scattered all around it. The wheels were turning at maximum speed as if they were fans, and sounds of knocking, clobbering, and banging could be heard all over the body of the car.

Galal got there first and looked through a window. Azza had buried her head in Ghada's arms. They were shaking violently, completely stuck together as if they were inseparable twins in a narrow womb. At the same time he saw Sarah holding on to Tamer, who had started kicking the door hysterically with his feet to open it. Galal shuddered when he saw Ghada's face behind the window and heard her screaming in a shrill, high, shaky voice. They suddenly realized that their friends had arrived when they saw that the doors were shaking violently from the blows of their heavy shoes. Karim became obsessed with trying to open the door when he saw Sarah drenched in tears and mucus, with a horrified dead gaze in her eyes. Wael suggested that they lift the car so they could get them out. Galal got Wael's point, so he started running toward his car. Karim ran behind him mumbling, "Sarah is here. Did you see that?"

His legs were numb, almost paralyzed. Galal patted him on the shoulder, which petrified him even more and intensified his sudden hatred for Galal.

"Don't be scared. We will tow their car with mine and get them out immediately."

For no apparent reason Galal suddenly froze in his place by the trunk of the car. Did he scream? Karim couldn't exactly identify the sound that filled the air between him and Galal as he was shuddering with fear. Galal disappeared behind the car, then peeked at him with a look full of horror and pain. Karim asked, "Galal, why are you so tense?"

With the same horror he responded, "Come and take a look."

Karim moved slowly as if paralyzed, so Galal moved toward him and grabbed his hand violently to help him walk steadily. He dragged him forcefully toward the back of the car. Galal looked at the ground and so did Karim. He bent over and so did Karim. He placed his palm underneath the car, where red blotches started dripping onto his hand. He withdrew his hand so that the drops continued to fall to the ground, gradually forming a thin line of dark red, heavy, sticky liquid that spread over the asphalt. The blotches got bigger and spread further.

Karim stuttered as he asked, "Is this engine oil or is it gas?"

Galal looked at him with his hand completely covered with the liquid. "Probably blood."

"What?"

"This is neither oil nor gas: oil is dark yellow and gas is transparent. But this is red and sticky. Probably blood."

He stopped talking suddenly, then resumed as he got into his seat, "Let's get the car out of that horrible fix."

He got in and quickly turned his car around, making deep marks on the ground with his tires as he headed toward Azza's car. Wael had succeeded in dragging Ghada out. She was screaming at the top of her voice:

"Ghosts! We saw ghosts!"

Azza finally said, "I want to go back to Cairo. Turn around and take us back, Galal."

Galal tried to pull himself together, "We only have twenty kilometers to go before we arrive at the compound. Let's get there and relax and talk, and then we can decide whether we want to go back."

Karim's voice rose like fire, "There's a car coming behind us, guys!"

They all turned their heads while Galal looked intently through his rear-view mirror. What he saw was a white Peugeot cab.

Having decided to ask the driver to stop, Karim said, "Galal, give them a signal to stop so we can talk to them and find out what they saw."

Azza held on to Ghada's arms.

"No, I don't want the car to stop."

Everybody said, "Calm down, Azza. We want to know what exactly happened to us."

Galal gave several repeated high-beam signals to the white car, which signaled him back. From the window, he pointed his arm toward the side of the highway for the car to stop. It slowed down, bore to the right, and came to a complete stop. He saw that the other car had stopped a couple of meters behind him. He opened his door, and so did Karim and Wael, in order to get out, while Tamer remained seated. No one got out of the white car as the three of them walked hesitantly toward it. Suddenly, the driver of the white car turned the high beams in their faces, blinding them completely. When he turned off the lights, they rubbed their eyes and tried to see clearly, as the horn of their car went off frantically. They looked toward their car, from where they could hear shrieks; suddenly it started moving wildly toward them with its doors open, as Azza and Tamer yelled, "Hurry up, get in! Come back!"

When Galal turned toward the white car he was astounded to see tall, robust, colossal men, dressed in fluttering black cloaks with green shawls and sashes carefully wrapped around their shoulders and heads, moving closer with the wind following on their trail.

Tamer screamed, "Ghosts! Ghosts! Get in, you crazy guys!"

Translated by Samia Mehrez

Public Spaces

Every city has its own distinguishing landmarks and every one of those is invested with its own historical, cultural, sociopolitical, and symbolic significations. However, urban landmarks are not necessarily immortal and unchangeable. Rather, their histories are fluid: as urban space expands, new urban signs are invented so that these city signs come to represent transformations of the cityscape, and the ever-changing historical and symbolic reading of the city. Together, these urban signs provide a visual inventory that renders the city legible, knowable, and more meaningful. They also map out the layering of the cityscape and its representation through overlapping, at times conflicting, signs.

But, landmarks are not simply real physical artifacts in the city that are readily decipherable and legible at the same level by all. In fact, the accessibility and readability of these urban signs will depend to a great extent on the position of the urban readers themselves: for the city dweller such signs may be part of a collective memory; for the tourist or the outsider they may remain opaque and mystifying. In both cases, however, these landmarks are never completely transparent: their signification is always incomplete and their reading unfinished. Furthermore, like magnets, city signs attract human crowds and social groups and become sites for manifold human interaction and expression. They are therefore at once part of the city's architecture and thoroughly part of its public sphere.

The process of reading the city through its signs becomes doubly complicated when these real urban landmarks are represented, indeed reinvented, through literary language and vocabulary that invests them with new levels of symbolic signification. Indeed, creative writers represent a very special group of urban readers: given that they belong to several generations and multiple socioeconomic classes they are bound to develop a special relationship with certain city signs over others, a relationship that bespeaks their background and position as city dwellers and is represented through the very form, language, and idiom of their literary texts. These multiple, colliding imaginative reconstructions of city signs further confirm that literary representations of urban landmarks depend on the ideological, cultural, and social positions of city writers.

The selections in this chapter provide at once a diachronic and synchronic spectrum of Cairo's urban landmarks whose representation in literary texts of the twentieth century map out a highly layered and complex reading of the city: from its ancient Egyptian signs to its Islamic, colonial, modern, and even postmodern ones. These literary representations are further nuanced and complicated through the language in which they are reinvented. While most of the selections were originally written in Arabic, a handful were written in either English (Waguih Ghali, Anne-Marie Drosso) or French (Robert Solé). These cosmopolitan reinventions bespeak Cairo's multi-ethnic, pluri-lingual literary inventory, which must be read against the more local renditions and readings of city signs.

Gamal al-Ghitani's Sufi and mystical representation of the pyramids recaptures their distant past as well as their eternal grandeur and mystery in a deliberate archaic literary language that is pitted against their present reality in which they are now embraced, if not besieged, by the city and dwarfed by its never-ending expansion. Sonallah Ibrahim's reading of the Citadel provides a cumulative history of this architectural conglomerate and renders it a metaphor for the history of Egypt, which has always oscillated between resistance and despotism. Muhammad al-Fakharani humanizes the colossal statue of King Ramses, "the owner of the square," who is uprooted and imprisoned in a museum leaving behind him severed imaginary friendships with Cairo's marginals who live at the foot of his pedestal and with whom he had many intimate relationships.

Cairo's cosmopolitan signs are at once linked to Egypt's colonial history with its privileged communities as well as the mass exodus of these communities and the transformation that besets colonial icons. The Shepheard's Hotel, the snooker club, Groppi's, and the Gezira Club are spaces for the select few, with well-guarded boundaries with the streets of the city and its inhabitants. These elite icons of the city with their foreign communities and languages are juxtaposed against the more local, spiritual and popular icons of the mosque, the traditional bath *(hammam),* and the venerated shrine that are the sites for radically different literary representations, languages, and interactions.

Indeed, the literary representation of city signs over the twentieth century eventually marks a shift in the social and ideological position of the writers themselves and their relationship with elements of the cityscape. One good example of this relationship is Cairo's coffee shops and their symbolic function for city writers. Naguib Mahfouz's traditional coffee shops that provide a site for social dialogue and integration across different classes compete with coffee shops that are invested with the city's cultural and political history: the social function of the traditional coffee shop such as the Zahra Café in Mahfouz's *Khan al-Khalili* co-exists with the Café Riche, Zahrat al-Bustan Café, and Sheikh Ali's Bar, each of which redefines and expands the traditional social function of coffee shop culture while becoming metaphors for Cairo's modern political history, sites of resistance and of oppression.

Likewise, downtown's exclusive ethnic community clubs are begrudgingly obliged, given the dwindling size of their communities in post-revolutionary Egypt, to open their doors and gates to a local middle class that had been formerly looked upon with contempt. In so doing the new occupants rewrite the histories of former colonial urban landmarks: the Gezira Club becomes a sign that pits a new world against an old one, a space that introduces new social mores that challenge a more traditional social order; the Greek Club and the exclusive Grillon restaurant are taken over by Cairo's intelligentsia and, rather than continue their existence as isolated islands in the bustling city, become an integral part of its public sphere with its sociopolitical and cultural concerns and conversations.

As the city of Cairo expands it invents new urban signs that seduce the literary imaginary. We move away from the ancient pyramids to the postmodern mall that becomes the symbolic site for the city's new and contested social mores: the mall as a haven for anonymity and the freedom of human relations in Ahmed Alaidy's *Being Abbas el Abd*, but also the mall as a nightmare of distorted historical representation of the city, as in Mahmoud Al-Wardani's *Mall Music*. As we move among these coexisting signs we witness a variety of social interactions and we learn an endless number of languages with which to read the city.

Gamal al-Ghitani

from *Pyramid Texts*

WHAT THE EYE CANNOT apprehend, the heart may find a way to.

Every time he became acquainted with one new thing, another would appear. Whenever he felt he had gathered information about the pyramids that would gladden the heart of his Sheikh in the Farthest West, some new insight would appear to him that encouraged him to stay. Much lore found its way to him and went no further. He would listen and interpret, staring by day, stealing glances by night. In the depths of his sleep, divers solutions to problems with which he had long been preoccupied would occur to him, until there came that instant, resembling a desire for some ill-defined woman, that would well up from within him, gushing, arousing, agonizing, irresistible, and inescapable.

In such a state, on a quiet, cold night whose iciness slowed the passing of time, he arose and made his way to the pyramids. He came to the Great Pyramid from the east, certain that something human existed in those seemingly mute stones, and that if he spoke, he would hear someone answer.

The mountains appear firm and solid, but they are continuously withering away.

On that night he understood many things, some of which may be stated openly or at least hinted at. Among them: that it is impossible to apprehend the pyramids with the eyes when standing close to them, within their shadow. And the way they look from a distance is an illusion, because they do not appear as they really are. It is impossible to take in their height by looking, observation from any point being incompatible with their angles of inclination. The structure is too all-embracing to be comprehended in a single glance. Thus, wherever a person stands, whatever his point of view, he can apprehend only a part of the whole. If he stops at widely separated places, including some (such as the Muqattam hills, Fustat, and the eastern bank of the Nile) that are elevated, and he stands there for varying periods of time, he will see, on each different occasion, a scene that differs from that which he saw on previous occasions.

Indeed, what he sees at the end will conflict with what he sees at the beginning.

Everything is relative. Everything is relative.

That night he stood directly beneath the Great Pyramid.

He walked around it. What he saw of its unaccustomed size, merging with the night, terrified him, for it was like a part, or an extension, of himself. Slowly he started to measure the east side. He confirmed that each side faces one of the points of the compass. The height, however, cannot be apprehended through observation. The one who would do so finds himself ill at ease, off balance, torn between the desire to commence and the desire to be done, between intention and execution, ever asking himself, would he never pass on through to the other side?

From that night on, he began to direct his sight toward the pyramids even when they lay beyond his vision. However, he would become disquieted and shaken whenever he moved to take action.

"Man walks and time rides." How then can the ephemeral catch the eternal?

Having once determined that each side was facing one of the primary directions, he started measuring.

His unease began when he came to the second attempt. After the third he was certain of the discrepancy; discrepancy is not something susceptible to doubt. For three days he didn't dare to repeat the attempt, three days during which he doubted himself, his name, whether he really belonged to the town from which he came, or even to that in which he resided. The Valley of Zamm, with its facades, street corners, treetops, clear skies, and beloved faces, vanished from his memory. He started to ask himself, had he really lived there? Had he followed his sheikh so slavishly that he would abandon his own country? Had that really happened? He continued trying. At the seventh attempt, which took place after the elapse of a lunar month, he was surprised to find an exact correspondence with the results of the first. But at the eighth, everything was completely different. This clear variance in something tangible astonished him.

To feel at home in a country other than one's own is to lose all certainty.

During this difficult period, whenever he suffered from the ache of his aloneness or on the rack of his solitude, he shed secret tears. However, his eyes had only to fall on the pyramids for serenity to well up inside him once more, and he would surrender himself to the contemplation of their awesome forms, to the rehearsal in his mind of the information he had gathered about them from the people. These told of their hereditary sanctity; of how, were any couple, male and female, to enter and attempt to perform the act, they would be turned to cinders; of mysterious birds flapping through their interior spaces and of magic traps, set long ago and known to be effective still. The people still held in awe and respect any who approached or demonstrated interest, but they would not divulge their secrets or teach them to a stranger, and especially not those of the visible but hidden pathways that they took toward the summit.

Those who specialized in these matters considered these pathways to be their inalienable possession, one whose secrets they passed on, in stages, to those among their children or relatives who bore the marks of a higher calling and a willingness to make the ascent.

Translated by Humphrey Davies

Sonallah Ibrahim

from *Cairo from Edge to Edge*

ONE CAN DISCERN Cairo's Citadel from any vantage point, even through the permanent veil of dust and waste. How can the eye mistake the two elegant minarets with the dome in between? But the Muhammad Ali Mosque is only the tip of the iceberg of this unique architectural conglomerate that was constructed over centuries and whose history, so closely related to that of the city, has become symbolic of its very being.

The oldest parts of the Citadel were constructed eight centuries ago by Salah al-Din al-Ayyubi, who through his victories during the Crusades became a symbol for the resistance to foreign occupation. The actual building of the structure was executed by Qaraqush, one of his aides, who became a symbol for pointless despotism. Between them, perhaps, they sum up the essence of Egyptian history.

Moreover, the Citadel marks the beginning of a unique period: five and a half centuries during which power was held by several dynasties of Mamluks—the slaves, imported from Asia Minor and central Europe, who became warriors and princes. The Citadel also witnessed the end of this period at the hand of the famous Muhammad Ali, the first ruler chosen by the Egyptians themselves and imposed on the Ottoman sultan in Istanbul.

After several bloody confrontations that put an end to many of them, Muhammad Ali invited the remaining Mamluks—twenty-four princes and beys and four hundred of their followers, aides, and confidants—to a banquet at the Citadel on March 1, 1811, which was attended by several thousand dignitaries. After they had drunk their coffee, smoked their waterpipes, and listened to music, they prepared for departure. They stood and saluted Muhammad Ali and formed a procession lined by two regiments of guards. The procession descended from the Citadel along a narrow passageway that led to the gate of Bab al-Azab. The vanguard rode at the head of the procession, followed by the chief of the police force, the governor, and his cortège. Here the music came to a halt, and suddenly the great gate of Bab al-Azab thundered shut and was bolted on the outside, blocking the passage of the Mamluks. Meanwhile, the guards mounted the rocks overlooking the passageway, took position along the walls above it, and opened fire on the Mamluks from above and from behind. It was a complete massacre from which no one escaped.

Muhammad Ali added a palace, a mosque, army barracks, and storage houses to the structure of the Citadel. Those who succeeded him followed in his footsteps: the British—the last of the foreign powers to occupy Egypt (and for the shortest period: only seventy-four years!)—constructed a military prison inside the Citadel that continued to receive occupants from among revolutionaries and politicians until the departure of the last British soldier from Egypt in 1956 at the hands of Gamal Abd al-Nasser, the first Egyptian ruler known to the country in over two thousand years. The last occupants of this small prison were the assassins of Sadat in 1981. In 1983, the prison was closed and transformed into a police museum.

The prison comprises a number of small cells constructed along the sides of two open passageways. In four of these cells have been placed life-sized figures that represent prisoners from various historical periods, distinguishable from one another by their dress and the signs that have been posted beside the doors. The signs for the Mamluk, Ottoman, and Muhammad Ali periods represent a historical falsification, since the prison was built only during the 1880s. Only one sign corresponds to historical truth: that which announces "A

Prisoner from the Modern Period," represented by a figure dressed in modern clothes, with eyeglasses and a book in hand. This is the same cell I occupied some time ago.

It was two years after the last British soldier had departed from Egypt. In the middle of the night, we went up to the Citadel, the site that conferred authority on those who ruled Egypt. But we were not triumphant conquerors, nor were we defeated conspirators or voyeuristic tourists. We entered, one after the other, through a small aperture in a huge wooden gate that may have been the ancient Bab al-Azab, then we were assigned to the different cells.

This was only the overture, for the city was big, and not short of prisons: one was just meters away and was aptly named (at least until the seventies when it was demolished), Prison of Egypt; the others were scattered around the northern and southern edges of the city. These prisons present their political occupants with elaborate reception ceremonies that are prepared with great care, in whose production many specialists participate and which are attended by distinguished state representatives who usually sit around an oblong table that overlooks the outer courtyard of the prison where the guests wait in the corner. The reception ceremonies then begin: the guests proceed between two lines of guards armed with sticks that increase in size until they become cudgels, at which point the guest is already naked, heavily wounded, unconscious—or in many instances dead.

Near the prison there is a spacious terrace that overlooks Cairo and from which a spectacular view is visible through the dust that envelops it: to the left are the remains of Fustat, the initial heart of the city built by the Arabs after the conquest of Egypt in 639 CE; straight ahead and to the north extends the old city with its thousand minarets announcing, besides the call to prayer, the various historical periods that succeeded each other within the city: the Fatimid, the Mamluk, and the Ottoman.

The oldest minaret dates from the year 877 CE. Built by Ahmad ibn Tulun, it is characterized by its conical shape and its external stairway, reminiscent of the minaret of the Samarra Mosque in Iraq, Ibn Tulun's place of origin. Most of the minarets belong to the Mamluk period, with its elaborate ornamentation. As for the two slim, spear-like minarets of the Muhammad Ali Mosque in the Citadel, they belong to the dry Turkish style. There are another two elegant minarets that tower—since the fifteenth century—not on a mosque but atop Bab Zuwayla, one of the gates of Old Cairo, though they actually belong to the famous mosque of al-Mu'ayyid, whose story encapsulates the entire Mamluk period.

Like all other Mamluks, al-Mu'ayyid was brought to Cairo by slave vendors, when he was still a twelve-year-old boy, where he was sold on its markets and bought by the Mamluk sultan Barquq, who schooled him in reading, philology, the arts of war, and wrestling. Thus he came to participate in the ongoing conflicts between the Mamluk princes. He ended up in a prison attached to Bab Zuwayla, where he was put in a dirty hole in the ground with hands, feet, and neck chained to the wall. During this crisis he vowed that if he were to become ruler of Egypt he would build a mosque and a school on the site of the prison.

It seems that God did respond, and he took over the sultanate in 1412. Within three years of his reign he began to fulfill his pledge. He started by demolishing the prison, then his men began raiding people's homes to remove the marble necessary for the construction of the mosque.

Five years later, the story came to a familiar close: he discovered that the princes wished to depose him and appoint his son, Ibrahim, so he put poison in the latter's dessert. Not a year had gone by before he joined his son and was buried by his side, under the dome of the mosque. Only Bab Zuwayla, whose history is no less bloody, remained erect. It had been the very heart of Old Cairo and a focus of life and death within it: upon it hung the bodies of crucified thieves and rebels, and into it sterile women hammered nails in hope of a God-given child.

Translated by Samia Mehrez

Ismail Wali al-Din

from *Hammam al-Malatili*

THE SUN ROSE. THE lights of the hammam were turned off. The men emerged from a small opening painted with striking colors. The noise rose on the narrow cobbled street. Only a few meters away, near the hammam, where the space was wider and more open, there were modern buildings where long-distance cabs were stationed.

Ahmad walked out of Qasr al-Madina Hotel after having paid three pounds and sixty-five piasters for his ten-day stay. He had a small suitcase. He walked toward the "small city," as he liked to call it: the alleys, teeming with kids and women. Crowds of buyers and sellers, each with his own distinctive call, merchandise from a hairpin to a silver tray, from a gold earring to a child's toy, from a marvelous wooden cart to different facial and hair cosmetics sold by a swindler. A woman called out searching for a lost child.

It was noon and the call to prayer could be heard from a distant mosque. "Why not go there?" he said to himself, as he made his way through a long, bland passageway. He performed his ablutions. An elderly woman was being sprayed with water by the mischievous child in her company as she washed a tattered black dress.

He headed for the courtyard of the mosque . . . with his small suitcase, in which he carried two pairs of underwear, a towel, a white shirt, a pair of trousers, and a toothbrush.

Blue lanterns with pendants hung from a marvelous ceiling. He was too timid to approach the man praying in a corner. A few people entered the mosque. They chose a stout man in a shirt and a pair of slacks to be their imam and lead them during prayer.

Ahmad stood next to a young man in wornout overalls with a pair of big, wide feet. His face betrayed the marks of misery and humiliation. Ahmad felt very sorry for him.

The imam began leading the prayer. Ahmad recited the Fatiha to himself with his eyes fixed on the imam's big feet. He thought of his mother and father and his younger siblings.

He prostrated with the others. He buried his nose in the old carpet. He was almost in tears. When he got up he had forgotten that he wanted to cry. He began the Fatiha while contemplating the blue and red colors of the old mihrab and the marvelous old corrugated iron window that could not possibly be reproduced in this age.

When he knelt again in his prayer his heart was cleansed, and he suddenly felt love toward all the others kneeling beside him. Their feet caught his eye again with their dirty, rugged toenails. He could see, through the slit in an old blue pair of trousers, part of the plump legs with long, bushy, fair hair.

The group rose at the end of the prayer. The young man beside Ahmad greeted him. The imam in western clothes began his sermon with poised, well-measured words. But the people didn't want to listen; they wanted to escape to the hubbub outside.

Now he was alone in the mosque. An old man lay down by the mihrab, resting his head on a bundle of clothes. In front of him, Ahmad could see a dome with inscriptions, but he could not make out who the founder of the mosque might have been.

He took a long look at the ceiling: a splendid, intricate design in gold and blue with a circle in the middle and four smaller ones on the sides. Birds chirped inside the empty mosque; children's soft voices playing at the ablution sink. His eyes almost popped out of their sockets as they tried to take in all this beauty.

He stretched out his arms. He wanted to fly to the ceiling, to embrace it, to touch it with his lips. He lay on his back. His eyes sharpened and wandered as he contemplated the engravings and the intricate colors. The dome had two circles and a crescent, eight pillars, and pendants holding illuminated cups.

A group of heavy men entered the mosque. They did not pray immediately, as he had imagined; rather, they lay down to stretch out their bodies and arms, then they fell asleep. He watched them suspiciously. He picked up his shoes and suitcase.

He did not forget to touch the door before leaving. He read: "Sultan Qalawun, May Allah Grant Him Victory."

The street was crowded: the neighing of saddled horses carrying wheat sacks; a waterpipe vendor; the sound of the cymbals of the tamarind vendor. The monuments were in bad shape on the outside because of the humidity. A lot of people were talking. A minaret, the mosque of al-Salih Ayyub; an old man sat on a bench near a hammam, a traditional one, for women only.

He moved toward a narrow street that smelled of perfume and incense. Shops overflowing with herbs, most of which had small paper signs with low prices: sieved fennel, Sudanese hibiscus, and celery seed.

He overheard one woman saying to another as she rubbed against his body in the crowd, "I took a shot in my vagina today."

A huge mosque. Vendors sat around its walls selling syringes, children's toys, plastic whistles, sheets and slippers, women's lingerie, earrings, and square rings. The smell of new shoes; a man dragged his son away from the crowd. His mouth was wide open, almost drooling over the fitir and basbusa in a shop. A foreign man and woman, with a tour guide hurrying in their footsteps. He overheard the guide saying, "We will now go to Sultan Qalawun mosque. It has a high minaret from which you can see the entire Old City."

A pot and cauldron store, a seller of milk, bracelets in pure gold, a snake, a horseshoe, and the hand of Fatima. A young woman bargained with an old man in front of the silver-rimmed tea sets. An old shop for tarbush pressing. An old mosque was being transformed into a row of squat, consecutive book stalls selling old books: *Manhaj al-azkar fi dustur al-a'yan, al-iqna' fi hifz alfaz Abu Shuja'*.

At al-Husayn Square he found a spot flooded with sun. There were crowds at the bus stop and kushari and taamiya vendors. Ahmad ate his lunch quietly and without interest. Time was almost at a standstill.

He walked toward the gardens and sat on a marble bench with a magazine he bought from an old newspaper vendor in front of al-Azhar mosque. The magazine cost two piasters and the book cost only one. It was a celebrity magazine: Elizabeth Taylor, a Canadian woman with her child and new husband, a black actor whose name he could not remember embracing an almost-naked white woman. He smoked a cigarette. He couldn't enjoy the clear weather.

Translated by Samia Mehrez

Naguib Mahfouz
from Khan al-Khalili

NEXT EVENING HE LEFT the apartment building, heading for the Zahra Café. He found it at the start of Muhammad Ali Street, just before it turned into Ibrahim Pasha Street. It was as large as any store, with two entrances, one of which was on Muhammad Ali Street itself, while the other was on a long passageway leading to the New Road. There were dozens of cafés like this one in the quarter; he estimated that there must be a café per every ten inhabitants. He approached the café with a certain hesitation because he was not a habitué of such places and was not used to their atmosphere. But no sooner had he entered the place than he spotted Boss Nunu sitting in the middle of a group of government officials, including some locals as well. Nunu noticed him and stood up with a smile.

"Welcome, Ahmad Effendi!" he shouted in his usual loud voice.

Ahmad moved over in his direction, with a bashful smile on his face. He held out his hand in greeting, and Nunu grabbed it with his own rough palm.

"This is our new neighbor, Ahmad Effendi Akif," he said, turning to the assembled group. "He's a civil servant in the Ministry of Works."

Everyone stood up in unison out of kindness and respect, something that made Ahmad even more nervous and shy. He went round shaking hands with everyone and being introduced by Boss Nunu: "Sulayman Bey Ata, primary school inspector; Sayyid Effendi Arif from the Survey Department; Kamal Effendi Khalil, also from the Survey Department; Ahmad Rashid, a lawyer; and Abbas Shifa, an eminent figure from the provinces."

They cleared a space for him and made him feel very welcome. He started to feel more at home and forgot about his shyness and discomfort at coming to the café. Before long he was feeling happily superior to them all, although he managed to keep it well hidden by smiling sweetly and exchanging amiable looks.

There was not the slightest doubt in his mind that he was superior to these people in every conceivable way. After all, he was from al-Sakakini, and families who lived there were the children of quarters like al-Darrasa and al-Gamaliya. He was an intellectual, with a fully fashioned mind, while these folk had none of that. Indeed, he pictured his presence in their midst as a nice gesture of sympathy, an engaging display of humility on his part. What continued to baffle him was the question of how he would make these people aware of his importance and introduce them to his sterling intellectual and cultural qualities. How on earth was he going to convince them that he was a person of real significance and earn their respect? Needless to say, as long as this new friendship developed and they continued to get together, such respect would inevitably follow; so there was no harm in delaying things for a couple of sessions. . . .

Even though the group was fairly small, it took up a good third of the café. The café owner sat by the cash register nearby as though he too were a member of the assembled company and one of the participants in their conversation.

Boss Nunu and Kamal Khalil extended the warmest of welcomes to Ahmad Akif, but Sulayman Ata maintained his frowning posture as though he had completely forgotten about the new arrival. Ahmad Rashid started listening to a broadcast on the radio.

"We've heard that you've just come here from al-Sakakini," said Kamal Khalil to open the conversation.

"Yes, sir," replied Ahmad, lowering his head, "that's correct."

"Is it true," the man asked anxiously, "that very few people made it out of their houses?"

"The truth of the matter is," replied Ahmad with a laugh, "that only one house was destroyed."

"So much for rumors! What was it then that made such a terrible noise, the one that sounded as though it was inside our very homes?"

"That was in the sky!"

At this point Ahmad Rashid turned away from the radio; he obviously had not been paying much attention to it. "Is it true that a bomb landed but didn't explode?" he asked.

Ahmad was delighted that the young man was now talking to him. He replied, "People say that two bombs did fall, but they were cordoned off and experts defused them."

"What we need," Ahmad Rashid went on, "is that Canadian specialist whom we've read about in reports on war news. Apparently he's saved whole quarters in London."

Sayyid Arif was an admirer of the Germans. "Are there any whole quarters of London left?" he asked with a scoff.

Ahmad Rashid smiled. "As you can tell, our friend supports the Germans!" he said.

"For medical reasons!" laughed Boss Nunu, completing Ahmad Rashid's comment.

That made Sayyid Arif blush, but Boss Nunu refused to spare him. "Our friend, Sayyid Arif believes," he went on with one of his enormous laughs, "that German medicine can restore one's youth."

Sayyid Arif frowned angrily. Obviously it was utterly inappropriate to make such a statement in the company of someone who had only just made their acquaintance. Ahmad Akif was well aware of what Boss Nunu's motivations were in saying it, and yet he made sure that his facial expression showed no sign of having heard anything. Boss Nunu was anxious to repair any damage his remark may have caused, so he started telling their new guest about the new quarter he was living in, praising its virtues to the skies.

"This quarter is the real old Cairo," said Ahmad Rashid, commenting on Boss Nunu's description. "Crumbling remnants of former glories, a place that stirs the imagination, arouses a real sense of nostalgia, and provokes feelings of regret. If you look at it from an intellectual perspective, all you see is filth, a filth that we're required to preserve by sacrificing human beings. It would be much better to knock the whole thing down so we could give people the opportunity to enjoy happy and healthy lives!"

Ahmad immediately realized that his new conversation partner had a seriousness about him that suggested that he might well be a smooth talker, and indeed someone of genuine intelligence; especially as his law degree gave him the kind of prestige that ignorant and naive people respect enormously. He was afraid that this man might outshine him, so he immediately assumed the offensive, ready to counterattack at any cost: "But old quarters do not necessarily imply filth; there are the memories of the past that are far more worthy than present-day realities, memories that can serve as the impetus for any number of qualities. The Cairo you're anxious to wipe off the map is the city of al-Mu'izz, reflecting the glories of eras past. Compared with that city, where does today's Cairo, all modern and indentured to others, belong?"

Translated by Raymond Stock

Yusuf al-Sibaie

from *We Do Not Cultivate Thorns*

FINALLY THE PROCESSION GOT going: she carried one basket on her head and the woman carried the other and ordered her to follow her. The two baskets were full of ful sandwiches.

She didn't know when she would give her her share of meat, for she had left the meat basket behind. The small procession moved along toward the shrine of Mawardi. The crowds had started to arrive, and the rising sound of swings mixed with the moans of the disciples and the calls of peddlers and the beat of circus drums.

Umm Abbas made her way through the crowd with arm and tongue. Her rebuking comments resounded amid the crowds, "Get out of the way, you dirty tongue."

Her rebuking comment would be followed by an order to Sayeda. "Move faster, girl. Are you walking on eggshells?"

Finally the pair arrived at the shrine with the two baskets. Umm Abbas lowered her basket and pulled the other one off Sayeda's head. She then placed them in front of her and started distributing its contents.

The Mawardi mulid disciples and participants in the celebration of the saint's birthday rushed toward the baskets so that the small procession could no longer be seen. It all disappeared in the crowd and in the blink of an eye not one piece of bread was left in the baskets.

Sayeda got lost in the crowd. She didn't know where Umm Abbas had gone and she didn't care to know, after she had given up hope on the loaves of bread with meat and after having spent her day working hard at Hagg Boraie's house. . . .

She might as well take off into the mulid, come what may.

What will you do, Sayeda?

She had to get organized.

But there was nothing to think about. The Ali Louz cart that sold almond paste with lemon and cinnamon was parked right in front of her. She mustn't lose time thinking. She pushed the kids who surrounded the cart until she got to its side, then yelled to the owner, "Hey, mister!"

The man did not answer her, for he was busy putting the paste into the mouth of one of his young customers who surrounded the cart. Sayeda did not wait: she extended her arm to the metal pointer that rotated in a circle on top of the tray that was divided into several compartments, each of which constituted a separate container that joined the others at the center of the tray, where the pointer was fixed. On each container there was a number that showed the players the number of times they could eat from the paste if the pointer stopped at that number.

The pointer started rotating until it stopped at the number four. Sayeda yelled at the man, "Four!"

The man looked angrily at her, "Your money, girl."

Sayeda responded even more angrily, "Here it is. What do you take me for, a thief?"

She pushed forward the piaster that she had been given by Sheikh Boraie.

The man examined the piaster carefully, then put it in his pocket. Sayeda started yelling again, "Give me the change."

"How many turns do you want?"

"Two."

The man put his hand in his pocket and brought out a couple of millimes and handed them over to her, as he refilled the spoon and put it into the boy's mouth, saying,

"This is your last turn."

"How about a little more?"

"Make room for the others. Let me get on with my work."

He then dipped the spoon into one of the containers and brought out a sweet paste of lemon sprinkled with cinnamon and decorated with almond.

Sayeda looked at the spoon and said, "Put more almonds, and fill it."

"Get on with it, girl, I don't have time for this."

"I swear to God, I'm not gonna take it except if you put more almonds."

The man dipped into the container again and brought out an almond. "You look like you're a troublemaker."

He shoved the spoon into her open mouth that was ready to devour the contents. Sayeda finished eating the Ali Louz and took off into the crowd, tightly gripping the money in the pocket of her gallabiya. Sayeda started eyeing the swings as they flew in the air and then she shifted her gaze between the wobbly swings and the swinging ones. Should you get into the goose, or the boat, or the water wheel? Should you go to the circus, Sayeda, or go to see Sheikha Zebeda, the marvel of her time, whose size has never surpassed that of a child? Should you have some hot liver or kushari with hot sauce, or kebab and kufta? The smell of grilled kebab rose from the white cart and filled the air of the mulid. How about sausages and head meat, Sayeda?

She spotted the sausage cart and remembered how the sausages would be arranged on the brass tray on top of a layer of parsley in the shop on Sadd Street, where the glitter of the trays mixed with the mirrors, and she remembered how she had longed for the sausages.

The girl was confused: many wishes filled her head and sounds crowded in her ears and scents mixed in her nostrils. She made up her mind and rushed toward the swings. She'll take a ride on the goose swing, then she'll see. The swing tossed her in midair and the mulid looked packed with lights and banners, the cries of the possessed disciples, the calls of the peddlers, the sound of the drums, the music of the reed mizmar, and the sound of the cymbals. A festive world in the midst of which stood the shrine under which lay or did not lie Sidi Mawardi. All this was for him but he certainly didn't know. And if he did, big deal!

True, some of the disciples called upon him in feverish moans, but what could he do for them? Some of the ailing and aggrieved called upon him to intervene on their behalf so that God might grant them their wishes and alleviate their problems, but he didn't know how to. God heard them, no doubt, and he certainly didn't tarry to do justice. Intervention, by a dead man?! Anyway, the moaning had started right at his grave.

The swaying began and the screaming, what they call zikr, which takes place inside the shrine on top of his body, if anything still remained of it or if it existed in the first place. The screaming swayers no doubt believed that he existed and that he felt their presence; otherwise, why did they choose his shrine to sway so noisily, believing that he could stand their clamor and their cries all night and then ask his intervention and his good word on their behalf to God?

Damn them! If only he felt their presence, all they would have merited would have been a prayer to God to take them to his side so that he might have some peace, even though he didn't really feel anything. Why all this screaming at the ruins of his grave?

The swing stopped and the man yelled at Sayeda, "Get off, girl."

And the girl got off.

Why were they all yelling at her as if she hadn't paid? She felt the pangs of hunger again and asked herself once more: sausages, Sayeda, or kebab, or kushari? Wow, the smell of kebab and kufta was so good! But also scary, for she did not know how much it would take out of her piasters. She truly had a fortune with which she could do whatever she wanted. But kebab seemed beyond her means and she was afraid that a kebab meal, if she really thought about it, would consume everything that she had left. But maybe she had enough for a kebab meal.

If only Umm Abbas had given her a couple of loaves with meat, or even just half a loaf, in exchange for all the hard work she had done, she would have saved her the cost of kebab and the anxiety of confusion. But why not have kebab and defy Umm Abbas with her money? Come on, Sayeda, calm down, don't be rash. She found her legs leading her to the kushari cart. What's wrong with kushari with hot sauce and fried onion? On her way to the kushari cart she passed by the gate of the shrine. She saw her father with Hagg Boraie among the swayers in the zikr celebration.

He didn't see her, of course, for his eyes were closed and his head was shaking and his body swaying without a swing; his voice grew louder along with the other chanters: "Allah hayy, Allah hayy."

She walked toward the kushari cart. Once again she hesitated. A question leapt to her mind, "Kushari or macaroni?"

She did not hesitate for long before she yelled, "One order of kushari and one of macaroni! Why not?!"

Sayeda ate the kushari and the macaroni. She went to the circus and watched Shawwal as he paraded his muscles, saying, "I am Shawwal, the featherweight champion of Imbaba." She saw Sheikha Zebeda and heard her speak. Sayeda did everything until the very last millime was spent. And now what, Sayeda? The only thing left was the spanking, awaiting you at home at the hands of Dalal for free. Go home quietly now so that you may be spanked and then go to bed, and dream about everything you've done at the mulid.

Translated by Samia Mehrez

Anne-Marie Drosso

from *Cairo Stories*

IT WAS QUITE A scene in front of the Mugama that morning. Hundreds of men and women clustered in loosely formed lines, some accompanied by children, were standing, sitting on stools and folding chairs, drinking, eating, or reading the morning news in front of the massive fourteen-story, ugly government building, erected at the end of the monarchy and the butt of countless jokes since. It was not yet eight in the morning. The men and women had roused themselves at the crack of dawn to make it to the Mugama so early for the same reason: to apply for an exit visa. The government was issuing exit visas to Egyptians wishing to travel abroad. No visa, no travel! Visas were issued only intermittently. There was no way of knowing when the door to the outside world would slam shut again. Leaving the country was a difficult affair for Egyptians in those days. Adequate letters of invitation from friends or relatives abroad had to be provided—letters in which the friends or relatives promised to support the applicant, as travelers would be permitted to take only a nominal sum of money out of the country. And, if the visa materialized, air travel would have to be on EgyptAir.

Some of these people were not even certain that they would actually be traveling. But that did not seem to matter. They wanted the freedom that the visa represented. And they had come fully prepared to wait for hours, to elbow their way into the building, to run from one office to the next in search of stamps, signatures, and seals, and once all this was done, to struggle out of the building, with the visa in hand—or almost in hand.

Among them there were well-to-do Egyptians whose economic assets were under assault from the new regime—Egyptians who, in the eyes of the country's new leaders, were suspect for being too enmeshed in the old order, or not Egyptian enough.

In a sense, the country's new leaders were correct. There were certainly those in the crowd waiting in front of the Mugama that morning who were imbued with a sense of superiority by virtue of their social background and considered themselves a cut above ordinary Egyptians; and those who, from the outset, had only contempt for the new leaders; and those who had turned bitter because they felt dispossessed even of their Egyptianness, as their loyalty and commitment to the country came under attack daily from the new leaders.

One of the first to arrive in front of the Mugama the day so many Egyptians flocked to its doors in the hope of obtaining an exit visa was Mrs. T, a slight, middle-aged woman with a parasol in hand—a vestige of this old order that the new one was so keen on dismantling. Though without a shred of old regime elitism, this lady stood out, paradoxically, as a caricature of the much-desired old order and its western orientation. She was an Egyptian who had lived all her life in the country yet spoke its language very poorly, and could neither read it nor write it—one of those Egyptians who spoke virtually only French, thought and felt only in French; an Egyptian who, by the standards of the new regime, did not belong in the country. Of that Mrs. T herself needed no convincing. She was quite aware that people like her had become anachronistic in post-1952 Egypt. She also knew that the old order of things had been both unfair and unsustainable; so she was not altogether opposed to the changes that the country was undergoing. She had that rare quality of being open-eyed about the world she belonged to—as open-eyed as one can be when change is about to engulf one's world. Her lucidity, sometimes but not always a blessing, did not make life any easier for her, as it intensified her sense that the new Egypt taking shape was leaving her in an untenable situation.

Anxious by nature, Mrs. T was full of big and small anxieties the morning she arrived at the Mugama so early. Her chief concern had to do with a major issue hanging over her. She was at a difficult crossroads. Were she to get the magic visa, she could start her life afresh in Geneva, working in a bookstore to be opened soon by a friend of hers. To be offered employment at her age was, she realized, a rare opportunity. But would she have the energy and courage to take that step. . .?

The more immediate reason for Mrs. T's nervousness that morning was the prospect of having to deal with the Mugama's bureaucracy. Any time she was about to find herself in a situation where her deficiency in Arabic was bound to become evident, she worried that some bureaucrat might quiz her—even if not in an ill-meaning way—about her lamentable Arabic. Her fears had some basis: that was happening more and more often. It usually went this way: "So you're Egyptian." the bureaucrats would say, sounding surprised, after looking at her identification papers. "It must be by marriage!" they would declare, only to exclaim, once they had looked more closely at her documents, "Your father was Egyptian and you were born here!" Then, some would conclude, "So you must have lived much of your life abroad!" While others would ask—sometimes innocently but not always so innocently—"But then tell me why is your Arabic so poor and so foreign sounding?"

How to begin explaining to them her appalling Arabic? Blame her Syro-Lebanese father's fixation on France, even though the man himself, a journalist, had been as fluent in Arabic as in French? Tell them that, throughout her childhood, her father had heaped French books on French history upon her—never once a book on Egyptian history? Blame it on her mother's Swiss origins? These were not good enough excuses. After all, she had lived all of her life in Egypt, so why hadn't she learned the language properly, later on in life? Sure, it was a very difficult language. And yes, she was not particularly gifted with languages. Still, she had been remiss. She had done absolutely nothing to lessen her foreignness in her own country, behaving all along as if she thought it was a lost cause—now clearly a self-fulfilling prophecy.

While waiting for the Mugama to open, Mrs. T made no attempt at conversation with those around her; nor did she pay any attention to their animated talk. Every so often she would glance at a page or two of the book she had brought along, Marguerite Duras' *Moderato Cantabile*. She didn't try to read properly: she was too nervous for that.

The Mugama finally opened its doors slightly after eight and the crowd of impatient applicants thronged the building. Mrs. T was fortunate—she was among the first to enter—yet her anxiety did not ease. On the contrary, it became more acute. For a brief moment she thought of turning back, but the swarm of bodies behind her pushed her further inside. "The die is cast," she told herself. And, all of a sudden, she was determined to get that visa. She felt that it was imperative for her to decide for herself, visa in hand, whether or not to leave Egypt and give up for good a life she had grown uncomfortable with but was—for better or worse—accustomed to.

Muhammad al-Fakharani

from *An Interval for Bewilderment*

AFTER YOUR IMMEDIATE EXIT from the main entrance to Misr Railway Station you find the entrance to the metro station and a relatively big glass kiosk with its own pay phone, that sells cookies, cigarettes, Doritos, chips, chocolate, and cold drinks to students and passengers.

You will not make a phone call at the kiosk because he rips you off on the number of minutes . . . you don't know how he does that. You will not buy cookies or chips because they are not filling and because the kiosk sells its merchandise for twenty-five piasters more than the real price . . . you don't quite know why. Is it because it's at the entrance to the station? Big deal!

After you walk past the kiosk, you hesitate for a few seconds: how will you walk past the cabs that have been washed and lined up side by side, waiting for someone other than yourself with an expensive briefcase and an affluent look? The drivers ignore you and you ignore them back. You walk quickly through the line of cabs. You look intently straight ahead, squinting your eyes enough to seem like someone interested in deciphering the number on a twenty-five-piaster or, maximum, fifty-piaster-ticket bus.

After you leave the train station, the kiosk, and the cabs behind, you expect to enter immediately into a scene where a specimen of people that reflect the spirit of the city roams around.

This is what all big cities do, especially the older ones: they greet you with a very open spirit that immediately makes you feel their boisterous heartbeat before all else.

While you expect, indeed wish, for this, you also somehow know what has happened to that spirit and that heart that you mean. Your eyes are assaulted by a big ridiculous space that you never quite got used to or accepted. That's why it surprises you every time you see it.

This ridiculous space is in the form of a circle surrounded by two walls—God damn them both—that are a meter and a half high and to which you can see no beginning or end. You are certain that it's another labyrinth. . . .

Labyrinths . . . the only well-made thing around here.

These damned things, and they are so many, teach people to cuss and use rotten language.

Now you have to jump over the wall or walk around it, only to find another, higher, and more stupid wall. Don't cuss now. You can do this a lot later. Don't worry.

You remember two side-by-side openings that have been made possible by the removal of four bars from the wall by the crushed commoners who were used to being imprisoned over the long periods of oppression and developed the taste for escape . . . escape from everything.

When you emerge from the labyrinth, you will see the statue of Ramses—the owner of the square—before they had moved him, standing informally in a way that safeguarded the humanity of a king surrounded by poor people with whom he had a real friendship, especially Umm Hanan, who considered herself his partner in the space through a secret contract between them. On the back of the contract she added her marriage to him.

Every day before dawn she would set up her tea joint in the small garden to the right of Ramses, where she could see him well without any obstruction and from where he could reach down and grab a glass of tea.

Umm Hanan unfolds a family-size Chipsy cardboard box on the withering grass. She occupies it with her huge buttocks that overflow to the sides of the box. Her dress is tight in the back along her vertebrae and obstinately pulled up between her breasts.

Tanned lips mutter white morning greetings to Umm Hanan; wet hands line up extended over the flames of the kerosene heater; a small kanaka is dipped into the boiling water on the heater; the water is then emptied into clean glasses with two spoons of sugar and a spoonful of tea.

Umm Hanan's clients are the drivers of the cabs, microbuses, Peugeot taxis, and buses, wretched construction workers, traffic policemen, some students, and passengers awaiting deliverance that is hard to come by. . . .

Ramses. . . .

You don't stand a chance with Umm Hanan and your friends now that they have moved you from Bab al-Hadid/Ramses Square to the New Egyptian Museum by the pyramids.

What is this strange place, you wonder?

A museum?

A slick, air-conditioned, perfumed place. The sun will not touch you there, nor will the smoke and dust gather on your face. People will treat you with what is known as 'civilized behavior' and will bestow upon you the respect of which you are worthy.

They will treat you with disgusting fineness. Will you be able to stand that?

You are no longer there.

One has to pay to see you.

But you will not feel your glory when all these faces look at you and whisper words you will never know. You feel something strange, as if you were an antique, a spectacle, or just a statue of an old king.

If you try to run away you will never succeed.

You have been deprived of Ramses Street.

When you were among the people, you used to leave your cement pedestal and walk happily among the oppressed. You were just like them: you would eat sunflower seeds and taamiya sandwiches; you would crouch by the newspaper vendor and leaf through the old magazines; you would quickly tear off a colored page that you would stick in your back pocket; you would get on any bus or microbus bumper, where the wind would whisk your face and your hair would fluff up into curls; you would touch the shoulder of a girl in a hurry or brush up against her breast in the crowd; you would make a pass at a pretty one, saying, "I dig you, fair one," or "I adore you, golden one"; you would try your luck with Sayeda; you would show her the tip of a ten-pound note in your pocket and tell her that you are at her disposal and that your apartment is nearby; you would enter any hashish den to fix your head with an eighth of hash; you would treat yourself to a plate of hot kushari, after which you would be filled with that warm desire for your partner Umm Hanan and would take a special glass of tea from her hand.

You eye her seductive tanned thigh.

She eyes your impressive pharaonic erection.

Suddenly you hide your face between her breasts. You lose yourself until she absorbs your anxiety; you lie down on the ground to clear your head on her lap.

At night, you used to steal into the small garden; you would lie with Hanan underneath her blanket, or in the arms of any one of the oppressed and sleep. If you felt hungry when you were penniless, you would stick yourself into their midst and share their food.

Your laughter would mix with theirs; you would wipe your tears on anyone's sleeve or the edge of a nearby dress.

With ease you would pull down your wraparound to piss or masturbate without anyone paying attention.

In the museum, forget the taste of tea, of kushari, ful, taamiya, mixed pickles, fitir, mish, black honey, sugar cane juice, the smell of liver, sausage, the fix of hash, the noise, the crowds, Umm Hanan's snort and her loud laughter.

You will not see the posters of film stars, the music, the ads.

You will be deprived even of the touch of a hand on your body.

No one will come close enough for you to feel alive and throbbing.

You are not allowed to move . . . to speak . . . to breathe . . . to wink . . . to cry . . . to sweat . . . to wash . . . to starve . . . to crave water . . . to feel . . . and sex, of course, until you are transformed into a long piece of stone.

They bestow upon you a title that makes you chuckle. King.

King? What is that?!

No one will keep you company during your night that begins very early: very quiet, very dark in a frightening way you are not used to. Are you afraid? Do you cry?

Umm Hanan is not here. No other woman will arouse you ever: her tea, her warmth, her thighs, her breasts, her desire for you, her warmth toward you.

Instead of you in the middle of the square, they now have stupid cement blocks in which they planted very short grass and prohibited the people from using the space.

Your friends have been disbanded.

Umm Hanan has moved to the nearby Sabtiya car park. She will not have a problem finding clients as soon as she sets up her tea corner. She just needs to practice her snorting for a few nights to establish her presence in the place and secure her tea joint. . . .

Poor Ramses.

The square still has your name: Ramses Square . . . until when?

You will not have a chance to see Umm Hanan, or Hanan/Hannouna, or Sharnubi, or the rest of your friends.

They will not have a chance to see you, either.

They miss you a lot.

Your friends.

You miss them a tremendous lot, almost to death.

Translated by Samia Mehrez

Robert Solé

from *Birds of Passage*

IT WAS THE MOST charming hotel in the Middle East. Founded by an Englishman in 1841 and rebuilt half a century later, when the premises were extended and equipped with electric lighting, Shepheard's incorporated the ancient palace in which Napoleon Bonaparte had once installed his headquarters. The management had carefully preserved the sycomore behind which General Kléber's assassin had hidden, and the splendid grounds, with their palms and banana trees, were home to a score of frisking antelope.

The hotel's famous terrace was guarded on the street side by two small stone sphinxes purloined from a temple at Memphis. It made an exceptional observation post. Édouard Dhellemmes spent the whole of Monday morning there, sipping chilled beer and watching Cairo parade past before his eyes.

A small crowd was permanently encamped at the foot of the steps: cabbies, guides, monkey showmen, beggars of every description. Water carriers trudged along the street bent double beneath the weight of their bulging goatskins. They were quickly overtaken by effendis in Turkish jackets, erect and ultra-dignified figures mounted on donkeys. From time to time a shiny limousine came gliding up to the curb, and the Shepheard's bellboys, with a deferential air, would hurriedly open the door for some pasha or other.

The hotel's English lady guests missed no detail of this spectacle. They would rise and crane their necks to watch coffins being borne along in the midst of hired mourners in black veils. Two minutes later they would be back on their feet, all of a flutter, to observe the arrival of a luxurious landau preceded by barefoot grooms who ran out into the roadway brandishing canes and yelling at pedestrians to stand aside. . . .

"So you're staying at Shepheard's. . . ."

Édouard Dhellemmes thought he detected a mixture of approval and envy in my grandfather's expression.

"We used to go there on Sundays when I was a child," Georges said pensively.

His father, Élias Batrakani, had then been employed by a Syrian merchant in the Muski district. No businessman himself, he watched others growing rich around him. Élias was not mercenary. He simply liked to observe money at close quarters, to toy with and talk about it.

That was why, every Sunday afternoon after his mulukhiya with onions, my great-grandfather would walk his family past Shepheard's and down Shubra Street. It was a way of rubbing shoulders with affluence, a free show that would help to cultivate his children's tastes.

Stationed outside the hotel in the shade of a mimosa tree, the Batrakanis would scan the terrace with the two little sphinxes, hoping to spot some Austrian prince in transit or some Italian diva on tour. They pictured all the marvels concealed behind those apricot-colored walls: the arabesques, the Persian carpets, the gilded bathtubs in which wealthy Englishwomen wallowed while listening to the call of the muezzin.

"The sun will be setting soon," Linda Batrakani would say after a while. "If we want to go to Shubra. . . ."

Having hailed a cab and negotiated a fare, Élias would hoist fat Nando on to the seat beside the driver, and they would trot the length of the famous thoroughfare in which all Cairo's most luxurious carriages assembled at the close of day.

Shubra Street was a broad avenue that ran along the Nile, flanked by ancient sycamore trees whose branches joined hands to form a vault overhead. To be seen there were princes out riding on horseback, their white silk kufiyas embroidered with gold thread, or teams of thoroughbred mares drawing carriages in which black, frock-coated eunuchs watched over conveys of harem women, their doe-eyed faces screened from view by transparent veils.

All along the avenue, Élias Batrakani would tell stories in Franco-Arabic, laced with Italian exclamations, in his fine baritone voice. They were wondrous tales replete with gold and tears, exciting anecdotes in which the protagonists—princes, princesses, or slaves—fulfilled their destinies aboard majestic feluccas or behind impenetrable mashrabiyas. Élias did not have the dispassionate approach of the ordinary storyteller. His stories were still fresh, having unfolded on his doorstep some years earlier; he himself trembled with pleasure or dismay as he recounted them. And if he sometimes exaggerated, it may simply have been for the sake of veracity, of fidelity to his own awakened dreams.

Georges never tired of hearing about 'Ain al-Hayat, the young orphan girl who was given a home by Khedive Ismail and destined to marry his son, Hussein, the future sultan. He knew the story of their wedding in every little detail.

"The khedive wanted to marry off four of his children at the same time," Élias would say. "He decreed that the wedding celebrations should go on for a whole month. Throughout the weeks preceding the signature of the marriage contracts, countless trunks and chests filled with crockery, silver, and precious objects—necklaces, bracelets, tiaras, chibouks, censers—could be seen arriving at the four palaces. These marvels were displayed on silk cushions and protected against theft with steel mesh. Then, for four days, they were paraded through the streets of Cairo under escort, to enable us to feast our eyes on them. I've no need to tell you how sumptuous they looked!"

We, too, were treated to these stories several decades later. They had been enriched in the interim with a number of episodes that rendered them still more coherent, still more true . . . .

During the 1860s, after their arrival in Egypt, Élias and Linda Batrakani had seen the modern city take shape before their eyes. Of course, Cairo had already ceased to be the big, chaotic medieval village whose sole horse-drawn carriage caused panic in the streets whenever it emerged from Shubra Palace. Muhammad Ali and his successors had removed the mountains of garbage that used to rot away in the middle of the city. They had installed road-sweeping, water and lighting systems, drained the Azbakiya marshes, built a number of palaces beside the Nile, and enclosed them with plantations of palm trees and carobs, mulberries and acacias.

Generally speaking, however, Cairo had retained its ancient structure intact. The capital's outward appearance, if not its character, did not really change until the time of Khedive Ismail. "My country is in Africa no longer. We form part of Europe. . . . "

Translated from the French by John Brownjohn

Ihsan Abdel Quddus

from *Let the Sun Shine*

THE CAR HEADED TOWARD Lazughli Square, then turned on Qasr al-Aini Street, then went off to Qasr al-Nil Bridge. Ahmad started humming the song "Mal il-hawa yamma mal" (Love Came By, Mom, It Came By), then quickly felt self-conscious and stopped singing. He looked at the back of the driver's head as if he feared he may have been listening to him singing. He looked out of the car window and looked at the passersby without really seeing them: they were like ghosts to his wandering eyes.

He arrived at the Gezira Club. He got out and paid the driver, then he turned around and found that the club controller was eyeing him. He hesitated: should he raise his hand and greet him? He didn't and then thought it was too late to greet him. So he walked in front of him, knitting his brow to look more distinguished. He walked toward the courts and strolled on the open lawn. He loved walking on the grass; it felt as if he were walking on silk cushions, a path paved by God himself; he felt more human than when he walked on asphalt. . . .

He headed toward the lounge chairs that were scattered everywhere under the willow trees. It was a quiet area of the club frequented by the more elderly members, where they could read or digest their lunch in peace or sleep.

Ahmad strolled past the elderly club members who were lounging on the long chairs, looking for a seat for himself and feeling heavy: he felt he was shouldering more than he can stand. He felt even heavier and he stopped walking suddenly. He knew why he had come to the club. He did not come to lounge on a chair among these old people, nor did he come to read a book. He came to look for a girl, a particular girl. He knew that.

He had spent many days watching her. More than a month and a half had passed since he had first seen her and been attracted to her. He had started going to the club to watch her from a distance. He used to feel the quiet, beauty, and calm of his soul every time he saw her. He started imagining the world in which she lived. Sometimes he would imagine her world like that of his sisters: a stable, conservative family life. He used to ask himself: why didn't he bring his sisters to the club like her? He used to feel danger when this question came to his mind, as if part of his mind were rebelling against him. No . . . his sisters could not possibly come to the club. They cannot be like this girl; they cannot sit among men like her as if they were in a coffee shop. His sisters were liberated: the eldest had joined the Faculty of Science, the second was in the Faculty of Letters, and the third was studying music. But their freedom still did not mean that they could become members at the Gezira Club, where they would spend their day lounging around and showing off in front of the gaze of men like himself.

He did not feel any kind of revolt as he compared his sisters and the girl of the club: not a revolt against his sisters nor one against the girl of the club. He was simply expressing his opinion about this life and that one. His many readings had convinced him that there were many kinds of societies in life, many kinds of traditions; that there was no good or bad society, but simply good and bad in one society, whether that was in a conservative or liberal context. There were no right traditions and wrong traditions, but right and wrong in every tradition: to dance was at once right and wrong, not to dance was similarly not right or wrong. If his mother believed that her daughters should not go to the club, there were other mothers who believed that their daughters should not go to university, and others still who believed that their daughters should not be allowed to look out of the window!

He just felt that his mother and sisters lived in another world, one that was different from the world of the Gezira Club girls. When he used to leave his home to go to the club, he would feel that he was traveling from one country to another, from Egypt to Italy. He used to love going to Italy, but he preferred living in Egypt.

All he wanted was to be able to go to the club and watch this girl from a distance. He watched her carefully: when she was with her girlfriends, when she went to the ladies' room and came back, when she moved from the sun into the shade, when she was joined by young men at her table. What did these young men say to her? What did they talk about? He used to try to eavesdrop, but couldn't hear a thing. But he was convinced that the table at which this girl sat, even with all the young men, was more respectable than the rest of the tables where other girls sat.

The girl would end her outing at the club and leave, and he would also happily head home as if he had been armed with a personal boost that would help him survive. He didn't think beyond that. He would think of her sometimes when he was home or when he was in his office at the Pension Administration. But it was always an image that was more like a film he had just finished watching. He would return to the club the next day to watch her again as if he were watching a new film.

Translated by Samia Mehrez

Hala El Badry

from *Swimming in a Hole*

I USED TO ADORE that place. I used to prefer it to both home and school. Even though our home was a happy and comfortable one, even though I loved my school, I still felt that my life was there. I was so attached to the place that it became the main axis around which all other details revolved.

The first time I went there, I was a little girl who loved swimming and hoped to join a team that would make a champion out of her. The club that brought us together was of a special kind. It was not a club for the elite, but it also wasn't a club for the more popular classes. It was a middle-ground club that brought together a mix of several classes.

For the more affluent middle-class families, it represented a kind of transit to the more aristocratic clubs of which they craved to become members. It was a waiting room before they could catch the train to the bourgeois clubs.

The somewhat lower class members represented the core of activities in our club. Socially they were intimidated, but in the realm of sports they dashed forward to the challenge.

The aristocrats represented a kind of symbolic membership. They predominantly belonged to other clubs that were more suitable for their class, where they practiced their favorite sports.

The club was situated at the edge of a popular neighborhood in Cairo where a battle between the soldiers of the French Expedition to Egypt and the Egyptian people had taken place.

White, low-income high-rises surrounded the club, as if to protect it but also to become its main and faithful supporting audience. When a tournament took place in the club, the balconies would fill up with fans, and so would the surrounding walls fill up with youth from the low-income high-rises.

The other wall, opposite this one, was situated in another new neighborhood where the aristocrats resided, and where there were beautiful villas with gardens so big that the wall of one villa ran parallel to two-thirds of the wall of the club.

Even though I spent my entire childhood and youth daily at the club, I did not know all of its surroundings. Was it a producer's villa, as they said? Or did it belong to a rich old man who lived alone? All I know was that I never saw any of the inhabitants of the villa during that entire period. We used to call it 'The Mysterious Villa.'

The third wall was situated on a quiet street that separated the club from a big hospital that was part of the aristocratic neighborhood. The Nile was a few steps away from the club and it separated the lower-class neighborhood from Cairo's most affluent one.

The gate to the club was in the quiet neighborhood. The main building was made up of two levels. The first level comprised the office of the director, a reception hall, the restaurant, and a spacious winter sitting room with a wide terrace; the second level comprised the library, the billiards room, and a big balcony that was sometimes used for weddings.

From the balcony on the second level, we could see the swimming pool: a small twenty-five-meter pool that was divided into eight lanes. These were dominated by the diving tower, a three-level structure that was divided into five-, seven-, and ten-meter levels consecutively. One of the sides of the pool was built in the shape of a stadium to allow the largest number of spectators to follow the swimming competitions.

The water in the pool was grass-green in the sunlight; it turned olive green with sunset and then even darker still, like the seaweed that grows in the depths of the ocean.

The water seemed heavy from whichever angle you looked at it, just like the water of the Nile. Every time I looked at it, I imagined that it was an immovable body. Even if you were to look at the water from the ten-meter level of the diving structure, you would not see the bottom of the pool; rather, you would see the reflection of the sun's rays into nothingness.

This color was due to the stagnant water because the pool was not equipped with a filter to purify it. The supervisors had to change the water regularly every Monday and add chlorine daily.

An aluminum pipe with holes at regular intervals ran alongside the edge of the pool and spouted water that transformed the swimming pool into a beautiful water fountain that sprayed water from all sides into the middle. This only happened on special occasions.

The swimming pool reflected the class structure at the small club. The club team comprised a number of sons and daughters of the new class that was competing with the old aristocracy. It also counted some children from the lower classes.

The main garden was situated to the left of the swimming pool, where tables were scattered and used by the non-athletic members of the club, since the team members were always in their respective courts until rest time. During the summer the tables were shaded with bright-colored umbrellas.

The main garden led to the soccer field. It was a small field used by the club's second-rate football team. Behind the football stadium there were cement passageways that constituted the golf course.

Our club was small and simple. Even though it was small it did not feel crowded. It felt peaceful, unlike bigger clubs. Simplicity was its main characteristic; in particular, it lacked the feminine social presence that constituted the core of aristocratic clubs. Each member in our club practiced a sport. There was no time for worthless gossip that only served to hurt others. Rumor was not one of our club's characteristics, nor were slander and intrigue. The youth had left their stamp on the club: mirth, and innocent love stories that were mostly secret. That is why one could say that our club succeeded in safeguarding the original raison d'être of clubs, namely, the spirit of the game and a healthy social space for both sexes to spend their free time.

Young groups had their own unwritten traditions and laws. A given love story could remain known only to the members of one group, who all made sure it remained a secret.

All the familiar harassment known to bigger clubs was simply rejected from the society of the small club. Romantic love was the only accepted thing, along with healthy, innocent friendships among the youth.

Gradually, I began to be integrated into this new milieu after I had been watching from a distance. In the beginning, I was drawn to the swimming pool, for that was the reason my father had intervened to get me a membership in the small club, since the big club had not yet finished constructing its swimming pool and I just couldn't wait and my father could stand my nagging no more.

Such was the beginning of my story with the club.

Translated by Samia Mehrez

Ihab Abdel Hamid

from *Failed Lovers*

WHERE SHALL I BEGIN?

Let me begin here and now.

I will say that my life, by any standards, is depressing. First of all, I no longer see myself as a great writer whose fame will spread like an epidemic all over the world. Before, I used to set free the bounds of my dreams so they could take off to wherever they wanted. I used to practice by myself the speech I would deliver in celebration of my Nobel prize for literature. Please do not laugh. This is an embarrassing confession.

But it is the truth. Yes, I had dreams and I believed that they would, no doubt, come true: that I would become a famous writer whose works are translated into a dozen languages; that women of a different color would fall in love with me; that I would travel to the East and the West and place them in a bundle that I would hang on the wall of my room full of incense. . . .

The day before yesterday, I went to a dance party at the Greek Club. The spacious hall was full; the lights were dim, the music loud, and the young crowd was ready to dance all night. I looked my best in my white shirt and jeans. I was perfumed, shaved, and confident. I found myself sitting at a front table with a bottle of scotch and an interesting woman. He greeted me and hugged me and asked me to join him. Even though I desperately needed an old friend, I could not accept his invitation. I told myself that this must be the outcome of drunken generosity and, at the end of the day, it wasn't really appropriate for me to sit with someone who knew I used to sleep with his wife. I sat far away and the drinking partners came by one by one to greet me and I started drinking.

Damn alcohol! The first drink was enough to set off the depression that was stored inside me for a thousand years. I had several drinks until I embarrassed myself. I went to the dance floor. I tried to dance with Laila; she looked very sexy but she tried to avoid me and danced with another beautiful woman who turned away every time I tried to move close to her. Not important. I tried with another girl, and a third, but they all moved away from me. I dragged myself to the restroom and looked at the mirror. Everything looked normal and I looked handsome. So why did they move away from me?

Perhaps, Salma, you were the best one to understand. Girls are afraid of emptiness; they are searching for a full man who would overflow into them. They would never be attracted to an empty heart or a dead soul.

When I came back from the bathroom I understood that truth. I suddenly realized that I was like a sick dog. You know, alcohol helps transform dreams into colored images. At that moment, I could have barked. I could have put my tail between my legs in shame. But I sat in a corner on the floor and started scratching my skin and weeping. Abu Isba' came by to console me. He sat by my side and patted my head with his four-fingered hand. I tossed my head on his shoulder and wept. I could not stop myself from throwing up on his trousers. I cannot remember what happened later, but I decided that I would commit suicide next time if this drama were to reoccur.

Translated by Samia Mehrez

Mahmoud Al-Wardani

from *Mall Music*

I HAD ARRIVED AT what resembled a spacious, dazzlingly lit hall with an archway that led inside, where tall ushers in dark suits and pastel ties were scattered, having painted broad smiles on their faces that revealed their teeth. It was a huge reception hall where men and women stood in groups, submerged in conversation and gestures. The space was filled with seats, armchairs, and sofas, but most of the people conversed standing.

In the beginning, I couldn't believe it, even though it was impossible for me to misidentify the smell. It was, without a doubt, the smell of ful. And here in the entrance to the hall was a small ful cart around which people were gathered, yelling and snatching the sandwiches from the smiling, heavy, fair-skinned man with a spotless chef's hat and vest. It was a real ful cart with big yellow brass ful containers. Behind it, definitely, hid several workers who were making the sandwiches and handing them to the heavy fair-skinned man who, in turn, handed them over to the hungry clients. I stood among them, for the smell of ful was irresistible.

I started looking at the walls, where similar-looking posters were hung here and there. I moved closer to one and began to discover what was actually taking place. They were announcing a conference, under the auspices of the Ministry of Culture, about folklore and social change in rural areas. There were names of well-known Egyptian and foreign personalities. Only then did I understand what was happening: the mall rented out its halls just like shops and wedding reception halls. How lucky I was! This way, I could kill time until eight o'clock, when the Two Cats nightclub was due to open.

When I spotted a great baladi coffee shop that served tea and shisha, I walked right in and called the waiter. The men were wearing suits and the women were in morning dresses and suits. They sat around me talking loudly. Men and women alike were smoking shisha all the time. The smell of apple tobacco filled the coffee shop as I sipped my glass of tea that the well-mannered waiter had brought me, as I waited for another waiter to bring the shisha. The women radiated an intimate, even exciting, ambiance in the coffee shop, especially in their clothes that revealed their arms and legs. I tried to resist staring at their bodies as I whiffed their perfume. The idea wasn't bad, but the most important thing was that it would offer me several hours before they opened the nightclub.

I couldn't resist smiling when I saw the garbanzo-bean cart in a nearby corner with vapors rising from its huge brass container where people had gathered around in boisterous conversation. In the opposite corner, I also spotted a kushari cart! Yes, a kushari cart! But it was naturally bigger than the garbanzo-bean cart. There were big bowls of rice, macaroni, and lentils. The vendor stood behind the cart plunking his aluminum utensils. The only thing we were missing in order to really be in the heart of an authentic Egyptian alley inside the mall, I said to myself, was a cotton-candy vendor.

As I sat in the coffee shop smoking my shisha, I noticed an unusual commotion: people started to get up and leave their seats, so I got up with them and looked in the direction they were heading. Gradually, I heard the sound of the mizmar and the tabla approaching. Then the organizers entered with broad smiles on their faces, followed by the mizmar troupe that was, itself, followed by a real horse and a rider who held the reins and swung them from side to side as the horse danced to the music of the mizmar, lifting its front and rear legs playfully. The audience applauded when the cameramen approached with their high-beam lights as the photographers jumped around with their shining flashbulbs. With great elegance, the delegated authority figure cut the inauguration ribbon, and instantly hands went wild with applause. He turned to greet the audience with a broad smile and a nod. He looked as if he had forgotten something, so he turned around again and bent over two children who were dressed as peasant girls with bright-colored head scarves. He took the bouquets of flowers from their hands and proceeded inside the hall with his entourage. They were all wearing dark suits, but I noticed their bright-colored ties glowing under the flashbulbs.

I found myself following the crowd until they got to an auditorium, so I followed in their footsteps. When they were seated, I took the first available seat, like them. They did not waste time: they turned off all the lights except for one spotlight that dominated the front of the stage. There was a man in a black suit and bow tie smiling with a gleaming face. He spoke for a while and then raised his voice as he greeted the delegated authority figure; there was a thunder of applause and the stage was dimmed for a moment.

The curtain opened to a group of peasant girls who were belly dancing. They were followed by a second row. They were all wearing colored costumes with various shades of orange that exposed their slender fair legs. I counted them: there were seven dancers in the first row and another seven in the second one. Their bodies were very similar and they were all quite slim. The two rows made way for a solo dancer who swayed slowly wearing a light, sky-blue gallabiya that uncharacteristically revealed part of her breasts and her thighs. She was the most beautiful. She came upstage and belly danced alone, as the spotlights illuminated various parts of her body that shook flexibly as she danced across the stage. Her headscarf slid and revealed part of her hair. Slowly I began to realize why I felt there was something wrong. The music was perfect and the dancers convincing, despite their exaggeratedly slender bodies. But the solo dancer had straight blond hair that fell in locks over her shoulders. I focused my gaze and discovered that they mostly had colored eyes. This was not an Egyptian troupe. Something about the dancers was not right; I immediately felt it in the way they danced: the colored eyes and the blond hair that showed from underneath their head scarves.

This is undoubtedly a Russian troupe. I had heard about similar troupes in Cairo that had specialized in five-star-hotel entertainment. In fact, I had read in the papers that these troupes have become a threat to national ones because they were more popular with audiences, who preferred fair-skinned blondes with colored eyes. I also remember having read, in the leftist weekly that I occasionally buy, that these Russian troupes include girls who have studied ballet since their childhood at the Russian people's expense, only to end up in this situation after the fall of what used to be the Soviet Union.

The audience had been swept off its feet by the beautiful slender peasant girls and kept applauding enthusiastically. The dancers were moved by this and redoubled the greeting by showing more of their well-formed thighs, while the solo dancer exaggerated her back-bending movements in what seemed very convoluted and difficult movements. At the same time, she revealed more of her breasts, and kept winking and making blatant sexual gestures as she danced.

The troupe finished its inaugural performance and greeted the audience, which continued to applaud even after the curtain came down. So the peasant girls came back for a second call in front of the curtain. I saw their features clearly; they looked very young, teenagers despite the heavy makeup that they had smeared all over their faces.

Their departure apparently signaled that of the inaugurating authority figure with his bodyguards, who surrounded him so closely they almost suffocated him, until they exited completely amid feverish applause. Soon the curtain opened to a panel table, to which those whose names were called by the man in the white bow tie ascended. They were five: two women and three men, among them a European or an American with a flushed face, wearing a suit like everyone else.

They started a very serious discussion and consulted the papers in front of them. There was a man whose role was to preside over the session. He alerted those around him that they each had ten minutes to present their points of view, followed by a discussion with the audience. But in less than ten minutes they became quite rowdy. I finally understood that the topic of the session was what the chair of the panel had called "Social Change in the Egyptian Village and its Effect on Songs and Popular Sayings."

Translated by Samia Mehrez

Khaled Al Khamissi

from *Taxi*

"Do you go to the cinema?" I asked him.

"The cinema, ah, it's been a million years since I went to the cinema. Wait a second. I remember the last time I went to the cinema was in 1984. It was Cinema Cairo or the Pigale in Emadeddin Street.

"After that life really minced me up. I became like Faragallah mincemeat and since then I haven't been to the cinema or the theater, although I used to go to the cinema often at the end of the 70s. I was living on Geish Street. You know Mahmoud, the guy who sells salted fish?"

"Yes, I know him," I said.

"That's the best place in the world for salted fish."

"And you were living next door?"

"Yes, I was living right next door," the driver said.

"There in Geish Street there was the Hollywood Cinema that used to show five films in the program—two foreign and one Arabic, then it would repeat the two. We used to watch three films and then the repeats, and other times after the three films were over we would cross the street and on the other side there was Cinema Misr, may it rest in peace and all the others too. That one was both winter and summer. The open-air summer cinema was upstairs. We would pay the man anything and jump over and watch the repeats at Cinema Misr. Those were the days. At that time a ticket was five piasters."

"Do you still remember the films you used to see?"

"There are films one can't forget. My favorite was *Red Sun* with Charles Bronson. Bronson had a look from under his hat, like this, that we would sit and imitate. Remember that film . . . ? How come? In that film he had caught a Japanese guy and he didn't trust him so before they went to sleep he tied his shoes to the laces of the Japanese guy's. The Japanese guy tried to escape. He walked a little, as far as the laces would go—Bronson had let them out a bit—and then he fell down and Bronson woke up.

"As for my favorite Egyptian film, that would be *Bus Driver* with Nour al-Sherif. That I've seen ten times. There was also a great American film, but I don't remember who was in it, called *Duel of the Space Monsters*, and of course *Godzilla* and *The Atomic Monster* and Bruce Lee's *The Big Boss* and the Indian film *Two Friends*. When *White Elephant* came out we went to Cinema Chark in Sayeda Zaynab to see it."

"Didn't you go to the theater?" I asked.

"What do you mean? I used to go the Vanguard Theater and we would get tickets for ten piasters. I was just crazy about art. Say what, you a believer?"

"There's no god but God."

"I was part of a theatrical group. It was called the New Revolutionary Group and it was in Galal Street."

"Where's that, Galal Street?"

"That's a side street of Emadeddin Street, right in front of Cinema Pigale. One day I was eating kushari in Goha's—that's the most famous kushari shop in Cairo—and I saw lots of young guys standing around and I found out that they were from the New Revolutionary Group. They told me they were a group from which many very big actors had graduated, like Khairia Ahmed, and they were part of the Ministry of Culture."

"And then?" I prompted.

"I applied to join and started doing rehearsals. There was one scene where we come into a hotel and sit down and shout out: 'People of God, you here! People of God, you here!' Then they told us as well that we had to bring clothes from home."

I said to myself, this group could never have been part of the Ministry of Culture.

The driver continued, "We had to bring the clothes and the customers too, so I quit."

"And what happened after that?" I asked.

"I don't know what happened. The world changed, or it was me that changed. Say what, you a believer?"

"There is no god but God."

"This is the first time I've spoken about this. I hadn't realized that I haven't seen a film in about twenty-something years."

"And all these memories, will they make you go to the cinema again?" I asked.

"Just by chance, I was taking a fare about a week ago to the Sawiris Tower on the river and I heard that a cinema ticket now costs twenty-five pounds, that means exactly one thousand times the price only twenty years ago. Imagine, one thousand times. You know, sir, even the expensive cinemas, until after 1980, the biggest of them was sixteen-and-a-half piasters for a ticket . . . like Cinema Metro, the Radio, Qasr al-Nil, Cairo, and Miami.

"And now most of our cinemas have gone and closed. The Hollywood's turned into something else, the Misr, the Rio in Bab al-Louk, the Star on

Kheirat Street, the Isis, the Ahli, and the Hilal summer cinema in Sayeda Zaynab, and very many others, have all closed.

"Anyway, what I've seen I've seen and what I haven't seen I might as well not have seen. I've had my time and it's the kids' turn. They've never been to the cinema or the theater, and they never will. They watch satellite TV at the coffee shop downstairs, God help them. Personally, I don't know what will grow in their brains, other than cactus."

Translated by Jonathan Wright

Waguih Ghali

from *Beer in the Snooker Club*

I LEFT AND WENT to Groppi's. I drank whiskey and ate peanuts, watching the sophisticated crowd and feeling happy that my aunt had refused to give me the money. I had asked simply because my conscience was nagging. It was something I vaguely had to do but had kept putting off. Soon Omar and Jameel came in, then Yehia, Fawzi, and Ismail. Groppi's is perhaps one of the most beautiful places to drink whiskey in. The bar is under a large tree in the garden and there is a handsome black barman who speaks seven languages. We drank a bottle of whiskey between us and I watched them fight to pay for it. Yehia paid, then we all left together. They each possess a car.

I am always a bit bored in the mornings because they are all either at the university or working. Sometimes I go and play snooker with Jameel at the billiards' club. You can find him there any time—in fact he owns it. I would go there more often if it weren't for Font. Whenever I reproach myself for drinking too much, I tell myself it's Font who is driving me to drink. "Font," I told him once, "just tell me what you want me to do?"

"Run away, you scum," he answered. So I went to Groppi's and drank more whiskey. There you are, although, of course, I still read *The New Statesman* and *The Guardian* and mine is perhaps the only copy of *The Tribune* which comes to Egypt.

"Font," I said another time, when I was nicely oiled and in a good mood, "Font," I said, "you're about the only angry young man in Egypt." And I laughed. It struck me as very funny.

"Go," he replied. "Go and sponge some more on these parasites. . . ."

I went from Groppi's to the snooker club. It is a large place with thick carpets in between the tables, a cosy bar and deep leather armchairs. It impresses with its subdued luxury and one feels bad manners would be sacrilege there. Jameel's father, having accepted defeat in educating his son, gave way to the boy's passion for snooker and built this place for him; which turned out to be excellent business. He is a strange man, Jameel's father. Believe it or not, he's a sincere socialist, a genuine one. Not a rich 'Liberal' nor a wealthy *The Nation* reader; no, he is active in his ideas and was once imprisoned by Farouk's gang. He often comes for a game: a tall, lean, elegant man who had a French education and who writes to *L'Express* of France. I like Dr. Hamza; as a matter of fact I'd like to be like him: well-dressed and soberly aristocratic and having been imprisoned for socialist views. I would not like to go to prison, but I'd like to have been. Of course Font isn't going to be patronized and Dr. Hamza isn't going to be patronizing; so there is a layer of sympathy separating them.

As I said, I went to the snooker club. I went behind the bar and watched Font run the vacuum cleaner over the carpets. There is a perpetual look of amazement on Font's face which makes one want to answer an unasked question. The way he works the vacuum cleaner over the carpets with his eyebrows lifted and his eyes wide, probing into the difficult turns and corners between tables, gives the impression that if he could only get the machine into that particular corner, he'd find the answer to whatever was puzzling him.

"Draught Bass, Font?"

"Yes, all right."

I opened two bottles of Egyptian Stella beer and poured them into a large tumbler, then beat the liquid until all the gas had escaped. I then added a drop of vodka and some whiskey. It was the nearest we could get to Draught Bass.

There is a street off the Edgware Road in London where a gang of Teddy boys, Irish laborers, and other odds and ends used to play dice on the pavement. We Egyptians are gamblers. Wherever Egyptians are gathered, you can be sure that sooner or later they'll start gambling. It's not that we want to win money or anything, we just like to gamble. We're lazy and we like to laugh. It's only when gambling that we are wide awake and working hard. Font and I won a lot of money on that pavement once, and went to a silversmith in Edgware Road and bought the two silver beer mugs we now keep behind the snooker club bar. We had our names engraved on them and vowed to drink nothing but Draught Bass from them. I now poured my concoction into the mugs and waited for Font to switch the sweeper off.

"It's not bad," Font said, "How much did you make?"

"About two pints each."

"I'm going to be nicely boozed all day."

"I'll spend the day here, too," I said.

If Font hadn't been so lonely, he would never have spoken to me. But he is lonely and he wants to discuss something with me; I knew that, or I would have known better than to come and chat with him.

"The real trouble with us," he said (when Font says 'us' for him and me, it means he's exceptionally kindly disposed toward me), "is that we're so English it is nauseating. We have no culture of our own."

"Speak for yourself," I said. "I can crack jokes with the best of Egyptians."

"Perhaps you're right." he said. "Perhaps our culture is nothing but jokes."

"No, Font, it isn't. It's just that we have never learned Arabic properly." That is the way I have to speak to Font. I have to contradict him, at least in the early part of any day we are to spend together, and I have to speak slowly or he'll accuse me of trying to be eloquent instead of carrying on an ordinary conversation.

"Then what do you mean by saying that cracking jokes is culture?"

"What I mean is," I replied, "that jokes to Egyptians are as much culture as calypso is to West Indians or as spirituals and jazz to American Negroes. In fact," I continued, saying whatever came to my mouth, for that is the way to coax Font into trusting my sincerity, "it is no less culture than playing the organ is culture."

I filled our beer mugs again and started preparing some more Bass. Font pondered over what I had just said. I sometimes say such things and then a moment later they sound less silly than they do when I utter them.

It was past eleven, and the first two customers came in; Arevian and Doromian, two rich Armenians who own the shoe store downstairs. Two fat and greasy individuals with a sense of humor.

"Good day, good day, professors," they said to Font and me (Font's degree is a source of great amusement to them). "We have come to play marbles for your amusement, Herr Doctor Professor Font. It is the ambition of our humble life to divert your knowledgeable eyes with our childish efforts, thus allowing your brain to dwell upon lofty matters." They bowed down to Font and made as though to kiss his hands—an ancient custom in government circles.

"Look at them," Font said, "they pay that miserable man downstairs six pounds a month to work twelve hours a day for them, and then they come here and gamble for thousands as though for peanuts."

"Forgive us, forgive us, Herr Doctor," Doromian sang. "If our Hassan had so much as a minor degree from Heidelberg or the Sorbonne, we would give him . . . eight pounds."

When I said they owned the shoe store downstairs, I wasn't quite exact. One of them owns it and the other has lost it. They play for fantastic amounts of money, and when money has been exhausted, they play for their share of the shop. They never lend money to one another. I remember Doromian losing everything including his car, and Arevian refusing to lend him the price of the tram home.

Font started laying out the snooker balls for them. I finished two pints of this Bass which makes me comfortable and allows my oriental brain to wonder over non-Oriental things such as Font, and other Fonts I've known, and even the Font that I am myself at times. Fonts who are not Keir Hardies but Jimmy Porters in the Egyptian Victorian age; Fonts who are not revolutionaries or leaders in the class struggle, but polished products of the English 'Left,' lonely and without luster in the budding revolution of the Arab world.

These thoughts on the one hand and, on the other, the having to pay for it, or of coming to the snooker club and sitting within reach of the bottles. Thinking of this, I reached out and swung the Martell bottle to my lips. Life was good.

Sonallah Ibrahim

from Cairo from Edge to Edge

THE NATURAL WAY FOR any writer to begin the day is to grab a pen and paper or to sit at the computer—if, like myself, he is very modern. But many Cairene writers prefer a more pragmatic beginning, capable of uplifting the creative powers: Tahrir Square is their point of departure. The importance of this square does not lie in the fact that it constitutes the center of the city, or that it is surrounded by strategically important buildings like the Hilton Hotel, the Egyptian Museum, the Mugama (which comprises 1,400 offices occupied by thirty thousand employees who deal with sixty thousand people per day), and the American University. Nor is it important because at its center stands an empty statue base erected twenty-five years ago, after the death of Abd al-Nasser, for which the Egyptians have yet to choose a personality to occupy it; nor because, according to a popular joke initially targeting one of the Arab kings, it is the space used by the prime minister to distribute the national budget: he stands at the center of the square and hurls the national budget into the air, taking what lands on the ground for himself and giving what remains in the air to the people.

For one thing, the importance of the square lies in the fact that it leads, just a few meters from the underground Metro station, to the café where the Nobel writer Naguib Mahfouz was accustomed to sit, every morning, to read the papers and have coffee. This is also the only café in the area that has designated a dark corner, with a curtain, where one can order beer. Just a few steps away begins—or ends, depending on the direction one is taking—an ancient street that during the monarchy witnessed the drunken soldiers of the British occupiers and their allies, aristocratic night clubs, high society ladies, and the most luxurious stores for clothes, furniture, and jewelry, before it came to carry the name of Talaat Harb, the pioneer of national industrialization during the thirties and forties. Now the many shops that line the street contain the scum of imported goods beside bottom-of-the-line local products—the result of drug money laundering attempts. But this is also the street that used to harbor Café Riche.

This café, of Greek ownership and atmosphere, was the meeting place for intellectuals during and after the sixties. In the mornings it would be filled with retired judges and distinguished civil servants escaping their homes and their wives' reminiscences about the long lost years to have some coffee and cake as they reminisced about their own lost years.

The ritual of breakfast would be repeated at midday as journalists and artists awakened. In the evening, beer bottles and Egyptian brandy would appear and the place would be packed, especially on a specific day of the week, designated by Naguib Mahfouz for an open discussion with his friends and admirers. At least, this used to be the case. For here we are remembering the golden age of this café, during the sixties and seventies, when it used to bustle with the most vital literary debates: committed literature, social realism, and the absurd, when small literary journals, some of which never saw the light (or did for a short while) would be concocted at its tables, when film scripts and plays would be discussed in small groups, and when many were taken to detention camps or prisons because of a word or a joke recorded in a secret report, written at a neighboring table.

This is how it became a symbol for intellectual small talk that actually matters very little. A well-known poet, who writes in the Egyptian dialect, reflects this general ambiance in a poem that begins: "Long live the intellectual at the Café Riche/ Hurray, hurray, hurray/ Stuck up and sleazy/ A bag full of words/ With a few empty ones and a few other terms/ He fabricates quick solutions to problems."

This may also explain why today, and for the past ten years, the café is surrounded by planks of wood, as it is said to be undergoing complicated renovations that have yet to be completed, the reason for which is unknown and around which several rumors have arisen. Naguib Mahfouz has been obliged to relocate, with his admirers, to a cafeteria on the nearby island of Gezira on the Nile, where he is guarded by two lions made of bronze, two of the last and most important remaining symbols of modernization under Khedive Ismail. As for the other regular customers of the Riche, who found it difficult to cross over to the other side of Tahrir Square, or to pay the expensive prices at the cafeteria on Gezira, or to deal with the Israeli presence at the kind-hearted and generous Nobel laureate's open discussion—all these have withdrawn to a small alley behind the Riche, to a popular café called al-Bustan, frequented by drivers, doormen, and neighboring shop vendors. From there, they have spread into what has come to be known as the "Triangle of Horror."

This triangle begins at al-Bustan café, extending north on one side to the old Grillon restaurant, which continued to deteriorate until it was taken over by an active Iraqi who had been displaced by the American attack on Iraq. He renovated it, and transformed its garden into an elegant, covered cafeteria that serves beer at Riche prices. Quickly, it became the meeting point for a group of writers, painters, and journalists. From the restaurant extends another line toward the east, leading to the rooftop Odeon bar, which remains open all night, thus allowing the theater crowd to drop in. At this point begins the third arm, on the return trip to al-Bustan café.

The principal center of the famous triangle is the Atelier—full name the Atelier of Writers and Artists—a hip club in a small two-story building surrounded by a small garden, with several exhibition halls for the plastic and musical arts, the largest of which is used for a weekly literary debate. During such debates, literary critics will eulogize a collection of poems, thereby guaranteeing themselves one of two things, or both: a set space (in exchange for an attractive fee) on the literary page edited by the eulogized poet in one of the daily papers, or regular coverage of their own activities and publications.

This place, which has received every single Egyptian or Arab writer or artist, witnessed glorious days during the sixties and seventies, before alcoholic beverages were deleted from its menu under the pressure of fundamentalism. But the disappearance of alcoholic beverages did not affect the legitimacy of the place, which during recent years has witnessed some historic events, the latest of which was the meeting of around one thousand intellectuals after the armed attack on Naguib Mahfouz, and their decision to organize a march in protest, which did not materialize because the police, always on the alert, besieged them, detained some, and dispersed the ranks of those remaining.

From whichever direction the writer tries to penetrate this triangle, he or she will arrive in the midst of storms and burning flames that confer upon the area its well-deserved description of the Triangle of Horror. Further, it is armed by a broadcasting service no less powerful than CNN. Like CNN, it has all-day coverage of the various literary and artistic battles, with their accompanying pacts, besides a summary of the daily news: that is, what even the opposition papers have not published with regard to the secrets of political events, the latest political scandals, the astonishing deals, and the dubious projects, all topped with the necessary dressing of marital betrayals and sexual relations. This broadcasting service is supported by an invisible express-mail service: should you begin your trip from al-Bustan café, within minutes, when you arrive at another focal point of the triangle, you will find an angry colleague ready for battle, after news has reached him of what you said moments ago concerning his literary honor, or that of his wife.

However, the world of the Triangle of Horror is not always this serious: there is room for entertainment and pleasure. By this I do not mean just a couple of drinks, or participation in harmless gossip, for the atmosphere within the Triangle is besieged by a permanent sexual fever. Those who bring their manuscripts, or their gossip, for discussion or comments are also in search of a perennial goal, that may not exceed listening to a lengthy monologue by a member of the opposite or the same sex on the latest theories of aesthetics, sufficient to exhaust the listener before the speaker. Usually, such conversations terminate by the turning of the page to another theory in the same field, or by resuming the conversation in a more intimate place, where obscure barriers worthy of the attention of Freud's disciples are discovered, thus hurling the parties concerned back to the point of departure, the heart of downtown.

It would be a mistake to believe that intellectuals are the main players in this arena. This may have been true some time ago when downtown Cairo was the stronghold of foreigners and the upper classes. Then came social mobility, which brought with it new kinds of profiles. When in 1957 foreign companies and banks were nationalized and the public sector was established, the new, ascending executive managers chose the downtown area for their work and residence. Because the public sector was established under a rigid economic system, it immediately gave rise to a parallel class of traffickers. The

Open Door policies then allowed for the accumulation of spectacular wealth that was the result of smuggling and black market money, whose owners were known, during the seventies, as the 'Fat Cats' and who have now grown to become whales and crocodiles. It is they who packed downtown Cairo with appliance, clothes, shoe, and pastry shops. In the evening, you see them in front of their shops, with enormous bellies, relaxing from the day's battles; they are joined by foreign company and tourist business representatives, easily recognizable by their uniform-like clothes, their colorful ties, their shaven heads, and their quick step in search of commissions.

Translated by Samia Mehrez

Naguib Mahfouz
from *The Day the Leader Was Killed*

CAFÉ RICHE IS A refuge from the pain of loneliness. I sit and order a cup of coffee, and prick up my ears. This is a temple where offerings are made to the late hero, who has become a symbol of lost hope, hope for the poor and the alienated. Here, too, torrents of indignation are poured upon the hero of victory and peace, victory that has turned out to be but a dirty game, and peace, surrender. All this within earshot of Israeli tourists. I find solace in just sitting there listening.

If this kind of talk disturbs you, then just take a look at the street. Watch the passersby closely: ceaseless, uninterrupted, brisk motion. Sullen faces. What do they conceal? Men, women, children, and even pregnant women no longer stay at home: the tragic or the comic sums them all up. Furniture stores and boutiques are all crammed with goods. How many nations live side by side in this one nation? The lights in the square are bright and nerve-wrecking, and equally exasperating are the bottles of mineral water on the tables of tourists. And what about us. What do we drink? And then the weirdest songs blast out from crazy radio stations in taxicabs. Only the trees and buildings remain the same. Some speech on the radio is being broadcast from some place. Lies fill the air and mingle with the dust. Fatigue, fatigue. . . . Let's return to the gossip: a tiny place falling in ruins selling for a hundred thousand pounds, academic crimes in university circles. How many millionaires are there? Relatives and parasites, smugglers and pimps. Shiites and Sunnis. Stories far better than the *Thousand and One Nights*. The waiter has a story and so does the shoe-shine boy. When will the famine begin? Open bribes at top voice. The confiscation of lands. And who will cause sectarian rifts to flare up again? The People's Assembly was a place for dancing; it has now become a place for singing. Imports with no transfer of funds. Different kinds of cheese. New banks. What do eggs cost today? The showering of banknotes on singers and dancers in nightclubs on the Pyramid Road simply as a token of appreciation. And the breakup of the engagement! What did the imam of the mosque say within earshot of the soldiers of the Central Security Forces? No public lavatory in the entire district. Why don't we rent it furnished? He's nothing but a failed actor. My friend Begin; my friend Kissinger. The uniform is Hitler's; the act, Charlie Chaplin's. Total silence as a woman coming up the street proceeds toward a brothel behind the café. A parallel is drawn between the swelling of her buttocks and public inflation in general. An optimist insists that she works in order to amass the necessary funds for her doctoral dissertation and that her heart is as good as gold. A homosexual proposes homosexuality as a means of solving the crisis of love among the classes with a fixed income and also as a means of achieving the objectives of family planning. A return to the Arabs and war, an everlasting war, and woe unto the agents of normalization. Enough, enough!

Translated by Malak Hashem

Miral al-Tahawy

from *Blue Aubergine*

SHEIKH ALI'S BAR ISN'T too rough, except that the regulars are like me and him. They chant slogans against rising prices and unemployment in demonstrations that end with truckloads of Central Security Forces and troopers chasing us with electric cattle prods and tear gas. They make grand statements about revolutionary justice and the conspiring with America, they boycott KFC and hamburgers and frozen chicken and sit around at ridiculous meetings talking about Marx and Trotsky and frustration. All their poems sound the same, their rhetoric even creeps into the stuff I write about ideological adherence and the revolutionary text.

He always reads his poems in Sheikh Ali's bar after expending all his energy in writing them. "A reasonable effort," they say, and tell him about the genius that comes from perseverance. His greatest passion is to be carried on their shoulders and improvise the slogans it takes to get the crowd going.

"Wearing sackcloth, barely fed, now they're coming to take our bread."

"They drink whiskey, they eat meat, but it's starvation for the man in the street."

"America, America, take your cash, tomorrow the Arabs will make you crash."

The sweat on his forehead is glistening in the sun, and after running and hurling stones we retreat exhausted and check the names of those who have been arrested and those who are hiding, and I see him grow and become a man the size of my dreams.

In Sheikh Ali's bar is a woman who plays the oud. She only sings one song: "My soul and your soul have been lovers since before this world, by God." When he isn't drunk he opens my bag, puts his hand in my purse, and buys me a string of jasmine, and kisses me. His friends laugh and clap and ululate, and he keeps drinking until he says again, "Come on. We have to finish the picture."

We walk down dark streets. He's probably so drunk that he undoes his trousers and urinates against a Central Security Forces truck parked outside the American University while holding my arm. He urinates a lot outside Bab al-Sharia police station because the duty officer there is fond of stopping him and searching him. He calls him a communist dog. The sergeant also likes to pick him up if he finds him wandering about the streets and he spends many a night in the cell.

I am drinking tonight . . . a lot, so we can chat away. We give the paper my blood has dried on a rest and enjoy our drunken state. When we wake up in the morning he has a headache. I am worried. I have to face the same questions about spending the night outside the halls. I have to arm myself with enough insolence to spit on the floor when I see the supervisor. Then she will think twice before she gets involved in an argument. And I have to forget what he says too, because with the passing of time, and the same old scene repeating itself, I will get used to the pain and will not always feel the full horror of what is happening to me. . . .

He knows how to speak a lot and laugh a lot and get the whole audience worked up, then he is asked to leave the lecture hall. He slumps out and sits on the stone bench where he reiterates in a more futile tone that all things are trivial, frustrating, and inhuman.

"All struggles are essentially class-based." He looks at my head covering and continues: "Your Lord rules us from a superior position. They invented him so our necks would remain yearning for above, crushed by his teachings. They invented him to endorse the existence of social classes."

His words were provocative but I didn't disagree. I did not dare tell him that the secularists and the communists are all out to get at Islam with this intellectual assault on the minds of young people, and that Islam has come to be a stranger in the world, as it was in the beginning, and that the establishment of the Islamic State is an obligation of the Faith, and that the warriors of God must revive the sacred jihad, for careful and precise organization and unswerving adherence and unceasing work are the only way. All those ideas were hanging on banners around the university for him to see and could be heard everywhere on the tapes and cassettes the Islamic bookstalls were playing.

I was flustered and confused. I bit my lip because I did not want to get into a fight with him. I wanted to say other things that would make him love me, like I was a coward, or I might be embarrassed about my body, or I might not know how to behave like a normal girl because I was always a lump of doughy flesh with features, and I might cry and he would say: "You're more beautiful than you think," but in the end I did nothing, just stood there trembling.

Translated by Tony Calderbank

Ahmed Mourad

from *Vertigo*

April 2005,

Grand Hyatt Hotel . . . ten-thirty in the evening.

The noise of the wedding procession filled the reception hall, announcing another victim whose name was written along with his bride's on a gold-plated sign in front of the door (Khaled and Nancy). The wedding procession moved slowly to allow the dancers with head-fitted chandeliers, heavy bellies, and very bored faces to perform some movements, by way of entertainment and duty, that have nothing to do with dancing.

The master of ceremonies was the tabla player, who wore a bright blue vest that clashed with the colors of the froufrou dangling from his sleeves and made him look different from all the members of the group, who were wearing Indian pink. It gave him the appearance of a maestro, with his long kinky hair dangling over his forehead, as his colleagues brushed away the guests, as if he were an astronaut, while he was completely submerged in playing the tabla.

Ahmad Kamal was the wedding photographer. And like every wedding photographer, he knew exactly how important he was for the event, but unfortunately he did not receive the appropriate treatment, even though a wedding is no easy matter. It is a battle to capture the moment that will become a lasting memory. No one will remember him afterward, like a male bee that contents itself with its fertilizing role and dies a martyr as life continues and others eat the honey, thanks to him.

He is dark and never wears anything but jeans with a light-brown jacket on top in order to look like a TV soap opera star from the eighties. He's only missing the dark brown leather patches on the elbows to become Jack Norris even though, deep inside, he was convinced that he looked very much like Amr Diab, but no one had noticed that before, despite his efforts to copy Amr Diab's clothes and the way he carried himself. He is obsessed with his appearance, which costs him most of what he spends, down to the very last pound note in his pocket. In addition, he does some weight-lifting once in a while at Salah's Golden Gym in order to look fit. He is of medium height, with eyeglasses that mask the mischievousness in his eyes, which are surrounded by the two recognizable black rims characteristic of night birds. They also hide his very weak eyesight that would have won the complete sympathy of Taha Hussein himself. He never sleeps before six o'clock in the morning, and does not leave a wedding without the memory of a beautiful girl who he imagines had been following him with her eyes throughout the evening. He contents himself with taking her photo in the hope that he might meet her elsewhere. He shows it to his friends and touches up the story, adding that it was she who asked him to take her photo, had asked for his number, and had fallen head over heels in love with him. He might even tell them that there were tears in her eyes because she was betrothed and her fiancé was right beside her, that she hoped time would rewind so she could get to know him. He feels the camera with his hand and holds it at his belt, looking confident, as if he had been born with it in that position. He uses the weight of the camera to tighten his biceps to show off the money he pays at the gym.

The wedding procession had ended and the DJ began doing his job (to exorcise the evil spirits from the bride and groom and their relatives, not to mention the sauna effect that will leave the groom exhausted and will chase away his dreams for the night). Ahmad Kamal started his daily battle of trying to take a photo of the bride and groom without the teeming hands, shoulders, or heads that would ruin the shot, not to mention the unsympathetic guests. He focused on the bride's girlfriends, for whom this special occasion was like a Coco Chanel fashion show, during which they parade low-cut dresses covered with transparent shawls. Who knows, they might meet Prince Charming. But even if that were not to happen, it will suffice to have been seen by the guys. Ahmad had grown accustomed to reading all these gazes and signs so that he became an expert in communication skills, like the telegraph officer during the Second World War who was able to decipher the Germans' secret codes. When it was time for the dinner buffet, Ahmad used to withdraw for a cigarette on the terrace of the reception hall that overlooked the Nile, especially in the wake of a row between him and Mr. Rifaat, the manager, who had found him at the tail end of the buffet among the guests. He scolded him in a voice everyone could hear as if he were a serial killer ("When the guests have finished, YOUR HONOR CAN EAT"). Since then, Ahmad has not come near the buffet.

Today he did not feel hungry, so he only took some Umm Ali and went out for a cigarette, trying to make ringlets and other geometric shapes in the air and then quickly disperse them with his hand, remembering his father, Kamal Ibrahim, who left him when he was nineteen years old along with his mother, Aya, his little sister, the camera, and the films that Ahmad sold. He gave up the lab to a new tenant who could pay the monthly rent. His father had many debts that he could not repay, so in the end he was forced to give up the place. In the spirit of the time, he bought a digital camera and a computer, even though he regretted parting with his father's equipment, for it represented his memory. He had nothing left but his father's relationships with the hotel's old personnel, who were moved every time they laid eyes on him, remembering his father and his good nature; all except Mr. Rifaat, who deliberately derided him, for he was not of his father's time.

It was already past three-fifteen when Ahmad withdrew from the reception hall, content with what photos he had taken during the wedding festivities as agreed with the groom. As usual, he made his way up to the fortieth floor after he put his equipment in the bag, and handed over the photo

CDs to Selim, who had exclusive photography rights in the hotel after his father—that short, fat, sweaty being with his inseparable large kerchief, who wore a three-piece suit all year round and provocatively shiny moccasins, a thick gold chain dangling across his hairless chest with a big sagging belly like a vendor of licorice, and his heavy-handed, sexually laden comments to both the waitresses and the dancers as well as business guests of the hotel. He could befriend even the stairway railing . . . as if he were a spy network that noted everything, big and small, about the hotel guests. He had kinky hair that covered his forehead in front and his yellow or bright red shirt collar in the back, to look artistic and to fulfill his desire to attract attention. He had a new cell phone with earphones glued to his ears. He was the assistant to the celebrity agent. He disappeared from the office one day with all the celebrities' private cell phone numbers and he rented the hotel reception hall, even though he had no notion of photography, to have a space from which he could spread like a flame and extend his tentacles all around.

He was married to two and had an affair with a third. He squandered his money on his nightlife and his cellophane-wrapped drugs. But he was stingy with the wages of photographers who worked for him. Ahmad worked for him after his father's death. He was happy to have him since he knew the place and the nature of the job. His liking for Ahmad was not without caution, since the place once belonged to his father and he did not want him to seek it again. That was why his pay, and that of his colleagues, remained barely enough to cover the necessities of life, so that they would all remain dependent on him.

The fortieth floor overlooks Qasr al-Nil Bridge, the Gezira Tower, and the far end of Zamalek. The special ambiance of the bar is complemented by the quiet Garden City streets, light music, flowers, and candlelight. The Vertigo Bar is the most famous and luxurious in Egypt. It hosts the elite and celebrities as well as foreign guests, where Husam Munir, Ahmad Kamal's only friend, works. They always meet after work to spend the remainder of the evening together until dawn, since they have both been night creatures for a long while now. Husam did not physically resemble Ahmad: Husam was fair with fine features, a bit bald, with long hair tied in a ponytail with a rubber band like all those night artists. His triangular beard had the shape of a boat anchor. It was as if he would lose his very creativity if he ever gave up any of these details. He had fine hands like a surgeon's blade, created especially for the piano. He wore a very small pair of eyeglasses and, because of the nature of his job, he wore a suit and tie every night. He owned only two suits, but he changed the ties from the bouquet he had bought at Fawzi's Boutique downtown, ties that looked slick even though they were cheap. So he looked good every night. . . .

The bar pianist, as he liked to be called, is not married or even in a relationship until quite recently, except for a couple of times when he came to know one or two of the waitresses of the restaurant attached to the bar. These relationships never went far, for they would quickly end because of Husam's sense of boredom, which he had exercised since he was a child: flighty, his eye hardly settles on the same one twice, especially if one of them was generous enough to let him have a taste, or if she did not understand his unpredictable nature and made marriage plans. Husam does not save a penny from his salary: there is his bedridden mother in one of the high-ceilinged apartments in Bab al-Luq that rents for seven pounds a month. The day came when his agent asked to see him about doing a good deed. They had a friendly relationship besides their professional one. He told him about Christina, this girl who had just come from Moldavia with the ant-like deluge of former Soviets during the summer to escape from the difficult economic crisis. He told Husam that he wanted him to marry her: she was clean and respectful and did not work in a dance hall; like him, she was a pianist, so they would have a good rapport; she would shoulder her own expenses and at the same time Husam could help her with her residence in Egypt. And so it was. . . . Husam was introduced to her during a business meeting, and even though he had heard about the beauty of these people, not in his wildest dreams had he imagined that their genetic heritage could achieve the kind of invention that was called Christina: she was translucently fair, with auburn hair and a slender figure. Makeup could not add to that. Her eyes betrayed a profound sadness, even though she tried to overcome that with her dimpled smile that mesmerized the beholder. She spoke a carefully articulated English to try to conceal her Russian accent, but she would always fall prey to the 'h' sound that she transformed into a 'kh' ("I don't know"). But more importantly, she was a pianist and was not going to be financially dependent on him; she owned an apartment that could serve as his rest stop at any time.

Husam agreed on condition that he got to know her first for a month. . . . But for the first time in his life, he fell in love. He fell in love with her because he failed to be bored with her. She was different from the girls that he knew: she was liberated, simple, and conscious of her good looks but not conceited, for among her own people she was not a beauty. Had he met an Egyptian woman of the same level of beauty, she would have been utterly superficial. More importantly, Christina would not besiege him with "Where were you?" or "Don't be late, I won't sleep until you come home," or "Give me a missed call when you're on your way home," and so on.

Despite the differences between Husam and Ahmad, they were best friends, as if their differences served to make them complement each other. They had the same upbringing, the same social class, until life separated them. Ahmad graduated from the Faculty of Commerce and Husam studied music at the Faculty of Education. When Husam graduated he couldn't find work until the agent who was Ahmad's friend asked him for a bar pianist; he, in turn, brought in Husam.

Translated by Samia Mehrez

Ahmed Alaidy

from *Being Abbas el Abd*

An Introduction You Can Suck or Shove

SHE WASN'T A CORPSE YET.
Hind doesn't like wasting time because she's never been like other girls.
Place: Geneina Mall, the Ladies' Toilet.
Hind writes the mobile phone number on the insides of the doors of the toilets with a waterproof lipstick, then passes a Kleenex soaked in soda water over it, 'cause that way, cupcake,
it can't be wiped off!
I told her to write it at the eye level of a person sitting on the toilet seat.
Above it, two words: **CALL ME**
Why?
Because these things happen.
The woman goes into the toilet to relieve herself.
The woman goes into the toilet to use something that emerges, from her handbag, to protect her.
Her sin, of which she is guiltless.
A naked fragile butterfly—and
Enter the terrible number.
The number gazes at her weakness.
The number *permits itself* to intervene instantaneously.
The number asks no permission and has no supernumeraries.
The number is

Zero-one-zero, six, forty, ninety, thirty.

CALL ME

010 6 40 90 30

Arkadia Mall:

CALL ME

010 6 40 90 30

Ramses Hilton Mall:

CALL ME

010 6 40 90 30

The World Trade Center:

Accept no imitations.

Zero-one-zero, six, forty, ninety, thirty.

CALL ME

There's a thing I like to get up to from time to time.

As though I was living like any other lunatic.

As though I was myself, with all the little stupidities I like to commit.

And with all the stupidities that have become—by now—part

of my makeup, it was obvious I'd ask her to push it.

How far?

You guess. . . .

A Postscript You Can Neither Stop nor Get Around

HE WASN'T A CORPSE YET.

Abdallah doesn't like wasting time because he's never been like other boys.

Place: Geneina Mall, the Men's Toilet.

Abdallah writes the mobile phone number on the insides of

the doors of the toilets with a waterproof Parker pen, then

passes a Kleenex soaked in soda water over it 'cause that way,

Neddy, it can't be wiped off!

I told him to write it at the eye level of a person sitting on the

toilet seat.

Above it, two words: **CALL ME**

Why?

Because these things happen.

The man goes into the toilet to relieve himself.

The man goes into the toilet to aim something that emerges from his pants.

His guilt, for the sin he did indeed commit.

A fragile naked cockroach, stompable—and

Enter the terrible number.
The number gawks at him sneakily.
The number *permits itself* to intervene instantaneously.
The number asks no permission and has no supernumeraries.
This is the number:
Zero-one-zero, six, forty, ninety, thirty.
CALL ME
010 6 40 90 30
Arkadia Mall:
CALL ME
010 6 40 90 30
Ramses Hilton Mall:
CALL ME
010 6 40 90 30
City Stars Center:
Accept no imitations.
Zero-one-zero, six, forty, ninety, thirty.
CALL ME
There's a thing I like to get up to from time to time.
As though I was living like any other lunatic.
As though I was myself, with all the little stupidities I like to commit.
And with all the stupidities that have become—by now—part
of my makeup, it was obvious I'd ask him to push it.
How far?
You guess.

Translated by Humphrey Davies

Muhammad Salah al-Azab

from *Frequent Stops*

YOU AND MIN'IM WORKED as salesmen for a medical supply warehouse in Marg.
You took quantities of medical supplies and toured the pharmacies throughout the week and you delivered on Fridays. Two months later, the warehouse

was shut down and the owner arrested because he was using the warehouse as a cover for dealing drugs. When the warehouse was shut down, you each had in your possession supplies that were worth eight thousand pounds. In two weeks, you distributed the medical supplies and you made sixteen thousand pounds that had no claimant.

You rented out an apartment on the ground floor in the army officers' residences across from al-Salam Hospital right in front of Suzanne Mubarak's High School for Girls. You opened a games arcade. You plastered twenty rolls of bamboo sheets across the walls and hung huge posters of Haifa Wahbi, Amr Diab, Elissa, Ruby, Nancy Agram, and Muhammad Hamaki, as well as old posters of The Four Cats, Spice Girls, Backstreet Boys, all torn out of *al-Shabab* and *Kalimatna* magazines, along with dim spotlights, a pool table, four TV screens, four Play Stations, and a big lit sign on the outside that read:

Friends' Games

Your main clientele, as Min'im had put it, were the good-for-nothing kids who skipped school to hang out in front of the girls' school. Being on the street was dangerous for them, for the Atari truck was regularly parked in front of the girls' school in order for the police officers to fulfill their pleasure by slapping these kids on the back of their necks in front of the satisfied, giggling girls. These guys found a refuge in the game arcade.

You also purchased a business line and several Ericsson 688 cell phones and placed them in the arcade as a means of luring in the girls.

Your grandfather used to have a big photograph of himself in a golden frame that hung in the sitting room. During the 1992 earthquake it fell and the glass and the frame broke. Since then, it had been put away with a lot of other junk. You brought it out and wrote on the back with a black marker that you took from your sister's coloring box:

Take Your Time Calling
One minute for the cell phone
Is
50 Piasters

You hung up the sign outside the arcade door with your grandfather's face, his turban, and the prayer mark on his forehead, turned toward the wall.

In one week the place was transformed into an unexpected brothel, and your main clientele became the girls who skipped school to play pool and Play Station like pros, tell dirty jokes, and smoke cigarettes in secret.

In the beginning, the good-for-nothing guys were scared to come in when they saw that the girls had invaded the place. So they used to stroll in front of the arcade to watch what was happening inside, as if it were a women's hair salon.

Gradually, they got used to the place, and they started mixing easily with the girls inside through the games, instead of following them and harassing them on the street with no results. But you did not allow any off-limits inter-action between the guys and the girls. At the same time, the inner space of the apartment was transformed into a den: one of you would stand outside in the arcade to oversee the game space, while the other would be inside with a girl. When one of you was done, he would come out to oversee the arcade while the other went inside.

Everyone felt relaxed in the place, especially since the building's security was restricted to the military police.

The place became well known among high schools in al-Salam City, Nahda, and al-Ubur, and it became commonplace for someone to ask their schoolmate, "Are you going to school tomorrow?"

And the answer would be, "No, I'm going to Friends' Games."

This only lasted for a month and a half, after which the complaints of the girls' parents multiplied, as did those of the school principal and the neigh-borhood residents. The place began to smell, so an old beige police jeep came by and closed down the arcade.

19919

You dialed the number and a girl with a melodious voice replied, "Al-Wasit . . . Rania speaking, sir."

"I want to place an ad in the hobby section. May I know how much it will cost?"

"Twenty pounds, sir, for normal font and twenty-five for bold font, per six-teen words."

"How do I pay you?"

"Sir, there are two ways to make payment: you may come to any of our branches or we can send you, sir, a collection officer wherever you please. If you choose the latter, sir, the sum will increase by five pounds."

"Done, okay. Normal font and the collection officer."

She took your details and said, "Could you please dictate to me the text of the ad?"

"Due to travel, selling a complete pool table, four 20-inch Toshiba TV sets, four Play Stations, four TV tables."

Min'im, who was sitting beside you, said, "Why didn't you tell her about the bamboo sheets and the posters?"

"No, those you can take to decorate your apartment."

The ad was run with your cell number attached, so you were flooded with phone calls. The items were sold separately: the four TV sets one after the other, then the pool table, then one Play Station, then one TV table, then another Play Station, and a TV table.

You received strange phone calls. One said, "Do you have a gym machine?"

And another, "Do you have a movie projector?"

A third called to find out why you were leaving, without asking to buy anything, and then asked you insistently about the details and said, "Do you know someone who could send me a work contract in the Gulf? I am ready to pay up to seven thousand pounds. I'm a graduate of the Faculty of Commerce and I have English and computer skills."

Only one Play Station and two TV tables were left. Each of you took a table and you took the Play Station for your brothers, who taught your mother how to play and she eventually became addicted to it.

You went back to sitting in your old hangout at Central Coffee Shop, where you calculated your gains and losses. You discovered that the sum had shrunk to 14,600 pounds. You ripped off the cell phone company on the bill that had exceeded one thousand pounds, so they cut off the line.

You began thinking about a new project and you avoided talking about dirty money. You each knew that this was precisely what the other was thinking, but you did not say it.

Translated by Samia Mehrez

Private Spaces

UNLIKE PUBLIC SPACES, PRIVATE ones in the city are less accessible and legible to both city dwellers and outsiders for they are hidden from the gaze and mystifying with their simultaneous presence and absence. Private spaces are a demarcation between the inside and the outside; they are intimate microcosms of social order, decorum, and rituals within different urban classes. The higher up on the social ladder the more private the 'private space' becomes. As we move down the social ladder, the strict divide between inside and outside, between home and street gradually recedes to the background and opens up the private to the public in many ways.

This chapter provides a network of such urban private spaces, with their symbolic spatial maps as well as their social hierarchies, social order, gender divides and daily internal lives. Because of the inaccessible, 'private' nature of these spaces, the chapter also includes autobiographical texts whose authors open up their homes and private lives to our gaze. As we read through this rather voyeuristic chapter, we will discover that the literary reconstructions of private space oscillate between its representation as a haven and a prison, a shelter and a cage, a space of belonging and one of estrangement, one of freedom and one of constraint. Each of the representations of private spaces in this chapter is anchored in a particular public one (a geographic area or a neighborhood) whose history is not only written into the private spaces themselves but is also responsible for shaping, and defining their very existence as private spaces.

The representation of Muhammad Ali's Palace of Shubra on the northern outskirts of Cairo by Prince Hassan Hassan depicts the ultimate privacy of the private. Shubra, now an industrial lower-class, crowded suburb of the metropolis, was then more village than city, more rural than urban. The palace and its environment was a world apart: large parks, immense gardens and fruit groves surrounded the various interconnected spaces of the palace that was home to a highly rigorous domestic order, the hallmark of an aristocratic lifestyle. Prince Hasan escorts us into this isolated haven from the *haramlik* (the exclusive women's quarters) to the all-male *salamlik* where the author's father entertained political guests. There were also separate servants' quarters, a main kitchen, laundry rooms, and garages. The staff of the palace themselves represent an entire world, at once multiracial and multilingual. The domestic men servants were Egyptian, Nubian, and Sudanese, while the more technical staff was Turkish, Albanian, Italian, or Armenian who all spoke their own native languages. A similar hierarchy existed for the female servants with the *kalfas*—the white maids and housekeepers of Circassian or Turkish origin who always spoke Turkish—as the most privileged in the hierarchy of women servants. This huge cocoon and rigorous, undisturbed order is responsible for the Prince's politically naive conclusion that "these multinational households got on well together—people not yet being influenced by political causes that cynically exploit color, race, or religion to divide and misrule the world."

The literary reconstruction of the palace at the beginning of the twentieth century in pre-revolutionary Egypt, along with other literary representations of similar aristocratic models with clear boundaries with the outside world, reemerge at the turn of the twentieth century when we witness the mushrooming of gated communities for the rich and famous on the outskirts of the mega city; communities like Utopia that we encountered in the first chapter "Mapping Cairo," where the newly rich are as isolated from the outside world as the pre-revolutionary aristocracy and protected from its fearsome intrusion not by Turks, Italians, and Albanians but by former U.S. marines.

At the beginning of the twentieth century the palace with its hybrid European/oriental architecture and furnishings is juxtaposed against the traditional Egyptian middle-class home with its typical traditional furnishings, kerosene lamps, and lattice windows that hid the female members of the family from the gaze of the street. While the palace is situated on the outskirts of the city in an idyllic, remote spot, Ahmad Abd al-Gawad's house in Naguib Mahfouz's *Trilogy* is situated in the heart of Islamic Cairo with its meandering alleys and "houses bunched together untidily on both sides of the road." For Amina, Abd al-Gawad's wife, who has never set foot outside her home, this private space is more like a prison, a haunted abode inhabited by jinn and ghosts that she has to confront alone.

Only the men have free access to the outside in these traditional bourgeois settings where they can enjoy other private spaces like brothels, alternative abodes with alternative mistresses with whom their conservative patriarchal demeanor that dominates the home gives way to more playful behavior and leaves Amina, the traditional wife, wondering, as she stands behind the *mashrabiya* watching Abd al-Gawad returning from his routine late evening outings, "How did he come by these joyful, jesting sounds, which flowed out so merrily and graciously?"

These havens/prisons coexist with other private spaces whose relationship with the public space is redefined by the city's new realities: geographic expansion and population mobility, rural–urban migration that led to the appearance of informal and illegal housing during the 1980s and the ruralization of urban areas not to mention new capital flow, specifically from the Gulf region and the transnational, mega capital of the city. The fragmentation of old familiar spaces and the encroachment of new unfamiliar ones led at once to a new sense of mobility and anonymity as well as an imminent sense of alienation and isolation that is ultimately defeated through newfound solidarities and communities that are brought together through various reasons and levels of displacement. From Sonallah Ibrahim's representation of Zaat's building during the pre and post-*infitah* period to Alaa Al Aswany's colonial/postcolonial Yacoubian building, to M.M. Tawfik's Tower of Happiness that is planted like an alien body on the Nile, all the way down to Hamdi Abu Golayyel's reconstruction of Abu Gamal's informal mud brick house in Manshiyat Nasser and Hani Abdel-Mourid's illegal garbage collectors' abodes in Zabbalin, we witness the blurring of the once well-guarded boundaries between inside and outside, private and public, until the garbage collectors' homes in Abdel-Mourid's representation literally become part of the street, where the walls of the ground floor of a house are knocked down to make room for the garbage with which they co-habit while members of the family sort it out inside the 'home.'

The literary reconstructions of private spaces in this chapter provide not just a map of urban dwellings and a panorama of architectural inequality and cacophony but more importantly perhaps, since we are invited into these private spaces, they offer memorable examples of new and colliding modes of consumption and social behavior. Likewise, of course, these representations reveal an interesting class cross-section of the actors within the literary field itself who, together, attest to the changing structure and boundaries not only of the city but also of the literary field, and the wide spectrum of literary profiles that co-habit the same space.

Another fascinating aspect of reading these private spaces against each other is the emergence of a complex map of urban language(s) in the texts. Even though they are all situated in the mega city of Cairo, the linguistic lexicon and symbolic signs, depending on where these private spaces are located, become important distinguishing markers that immediately identify the colliding economic, social, and cultural spaces that their occupants inhabit: from the Babel-like linguistic world of the palaces, to the chic francophone of the beginning of the century, to the Anglicizations of the sixties, to the Islamization/globalization of the eighties and nineties side by side with the most popular levels of Egyptian Arabic where certain expressions would require 'translation' for a middle-class Cairene.

Furthermore, when read against each other, the archival nature of many of these selections is striking. Among representations of more affluent private spaces, we are provided with an archaeology and history of the artistic and the culinary. We have descriptions of private concerts, the deliberate painstaking recording of popular lyrics that have been sung for over a century and hence inscribed in these private spaces; lists of foodstuffs, pastries, traditional dishes and drinks pile up in the ease of some of these homes. As we move down the economic ladder, however, mention of food practically disappears except for the very basic *ful* and *kushari,* of course.

Finally these selections are an invaluable repository of household lives and interactions: restrictive bourgeois family relations, gender divides, household rituals, as well as displaced affiliations, the human intimacies of the underworld of the urban poor and the intensely moving and individuated experiences of confronting *al-Qahira* (The City Victorious), all of which are placed on the map of the mega-city beyond impersonal statistics and figures.

Hassan Hassan

*from In the House of Muhammad Ali:
A Family Album, 1805–1952*

THE PALACE OF SHUBRA is situated on the northern outskirts of Cairo. The palace consisted originally of a large park reaching down to the Nile, carefully planted in extremely diverse sections: some were formal gardens, others were fruit groves of mangoes, guavas, and citrus trees. Muhammad Ali took an almost childlike delight in seeing orange trees in fruit and could not bear to have them picked; only the ones that fell to the ground were collected. In my childhood the place had been abandoned for many years and some of the lands sold and set back to agricultural use. The park was running wild, all the different elements intermingling in a romantic and informal manner. I remember the eucalyptus trees swaying in the wind, the mango trees with their thick, handsome foliage motionless at noon—big sacred beetles moving clumsily in their shade—and the elegance and scent of pine trees silhouetted against a striped evening sky.

The main building, the haramlik, was demolished well before my birth (I was born on February 22, 1924). This building had been Aunt Aziza's share of my grandparents' property. She had had it demolished when it was rumored that the British were thinking of taking it over. She felt it would be wrong to have the British use Muhammad Ali's palace for military purposes and the occupation of the country. It had been an early-nineteenth-century European's idea of Arab style, built in white marble, with loggia and balcony adorned with metal and stucco arabesques. As the palace was reputed to have been of great splendor in decoration and furnishing, fortunes are said to have been made in town from the materials salvaged when it was demolished, including paintings that were framed in the walls.

What is known as the Palace of Shubra now is a pleasance, its main feature being a vast square pool with a marble island in its center. Fountains play on it, and the pitter-patter of water on stone, or the steadier rhythm of running streams finishing in the pool, are the only sounds that breaks the silence and calm of the place. Surrounding the pool is a cloister-like colonnade broken up by four advancing terraces, all in white marble, exquisitely sculpted in a neoclassical, almost Pompeian style, the work of the French architect B. Coste.

The building and colonnades are enclosed on the garden side by a wall composed mainly of amber-colored windows and four doorways opposite the advancing terraces. In the four corners of the colonnade, on semicircular platforms, stand marble lions spouting water into the pool. The ceilings of the cloister are painted with decorative motifs, among which there is a portrait of Muhammad Ali set in a medallion and, in the opposite ceiling across the water, a corresponding one of his son Ibrahim.

The rooms of the building are grouped in its four corners. On the right when entering the colonnade is a drawing room with an exceptionally beautiful parquet floor inlaid with intricate designs made of rosewood. It is surmounted by a heavily sculpted ceiling painted dark blue and gold with a handsome chandelier hanging from its center. The room is furnished with nineteenth-century armchairs and chairs in the style of Louis XV lined up against the walls. Two ornate consoles, topped by high mirrors, are to be found on the left as one enters, and on the opposite wall another console completes the furniture of the room. On the darkly paneled wall between the two consoles should hang a full-length portrait of Muhammad Ali. The remaining three walls are almost exclusively composed of windows and striped carnation-red and silver-grey curtains. Bronze wall brackets give additional light, their crystal festoons intermingling with the floor-length draperies of the curtains.

Two other suites in the corners of the building were used as bedrooms, all walls and ceilings gaily painted with oriental arabesques. In the fourth corner is the billiard room. The wall on the right when coming in is decorated in the Italian manner of the period, depicting a romantic landscape with classical ruins, almost a trompe-l'oeil, but the flowing architectural lines that frame it are very Turkish. The three remaining walls are almost all windows, with, on the whole length of the facing wall, a deep divan.

Originally this had been the dining room, but when King Louis-Philippe of France (1830–48) sent Muhammad Ali the billiard set, with its superbly sculpted bronze-handled cues, he housed it there. This was one of the many presents exchanged by these two rulers of such different worlds but who seemed to have been staunch friends. For in 1848, Muhammad Ali, during a Mediterranean cruise, landed at Naples, where news reached him that Louise-Philippe had been obliged to abdicate; it is said that this shock provoked the first signs of senility in Muhammad Ali. . . .

Muhammad Ali's well-loved Shubra had changed considerably when we were there in the early 1920s. We lived in two perfectly simple modern villas that my father had built on his share of the grounds. (The only words embossed on my parents' stationery were "Shubra Village.") I have no memory of the furniture, but I suppose it must have been the same that we had when we moved to town. This was heavily sculpted dark Chinese, monumental and uncomfortable. But there was another set I was particularly fond of which dated back to Muhammad Ali: some of the consoles and a very beautiful round central table made of porphyry, with cornflower-blue, enameled bronze bands encircling the pieces. From one or two old photographs, I see there was also quite a lot of furniture in hybrid 'Arab' style and, as always with my father, an enormous collection of arms on big, red-felt-covered panoplies.

The dining room was again in hideous arabesque adapted to European forms—a merger that should have never occurred. It had two large sideboards with mirrors in the middle; these were surrounded by shelves which, to my childish eyes, seemed to go upward almost to the ceilings but which, of course, did not, as the ceilings at Shubra were very high.

The second house was the salamlik, where, for the most part, my father entertained political guests. On the ground floor were spacious reception rooms with armchairs and couches, usually staked against the walls, a study for my father's business activities, and this time a much more sensible dining room in a fine, polished dark wood. The floor above was given over completely to a vast library and a few guest rooms.

It was perhaps in this house that the Wafd Party came to life, as Prince Omar Toussoun, my father's brother-in-law and cousin, had been the one to suggest to Saad Zaghloul Pasha the founding of this political party that at its origins was to have the unanimous backing of all the people, in all the different strata of society. My father, among many others, was to help finance it, and Shubra was to become one of its active rallying points.

A third house was the servants' quarters and the main kitchens, where reigned two head cooks and their underlings. (My mother said to me, "In my father's house we ate very well, in your father's house we ate supremely well!") There were, of course, also some outbuildings for the laundry, the garages, and other utilities.

The three buildings were grouped together in a perhaps not impeccable garden; in its farthest corners, it was very 'countryish,' but formal around the living quarters. It was an amusing place for us children, where we could be driven around in a horse-drawn carriage on sand-covered paths or play with some old cannons and other armaments too big to enter the house.

Our part of Shubra al-Balad (Shubra Village), as the district is called, was the farthest away from the city and still very much part of the countryside. In the farthest sections of the garden—those adjoining the fields—and also down on the water's edge, there lurked wolves, foxes, and jackals which at times would be hunted down. At night some would roam near the houses, and the foxes, strange to say, were the ones that attacked the night watchmen, who in the morning would exhibit their torn garments.

On and over the Nile there was a delightful two-storied wooden chalet, a sort of tea pavilion, which afforded a beautiful vantage point for sunsets. But my father also used it to sleep in when coming back late at night, his chauffeur valeting him so as not to wake up the household. It was built in a style which had details reminiscent of nineteenth-century medieval, simplified and not at all fussy, the whole construction appearing like a fragile cube painted a reddish, rusty color. On each side of it antique cannons pointed outward over the Nile. But we would go to the nymphaeum, or *fisqiya*, as the marble quadrangle with its fountains and pool is called in Arabic, to play about in, rowing on its water or lingering by its colonnades in an atmosphere of peace and tranquility.

In later years my aunts would give receptions in the nymphaeum for passing royalty, or huge charity balls, when the building would come to life for a brief moment, only to relapse again into its deathlike silence. Aunt Aziza, who was fond of the place, would go there regularly once a week to have tea with a few friends.

Aunt Iffet lived in another part of the garden in a most charming little house built on the top of what looked like a step-pyramid. The house had been elevated in this unusual manner so as to have a view of the Nile. But it turned out that, as the building was facing west, the afternoon sun was too hot to bear comfortably and a screen of eucalyptus trees was planted between it and the river, but in a manner which still allowed one to see the glimmer of water and passing sails. The platforms leading up to the house were planted with flowers, shrubs, and eucalyptus and pine trees. Stone stairs flanked by white marble urns overflowing with flowers communicated from the ground to the main door of the house facing the river, while identical stairs at the back façade led down to the grounds.

The central hall was of alabaster, with a little sunken fountain surmounted by a white dome ribbed with gold. In this room Princess Iffet would give small parties, each guest seated in front of a round silver tray for dinner, while around the fountain her Circassian or Turkish maids danced their national dances in their lovely native costumes. Often each tray would be arranged with different porcelain and glass so that the guest had an individual color scheme to suit his or her personality. In the evenings or afternoons when Aunt Iffet was not entertaining, one would sit on rocking chairs on the platforms surrounding the house while a flute player, hidden among the trees, played my aunt's favorite instrument. . . .

The kalfas were female servants ranging from a simple maid to a house-keeper or person of confidence; they always spoke Turkish, even if they were not of Turkish origin.

The men servants were Egyptians, Nubians, and Sudanese, with a sprinkling of Turks or Albanians, and sometimes a few Italians or Armenians, these last usually working in the garages; all spoke their own languages, but here Arabic was the common denominator among them. These multinational households got on well together—people not yet being influenced by political causes that cynically exploit color, race, or religion to divide and misrule the world. Even social barriers in those days seem to have been less self-conscious.

Naguib Mahfouz
from *Palace Walk*

SHE WOKE AT MIDNIGHT. She always woke up then without having to rely on an alarm clock. A wish that had taken root in her awoke her with great accuracy. For a few moments she was not sure she was awake. Images from her dreams and perceptions mixed together in her mind. She was troubled by anxiety before opening her eyes, afraid sleep had deceived her. Shaking her head gently, she gazed at the total darkness of the room. There was no clue by which to judge the time. The street noise outside her room would continue until dawn. She could hear the babble of voices from the coffeehouses and bars, whether it was early evening, midnight, or just before daybreak. She had no evidence to rely on except her intuition, like a conscious clock hand, and the silence encompassing the house, which revealed that her husband had not yet rapped at the door and that the tip of his stick had not yet struck against the steps of the staircase.

Habit woke her at this hour. It was an old habit she had developed when young and it had stayed with her as she matured. She had learned it along with the other rules of married life. She woke up at midnight to await her husband's return from his evening's entertainment. Then she would serve him until he went to sleep. She sat up in bed resolutely to overcome the temptation posed by sleep. After invoking the name of God, she slipped out from under the covers and onto the floor. Groping her way to the door, she guided herself by the bedpost and a panel of the window. As she opened the door, faint rays of light filtered in from a lamp set on a bracketed shelf in the sitting room. She went to fetch it, and the glass projected onto the ceiling a trembling circle of pale light hemmed in by darkness. She placed the lamp on the table by the sofa. The light shone throughout the room, revealing the large, square floor, high walls, and ceiling with parallel beams. The quality of the furnishings was evident: the Shiraz carpet, large brass bed, massive armoire, and long sofa draped with a small rug in a patchwork design of different motifs and colors.

The woman headed for the mirror to look at herself. She noted that her brown scarf was wrinkled and pushed back. Strands of chestnut hair had crept down over her forehead. Grasping the knot with her fingers, she untied it. She smoothed the scarf around her hair and retied the two ends slowly and carefully. She wiped the sides of her face with her hands as though trying to erase any last vestiges of sleep. In her forties and of medium build, she looked slender, although her body's soft skin was filled out to its narrow limits in a charmingly harmonious and symmetrical way. Her face was oblong, with a high forehead and delicate features. She had beautiful, small eyes with a sweet dreamy look. Her nose was petite and thin, flaring out a little at the nostrils. Beneath her tender lips, a tapered chin descended. The pure, fair skin of her cheek revealed a beauty spot of intensely pure black. She seemed to be in a hurry as she wrapped her veil about her and headed for the door to the balcony. Opening it, she entered the closed cage formed by the wooden latticework and stood there, turning her face right and left while she peeked out through the tiny, round openings of the latticework panels that protected her from being seen from the street.

The balcony overlooked the ancient building housing a cistern downstairs and a school upstairs which was situated in the middle of Palace Walk, or Bayn al-Qasrayn. Two roads met there: al-Nahhasin, or Coppersmiths Street, going south and Palace Walk, which went north. To her left, the street appeared narrow and twisting. It was enveloped in a gloom that was thicker overhead where the windows of the sleeping houses looked down, and less noticeable at street level, because of the light coming from the handcarts and from the vapor lamps of the coffeehouses and the shops that stayed open until dawn. To her right, the street was engulfed in darkness. There were no coffeehouses in that direction, only large stores, which closed early. There was nothing to attract the eye except the minarets of the ancient seminaries of Qala'un and Barquq, which loomed up like ghostly giants enjoying a night out by the light of the gleaming stars. It was a view that had grown on her over a quarter of a century. She never tired of it. Perhaps boredom was an irrelevant concept for a life as monotonous as hers. The view had been a companion for her in her solitude and a friend in her loneliness during a long period when she was deprived of friends and companions before her children were born, when for most of the day and night she had been the sole occupant of this large house with its two stories of spacious rooms with high ceilings, its dusty courtyard and deep well.

She had married before she turned fourteen and had soon found herself the mistress of the big house, following the deaths of her husband's parents. An elderly woman had assisted her in looking after it but deserted her at dusk to sleep in the oven room in the courtyard, leaving her alone in a nocturnal world teeming with spirits and ghosts. She would doze for an hour and lie awake the next, until her redoubtable husband returned from a long night out.

To set her mind at rest she had gotten into the habit of going from room to room, accompanied by her maid, who held the lamp for her, while she cast searching, frightened glances through the rooms, one after the other. She began with the first floor and continued with the upper story, reciting the Qur'an suras she knew in order to ward off demons. She would conclude with her room, lock the door, and get into bed, but her recitations would continue until she fell asleep.

She had been terrified of the night when she first lived in this house. She knew far more about the world of the jinn than that of mankind and remained convinced that she was not alone in the big house. There were demons who could not be lured away from these spacious, empty old rooms for long. Perhaps they had sought refuge there before she herself had been brought to the house, even before she saw the light of day. She frequently heard their whispers. Time and again she was awakened by their warm breath. When she was left alone, her only defense was reciting the opening prayer of the Qur'an and sura one hundred and twelve from it, about the absolute supremacy of God, or rushing to the latticework screen at the window to peer anxiously through it at the lights of the carts and the coffeehouses, listening carefully for a laugh or cough to help her regain her composure.

Then the children arrived, one after the other. In their early days in the world, though, they were tender sprouts unable to dispel her fears or reassure her. On the contrary, her fears were multiplied by her troubled soul's concern for them and her anxiety that they might be harmed. She would hold them tight, lavish affection on them, and surround them, whether awake or asleep, with a protective shield of Qur'an suras, amulets, charms, and incantations. True peace of mind she would not achieve until her husband returned from his evening's entertainment.

It was not uncommon for her, while she was alone with an infant, rocking him to sleep and cuddling him, to clasp him to her breast suddenly. She would listen intently with dread and alarm and then call out in a loud voice, as though addressing someone in the room, "Leave us alone. This isn't where you belong. We are Muslims and believe in the one God." Then she would quickly and fervently recite the one hundred and twelfth sura of the Qur'an about the uniqueness of God. Over the course of time as she gained more experience living with the spirits, her fears diminished a good deal. She was calm enough to jest with them without being frightened. If she happened to sense one of them prowling about, she would say in an almost intimate tone, "Have you no respect for those who worship God the Merciful? He will protect us from you, so do us the favor of going away." But her mind was never completely at rest until her husband returned. Indeed, the mere fact of his presence in the house, whether awake or asleep, was enough to make her feel secure. Then it did not matter whether the doors were open or locked, the lamp burning brightly or extinguished.

It had occurred to her once, during the first year she lived with him, to venture a polite objection to his repeated nights out. His response had been to seize her by the ears and tell her peremptorily in a loud voice, "I'm a man. I'm the one who commands and forbids. I will not accept any criticism of my behavior. All I ask of you is to obey me. Don't force me to discipline you."

She learned from this, and from the other lessons that followed, to adapt to everything, even living with the jinn, in order to escape the glare of his wrathful eye. It was her duty to obey him without reservation or condition. She yielded so wholeheartedly that she even disliked blaming him privately for his nights out. She became convinced that true manliness, tyranny, and staying out till after midnight were common characteristics of a single entity. With the passage of time she grew proud of whatever he meted out, whether it pleased or saddened her. No matter what happened, she remained a loving, obedient, and docile wife. She had no regrets at all about reconciling herself to a type of security based on surrender.

Whenever she thought back over her life, only goodness and happiness came to mind. Fears and sorrows seemed meaningless ghosts to her, worth nothing more than a smile of pity. Had she not lived with this husband and his shortcomings for a quarter century and been rewarded by children who were the apples of her eye, a home amply provided with comforts and blessings, and a happy, adult life? Of course she had. Being surrounded by the jinn had been bearable, just as each evening was bearable. None of them had attempted to hurt her or the children. They had only played some harmless pranks to tease her. Praise God, the merit was all God's. He calmed her heart and with His mercy brought order to her life.

She even profoundly loved this hour of waiting up, though it interrupted a pleasant sleep and forced her to do chores that should have ceased with the end of the day. Not only had it become an integral part of her life, tied to many of her memories, but it continued to be the living symbol of her affection for her spouse, of her wholehearted dedication to making him happy, which she revealed to him night after night. For this reason, she was filled with contentment as she stood in the balcony peering through the openings toward Palace Walk and al-Khurunfush streets and then toward Hammam al-Sultan or the various minarets.

She let her eyes wander over the houses bunched together untidily on both sides of the road like a row of soldiers standing at ease, relaxing from harsh discipline. She smiled at the beloved view of this road, which stayed awake until the break of dawn while the other streets, lanes, and alleys slept. It distracted her from her sleeplessness and kept her company when she was lonely, dispelling her fears. Night changed nothing save to envelop the surrounding areas with a profound silence that provided a setting in which the street's sounds could ring out clearly, like the shadows at the edges of a painting that give the work depth and clarity. A laugh would resound as though bursting out in her room, and a remark made in a normal tone of voice could be heard distinctly. She could listen to a cough rattle on until it ended in a kind of moan. A waiter's voice would ring out like the call of a muezzin: "Another ball of tobacco for the pipe," and she would merrily ask herself, "By God, are these people ordering a refill at this hour?"

They reminded her of her absent husband. She would wonder, "Where do you suppose he is now? What is he doing? . . . May he be safe and sound whatever he does."

It was suggested to her once that a man like Mr. Ahmad Abd al-Gawad, so wealthy, strong, and handsome, who stayed out night after night, must have other women in his life. At that time, her life was poisoned by jealousy, and intense sorrow overcame her. Her courage was not up to speaking to him about it, but she confided her grief to her mother, who sought as best she could to soothe her mind with fine words, telling her, "He married you after divorcing his first wife. He could have kept her too, if he'd wanted, or taken second, third, and fourth wives. His father had many wives. Thank our Lord that you remain his only wife."

Although her mother's words did not help much then, she eventually accepted their truth and validity. Even if the rumor was accurate, perhaps that was another characteristic of manliness, like late nights and tyranny. At any rate, a single evil was better than many. It would be a mistake to allow suspicion to wreck her good life filled with happiness and comfort. Moreover, in spite of everything, perhaps the rumor was idle speculation or a lie. She discovered that jealousy was no different from the other difficulties troubling her life. To accept them was an inevitable and binding decree. Her only means of combating them was, she found, to call on patience and rely on her inner strength, the one resource in the struggle against disagreeable things. Jealousy and its motivation became something she put up with like her husband's other troubling characteristics or living with the jinn.

She continued to watch the road and listen to the people chat until she heard a horse's hoof beats. She turned her head toward al-Nahhasin Street and saw a carriage slowly approaching, its lamps shining in the darkness. She sighed with relief and murmured, "Finally . . . ." It was the carriage of one of his friends, bringing him to the door of his house after their evening out before continuing on as usual to al-Khurunfush with the owner and some other friends who lived there. The carriage stopped in front of the house, and her husband's voice rang out cheerfully: "May God keep you."

She would listen lovingly and with amazement to her husband's voice when he said good night to his friends. If she had not heard him every night at about this hour, she would not have believed it. She and the children were accustomed to nothing but prudence, dignity, and gravity from him. How did he come by these joyful, jesting sounds, which flowed out so merrily and graciously?

The owner of the carriage teased her husband, asking, "Did you hear what the horse said to himself when you got out? He commented it's a pity I bring a man like you home every night when all you deserve is an ass."

The men in the vehicle exploded with laughter. Her husband waited for them to quiet down. Then he replied, "Didn't you hear the answer? He said in that case I'd be riding you."

The men burst out laughing once more. The vehicle's owner said, "We'll save the rest for tomorrow night."

The carriage proceeded along Palace Walk, and her husband headed for their door. She left the balcony for the bedroom. Picking up the lamp, she went to the sitting room and then to the hall to stand at the top of the stairs. She could hear the outside door being slammed shut and the bolt sliding into place. She imagined his tall figure crossing the courtyard as he donned awesome dignity and shed the mirthfulness which, had she not overheard it, she would have never thought possible. Hearing the tip of his walking stick strike the steps of the stairway, she held the lamp out over the banister to light his way.

Translated by William Maynard Hutchins

Samia Serageldin

from *The Cairo House*

THE FEAST OF THE Sacrifice must have been in winter that year. The sheep had arrived two days before amid much commotion, an incongruous sight in a residential neighborhood in Cairo. Sheep or cattle were sacrificed on the family estate, but it was also customary to carry out the ritual in Cairo. This imperative was never questioned: it was one of the many instances in our hybrid culture when western norms were unhesitatingly sacrificed on the altar of tradition.

I watched from the balcony when the van arrived with the two sheep in the back. The cook, his helper, the chauffeur, and Ibrahim the Nubian door-keeper then proceeded to drag the bleating, resisting beasts to the dog run where they would be penned until the morning of the Feast.

There was a sudden commotion and panic; someone had forgotten to chain up the dog, who had come flying at the throat of the ram. The howling German Shepherd was dragged away. Finally the sheep were safely enclosed. Two days later, before dawn on the day of the Feast, they would be taken to a shed in the backyard that was ordinarily used once a week by two washer-women who came to do the laundry, then on the following day by a man who came to do the ironing. The dog was also bathed there. But on that one day of the year, between dawn and daybreak, as tradition required for the sacrifice to be valid, the sheep would be slaughtered and skinned in that room, and the stench of blood would replace the scent of soap and starch. Then the walls and floor were hosed down and everything returned to normal for another year.

On the morning of the day before the Feast the bustle around the house had reached a pitch of controlled frenzy. In the salon, the Sudanese head suf-fragi stood on top of a tall ladder, painstakingly unhooking the crystal drops from the chandelier, one by one, to be wiped with vinegar and water. Mama supervised, hair in curlers under a chiffon cap, wearing one of her favorite déshabillés: a faded, blue satin, shawl-collared affair with a sweeping skirt. Mama only dressed to go out, and then she spent at least an hour in front of her tulle-skirted vanity and her modern built-in closets.

The under-suffragi was pushing a heavy contraption across the parquet floor to polish it; twice a year the hardwood floors were hand-stripped with steel wool, cleaned, waxed, then polished with a chamois cloth weighed down by a massive brick of lead at the end of a stick. He pushed the unwieldy contraption forward and dragged it back with a clicking, sucking sound. One of the maids was using a bamboo duster to beat the back of a rug slung over the railing of the balcony.

I stood on the balcony at a safe distance from the dust raised by the maid, watching the arrival of the sheep. I remember the scent of jasmine from the bushes under the balcony—jasmine and dust. The cook came up to the balcony with some carrots to coax me to feed the lamb. A large, garrulous man with terrible burn scars on his chest, he was sweating from his recent efforts and the general excitement. All the household help seemed to go around with unusually dilated pupils in the days leading up to the Feast. "Blood lust," my mother called it. The cook proudly pointed out the two animals to me, a ram and a lamb.

"See the pretty little one, I chose him just for you. . . ."

I had never been particularly curious about the ritual of the sacrifice. By the time I woke up on Feast Day mornings, it was all over. It was over by the time my father was roused, at about six o'clock, to attend the early prayers. Even Muslims who rarely set foot in a mosque during the year attend the Feast prayers, and, on these occasions, the carpeting is extended out into the courtyard of the mosque in anticipation of the overflow. Papa tended to be late, so he usually ended up in the courtyard, along with the cook and his helpers, who would also arrive late and exhausted, having just finished with the butchering.

Mama, who normally rose at about ten o'clock, would have been up at dawn, supervising the distribution of meat to the old retainers and the poor who regularly came to the house. A small crowd would have gathered by daybreak. The wetnurses were given the lion's share, followed by the household help. The sheepskins invariably fell to the lot of the Nubian doorkeeper, who took them back with him to his village in Nubia on his biannual visits home.

I would stay up in my room until it was time for me to dress and go with Papa on another round of visits. By the time I came home, calm would have been restored, and the people who had come for charity would have dispersed. Dinner would be served, with several dishes of lamb as required by tradition. I never touched it; the odor of freshly butchered meat still lingered about the kitchen, wafting into the dining room every time the door to the butler's pantry swung open. The household staff would be in a hurry to clear the table and be gone for the holidays, except for the governess, who did not celebrate Muslim feasts, and for the doorkeeper, who had no family in Cairo.

It had never before occurred to me to be curious about what went on in that shed, between dawn and daybreak. But now I could not get the idea out of my head, not even when Papa took me with him on the first round of visits to relatives. The routine never varied; the aunts and uncles were visited in order of their seniority. Since Papa was the youngest of his eight brothers and sisters, his turn to receive visitors came on the last of the three days of the Feast. On the eve of the Feast he took me to visit the Pasha, Papa's eldest brother and the head of the clan. He lived in the family home in Garden City, which everyone called the Cairo House.

On the way we passed a truck full of smiling, excited people from the country. They were standing up in the back of the truck, swaying with its movement, singing and clapping. The girls wore neon pink, nylon gauze dresses, the boys new striped pajamas. We also passed pickup trucks carrying bleating sheep marked for slaughter with a rose-red stain on their fat tails. By dawn the next day they would all be butchered. I stared at them with equal fascination and revulsion, trying to imagine the actual proceedings.

We drove down the Nile Corniche past the grand hotels and the long white wall of the British Embassy, then turned off into the narrow, villa-lined streets of Garden City. When we reached the family house, Papa stopped the car and honked for the gatekeeper to open the gate. He parked in the back of the villa, alongside several other cars.

I followed him round to the front, past the fountain with its statue of a reclining Poseidon. One of the two heavy double doors was open; normally the front doors were only used on Feast days, and for weddings and funerals. Inside the long hall the marble floor radiated cold. I looked up through the atrium at the blazing crystal chandelier suspended from the ceiling of the second floor, fifty feet above my head.

"Let's go upstairs to see your grandmother first." Papa headed for the wide marble staircase with the two curved balustrades. I followed him up, then along the gallery.

At the top of the stairs we were met by Fangali, the majordomo of the house. He adjusted the outmoded fez he wore on his head and tugged at his caftan as he came forward to greet us. There was something about him that eluded my understanding. The high-pitched voice, the ingratiating manner, contrasted with the thin mustache, the bold eyes. I wondered why he, of all the menservants, was the only one allowed to come and go freely upstairs, in the family quarters. I had vaguely overheard that, as a result of an accident at birth, he was not quite a man. I wondered if he was an agha. I had heard of the eunuchs of my grandmother's day, without understanding what the word signified. I didn't dare ask. Years later I thought I understood, but later still, Fangali would spring a surprise on us all.

Fangali knocked perfunctorily on the door to Grandmother's room and opened it, announcing in his peculiar whine, "Look who's here, Hanim. Shamel Bey and Sitt Gigi."

Grandmother was sitting on a chaise longue, her legs covered with a knit shawl. Fangali tucked the shawl around the childlike feet in satin mules, and left the room. It never failed to amaze me that this tiny woman could have borne my tall, strapping father and his eight brothers and sisters. But it seemed as though the effort had drained Grandmother completely; as far back as I could remember, she had always had that vague air of detachment about her.

Papa kissed his mother's hand and pulled up a chair beside her and I followed suit. She was saying to Papa, with an approving nod in my direction, "That little one can name her own mahr." I understood vaguely what the word meant: the dowry the bridegroom brings to the bride.

Papa laughed and rumpled my hair. "I'm going down to see your uncle in his study, Gigi. I'll send for you when I'm ready to go, and you can come to wish him a happy Feast before we leave."

I nodded and sat down beside Grandmother. Fangali brought us glasses of qammareddin, apricot nectar, and a tray with sweets. I nibbled absently on a glacé chestnut, my mind on the act of the sacrifice. Mama would never allow it if I asked to observe it, but she had never expressly forbidden it, so technically I would not be disobeying. I knew Mama's rules well enough though: whatever was not explicitly allowed was forbidden. As for Madame Hélène, she slept in the room adjoining mine, with the door ajar, but she slept heavily, with a smoker's nasal snore. I made up my mind: I would do it.

At that moment Fangali ushered in a shriveled old woman wrapped in black from head to toe. The sooty black eyes, ringed with kohl, darted sharply around the room. No one seemed to know how old Umm Khalil really was, but it was rumored that the secret of her spryness was drinking nothing but vinegar and water for one day a week. She went from house to house, making jam, pickles, rosewater, kohl from pounded roast almonds, or special concoctions for recovering new mothers. The servants in each household treated her with the awe commensurate with her reputation for an undeflectable evil eye.

I tried to resist an involuntary frisson when I set eyes on the black-shrouded figure. I knew this reaction to an old family retainer was highly reprehensible, but children, like animals, have not yet learned to override their instincts. Seeing Umm Khalil at the moment I had made my decision was a bad omen, and I hesitated again.

"How are you, Umm Khalil?" Grandmother reached for some money from a tasseled purse she kept beside her for the steady stream of family domestics who came to visit on feast days. She had phobias about certain things; for instance, she insisted on having the maid wash any money that she handled, whether it was coins or bills. "It's because she had such a bad experience during the cholera epidemic," Mama had explained. "She lost two children to cholera, they were just babies."

Fangali came to fetch me. I kissed Grandmother and hurried downstairs. The door to my uncle's study was open, and there were a dozen men sitting around the room. My eldest uncle sat behind his desk at the far end. He seemed even larger than the last time I had seen him, on the Lesser Feast a few months before. A big man, his bulk suggested power rather than obesity. His gray double-breasted suit fitted him perfectly, and the silk square in the breast pocket matched his tie. I went up to kiss him; he smelled of Cuban cigars and Old Spice, just like I remembered.

"Happy Feast, little one. What a big girl you've become." He patted my cheek and reached into his pocket for a handful of shiny coins. It was the custom to give children shiny new coins for luck on feast days, and my uncle always prepared great quantities of them for all the children of the clan, and the children of friends and retainers, who came to visit.

I had heard that in the old days, before the revolution, before I was born, when my uncle had been prime minister, he had once paid the Feast Day bonuses to some of the Cairo police force out of his own pocket—out of the family's pocket, really, since it was all one and the same. During the revolutionary tribunals of 1952, this had been brought up as proof of undue influence. The Pasha had countered that, there being a temporary shortfall in the budget, he had only advanced the money out of his own pocket, in order to make sure that the poor policemen and their families would have the wherewithal to celebrate the Feast. I did not understand what all the fuss had been about, I thought it was about the new coins that children were given.

Andrée Chedid

from *From Sleep Unbound*

THE ARRIVAL OF SUNDAY brought the taste of hope to the tip of your tongue. Even though memories of past disappointments assailed you, after a week of waiting, one began to hope once again. On those mornings I brushed my dress and did my hair carefully. The passing hours had a meaning, they brought me nearer to leaving.

Ali was waiting in front of the gate. From a distance I could see his black profile, his fine features, his fez planted straight on his head. He was usually alone, but sometimes his son was with him, wearing long pants even though he was only ten. The son was darker than the father; the same scars striped his cheeks, three on each side. It was he who opened the door and got out in front of the gas station while Ali leaned on the hood and discussed politics or the weather. He held the same views as my father on everything; for more than fifteen years he had not left my father's service for longer than a day.

On Sundays around twelve we crossed the city again in the opposite direction.

The car rolled past streetlamps, past shops, past carts creaking along as if time did not exist. Trees, pavements, and people were left behind. Nothing could stand firm against the motion of the car. Smoke rose from the railway station and mingled with the smoke of the factories, before dissolving above the rooftops.

Ali's back was immutable; not a muscle in his neck twitched. The car glided between obstacles, barely missed red lights, swerved sideways to avoid hitting a pedestrian. Suddenly Ali leaned out the window and yelled, "Son of a bitch! Wait till I catch you! I'll beat the life out of you!" Regaining control, he mumbled, "Sleepwalkers!"

The noises of the narrow streets mingled with the noises from the open balconies, growing thicker with each step of each passerby, with each new sound, taking on monstrous proportions before assaulting the public square. There this monstrous noise circled the equestrian statue, knocked on window panes, and swirled past a row of dozing carriage drivers. One could scream at the top of one's lungs; no one would hear. The noise was everywhere. Nobody paid any attention to it; it became a constant rumble, the tick-tock of a clock or the background music of a play.

The town flew by so quickly. It was nothing more than a succession of images drowned in this noise. The wish to capture these images one after another, to examine them, to understand them, these images of people, of forlorn façades and shop windows; this urge vanished with the car's flight. I was alone in the backseat, digging at the scaly worn leather with my fingernails.

The boulevard led to the house, which had a majestic air; two massive pillars supported the central balcony. At this hour my father and my five brothers were either taking a walk or chatting with friends on the terrace of one of the big cafés.

Hunched up on the bench, the porter was sleeping, barefooted; his Turkish slippers were lying on the ground. Nothing except the master's car could rouse him from his nap. As soon as it appeared in the distance, the very sound of the wheels seemed to pierce his eardrums. In less than a second he was standing up, his ivory turban straight, his slippers on, his hand ready to open the gate. He always kept his eyes fixed on a spot slightly higher than one's head, as if he were afraid his eyelids might drop of their own weight if he didn't hold them up by an effort. He slept all day long and sometimes in the most unique positions. His job consisted of opening doors and receiving insults from my father and brothers. Nothing affected him. He accepted their abuse with a great generosity of soul, eyes fixed on a spot a little above their heads. Then, as soon as the car passed through the gates and they were closed, he went back to squat on his bench.

Marduk, the dog, howled when we arrived. He never recognized me. Ali had to use his most persuasive manner to coax Marduk to let me pass. "This is the daughter of the house!" Ali would say. "Come, come, Marduk . . . ," he insisted gently. "This is Sitt Samia, the daughter of the house."

The white marble staircase was covered with ants. They were crawling over every step. Marduk was so used to them that he never hurt them. Ali led the way, carrying my bag. The soles of his shoes crackled as he crossed the gravel. Marduk sniffed at the hem of my dress. What was I doing here? Ali pushed open the door, and I followed him into the big hall with the domed ceiling. From this hall another marble staircase with wrought-iron railings led to the top floor. The bedrooms were on this floor. Mine faced that other room, the one whose door was draped with mourning crepe.

Ever since they had taken away my mother, her room had remained intact, but it was kept double-locked, and the door was framed by a large black border. For ten years now I had felt the presence of my mother behind this door which I longed to beat until it flew open. For ten years they had kept her buried while I struggled to will her back to life.

"But the mourning period is over," said my father. "Soon we'll repaint the door. We'll open up the room and fix it for one of your brothers. The first one to get married."

The time was over, he said. She had to be dead, forgotten. "Mother, Mother, my absent one, this black-bordered door is my only image of you!"

My room was stuffy. When I opened the windows, clouds of dust rose from the woodwork. I tore off my uniform and threw it far away into the darkest corner of this prison, from which I could not escape.

I could hear my father's voice as well as those of my brothers. All these voices echoed under the domed ceiling of the foyer:

"Abdu! Abdu!"

My brothers were hungry. They wanted to go to the dining room. My father restrained them, saying: "It is Sunday. We must wait for Samia."

I hurried. I took out my best dress from the closet, the one Zariffa had recently ironed.

"Samia! Samia!"

My name was resounding from the walls of my room. They were hungry. My dress was tight at the elbows, and I had trouble getting my arms into the sleeves. The seams ripped.

"Samia! Samia!"

They were threatening to sit down, to start eating without me. My father silenced them, and then he came to the foot of the big staircase and shouted up at me:

"Samia, my girl, your brothers are hungry. Hurry up! We are all waiting for you!"

I fought with the hooks. I didn't have time to change my heavy black stockings, and I couldn't help being aware of them as I walked down the stairs in my patent leather shoes. My hair had gotten messed up when I pulled on my dress; I hadn't the time to do it again.

"What a sight!" Karim mocked me, standing at the foot of the stairs. "I'm glad I'm only your brother."

The others laughed. "Well, you're finally here."

I ran but the staircase seemed endless. My father walked toward the dining room, whispering with Guirguis, the eldest. They looked alike. Seen from behind, one could mistake them for each other.

Before sitting down I went up to each brother and each one kissed me on the cheek.

"You have grown again," my father said.

I sat on his left at the carved wooden table; my place faced the buffet with glass doors in which the silver was displayed. There were circles on the glass shelves where pieces had been taken out.

The Sunday meal consisted of a sauce of green herbs which we poured over rice, of onions, lamb, and chicken. My brothers and my father consumed huge portions. I also ate a lot, compelled by a feeling of rage.

Guirguis was over thirty. He had dark skin and cunning eyes which enlivened his heavy, drooping features. Although there were six years between them, Karim and Yusef were inseparable. They knew they were handsome, and they admired each other greatly. They discussed ties, women, and cars. Sometimes they lowered their voices to spare me the details of their latest feats. Yusef was only twenty-two, but he already boasted of incalculable conquests and swore he would never marry until he was at least fifty.

"I," said Barsum, "have decided to get married this year." And he asked my father if he knew of any young girl he could recommend.

My father liked to be consulted; he replied, "That's good, very good, my son. I'll think about it." He would find someone, he would go to visit my aunts, he'd consult the bishop.

Barsum wanted a family; he would accept the wife his father chose but he wanted her to be young, very young.

"Certainly, my son, you must take a young wife, to train her."

Antun was silent. He was the youngest but he looked so serious, with his growing stoutness and his gold-rimmed spectacles, that he was consulted in spite of his youth.

"What do you think, Antun?"

"Do you have any suggestions?"

"One must marry young, don't you think so, Antun?"

"It isn't necessary to marry before you're fifty, is it, Antun?"

The conversation had taken off, and now "the family" was being discussed.

"Our cousin Suraya is over twenty and she's not yet married! Her brothers are so embarrassed they hardly dare to show their faces in society."

"Not yet married, in spite of her dowry!" affirmed my father.

"She's being difficult," Antun commented.

"Difficult?" questioned my father. "You can see that no one's in charge of that household. My sister has no control over her children. If I took the situation in hand, you'd see a difference!"

"Suraya's strong-willed," Antun reminded the others.

"Strong-willed!" exclaimed Karim. "She'll come to a bad end."

"A bad end," echoed Yusef.

Poor Suraya! Ticketed, labeled, and imprisoned by a rigid prophecy. "A bad end."

Translated from the French by Sharon Spencer

Yusuf al-Sibaie

from *We Do Not Cultivate Thorns*

BEFORE SAYEDA LEFT THE room, a voice rose high in the alley, breaking the silence of the morning with the call, "We polish brass."

Dalal sat up in bed and called Sayeda, "Get the brass pots from the kitchen and take them down to Amm Ali to polish them."

With enthusiastic joy Sayeda rushed to the kitchen and looked out of the small window and called out, "Amm Ali, Amm Ali!"

The emaciated old man raised his head toward the source of the voice as he repeated his call, "We polish brass."

Sayeda called out again, "Wait, Amm Ali!"

Amm Ali stopped and took the polish basket off his shoulder. He had two thin legs that showed beneath his pants, colorless from the amount of dust and soot that covered his body. He was wearing an old striped football T-shirt and his neck protruded from it with his face stuck on top as if he were a puppet. He gave her a wide smile with lips covered in bushy hair that extended from his head to make up his mustache and beard. He called to Sayeda after he recognized her voice, "Come down, Sayeda. May this first job, daughter of Gaber and Ruqayya, be as sweet as milk."

Sayeda came down carrying on her shoulder a bunch of pots, a tray, and a strainer, and put them all in front of him as she greeted him with a smiling face, "Good morning, Amm Ali!"

"Good morning, Sayeda. How's your father?"

"Fine."

"We didn't see him at the mosque this morning."

"He's still sleeping."

"Bless him. It's unusual that he should miss dawn prayer."

"I think he's tired."

"When your mother was alive, he never missed dawn prayer. He was as strong as an ox."

Ali brought out the tools and started preparing the hole in which he would bury the opening of the air pump. He covered it with a few bricks and said, resuming their conversation, "He had his days of glory. He once closed down the entire Sadd Street and beat up tough Rashwan, the futuwwa of the slaughterhouse, and made him run ahead in front of him."

Ali took out some pieces of coal from his basket and started to arrange them at the end corner of the hole he had dug as he said, "Only your mother's death did him in. She was the greatest of women! The fever and infection finished her off a couple of months after you were born."

Sayeda found nothing new in what Amm Ali the brass polisher had to say, for she had often heard it from him and from people of the neighborhood. She also knew what he would say next. After he had arranged the coal, he said, "Your mother's death did him in and that woman Dalal finished him off. I don't know where he found her!"

Ali pulled Sayeda over and sat her by his side, "I know her well . . . her and her mother. They're from the slaughterhouse area."

He lowered his voice and moved his lips closer to Sayeda's ear, whispering, "Once I was with her mother in Tall Zenhum. It was noon and the sun was scorching hot. We got into a hole to hide from view and be in the shade. We had just started when patrolling soldiers surprised us. I left my polish basket in the hole and we ran, but the soldiers caught up with us. They let me go after they whipped me on my back. The marks are still there."

Ali started moving the air pump to light the coal.

Sayeda found that this part of Ali's story was new to her, so she listened carefully.

She asked, "Then what happened?"

"Nothing. I stopped going to the hills and repented to God."

He was silent for a moment as he took out the tin from the basket. But then he said, "We started going to her place. Dalal had grown up and started to get into the business, too."

He shook his head regretfully and continued, "Later, fate hurled her into your father's path. And she was able to seduce him and then marry him."

Ali started brooding and sighed, saying, "Such is life! Who would have believed it?!"

Sayeda felt that the new bit in the story was finished, so she got up from beside Ali to go home.

Ali raised his head and asked, "Where to?"

Sayeda was used to sharing the polish session with Amm Ali. She enjoyed the lighting of the coal, and she used to stand inside the pots and shuffle her feet inside them as if she were playing hopscotch or jumping rope to polish them. But today she felt she had more attractive things to do beyond lighting the coals with the air pump and shuffling inside the pots.

She answered Ali, "Today is the mulid, Amm Ali."

"And so? The day hasn't begun yet."

"Sitt Zakiyya, Hagg Boraie's wife, is giving out ful and bread."

"So, what business is it of yours?"

"I'm going to help her."

The man was overjoyed, "Bring us a couple of loaves."

"Of course."

Ali got up and grabbed her arm, then whispered in her ear, "Is she gonna give out meat as well?"

"I suppose so."

Ali raised both arms toward the sky in prayer with a broad smile on his lips that revealed his remaining teeth, "May this job be as sweet as milk."

He then whispered in her ear, "Will I get my share?"

Sayeda was a bit hesitant as she said, "I can only bring ful, Amm Ali."

"Keep a loaf with meat on the side. Be smart. Hide it in your chest."

Translated by Samia Mehrez

Naguib Mahfouz

from *Palace Walk*

IN THE HOME OF the singer Zubayda there was a room like a hall in the middle of her residence that was dubbed the recital chamber. Actually it was a hall for which new uses had been found. Perhaps the most important of these for her and her troupe was rehearsing their songs and learning new material. It had been chosen because it was far from the public street and separated from it by bedrooms and reception chambers. Its size also made it a suitable location for her private parties, which usually were either exorcisms or recitals to which she would invite her special friends and close acquaintances. The motive for hosting these parties was not simply generosity, for any generosity manifested was almost always that of the guests themselves. The aim was to increase the number of fine friends able to invite her to perform at their parties or to help promote her by praising her in the circles where they were received. It was also from these men that she selected lover after lover.

Now it was al-Sayyid Ahmad Abd al-Gawad's turn to honor the festive hall, accompanied by some of his most distinguished acquaintances. He had displayed boundless energy following the daring meeting that had taken place between them at her house. His messengers had immediately taken her generous gift of candied nuts and dried fruit, which was decorated with silver plate. These gifts were all a token of the affection to follow. Leaving the guest list entirely up to him, the sultana had invited him to get-acquainted party in honor of their newfound love.

The chamber was remarkable for its attractive, Egyptian look. A row of comfortable sofas with brocade upholstery, suggesting both luxury and dissipation, stretched out on either side of the sultana's divan, which was flanked by mattresses and cushions for her troupe. The long expanse of floor was covered with carpets of many different colors and types. On a table suspended from the right wall, halfway along it, candles were arranged in a candelabra where they looked as lovely and intense as a beauty mark on a cheek. There was a huge lamp hanging from the peak of a skylight in the center of the ceiling. The skylight's windows looked out on the roof terrace and were left open on warm evenings but closed when it was cold.

Zubayda sat cross-legged on the divan. At her right was Zanuba, the lute player, her foster daughter. On her left was Abdu, the blind performer on the zither-like qanun. The women of the troupe sat on both sides, some clasping tambourines, others stroking their conical drums or playing with finger cymbals. The sultana had selected for al-Sayyid Ahmad the first seat on the right. The other men, his friends, found places for themselves without any hesitation, as though they lived there. This was not odd since there was nothing novel about the situation for them and it was not the first time they had seen the sultana. Al-Sayyid Ahmad presented his friends to the performer, beginning with al-Sayyid Ali, the flour merchant.

Zubayda laughed and said, "Al-Sayyid Ali is no stranger to me. I performed at his daughter's wedding last year."

Then he turned to the copper merchant. One of the men accused him of being a fan of the vocalist Bamba Kashar, and the merchant quickly remarked, "Lady, I've come to repent."

The introductions continued until everyone was presented. Then Jaljal, the maid, brought in glasses of wine and served the guests. The men started to feel a vitality mixed with liberality and mirth. Al-Sayyid Ahmad was undeniably the bridegroom of the party. His friends called him that and he felt it too, deep inside. At first he had been a little uncomfortable in a way rare for him but had concealed his discomfort with an extra amount of laughter and mirth. Once he began drinking, the embarrassment left him spontaneously and his composure returned. He threw himself wholeheartedly into the excitement.

Whenever he felt a surge of desire—and desires are aroused at musical entertainments—he would gaze greedily at the sultana of the soiree. His eyes would linger on the folds of her massive body. He felt good about the blessing fortune had bestowed on him. He congratulated himself on the sweet delights he could look forward to that night and following ones.

"'It's when a man is tested that he's honored or despised.' I challenged her with this declaration. I've got to live up to my word. I wonder what she's like as a woman and how far she'll discover the truth at a suitable time. In any case, I'll play by her rules. To ensure a victory over an opponent, you must assume she's vigilant and strong. I won't deviate from my long-standing practice of making my own pleasure a secondary objective after hers, which is the real goal and climax. In that way my pleasure will be achieved in the most perfect fashion."

Despite his great number of amorous adventures, out of all the different varieties of love, al-Sayyid Ahmad had experienced only lust. All the same, he had progressed in his pursuit of it to its purest and most delicate form. He was not simply an animal. In addition to his sensuality, he was endowed with a delicacy of feeling, a sensitivity of emotion, and an ingrained love for song and music. He had elevated lust to its most exalted type. It was for the sake of this lust alone that he had married the first time and then for the second. Over the course of time, his conjugal love was affected by calm new elements of affection and familiarity, but in essence it continued to be based on bodily desire. When an emotion is of this type, especially when it has acquired a renewed power and exuberant vitality, it cannot be content with only one form of expression. Thus he had shot off in pursuit of all the varieties of love and passion, like a wild bull. Whenever desire called, he answered, deliriously and enthusiastically. No woman was anything more than a body to him. All the same, he would not bow his head before that body unless he found it truly worthy of being seen, touched, smelled, tasted, and heard. It was lust, yes, but not bestial or blind. It had been refined by a craft that was at least partially an art, setting his lust in a framework of delight, humor, and good cheer. Nothing was so like his lust as his body, since both were huge and powerful, qualities that bring to mind roughness and savagery. Yet both concealed within them grace, delicacy, and affection, even though he might intentionally cloak those characteristics at times with sternness and severity. While he was devouring the sultana with his glances he did not limit his active imagination to having sex with her. It also wandered through various dreams of amusing pastimes and tuneful celebrations.

Zubayda felt the warmth of his gaze. Glancing around at the faces of the guests vainly and coquettishly, she told him, "Bridegroom, control yourself. Aren't you embarrassed in front of your associates?"

"There's no point trying to be chaste in the presence of such a prodigious and voluptuous body."

The songstress released a resounding laugh. Then with great delight she asked the men, "What do you think of your friend?"

They all replied in one breath, "He's excused!"

At this the blind qanun player shook his head to the right and left, his lower lip hanging open. He muttered, "He's excused who gives a warning."

Although the man's proverb was well received, the lady turned on him in mock anger and punched him in the chest, yelling, "You hush and shut your big mouth."

The blind man accepted the blow laughingly. He opened his mouth as though to speak but closed it again to be safe. The woman turned her head toward al-Sayyid Ahmad and told him threateningly, "This is what happens to people who get out of line."

Pretending to be alarmed, he replied, "But I came to learn how to get out of line."

The woman struck her chest with her hand and shouted, "What cheek! Did you all hear what he said?"

More than one of them said at the same time, "It's the best thing we've heard so far."

One of the group added, "You ought to hit him if he doesn't get out of line."

Someone else suggested, "You ought to obey him so long as he stays out of line."

The woman raised her eyebrows to show an astonishment she did not feel and asked, "Do you love being naughty this much?"

Al-Sayyid Ahmad sighed and said, "May our Lord perpetuate our naughtiness."

At that the performer picked up a tambourine and said, "Here's something better for you to listen to."

She struck the tambourine in a rather nonchalant way, but the sound rose above the babbling commotion like an alarm and silenced it. The noise of her tambourine teased their ears. Everyone gradually dropped what he was doing. The members of the troupe got ready to play while the gentlemen drained their glasses. Then they gazed at the sultana. The room was so silent it almost declared their eagerness to enjoy the music.

The maestro gestured to her troupe and they burst out playing an overture by the composer Muhammad Uthman. Heads started to sway with the music. Al-Sayyid Ahmad surrendered himself to the resonant sound of the qanun, which set his heart on fire. Echoes of many different melodies from a long era filled with nights of musical ecstasy burst into flame within him, as though small drops of gasoline had fallen on a hidden ember. The qanun certainly was his favorite instrument, not only because of the virtuosity of a performer like al-Aqqad, but because of something about the very nature of the strings. Although he knew he was not going to hear a famous virtuoso like al-Aqqad or al-Sayyid Abdu, his enthusiastic heart made up for the defects of the performance with its passion.

The moment the troupe finished the five-part overture, the singer began, "The sweetness of your lips intoxicates me." The troupe joined her enthusiastically. The most movingly beautiful part of this song was the harmony between two voices: the blind musician's gruff, expansive one and Zanuba the lutanist's delicate, childlike one. Al-Sayyid Ahmad was deeply touched. He quickly drained his glass to join in the chorus. In his haste to start singing he forgot to clear his throat and at first sounded choked. Others in the group soon plucked up their courage and followed his example. Soon everyone in the room was part of the troupe singing as though with one voice.

When that piece was finished, al-Sayyid Ahmad expected to hear some instrumental solos and vocal improvisation as usual, but Zubayda capped the ending with one of her resounding laughs to demonstrate her pleasure and amazement. She began to congratulate the new members of the troupe jokingly and asked them what they would like to hear. Al-Sayyid Ahmad was secretly distressed and momentarily depressed, since his passion for singing was intense. Few of those around him noticed anything. Then he realized that Zubayda, like most others of her profession, including the famous Bamba Kashar herself, was not capable of doing solo improvisations. He hoped she would pick a light ditty of the kind sung to the ladies at a wedding party. He would prefer that to having her attempt a virtuoso piece and fail to get it right. He tried to spare his ears the suffering he anticipated by suggesting an easy song suitable for the lady's voice. He asked, "What would you all think of 'My Sparrow, Mother'?"

He looked at her suggestively, trying to arouse in her an interest in this ditty with which she had crowned their conversation a few days before in the reception room. A voice from the far end of the hall cried out sarcastically, "It would be better to ask your mother for that one."

The suggestion was quickly lost in the outburst of guffaws that spoiled his plan for him. Before he could try again, one group requested "O Muslims, O People of God" and another wanted "Get Well, My Heart."

Zubayda was wary about favoring one bunch over the other and announced she would sing for them "I'm an Accomplice against Myself." Her announcement was warmly received. Al-Sayyid Ahmad saw no alternative to resigning himself and seeking his pleasure in wine and dreams about his promising chances for the evening. His lips gleamed with a sincere smile that the gang of inebriates cheerfully perceived. He was touched by the woman's desire to imitate the virtuosi in order to please her knowledgeable listeners, even though her actions were not totally free of the vanity common among singers.

As the troupe was getting ready to sing, one of the men rose and called out enthusiastically, "Give the tambourine to al-Sayyid Ahmad. He's an expert."

Zubayda shook her head in amazement and asked, "Really?"

Al-Sayyid Ahmad moved his fingers quickly and nimbly as if giving her a demonstration of his skill. Zubayda smiled and remarked, "No wonder! You were Jalila's pupil."

The gentlemen laughed uproariously. The laughter continued until Mr. al-Far's voice rose to ask the sultana, "What are you planning to teach him?"

She replied teasingly, "I'll teach him to play the qanun. Wouldn't you like that?"

Al-Sayyid Ahmad implored her, "Teach me internal repetitions, if you will."

Many of them encouraged him to join the musicians and he took the tambourine. Then he rose and removed his outer cloak. In his chestnut caftan he looked so tall and broad that he could have been a charger prancing on its hind legs. He pushed back his sleeves and went to the divan to take his place beside the lady. To make room for him she rose halfway and scooted to the left. Her red dress slipped back to reveal a strong, fleshy leg which was white brushed with pink where she had plucked the hair. The bottom of her leg was adorned with a gold anklet that could barely encompass it.

One of the men who glimpsed that sight shouted in a voice like thunder, "The Ottoman caliphate forever!"

Al-Sayyid Ahmad, who was ogling the woman's breasts, yelled after him, "Say: the Ottoman grand brassiere forever!"

The performer shouted to caution them, "Lower your voices or the English will throw us in jail for the night."

Al-Sayyid Ahmad, whose head was feeling the effects of the wine, yelled, "If you're with me, I'll go for life with hard labor."

More than one voice called out, "Death to anyone who lets you two go there alone."

The woman wanted to end the debate begun by the sight of her leg and handed the tambourine to al-Sayyid Ahmad. She told him, "Show me what you can do."

He took the tambourine and smiled as he rubbed it with the palm of his hand. His fingers began to strike it skillfully and then the other instruments started playing. Zubayda glanced at the eyes fixed on her and sang:

I'm an accomplice against myself
When my lover steals my heart.

Al-Sayyid Ahmad found himself in a wonderfully intoxicating situation. The sultana's breath fluttered toward him each time she turned his way, meeting the vapors which rose to the top of his head with every sip. He quickly forgot the refrains of the famous musicians al-Hamuli, Muhammad Uthman, and al-Manilawi, and lived in the present, happy and content. The inflections of her voice made the strings of his heart vibrate. His energy flared up and he beat the tambourine in a way no professional could match. His intoxication became a burning, titillating, inspiring, raging drunkenness the moment the woman sang:

You who are going to see him
Take a kiss from me as a pledge for my
Sweetheart's mouth.

His companions kept pace with him or surpassed him as the wine made its ultimate impact on them. They were so agitated by desire they seemed trees dancing in the frenzy of a hurricane.

Slowly, gradually, the time came for the song to close. Zubayda ended by repeating the same phrase that began it, "I'm an accomplice against myself," but with a spirit that was calm, reflective, and valedictory, and then final. The melodies vanished like an airplane carrying a lover over the horizon. Although the conclusion was greeted by a storm of applause and clapping, silence soon reigned over the hall, for their souls were worn out by all the exertion and emotion. A period passed when nothing was heard except the sound of someone coughing, clearing his throat, striking a match, or uttering a word that required no reply. The guests realized it was time to say goodnight. Some could be seen looking for articles of clothing they had stripped off in the heat of their musical ecstasy and placed behind them on the cushions. Others were having too good a time to leave until they had sipped every possible drop of this sweet wine.

One of these cried out, "We won't go until we have a wedding procession to present the sultana to al-Sayyid Ahmad."

The suggestion was warmly received and widely supported. Incredulous, the gentleman and the entertainer collapsed with laughter. Before they knew what was happening, several men had surrounded them and dragged them to their feet, gesturing to the troupe to commence the joyous anthem. The couple stood side by side, she like the ceremonial camel litter bound for Mecca and he like the camel. They were giants made less threatening by their good looks. Coquettishly she placed her arm under his and gestured to those surrounding them to clear the way. The woman with the tambourine started playing it, and the troupe along with many of the guests began to sing the wedding song: "Look this way, you handsome fellow." The bridal couple proceeded with deliberate steps, strutting forward, animated by both the music and the wine.

When she saw this sight, Zanuba stopped playing her lute and could not keep from emitting a long, ringing trill or shriek of joy. If it could have taken bodily form, it would have been a twisting tongue of flame splitting the heavens like a shooting star.

Their friends tried to outdo each other in offering their congratulations: "A happy marriage and many sons."

"Healthy children who are good dancers and singers."

One of the men shouted to caution them, "Don't put off until tomorrow what you can do today."

The troupe kept playing and the friends kept waving their hands until al-Sayyid Ahmad and the woman disappeared through the door leading to the interior of the house.

Translated by William Maynard Hutchins and Olive E. Kenny

Naguib Mahfouz

from *Palace of Desire*

THE CARRIAGE MADE ITS way along the banks of the Nile until it stopped in front of a houseboat at the end of the first triangle of streets on the road to Imbaba. Al-Sayyid Ahmad Abd al-Gawad descended at once, followed immediately by Mr. Ali Abd al-Rahim. Night had fallen, and darkness blanketed everything. The only exceptions were the widely spaced lights shining from the windows of the houseboats and other vessels lined up along either shore of the river channel downstream from the Zamalek Bridge, and the faint glow of the village at the end of the road, like a cloud reflecting the brilliance of the sun in a sky otherwise dark and heavily overcast.

Al-Sayyid Ahmad was visiting the houseboat for the first time, although Muhammad Iffat had leased it for the last four years, dedicating it to the romantic escapades and parties al-Sayyid Ahmad had denied himself since Fahmy was slain. Ali Abd al-Rahim went ahead to show him the gangplank. When he reached the stairs he warned his friend, "The stairway is narrow and the steps are steep with no railing. Put your paw on my shoulder and come down slowly."

They descended cautiously as the sound of water lapping against the riverbank and the prow of the boat caressed their ears. At the same time their noses were stung by the rank odors of nearby vegetation mixed with the scent of the silt that the floods at the beginning of September were lavishly depositing.

As Ali Abd al-Rahim felt for the doorbell by the entrance, he remarked, "This is a historic evening in your life and ours: the night the old master returns. Don't you think so?"

Tightening his grip on his friend's shoulder, al-Sayyid Ahmad replied, "But I'm no old master. The oldest master was your father."

Ali Abd al-Rahim laughed and said, "Now you'll see faces you haven't glimpsed for five years."

As though wavering, al-Sayyid Ahmad remarked, "This doesn't mean that I'm going to alter my conduct or deviate from my principles." Then after a moment of silence he continued: "Perhaps . . . maybe. . . . "

"If you leave a dog in the kitchen with a piece of meat, can you imagine him promising not to touch it?"

"The real dog was your father, you son of a bitch."

Mr. Ali rang the doorbell. The door was opened almost immediately by an aged Nubian servant who stepped aside to allow them to enter and raised his hands to his head in welcome. Once inside they made for the door on the left, which opened on a small vestibule lit by an electric lamp hanging from the ceiling. The walls on either side were decorated with a mirror beneath which a large leather armchair and a small table were placed. At the far end of the room there was another door, which was ajar. Through it could be heard the voices of the guests, and al-Sayyid Ahmad was deeply moved. Ali Abd al-Rahim shoved the door wide open and entered. Al-Sayyid Ahmad followed and had scarcely crossed the threshold when he found himself confronted by his friends, who rose and came forward to greet him joyfully. Their delight was so great it virtually leapt from their faces.

The first to reach him was Muhammad Iffat, who embraced him as he quoted from a popular song: "The beauty of the full moon is shining upon us."

Ibrahim al-Far cited another song title when he hugged him: "Destiny has brought me what I've longed for."

The men then stepped back to let him see Jalila, Zubayda, and a third woman, who stood two steps behind the others. He soon remembered that she was Zanuba, the lute player. Oh . . . his whole past had been assembled in a single setting. He beamed, although he appeared slightly embarrassed. Jalila gave a long laugh and opened her arms to embrace him as she chanted, "Where have you been hiding, my pretty one?"

When she released him, he saw that Zubayda was hesitating an arm's length away, although a happy light of welcome illuminated her face. He stretched his arm out to her and she squeezed it. At that same moment she arched her painted eyebrows reproachfully and, referring to yet another song, said in a tone not free of sarcasm, "After thirteen years . . . ."

He could not help but laugh wholeheartedly. Finally he noticed that Zanuba had not budged. She was smiling shyly, as though she thought their past acquaintance too slight for her to be forward. He held his hand out and shook hers. To encourage and flatter her he said, "Greetings to the princess of lute players."

As they returned to their seats, Muhammad Iffat put his arm around Ahmad's and made his friend sit beside him. He laughingly asked, "Did you just happen to drop by or has passion caught hold of you?"

"Passion caught hold of me, so I just happened to drop by."

At first he had been blinded by the warmth of the reunion and the jests of his friends when they welcomed him. Now his eyes could take in his surroundings. He found himself in a room of medium size with walls and ceilings painted emerald green. There were two windows facing the Nile and two on the street side of the boat. Although the windows were open, the shutters were closed. Hanging from the ceiling in the middle of the room was an electric lamp with a conical crystal shade, which focused the light on the surface of a low table holding the glasses and the whiskey bottles. The floor was covered with a carpet the same color as the walls. On each side of the room there was a large sofa divided in half by a cushion and covered with an embroidered cloth. The corners of the room were filled with pallets and pillows. Jalila, Zubayda, and Zanuba sat on the sofa farthest from the street, and three of the men on the one facing them. The pallets were strewn with musical instruments: lute, tambourine, drum, and finger cymbals. He took his time looking around. Then after sighing with satisfaction he said delightedly, "My God, my God, everything's so beautiful. But why don't you open the windows on the Nile?"

Muhammad Iffat replied, "They're opened once the sailboats stop passing. As the Prophet said, 'If you are tempted, conceal yourselves.'"

Al-Sayyid Ahmad quickly retorted with a smile, "And if you conceal yourselves, be tempted."

"Show us you're still as quick as you used to be," Jalila shouted as if challenging him.

He had intended his words to be nothing more than a joke. The truth was that he was anxious and hesitant about taking this revolutionary step and coming to the houseboat after the long period of self-denial he had observed. There was something more too. A change had taken place that he would have to unravel for himself. He would need to look closely and attentively. What did he see? There were Jalila and Zubayda, each of them as massively beautiful as the ceremonial camel when it set off for Mecca with the pilgrims. He had used that image to describe them in the old days. They had perhaps even added to their mass of fleshly charms, but something had come over them that was almost more easily perceived by his emotions than his senses. No doubt it was associated with the process of aging. Perhaps his friends had not noticed it since they had not been separated from the women as he had. Had he not been affected by age in much the same way? He felt sad, and his spirits flagged. A man's most telling mirror is a friend who returns after a long absence. But how could he pinpoint his change? Neither of the women had a single white hair, for no entertainer would ever allow her hair to turn white. And they had no wrinkles.

"Do you give up?" he asked himself. "Certainly not. Just look at those eyes. They reflect a spirit that's fading, no matter how they sparkle and flash. Fatigue disappears from sight momentarily behind a smile or a jest, but then its full truth is apparent. You can read in that look the obituary for their youth, a silent elegy. Isn't Zubayda in her fifties? And Jalila's several years older. She violently disputes that fact but will never be able to disprove it no matter how often she denies it."

There was a change in his heart too. He felt aversion and repulsion. It had not been that way when he arrived, for he had come in breathless pursuit of a phantom, which no longer existed. So be it. God forbid that he should willingly submit to defeat. . . .

Zubayda stood up to look for her wraps and check her handbag to make sure that her container of cocaine was still where she had left it. Ibrahim al-Far seized the opportunity provided by her absence to take the seat beside Jalila. He leaned his head on her shoulder, sighing audibly. Muhammad Iffat went to the windows overlooking the Nile channel and thrust the shutters aside. The surface of the water appeared to consist of a flowing pattern of darkness, except for still streaks of light traced on the undulating river by rays coming from the lamps of other boats where people were staying up late. Zanuba plucked the strings of her lute, and a rollicking tune sprang forth. Al-Sayyid Ahmad gazed in her direction for a long time. Then he rose to refill his glass. When Zubayda returned she sat down between Muhammad Iffat and Ahmad Abd al-Gawad, whose back she thumped.

Jalila's voice was raised in song: "One day you took a bite out of me. . . ."

Now it was Ibrahim al-Far's turn to shout, "Congratulate me!"

Muhammad Iffat and Zubayda started singing along with Jalila once she reached the words: "They brought me an antidote." When Zanuba joined the song, al-Sayyid Ahmad began looking at her again. Before he knew what was happening he was one of the singers too, and Ali Abd al-Rahim's voice lent its support from his corner.

His head still on Jalila's shoulder, Ibrahim al-Far called out, "Six performers and an audience of one: me."

Without stopping his singing al-Sayyid Ahmad told himself, "In the end, she'll comply with my wishes most willingly." Then he mused, "Is tonight to be a passing affair or the beginning of a lengthy relationship?"

Ibrahim al-Far rose unexpectedly and began dancing. The others all started to clap in unison. Then they sang together:

So take me in your pocket,
Between your belt and sash.

Translated by William Maynard Hutchins, Lorne Kenny, and Olive E. Kenny

Albert Cossery
from *Proud Beggars*

SITT AMINA'S BROTHEL WAS not a place of easy pleasure for Gohar. He never went there as a client, but only to fulfill an important literary function. Actually, it was an exceptionally diverting job to which he attached a symbolic value. To draw up Sitt Amina's business accounts and sometimes the love letters of illiterate whores seemed to him work worthy of human interest. So, despite his evident decay, he still preserved the role of a powerful intellectual which had been his glory in the past, when he taught history and literature in the biggest university in the country. However, the academic side of his nature, which was so odious then, here no longer had any excuse for existing. In this milieu where life appeared in the raw, unspoiled by established conventions, Gohar fooled no one; he no longer recited the endless philosophical lies he himself—alas!—once believed. The freedom of thought which accompanied his new job gave him an inexhaustible source of joy, a boundless, generous joy. The infinite human resources of a brothel in the native quarter kept him in perpetual ecstasy. How far he was from the sterile, deadly games of men and their hazy idea of life and reason. All the great minds he had so long admired now appeared to him as vile corrupters, stripped of all authority. To teach life without living it was a crime of the most detestable ignorance.

From this work—which he accepted as a lesser form of servitude—he made only a slight profit; for his exalted services Sitt Amina gave him only a ten-piaster piece from time to time. This was his only income and more than enough to live on. His lodging was cheap and local merchants were happy to give him all the food he needed. They were all enchanted by his conversation; some even considered him a prophet and cherished his peaceful vision of the world. But Gohar never took advantage of their kindness. He never asked for anything. If he happened to accept, it was so as not to offend his generous donors.

Out of breath, he stopped.

Behind the gate covered with climbing plants, which hid it from indiscreet eyes, was a yellow, two-story, middle-class house with a narrow façade. A little dirt courtyard full of rubbish separated it from the street. Gohar opened the gate, gripped his cane, straightened his tarboosh, then climbed the steps to the first floor with all the assurance he could muster. The door was closed from the inside; he knocked twice with his cane and waited, holding his breath. Nothing moved; the house seemed deserted. An ominous silence weighed on Gohar's soul. Clearly no one was there. Yeghen might have left long ago! A wave of anxiety swept over him, and all of his organs stopped at once, as though from a fatal injection.

Finally, the door opened, and Gohar breathed again. The girl before him was decked out like a sugar doll at a country fair. She was wearing a short-sleeved, rose silk nightgown embroidered with green flowers; she was heavily made-up, and her arms were covered with gold bracelets. Long, brown hair framed her face, strange and primitively beautiful like portraits on local café walls. Her eyes, exaggeratedly blackened with kohl, seemed fake. Gohar knew her; she was a new girl just arrived from her home village. She was named Arnaba and was perhaps sixteen. Since she'd come, all the clients fought over her and waited hours till she was free.

Gohar greeted her, and she smiled. When she smiled, she looked like a young girl disguised as a woman.

"It's you," she said. "Come in. No one's here. Sitt Amina went shopping in town with the girls."

Gohar entered the vestibule which served as a waiting room. Again he returned to shadows, and his jangled nerves calmed down. But he wasn't completely reassured; he didn't see Yeghen anywhere.

"Yeghen isn't here?" he asked.

"He was sleeping on the couch just now," the girl said, looking around. "He must have gone."

The disappointment made Gohar pale. He was about to ask her if she knew where Yeghen went, but changed his mind.

"I'll wait for him; perhaps he'll return."

"Wait if you like."

"You're alone here?"

"Yes. I didn't go, because I wanted to wash my hair. I'm sorry now; they took a cab."

She seemed to hesitate a moment, then entered one of the rooms off the vestibule and closed the door. Gohar was left alone. He looked around for a chair. The bare-walled waiting room was furnished in an improvised, temporary style. There was only a couch with a plain slipcover, four or five rattan chairs, and a big ashtray perched on a round table. This was the banal decor of brothels in the native quarter. Just now, without its disparate clientele and its atmosphere of stupor and facile gaiety, it was depressing. Gohar sighed, found a chair, and sat down. The waiting room's gloomy sadness acted on him in a treacherous, almost offensive manner. He'd never before come at this hour; everything seemed strange and hostile here. He tucked his cane between his legs, took another mint lozenge from his pocket, and began to suck it with a certain disgust.

His drug craving had somewhat subsided, as if the fact of being in a place touched by Yeghen constituted an assurance, a moral certitude against fate. He thought of him with real tenderness. The affection he felt for Yeghen didn't only have drugs as a motive; he loved him like an ideal. Yeghen was an impoverished poet, he led a life without honor or glory, made up of begging and joyful mishaps. Immoderate use of drugs had led him to prison several times. An infamous legend clung to him; he was suspected of betraying his own drug suppliers to police prosecution. This reputation as an informer plagued him with dealers; they all mistrusted him. Actually, it was difficult to find the truth to this story, as Yeghen hadn't bothered to clear himself. Whatever he was, Yeghen remained himself, full of humor and generosity, even in betrayal. His ability to disregard mental torture and conscience pangs made him a delightful companion. He was never humbled by the indignity of his acts; he accepted with fierce optimism all the abasements that fate brought him. He was without dignity, but that didn't prevent him from living. Gohar especially admired his true feeling for life: life without dignity. Just to be alive was enough to make him happy.

Translated from the French by Thomas W. Cushing

Amina al-Said

from The End of the Road:
A Real-life Tragedy

He turned to me and said, "Would you believe that our house was made up of twenty-three rooms?"

I said, "Where was it?"

He replied, "In Mounira, during its good old days. The most affluent people competed to have their homes built there, just as is now the case with Zamalek. My father conformed to the traditions of his class, so he chose to have a spacious garden surrounded by high walls, with the house that he wanted in the middle. My parents were married in this house and that's where I was born and raised. Our house was different from what you know today. It was an imposing structure with two levels: the upper one was the haramlik, the family women's quarters, and the lower one was what we called the salamlik, or the guest house, because it contained rooms for male relatives and guests of the patriarch. But the two levels were connected by a stairway that occupied a big space in the reception hall at the center of the house. I especially remember this stairway, since during my childhood I would crouch in front of it and stick my head between the rails to enjoy what was happening downstairs at the festive banquets my father would host during the feasts and other important occasions. I was told that when I was born, my father had the greatest banquet ever, for I was a male child after a long wait for my mother's pregnancy. It was the joy of his life! He slaughtered several animals as offerings every day of the first week of my birth. He gave away money and hosted banquets. Every single person in the neighborhood partook of his generosity or the festivities that he held.

"It was also said that during the subu', the seventh day after my birth, my father arrived at the house with tons of nuts, almonds, dates, and sweets of all sorts, and hundreds of big and small candles that women and girls would hold during such an occasion. He had a banquet for the male guests that included roast mutton in quantities equivalent to the number of guests. As for entertainment, the evening was animated by no other than Muhammad Osman, the master singer of his time. He sang a song that went:

Your garden of beauty is more sublime and more delightful than the garden itself.
Should your figure sway by one of the branches, it will teach the nightingale new songs.
Time graciously allowed me to meet my loved one in the garden,
So I said when he appeared: It's been a long time, my love, it's been a long time.

"I actually memorized this particular song because my Ethiopian nanny often sang it to me as a child. And she would say, time and time again, that the singer had written the lyrics especially for my subu', and that he sang it for the first time on that occasion. When my father found out about this courtesy, he gave him a hundred pounds in gold, which was a huge sum at the time."

I said to him, "Had your father not been madly in love with your mother, he would not have spent so much money to celebrate your birth."

He replied, somewhat confused, "I really don't know. His feelings toward her are a riddle to me till this very day. When I recall the little I remember of their life together, I am almost certain he hated her. But when I reflect on the meaning of his behavior toward her I can see that it bespeaks his adoration of her. In any case, she was a wonderful woman, or at least that's how I felt as a child as I saw her animate the house with her beauty and style. She was tall, well-rounded, with full breasts and hips whose beauty was accentuated by the corset that women wore in those days. She was neither fair nor dark, but naturally tanned, with a fresh complexion that heightened the glow of her rosy cheeks. She had very long and thick hair and she let it down, untied, most of the time except when she had guests. Her nose was delicate and small, her lips beautiful and full; when she laughed, her wide brown eyes twinkled along."

I said to him, when I saw that the description resembled him, "Like your own eyes?"

He answered, "That's what they used to say. Every single guest of hers who had seen me as a child said that I had my mother's eyes. I also inherited her silence and her quiet demeanor. She was very quiet and I seldom heard her say more than a few sentences. I remember that she used to spend her entire day circling the rooms of the house, a bit lost and confused, like a restless soul searching for its abode. From time to time I would see her heading for the dining room. She would stand behind its closed windows to sneak a look from behind the mashrabiya at the front garden where my father used to entertain his guests during the day. She would remain silent and still behind the window until she heard my father's laughter—for he was known for his gaiety outside our little kingdom—and her face would turn crimson and she would bite her lower lip in great distress. She would then fidget around like a caged animal in search of escape. At moments like that, I would feel that my mother needed me, so I would clutch her leg with my little hand to grab her attention. My strategy would work and she would turn toward me with a distracted look. She would quickly regain her senses, and would pick me up and hold me in her arms and would bury her face in my hair, pressing my body against hers, until I would feel as if my bones were about to break against her chest. I would kiss her in silence and she would whisper to me, 'You are my only treasure, Midhat, you are my life and my consolation.' Tears would stream down my face without my knowing the reason why. She would cover my tears with kisses, blaming herself for my anxiety. And she would say the sweetest things to calm me down. She used to consider me part of her own sensitive temperament and would not ask me the reasons for my distress.

"But she was not always like that. On a certain day every month, I used to see her smiling, happy, and active, like a bird that had suddenly just flown out of its cage. There is a story behind that day. For, at the time, women did not have the same opportunities of pleasure as today and their lives were constrained to homes away from the men, except their husbands. The only entertainment that was allowed to them was 'get-together' sessions, or regular women's social gatherings, that they would host in their homes once or twice a month. Traditionally these gatherings would start at seven o'clock in the evening. Women friends would arrive in their best attire and most expensive jewelry in order to spend three or four hours of loud and innocent women's mirth.

"My mother had chosen the first Monday of each month for such gatherings. But she would start preparations at least two or three days earlier. She would make subia, tamarind, and hibiscus in summer, sahlab and cinnamon in winter. She used to serve delicious homemade pastries like surra, balah al-sham, and mahallabiya sprinkled with pistachios. Strangely, she insisted on making the pastry herself, even though our cook was famous for his pastries in all of Mounira. My mother paid special attention to her appearance and dress during that day, just as you would when invited to a grand ball. I remember she had a new dress for every gathering, that she would excel in adorning with ribbons and lace. When she went to her friends' gatherings she would change her black veiling habara from lovely chiffon to transparent muslin or glossy silk. I remember that every time Umm Hussein the dallala came to visit—and she came once a week—my mother would buy one or two pieces of cloth from her in preparation for those special days: those Mondays.

"On these days, my mother would be at her best; she would tour the house with a bright smile on her face and would give orders to the servants, at times nicely and at others angrily. My life was like heaven during that period, for I was allowed to taste the subia, hibiscus, and pastries before the guests . . . not to mention my joy at seeing my beloved mother smiling with twinkling eyes.

"These preparations were like historic events in my small life. But most important of all was the day of the visit itself. Our reception hall on the upper level of the house was right next to the bedroom, whose wooden door had a window in the old style. My mother would invite me to sit with her and her friends during the visit but I would obstinately refuse, not because I wasn't interested in the goings-on in the reception hall, but because I preferred to watch things from a distance.

"Actually the reception hall—or the travelers' room, as it was called at the time—was magnificent: its floors were covered with wall-to-wall red carpets, its doors and windows were adorned with flowery silk curtains, and its walls were decorated with pictures of celebrity women, or of grandparents and uncles with long mustaches that defied time. Comfortable divan-like sofas adorned the four corners of the room: some were decorated with inlaid ivory and mother of pearl, others were covered in velvet and silk. There was a big marble table in the middle of the room with shiny gold-plated legs. Several silver chandeliers with crystal tops were placed in the middle. This room was opened only for the days of the visits or for a very special guest. I was not allowed inside the room, but I sometimes disobeyed and would steal into this magical place. I would walk around the room and try the seats or play with the lute or riqq that were hung inside gold-threaded velvet bags. I would remain in this stupor until I was discovered by my nanny, who would scold me for intruding on the most sacred space in the house.

"Despite all this, I still didn't like being in the haram room on visit days and preferred to watch from the wings. This meant that I would sit on my kind Ethiopian nanny's stool inside the bedroom near the door leading to the reception hall. We would leave the door ajar as if someone had forgotten to shut it. We would turn off the light and sink into the dark as events unfolded before us, as if we were at the Mounira theater.

"The women's society was filled with exciting events: sometimes I would see them dancing elegant Circassian-style dances or hear them singing in a mix of beautiful and ugly voices. My mother would sit with the lute on her lap, playing the sweetest melodies for her friends. I would hear their loud laughter when a singer went out of tune, and more laughter still with the stories they whispered in each other's ears. This would go on until for a while until the women servants brought in the delicacy trays. The women would drink, eat, and praise this delicacy or that. When they had had their fill of drinks and pastries, they would be overtaken by fatigue and the initial storm would die down. They would turn to quieter conversations, during which I overheard names I did not know most of the time. I would fall asleep before the end of the wonderful evening. I would open my eyes to find myself in bed with my mother beside me, with her hair loose against the pillow like a brown flood.

"My mother would wake up feeling abandoned by the mirth that had surrounded her for two days. I would see her resuming her life with her usual silence and helplessness. And I would feel she needed me once again. So I would begin brushing up against her like a cat against its owner."

Translated by Samia Mehrez

Bahaa Taher

from *The Drop of Light*

SINCE HIS CHILDHOOD, SALEM had lived with his grandfather, the Bashkateb. When he was little he didn't know the meaning of the title or the job itself, but he used to hear his father say, when answering the neighbors' questions, "I will ask my father, the Bashkateb," so he reckoned that it must be an important job.

Salem came into the world when his grandfather had already retired. The grandfather had the best room in the house, with northern exposure and a big balcony known in the household as "the terrace." Its floor, which was covered with small circular tiles, was enclosed within wooden mashrabiya-like windows that broke the bright morning sun and were opened by night for the breeze. The Bashkateb used to spend long hours on the balcony every night before he went to bed. He would sit in an armchair in front of the open window and would watch the crowded street and those on their way from and to Sayeda Zaynab Square. During spring, when the trees would blossom, the breeze would carry the scent of the tamarind tree that was planted in the narrow alleyway by the house.

The Bashkateb's room contained his big brass bed with its four poles that supported the mosquito net, a desk with many drawers that were always locked, piles of hardbound books on one side, and old faded green folders with yellowish borders on the other. When Salem grew up a little, he came to know that the apartment they lived in belonged to his grandfather, and that he was also the owner of the house itself, which comprised six rented flats. It was a four-story house that had been built at the beginning of the century by Hagg al-Saadi, the Bashkateb's father. The family occupied the third floor, and the other flats had been rented out, since the house was built, to the neighboring shop owners, whose children inherited both their professions and their homes. Those were a carpenter, an upholsterer, a druggist, an electrician, and a shoe vendor. The Bashkateb was the only civil servant in the house and they all respected and loved him.

Salem did not know the color of the façade of the house, for he only came to know it when it had turned grayish-brown like the color of the ancient mosques, tikiyas, and sabils that filled the neighborhood. But it was obvious that his great-grandfather had given much attention to its design when he built it. Besides the two spacious tile balconies on each floor, there were two smaller ones with wrought-iron railings decked with vine-shaped corrugated iron motifs. Between the balconies, and along the whole height of the house in two parallel lines, there were stone etchings in the form of braids in which were carved small round flowers. There was also a low iron fence that surrounded the entrance to the house and embraced the narrow alleyway that some residents called "the garden" because it comprised, besides the tamarind tree, two ficus trees with big flat shiny leaves (that were called elephant ears) and that were planted in many other gardens in the neighborhood. But Abu Zeid, the old bawwab, could no longer attend to these trees as he used to. In his old age, he spent most of the time in his room under the stairwell and he neglected watering them regularly. So some of their leaves dried and wilted, but the trees remained sturdy on the whole, preserving a bright green entrance to the house.

This was the façade of the house facing the main street that branched off from Sayeda Zaynab Square. As for the side that overlooked the alleyway, that was decked with parallel rectangular wooden windows.

In this house Salem was born, and lived with his elder sister Fawziya and his father Shaaban, who remained in the house even after he married and had children. Salem cannot remember his mother, who died two years after his birth, but he found her very beautiful in the photographs. Just like his sister Fawziya, she had a rounded face and thick auburn hair that fell down to her shoulders, with shiny olive-hued eyes that he and his sister had inherited.

Bashkateb Tawfiq had been accustomed to taking his grandson to Friday prayer at the mosque of Sayeda Zaynab since childhood. He taught him many things at that time: to walk to the mosque using a certain route and to walk back by another because that increased their reward from God; to buy certain things after prayer, like lime or fruit or incense. Fawziya used to protest that the house was cluttered with lime and incense, but the Bashkateb used to respond, smiling, as he patted her cheek, "Give some to the neighbors." Then he would look up and point with his finger toward the sky, saying, "Shopping after Friday prayer has a special reward up there."

The Bashkateb loved his granddaughter very much. She was the only one allowed to clean his room, even when they had a servant in the house. She would tidy and dust the old folders and books on the desk, but she was not allowed to change the order of these folders or to open the drawers, to which he alone had the keys.

He also used to go to the kitchen with her. He would give her advice and taste her cooking and suggest more salt or halt the blanching of the onions. He would recite poetry and proverbs about most kinds of food. On days when they cooked qulqas he would put his hand on his chest and say, "Idha sa'aluka 'an qalbi fa qul qasi wa qulqasi" (If they were to ask you about my heart, say it is hard like the qulqas); when Fawziya cooked green rigla he would feign limping and say, "al-'Aqil la ya'kul rigla" (The sane person will not eat his leg); or on the day they made mulukhiya, which he loved, he would spread his arms wide open and say in feigned pomp, "Ta'am al-muluk ya mulukhiya" (The food of kings, oh, majestic mulukhiya). Many of these sayings made Fawziya and Salem laugh, even though the proverbs and the gestures did not change most of the time.

There were certain things that the Bashkateb did only with his grandson but not his granddaughter: they would sit on the rooftop and tell stories in the sun during winter and in the evening during summer. The grandfather would ask his grandson to buy of lupine seeds that would be served in a bowl for them. The Bashkateb would top this with a lot of lime juice that he would squeeze, and say to his grandson, as if ordering him, "Eat . . . this cleanses the blood," and would then add, laughing, "So that your face does not become yellow like your father's."

Only on Thursdays were these rituals interrupted, for the Bashkatib used to go out in the afternoon and would return late at night. Most of the time, he would wear a baggy white linen jacket, but it was always clean and well pressed; over this, in winter, he would wear a brown woolen cloak. No one in the family knew where he went. Apart from that, his outings at night were quite rare except when he went to religious ceremonies and Sufi zikr sessions.

The Bashkateb also maintained some traditions he had inherited from his father: there was a blind Qur'an reciter who came to the house every Friday morning to recite verses from the Qur'an, sitting cross-legged on a sofa in the big hall as Fawziya toured the five rooms in the apartment with incense. He also kept up the tradition that his father had established, of slaughtering offerings on the occasion of the Prophet Muhammad's birthday and hosting munshids to sing Burdat al-Busayri on the roof in the company of neighbors and friends, who would be invited to a banquet as they listened to the Burda.

But after the Bashkateb retired, he could no longer afford all this, so he contented himself on this special occasion with hiring a number of Qur'an reciters to take turns reciting the entire sacred book on the rooftop of the house or in the hall. He used to attend this collective ceremony, which was called rib'a, and would volunteer to participate with other neighbors as well. On that day, Salem would accompany Abu Zeid the bawwab with loaves of bread filled with ful nabit to give to the poor and needy who surrounded the Umm al-Awagiz mosque.

Translated by Samia Mehrez

Alaa Al Aswany

from *The Yacoubian Building*

IN 1934, HAGOP YACOUBIAN, the millionaire and then doyen of the Armenian community in Egypt, decided to construct an apartment block that would bear his name. He chose for it the best site on Suleiman Basha and engaged a well-known Italian engineering firm to build it, and the firm came up with a beautiful design—ten lofty stories in the high classical European style, the balconies decorated with Greek faces carved in stone, the columns, steps, and corridors all of natural marble, and the latest model of elevator by Schindler. Construction continued for two whole years, at the end of which there emerged an architectural gem that so exceeded expectations that its owner requested of the Italian architect that he inscribe his name, Yacoubian, on the inside of the doorway in large Latin characters that were lit up at night in neon, as though to immortalize his name and emphasize his ownership of the gorgeous building.

The cream of the society of those days took up residence in the Yacoubian Building—ministers, big land-owning bashas, foreign manufacturers, and two Jewish millionaires (one of them belonging to the famous Mosseri family). The ground floor of the building was divided equally between a spacious garage with numerous doors at the back where the residents' cars (most of them luxury makes such as Rolls-Royce, Buick, and Chevrolet) were kept overnight and at the front a large store with three frontages that Yacoubian kept as a showroom for the silver products made in his factories. This showroom remained in business successfully for four decades, then little by little declined, until recently it was bought by Hagg Muhammad Azzam, who re-opened it as a clothing store. On the broad roof two rooms with utilities were set aside for the doorkeeper and his family to live in, while on the other side of the roof fifty small rooms were constructed, one for each apartment in the building. Each of these rooms was no more than two meters by two meters in area and the walls and doors were all of solid iron and locked with padlocks whose keys were handed over to the owners of the apartments. These iron rooms had a variety of uses at that time, such as storing foodstuffs, overnight kenneling for dogs (if they were large or fierce), and laundering clothes, which in those days (before the spread of the electric washing machine) was undertaken by professional washerwomen who would do the wash in the room and hang it out on long lines that extended across the roof. The rooms were never used as places for the servants to sleep, perhaps because the residents of the building at that time were aristocrats and foreigners who could not conceive of the possibility of any human being sleeping in such a cramped place. Instead, they would set aside a room in their ample, luxurious apartments (which sometimes contained eight or ten rooms on two levels joined by an internal stairway) for the servants.

In 1952 the Revolution came and everything changed. The exodus of Jews and foreigners from Egypt started and every apartment that was vacated by reason of the departure of its owners was taken over by an officer of the armed forces, who were the influential people of the time. By the 1960s, half the apartments were lived in by officers of various ranks, from first lieutenants and recently married captains all the way up to generals, who would move into the building with their large families. General al-Dakrouri (at one point director of President Muhammad Naguib's office) was even able to acquire two large apartments next door to one another on the tenth floor, one of which he used as a residence for himself and his family, the other as a private office where he would meet petitioners in the afternoon.

The officers' wives began using the iron rooms in a different way: for the first time they were turned into places for the stewards, cooks, and young maids that they brought from their villages to serve their families to stay in. Some of the officers' wives were of plebeian origin and could see nothing wrong in raising small animals (rabbits, ducks, and chickens) in the iron rooms and the West Cairo District's registers saw numerous complaints filed by the old residents to prevent the raising of such animals on the roof. Owing to the officers' pull, however, these always got shelved, until the residents complained to General al-Dakrouri, who, thanks to his influence with the former, was able to put a stop to this insanitary phenomenon.

In the seventies came the 'Open Door Policy' and the well-to-do started to leave the downtown area for Mohandiseen and Medinet Nasr, some of them selling their apartments in the Yacoubian Building, others using them as offices and clinics for their recently graduated sons or renting them furnished to Arab tourists. The result was that the connection between the iron rooms and the building's apartments was gradually severed and the former stewards and servants ceded their iron rooms for money to new, poor residents coming from the countryside or working somewhere downtown who needed a place to live that was close by and cheap.

This transfer of control was made easier by the death of the Armenian agent in charge of the building, Monsieur Grigor, who used to administer the property of the millionaire Hagop Yacoubian with the utmost honesty and accuracy, sending the proceeds in December of each year to Switzerland, where Yacoubian's heirs had migrated after the Revolution. Grigor was succeeded as agent by Maître Fikri Abd al-Shaheed, the lawyer, who would do anything provided he was paid, taking, for example, a large percentage from the former occupant of the iron room and another from the new tenant for writing him a contract for the room.

The final outcome was the growth of a new community on the roof that was entirely independent of the rest of the building. Some of the newcomers rented two rooms next to one another and made a small residence out of them with all utilities (latrine and washroom), while others, the poorest, collaborated to create a shared latrine for every three or four rooms, the roof community thus coming to resemble any other popular community in Egypt. The children run around all over the roof barefoot and half naked and the women spent the day cooking, holding gossip sessions in the sun, and, frequently, quarreling, at which moments they will exchange the grossest insults as well as accusations touching on one another's honor, only to make up soon after and behave with complete goodwill toward one another as though nothing had happened. Indeed, they will plant hot, lip-smacking kisses on each other's cheeks and even weep from excess of sentiment and affection.

The men pay little attention to the women's quarrels, viewing them as just one more indication of that defectiveness of mind of which the Prophet—God bless him and grant him peace—spoke. These men of the roof pass their days in a bitter and wearisome struggle to earn a living and return at the end of the day exhausted and in a hurry to partake of their small pleasures—tasty hot food and a few pipes of tobacco (or of hashish if they have the money), which they either smoke in a waterpipe on their own or stay up to smoke while talking with the others on the roof on summer nights. The third pleasure is sex, in which the people of the roof revel and which they see nothing wrong with discussing frankly so long as it is of a sort sanctioned by religion. Here there is a contradiction. Any of the men of the roof would be ashamed, like most lower-class people, to mention his wife by name in front of the others, referring to her as "Mother of So-and-so," or "the kids," as in "the kids cooked mulukhiya today," the company understanding that he means his wife. This same man, however, will feel no embarrassment at mentioning, in a gathering of other men, the most precise details of his private relations with his wife, so that the men of the roof come to know almost everything of one another's sexual activities. As for the women, and without regard for their degree of religiosity or morality, they all love sex enormously and will whisper the secrets of the bed to one another, followed, if they are on their own, by bursts of laughter that are carefree or even obscene. They do not love it simply as a way of quenching lust but because sex, and their husbands' greed for it, makes them feel that despite all the misery they suffer, they are still women, beautiful and desired by their menfolk. At that certain moment when the children are asleep, having had their dinner and given praise to their Lord, and there is enough food in the house to last for a week or more, and there is a little money set aside for emergencies, and the room they all live in is clean and tidy, and the husband has come home on Thursday night in a good mood because of the effect of the hashish and asked for his wife, is it not then her duty to obey his call, after first bathing, prettying herself up, and putting on perfume? Do these brief hours of pleasure not furnish her with proof that her wretched life is somehow, despite everything, blessed with success? It would take a skilled painter to convey to us the expressions on the face of a woman on the roof of a Friday morning, when, after her husband has gone down to perform the prayer and she has washed off the traces of love-making, she emerges to hang out the washed bedding—at that moment, with her wet hair, her flushed complexion, and the serene expression in her eyes, she looks like a rose that, watered with the dew of the morning, has arrived at the peak of its perfection.

Translated by Humphrey Davies

Sonallah Ibrahim
from *Zaat*

. . . THEIR STREET, WHICH HAD been so peaceful and shaded when they moved into it, had filled with small stores and car mechanics' workshops and was covered in sewage and rubbish. The adjacent spare land that had been planned as a garden was now a dump. The walls of the building itself had turned black, the windows in the back stairwell were all smashed, and street cats had occupied the lobby and the landings.

Because of the exodus of labor in search of pickings among the valuable refuse of the Gulf, local rubbish piled up in buckets left in front of apartment doors, which allowed the cats to hold riotous carnivals that went on all night. The contents of the buckets spilled onto the floor (over a wider area than when the rubbish collector emptied them), and residents would be compelled, when going up and down, to tiptoe cautiously through the mess with the bottoms of their trousers and skirts hitched up. Despite this inconvenience, however, not one of them ever thought to meddle with the cats' daily bread except Zaat.

We have to suppose (if we are to be completely honest about the fact that tolerance for dirt is a national characteristic of ours) that Zaat was sick or, at the very least, not normal. Or that, under the pressure of circumstances, she had decided to operate according to the golden rule of transmisson, which stipulates that, rather than waiting for something to happen and using it later in a subsequent transmission session, one should manufacture one's own material.

She spoke a number of times to the middle-aged bawwab (who came from the farthest reaches of Upper Egypt, where he enjoyed considerable prestige due to his position in Cairo): the first time, he announced that he was only responsible for cleaning the stairs once a week; the second, he proposed putting down poison for the cats but Zaat rejected the idea outright; the third, they agreed to replace the metal buckets with plastic bins with lids, according to a schedule that allowed the cats ample time to train themselves how to remove the lids. The fourth time they decided to call a residents meeting to discuss all aspects of the matter.

After long preparation and intense comunications, the first and last meeting in the history of the building was convened, in the flat of the police officer (it seemed that this would provide sufficient immunity from the emergency law). All the residents (the men only, of course) attended, except for the owners of the furnished flats and their tenants, and the man who worked at the Ministry of Agriculture, who refused to attend without giving any reason. Amm Sadeq the bawwab also took part, standing up (he later reprimanded Abd al-Maguid because no one had invited him to sit down). The meeting lasted a number of hours and ended with complete agreement on three points: one, no putting chicken and fish leftovers in front of flat doors (which Zaat used to do as her program of organization and administration called for reducing the element of wastage to the minimum degree); two, ceasing to provide special treatment for pregnant and newborn cats in the form of boxes lined with newspaper or rags (which Zaat used to do out of the kindness of her heart); and three, knocking nails twisted into the shape of the letter 'L' (the Latin one not the Arabic one of course) on the landing walls next to each flat, at an appropriate height, and hanging the rubbish buckets from them out of reach of the cats.

A special committee consisting of Abdel Maguid, the army officer, and a neighbor who worked for a building contractor bought the required nails and installed them, while Amm Sadeq oversaw the replacement of the existing bins and buckets with new ones that had lids and handles so they could be hung on the hooks, according to a schedule which allowed the cats to train themselves how to jump into the bins after removing the lids.

The final blow to the conference's resolutions, however, came from a totally different direction. Amm Sadeq was carrying out his duty overseeing implementation when he noticed that the emptying of the dirty, rusty cheese can that the police officer's wife used for her rubbish (it had still not been replaced according to the schedule), left a larger amount of rubbish scattered around it than the cats did playing in it when it was full. He decided to accompany the rubbish collector while he was emptying the receptacle, thinking that his negligence was the reason. He stood next to the man, observing him carefully as he lifted up the can to empty it into his basket, and the contents fell out onto the stairs. The can had no bottom.

Amm Sadeq felt that the powers granted him in the meeting, that had, after all, been held under the patronage of the police officer, gave him the right to remove the worn-out can, which he did with an impetuosity not in keeping with the wisdom of his years and without sufficiently taking into consideration the possible results.

When the officer's wife discovered what he had done she called her husband on the walkie-talkie while he was out in the patrol car. He drove home immediately, and from the entrance to the building, where he stood surrounded by his men, he issued the order to return the can to its place.

None of the residents thought to meet again, since they realized by telepathy the absurdity of trying to overcome the cats, and they went back to serving them chicken and fish leftovers on aluminium foil, and preparing padded boxes for the pregnant ones, and they took down the rubbish bins and even removed the bent nails, and they trained themselves once again how to lift up the bottoms of their trousers and dresses and pick their way skillfully through the filth. Zaat now turned her attention to a more serious matter: the march of demolition and construction. . . .

The march of demolition and construction in the building began with the Ministry of Agriculture man when his fortunes began to take a turn for the better after competition flared up between the foreign insecticide companies that supplied the ministry. The banner then passed on to the schoolteacher who had worked in Kuwait, then to Hagg Fahmy, the butcher who had joined the residents of the building more recently, and in the latest way, that is, buying rather than renting, until eventually it was picked up by the armed forces: the police officer after his return from a security mission in Oman, and the army officer after he took part in a training mission in the United States. The real leader of the march, however, was a refined and rather smarmy chief engineer who lived directly above Zaat and had no particular occupation apart from his marriage to a schoolteacher with a vicious tongue and huge chest. When he noticed the Agriculture man's fortunes had begun to take a turn for the better, he paid him a visit, dressed in his finest clothes, a gold chain dangling around his neck, and swinging a car key in his hand (one of his friends had asked him if he could sell his car for him), to offer his services as an interior decorator. Thanks to the chief engineer's efforts the whole building joined the march, except for the floor Zaat lived on (besides Zaat there was one furnished flat, another which was closed up, and a third which had recently been occupied by a couple who kept to themselves). She followed with interest the typical signs: sacks of cement, plaster, and sand and tins of paint; the din of falling rubble which mingled with the voices of the street hawkers, car horns, and calls to prayer on top of all the usual background noise; sinks, rolls of carpet, and wooden panels; and finally the rubbish: empty cans, broken sinks, and twisted pipes, bits of brick and porcelain, wood and cement, and dust piled up on the stairs until feet distributed it to the very doors of those neighbors who were still waiting their turn in expectant glee.

The residents kept successfully to the agreed marching timetable, for although no two flats ever joined in at the same moment, the time of departure never changed (this happened without any prior agreement and was in some senses telepathic). It began every year with the onset of the cotton spraying season, when the Agriculture man would change his wallpaper for a more up-to-date color, or add a new unit to the air-conditioning system. When he had finished, the teacher who had come back from Kuwait would take his turn and fit new carpets or add a latest electrical appliance to his rare collection. Then, according to the schedule, those next door or upstairs would follow suit, and when the next spraying season came around, the cycle would be complete and the banner would return to the Agriculture man, and he would replace his wallpaper with wooden panels, and so it went on.

There were certain exceptions of course, when the first move came not from the Agriculture man, but from the police officer (once, when he was transferred temporarily to the Drug Squad) and the army officer (twice, once when he got a new flat from a housing project belonging to the armed forces and sold it immediately for double its price, and once when he was transferred to the Military Apparatus for Civil Contracts, where he was brought into direct contact with the great construction market). Apart from these few cases the march kept to its well-ordered cycle, jumping every time from the third floor to the fifth without pausing on Zaat's. All of this got her ducts flowing, especially when she had to wrap a piece of cloth around the bathroom pipe to stop the water leaking, or when she noticed the layers of grease and smoke ingrained on the kitchen walls, and worst of all when her sister Zaynab, commenting with feigned innocence on the old iron cistern suspended near the ceiling and the metal chain that usually ended up dangling just above the head of the person sitting on the toilet, said,

"Goodness gracious Zaat, do you still have one of those?"

Translated by Tony Calderbank

Mekkawi Said

from *Cairo Swan Song*

I LOVE MANY PARTS of this city, but the neighborhood dearest to my heart is al-Talabiya off Haram Street. Not because I lived out my childhood, my adolescence, and my dreams there, as the romantic poets say, but because of the hidden links that bind me to it even when I can't grasp what they are. I just know that I fill up with the feeling of it, so that whenever I pass through it, or find myself there—even when I pass by it on my way to some other place—I can feel the grass, dry straw, and twigs crunching under my feet as I walk through its vast fields. I still feel the grass pricking my legs to this day. None of my childhood friends live there anymore except for Ahmad al-Helu's family. The name of the street we used to live on—where our little house still stands—is different now: it used to be Tutankhamen Street, but now it's Good Works street. The exteriors of the houses are still the same, but their corners and façades are crumbling now. New houses built on the same plan as the old houses have filled the street: four-story houses built garishly by a rough neighborhood contractor without a conscience. The ground floors have all disappeared behind the asphalt that rises year after year, so that now the windows look out onto the shoes of passersby and the bare legs of little girls. My father was one of the first to own a house in that neighborhood. We used to live exclusively on the second floor and use the ground floor for entertaining and storage. There was no third floor, only a few pillars that my father was planning to roof over in order to make a suitable apartment for when I or one of my sisters got married. But, of course, he never did, and the pillars remain, imploring the heavens to this day.

Our street is five meters wide and, nowadays, the distance between balconies on either side of the street is no more than a meter and a half. When my father built the house, there was a big, green field across from it, planted with corn. We never had any problems in that house when we were little, except for the flies and the beastly mosquitoes, but we got used to them. Most of the homeowners left the street because of difficult economic conditions. Once they'd removed the apartment doors and knocked down some of the walls, they rented the buildings out by the room to students from Cairo University or to villagers who came to work in Giza.

I lived in that house until my first couple of years at university. Most of my friends in the neighborhood had finished their schooling, be it secondary, trade, or technical, and had gone to work in Libya or Iraq. Ahmad al-Helu, whom we used to call the neighborhood genius, and I were the only ones to have completed secondary school. I studied literature and he studied engineering at Cairo University. Essam, our friend from secondary school, didn't much like Ahmad al-Helu. Essam didn't live on our street; he lived on Haram Street, the main drag. A while later Ahmad al-Helu succeeded—because of the extraordinary influence he'd had on me since secondary school and because of his structured, prolific reading and organized mind—in getting me to join one of the Egyptian leftist cells. Our relationship grew stronger than my relationship with Essam, which had cooled off a little since Essam was going to college in Zamalek. Ahmad al-Helu, on the other hand, used to spend his free time with me on campus, recruiting new students for his cell. He and I used to study together in secondary school and he would still come by the house to study even after he'd started his engineering degree. My father was really taken with his towering height, his athletic physique, and his clean-cut look, as opposed to Essam the hippie, as my father liked to call him. He used to criticize me, too, for my long hair and tight trousers, and when Essam started studying at the College of Fine Arts, my father said it suited a pansy like him. But in spite of everything he said, he was always very polite. He never scowled at Essam, or teased him when he saw us together or found him drawing in my room. He'd reserve his mockery and rib me at dinnertime when the whole family was together. The girls would laugh, but my mother was too embarrassed to laugh at one of my friends. My father was friends with Ahmad al-Helu's father, too, so that endeared Ahmad to him even more.

That all changed later. My father would come to despise Ahmad al-Helu and refuse to speak to Ahmad's father until he died. That was after we were arrested one dusty night and accused of establishing a cell to agitate against the government. we'd been ratted out by a nobody informant, one of the many people that Ahmad al-Helu had indiscriminately taken into his confidence, announcing the cell's principles the same way his father hawked oranges, watermelons, and fresh dates. (That informant later went on to become minister of one of the most important ministries in Egypt.)

Those days were tough for me and my family, but it wasn't as bad as when Hind suddenly disappeared from my life. My father cheated certain death after we were arrested, but his grave cardiac crisis left him a shell of his former self. As I was his only son, he'd hoped he could be confident of my future before he left this world, but instead he'd been ambushed by the worst imaginable news: I'd become a guerilla fighter, an enemy of the state, a jailbird. His reaction was the opposite of the country peasant Hamid al-Helu, Ahmad's father, who bore the news with the timeless patience of Egyptian fellahin, who never complain or chafe under oppression. Later, I heard that he'd boasted about his son's imprisonment, proud that he'd grown up to become an intellectual feared by the government.

I was released after three months on account of the triviality of a cell led by a recent college graduate (that was what the sardonic prosecutor had told me at the time). My father treated me as if I were a slave after that; like a father who locks his daughter up in the house because he's discovered she's been working as a prostitute. He refused to allow Ahmad al-Helu in our house for as long as he lived and he forced me to cut all ties with him, just as he'd ended his relationship with Ahmad's father before my release. Figuring that art was less trouble than politics, my father started treating Essam warmly, with genuine affection. He took to Essam's drawings and started discussing them with him. He promised Essam that, after he graduated, he'd put him in charge of decorating the Misr Insurance Company's apartments, which my father was responsible for marketing. That promise was never fulfilled, for reasons outside my father's control: he'd died by then.

I finished the school year as if I'd been serving an extension of my prison sentence under house arrest. Those difficult times, which had altered my view of life, got me thinking about Hind again and I was drowning in crushing feelings of defeat, injustice, and anger. I failed that year, too. I was becoming a real professional at it: failing one year because Hind abandoned me and another because the government summoned me. My father didn't yell at me because he didn't have any energy left for yelling. his solution was to move us all, over the summer, to an apartment downtown—my mother told me he'd spent his whole savings to rent it—in order to get me far away from al-Talabiya and Ahmad al-Helu, who'd ruined my prospects by making me cross the government. The apartment was spacious, taking up almost half of the sixth floor of a building on Qasr al-Nil Street. It was one of the things that'd been left behind by the wealthy from Egypt's royal era, co-opted by the revolutionary government who left it to Misr Insurance to administer. The apartment was a lucky find and I was very happy there. I didn't stop seeing Ahmad al-Helu on campus though, even if I no longer shared his political views, which had only grown more revolutionary and extremist after our arrest. My father didn't sell our house in al-Talabiya or rent it out to anyone, but he did leave me the upper floor, which we used to use for my two sisters, and the skeleton of the top floor for when I got married.

My father left the keys to the old house with my mother and insisted she not give them to anyone without telling him. He made her responsible for anyone who used it without his permission (meaning specifically me). After I passed my exams with distinction the following year, my father relaxed his surveillance a little, confident that Ahmad al-Helu was safely in the past. My sweet, loving mother would always give into my pleading and hand over the keys for a variety of excuses: to check up on the house, to go there to study because I was sick of my father watching me all the time. She'd conspire with me, too, sometimes lying to my father. I made a copy of the key and our old house became the setting of my sex and hashish adventures. The first thing I did after returning from overseas with some money was to buy out my sisters' shares in the house, and I still own it.

Whenever I enter the house, I breathe in my mother's scent, may she rest in peace. I remember her frailty, her fragility, her support. I can imagine the family gathered around the dining table and the smell of cooking coming from the kitchen. My memories are hidden in its corners and crannies; my poems and experiences are locked up tightly in the ground floor. Our childhood scampering has worn away the paint on the cheap tiles in the living room. I can almost hear the water sloshing on the tiles from Fatheya's bucket. She used to come, all forty years of her, to clean the apartment every Saturday. I was always sure to stick around on those days. I'd come in, reading out loud from a book I was carrying, pretending to memorize what I was repeating. I snuck looks at whatever I could see under the gallabiya, which stuck to her body. Like most poor maids, she used to roll up the bottom of her gallabiya and tuck it into the front of her panties so that it wouldn't get in her way. I watched her, the water flowing between her bare feet, her legs completely exposed, showing even the prominent blue veins. I'd stare at her round backside as she bent over to polish the floors with a steel wool brush. My heart would speed up and my eyes would almost jump out of their sockets when her panties would slip down and I could see half of her sexy, creamy ass and some chestnut down, which got thicker as it neared her anus. Then I'd break out in a sweat; my knees wouldn't be able to support me; I'd tremble as my voice trailed off. And at that moment my mother would notice and call to me from the kitchen, so that Fatheya would suddenly turn around and see me, stifling with her hand the loud laughter that made her breasts shake alluringly, as I retreated, embarrassed and damp.

Ahmad al-Helu laughed hysterically when I told him how Fatheya was fond of what I used to do, and one time, he said I should try talking to her. I saved up my entire allowance until Saturday came around and when, almost as soon as I'd started speaking to her, I began to stammer, she instantly caught on and whispered to me to wait for her downstairs in the sitting room beside the pantry. She followed soon after me. I don't know what excuse she gave my mother. She didn't even give me time to take my trousers off, pulling me toward her and putting me inside of her, raping me. Was it so wild, fun, and delightful that I didn't notice how dirty she was, how she smelled of sweat, how rough her skin was, how threadbare her underwear? I used to pine for her all week long as if my life were on pause except on Saturdays; as if I were waiting for Madonna.

My study was on the ground floor of our old house. My father set it up for me when I started university so that I could hang out with my friends far away from my sisters. I still keep a bunch of Essam's finished and unfinished paintings there because he used to prefer to stay with me at the house when he was preparing for an exhibition: that was before he'd rented the studio in Abdeen. I even used to leave it to him for long stretches so he could entertain his girlfriends and models.

The street's changed. Maestra Fakeeha, who lives at the head of the street, runs the show now. New houses have replaced the plant shops that stretched alongside it. Fakeeha runs the business for her husband, Maestro Fawzy, while he's gracing the penitentiary with his presence on charges of dealing in narcotics. Fakeeha has since added pills and Maxitone Forte syringes to the menu.

Halfway down the street, if we can still call it a street, lives Maestra Nasra, who specializes in pimping minors and advertises her skills as a disciplinarian to anyone who needs help with an annoying family member or neighbor.

I like this part of summer and the pleasant weather in the late afternoon when the women come out carrying buckets to sprinkle water in front
of their houses. Each group lays out a modest rug or country mat near the
others to sit on. A sibirtaya for boiling the water for tea or a pan for roast-
ing dried watermelon seeds sits in the center of each group, and occasionally
they buy sunflower seeds, one of the cheapest types of seed. They smoke,
passing around a gouza, which is a glass jar filled two-thirds of the way with
water and covered with a rubber stopper, with a hole just wide enough for
a reed to pass through. The women usually spend the majority of their time
gossiping and quarrelling with God's creation. If you happen to walk by carrying a bag of fruit, or anything else you've bought, you won't be safe from
their tongues: they'll start out by asking you what's in the bag and end up asking to have a taste. That's if you live on the street or if they know you. But if
you're a stranger, God protect us, they'll send a young child after you to snatch
some of what you're carrying, or stick a finger in your ass, or throw a rock or
a handful of dirt at you. At the very least, they'll hurl obscenities at you to
drag you into a fight that only you can lose. I thanked God that they knew
me and respected me because my father had been one of the first homeowners on the block and had always helped everybody. He was known for having
a good heart and a steady mind. People used to ask him for advice and they'd
listen to what he said, submitting to his wisdom. That respect for our family
was passed down to this sad generation, descended from the original inhabitants of the street. They respected me and they knew who my friends and
guests were so they never overstepped their bounds. They never made fun of
Essam and his ponytail or the models that came to pose for him and when
I took Marcia to visit the house, the female neighbors greeted her warmly
and treated her like a porcelain doll. No one even asked how long we'd been
together. Your wife? Girlfriend?

In the end, those women are pitiful. Most of their daughters are captivat-
ingly beautiful, even if it's hidden under filth, and when one of the girls turns
sixteen, she starts taking an interest in her appearance and adorning herself
with plastic rings and worthless necklaces. She starts going out to Haram
Street nearby and coming back a different person. As for the boys, they try
to outdo one another with their busted mobile phones or toy dart-guns, and
when they get a little older, most of them start out as lookouts before they
start dealing in pills and pot like big boys.

Translated by Adam Talib

M.M. Tawfik

from *Murder in the Tower of Happiness*

THE FOLLOWING MORNING, ASHMOUNI accompanied the police recruit sent by the investigator to summon him. The sergeant mentally cursed his fate. Here he was, condemned to spend his days among the rabid cars, his shoes sinking into the melting asphalt, with nothing to shelter him from the August sun. A trainer of beasts, protected by neither whip nor moral authority, only separated from the predators' fangs by destiny's delayed hand, yet united with them by the inevitability of his fall. And to make things worse, he had to contend with these mighty officers, who neither showed mercy nor allowed God's mercy to prevail.

The two men crossed the road, walking away from the sergeant's median and approaching the tower's sumptuous entrance with heavy steps. The sergeant fell two or three steps behind the police recruit, trying hard to conceal his anxiety. On this side of the road, there was not a trace to be found of the previous day's events. The Pasha's car had been towed away before the day broke. As for the remains of the piano, armchairs, china, and pillows, these had all been piled into a small pyramid on the pavement next to the Nile and left for the government to deal with.

A young woman suddenly blocked the sergeant's path and shoved a microphone in his face. The foreigner had black, silky hair and slanted eyes. Despite her unintelligible language it was not difficult for Ashmouni to classify her as Japanese. A man behind her carried a camera on his shoulder, which was also pointed at him.

The sergeant instinctively pushed aside the microphone and redoubled his pace to catch up with the police recruit. He signaled to the woman, by raising his shoulders and pursing his lips, that he did not understand a word she was saying.

As he followed the police recruit up the polished granite steps that led to the tower's entrance, he stole a look backward. The young woman was on the sidewalk talking into the camera and pointing to the pile of broken furniture on the other side of the road.

Then the sergeant entered the Tower of Happiness.

Ashmouni voiced customary greetings as he passed the security clerk, but the other did not bother to respond. The sergeant cursed him under his breath in the vilest of terms. The man had barely been here a few months and he was already looking down on him. He missed Abdelaty, the previous security clerk and a good man. Alas, some powerful figures had wanted him out of the way.

The police recruit pressed a button and a musical bell rang. The electric door rolled sideways and the two men stepped into the elevator. Their ghosts stared back at them through the tinted mirrors that covered the elevator's three walls. They felt embarrassed just being here amid all this opulence. The elevator sped toward the thirteenth floor, carrying them across barriers of time and space neither of them had dreamed they would ever traverse.

Since the previous day, Ashmouni had been unable to free himself of the piano's ghost-like image. Its specter had disturbed his waking hours and disrupted his sleep. He even started to suspect that Souma the Owl had cast a magic spell on him. Ever since he took a second wife, he had anticipated her rage and almost expected her to find a way to dampen his fire for Zuzu, the young lass with the bold eyes and the thighs like sculpted marble.

Zuzu would faint at the sight of these lights that glowed with every floor the elevator crossed. And, if her cracked feet were to tread the red marble floor of the tower's foyer, the Owl would surely lose the remaining quarter of her rusty mind.

A grin took shape on the sergeant's face as the thoughts raced inside his head. He is still here in the elevator, but all alone with Zuzu. The tip of her pink nightgown is showing beneath the edge of her loose cotton gallabiya. She has nothing on underneath her nightgown. The sight of only a few inches of her see-through nightgown is enough to set his loins on fire. He presses the red button and the elevator stops between floors. With eager shaking hands, he raises her gallabiya, then her nightgown. Her silken skin feels like warm cream. True, he married her in accordance with the laws of Allah and his prophet, yet he cannot escape the feeling that he's enjoying her in sin. At the peak of his arousal, the elevator door opens with a metallic ring. He pulls up his trousers and turns around to find the Owl staring at him with a smile that exposes her missing teeth. She sings in her coarse voice:

Let him take another wife, sister. . . .
We'll see who'll come out on top, me or her.

With the same metallic ring, the elevator door slides shut. Ashmouni turns to his young wife. She is lying on the floor with her body rolled to one side, naked as the day she came into this world, silent. There is no trace of her clothes or of her plastic slippers. Her black hair fans over her back and across part of the elevator floor. Her small body is fully rounded, its frozen white-ness starting to turn blue.

But this woman is not Zuzu. It strikes him like lightning that this is the corpse of Ahlam Shawarby, the deceased movie star. Fear's uncompromising fist grips Ashmouni, as though he were the accused murderer. He wants to cry out, "I'm innocent. As God is my witness, I'm innocent." But his voice is held back, incapable of finding its way to existence. He gasps for breath as if the air is about to run out. . . .

"Don't look so worried, sergeant! The investigator will just ask you a cou-ple of questions then you'll be free to go." The police recruit was already on the landing, holding the elevator door from sliding shut before Ashmouni had come out.

It took him a few seconds to pull himself together and gingerly step onto the thirteenth floor. Then he followed the recruit into apartment 1301, whose door had been left ajar. But no sooner had he crossed the threshold than he froze in his shoes.

Books, sheets of paper, music discs, broken liquor bottles, and torn-up curtains were strewn all over. Gilt chairs, missing seats and some legs, were knocked over. The sofas had been overturned with cushions, springs, and tufts of straw pouring out, as if a giant hand had pulled out their entrails, like women do to birds before cooking them. Video jackets were scattered everywhere: some of well-known movies, others showing naked women in obscene positions. Shattered tables, an eviscerated VCR with cogs spilling out and electronic circuits exposed, a TV with a smashed screen; everything bore the brunt of indescribable rage. Jagged shards of glass from the windows and mirrors and fluffy pillow-feathers equally defied all boundaries and were sprinkled in every corner, adding a dreamlike element to the destruction that inhabited the large apartment.

Were it not for two intersecting passages cleared of debris, one to allow the investigators to cross the wide hall from the entrance—where Ashmouni was standing—to the terrace straight ahead, and the other running sideways between the dining room to the left and the corridor leading to the bedrooms to the right, it would have been impossible for him to tell that the floor was a glistening marble. A pistachio-green marble that imparted a sense of depth and transparency as if one were walking on water, the sensation he'd often imagined of floating across the canal that separated his village from the Abaida farm. This was a floor whose extravagance he'd never seen the likes of, nor imagined in his wildest dreams.

"Wait here."

The police recruit left him and, with measured steps, crossed the green passage to the left side of the hall where another recruit stood under an archway draped in a thick curtain of olive-green velvet. The two young men exchanged whispers with the gravity of generals whose deliberations could alter the course of history.

The sergeant took a few steps along the marble passage. He stopped to contemplate a life-sized statue of a scantily clad woman. The brass figure was leaning on a sofa that had prevented it from falling to the floor. But the woman's head was not visible from the sergeant's vantage point, as it had gone cleanly through a large oil painting that had evidently been smashed against it. The sergeant's eyes toured the hall for the hundredth time but he could still not believe them. It was as though a raging tempest had been trapped in this apartment, and did not rest until it had left it in ruins.

A scene from hell. This was devastation on a scale the sergeant had never witnessed, and he was by no means a stranger to squalor; he had grown up with poverty as a friend and hunger a companion. The stench of sewage overflowing in the alleyways hardly disturbed him, nor was he moved by the sight of a child foraging for food in a heap of garbage. All these were situations that people had no choice but to live with. But what surrounded him in this apartment was deliberate destruction. All this affluence had been shattered on purpose.

The sergeant had witnessed people's anger in the alleys. But it was an anger generated by overcrowding and need. It came in instantaneous outbursts, understandable and soon dispelled. People's smiles would soon return and the music would resume. As for these rich people, he had never imagined that they experienced anything but joy and merriment.

He never imagined this pure loathing that today he could almost touch with his fingertips, this absolute evil that screamed from every corner. It could only be the devil's work.

The sergeant's attention was drawn to a corner of the hall next to the terrace overlooking the Nile. Closer scrutiny only increased his bewilderment. The corner housed a small circular side table with a spotless varnished surface. On a delicate white tablecloth, a porcelain vase with dainty floral designs held a vibrantly fresh white rose. The section of the balcony's windowpane next to the table, clean, intact, and partly covered with a white chiffon curtain, stood in stark contrast with the rest of the room's shattered glass and ripped curtains. Beneath the table also, the pistachio marble floor was crystal clear. This corner had, by some miracle, escaped the devastation that covered every inch of the large hall.

But how and why?

Searching for a clue to explain this mystery, the sergeant noticed a slim copybook on the table next to the vase. But he could not prevent his eyes from drifting back to the rose, which seemed to call out to him, as if saying, "Come! Here you'll find all explanations, in my perfumed nectar, in my magic touch, in my pristine beauty, here away from the madness that surrounds you."

Ashmouni invoked the name of God in a loud voice. If it were not for his fear that the police recruits would make fun of him, he would most certainly have unbuttoned his vest and spat inside his undershirt to dispel the devil.

"Boo!"

A shrill cry accompanied by a sudden movement from the statue's direction took him by surprise. The sergeant recoiled backward with hands raised to protect his face from the small body that approached him. Was this a ghost or a jinn? Ashmouni froze for a few seconds until he realized it was only a child who had been hiding beneath the painting that hung around the statue's neck.

"Yay! I got you, I got you, I got you!"

The little devil had wide black eyes, spongy disheveled hair, and two matchstick legs protruding from his shorts. Worn-out sandals exposing his dirt-blackened toes appeared and disappeared as he jumped in the midst of the diverse shrapnel that covered the floor. The boy—no older than six or seven—beamed with pride over his outrageous behavior.

"Yesss! One for me, one for me, one for me!"

"Shame on you, son. Like I don't have enough to deal with."

"But it was a good one, right? Right? Ri—"

"Antar! What are you doing there, you little devil?"

Before the sergeant could respond to the boy, a sonorous voice assailed him from behind. Its owner, a bulky man in a safari suit and leather sandals, with not a single hair on his head, was a teacher at university. The sergeant remembered him because of his broken-down Russian-made Lada. Of all the tenants, he alone did not drive a luxury car. The garage attendants called him "doctor," though he was no doctor, not even a nurse.

"Hello, sergeant, where have you been hiding? You never drop by. That's not right."

The sergeant could not grasp what the man was saying. He wondered if he had mistaken him for someone he knew well. The man glanced behind his back at the two police recruits then whispered in the croak of one who has swallowed a frog, "How rude! They keep me waiting for an hour in this dump . . . just to ask me a couple of pointless questions! Seriously, this country has no respect for people's intelligence or their time."

He went on in his thunderous voice: "I'll be waiting for you, as soon as the good investigator is finished with you. It's important. Remember, sixth floor, apartment 61."

Then he turned his narrow eyes and hooked nose to the child. "Come on, you little devil."

Antar was busy tearing yellowing pages from a thick book with a worn leather cover. It crossed the sergeant's mind that a book like this would fetch a hefty sum at the second-hand bookstalls of Asbakia. The boy dropped the tome, leaving it to its fate amid the accumulated trash on the floor, and rushed to the door. But the doctor was quicker and caught him by the nape of his neck. He maneuvered the child, like a doll in his steel grip, out of the door. The child's eyes were ablaze with defiance.

The man's voice came to the sergeant's ears after both of them were out of sight. "You've been molded in devil's water."

Translated by M.M. Tawfik

Shehata al-Erian

from *The Women of Others*

MORNING.

This is truly the most joyful moment.

The alarm goes off at six o'clock and awakens Shahab from deep sleep. Getting up promises many happy surprises. . . . He zaps through the radio stations in search of morning music. He can, while in bed, plug in the heater so that it glows underneath the tea kettle. He stretches and tries moving his joints underneath the light summer cover. The northern window was open all night, so the room was a bit cool that early and was faintly lit. Most of the time the song "Ya sabah al-kheir yalli ma'ana" (Good morning, you who are with us) brings him to his feet—the distance between the bed and the desk, that is, covered with a kilim rug folded in two. It would be so good if they played "Ya hilw sabbah, ya hilw tull" (Say good morning, pretty one, give us a look). It might wake him up completely and he might run a little around the room. The emotional drama in the song starts off the morning, just like the Umm Kulthum songs. . . . Andil's morning is good for lovers.

It will be necessary to go downstairs to take a quick shower, the water pressure permitting, or to content oneself with rinsing one's head with water as a minimum step to complete wakefulness. Even if the water is cut this early in the morning, the amount that Umm Muhammad will have saved for him should suffice.

The Hagga who is the owner of the house does not live on the same floor. The room where she stores her things, near the bathroom, is locked. The other room is for Mona, her daughter, for times when she has rows with her husband. She pays the rent to her mother "at the beginning of every month like any other tenant." When she sublet the room to him the Hagga had said, "There is a bathroom on the rooftop but downstairs might be better for you . . . with Umm Muhammad so that she would keep it clean. . . . Her son Muhammad goes to school, like you . . . they are good people from Mit Ghamr. I keep the bathroom on the rooftop locked . . . I have some stuff in it, so it's locked."

His features must have given away his objection, so she changed her tone, "And the couple of steps you have to walk down are no big deal. At least we'll get to see you."

The locked bathroom on the rooftop seemed to be a closed matter. And the idea of mingling with people seemed a chance to get to know them, he who had never had to live among strangers before. He had packed his books and left the student housing, which seemed like hell and where he had wasted a whole school year: never-ending problems and trivia all day long and incomprehensible trespassing on what he believed was his own privacy. He also resisted the idea of staying with relatives, to escape family surveillance.

He was elated when he found that room on the rooftop of a slim tall building that dominated all its surroundings inside the complicated maze of alleyways through which he loved to walk. During the first week of his stay he was able to count eight different routes that would bring him to the entrance of the house that represented this sturdy old woman's sole treasure, who, more than fifty years ago, had handed her husband the bricks, cement, and wood to build "the two rooms and the bathroom on thirty square meters of the house he had inherited from his father." Because he was "a great construction worker" he continued building year after year: the stairway and the second floor after he returned from the war in Palestine; the third to the fifth during similar occasions. "This room was the last one he built. He left four men and three girls behind, none of whom lifted a brick in the house."

It was Shahab's second summer vacation in Cairo and the first in his room. He had failed half his courses, so the next academic year promised a lot of free time. He decided he was done with the university lectures after the first year, since it was senseless to try and listen to presentations of books that you can read and understand on your own, if you wished, in an auditorium crowded with seven thousand classmates.

As he walked up "the two steps" with the towel covering his wet head, he tried to look out through the mist onto Cairo breathing in the morning fog with the breeze. In the meantime, the kettle would be bubbling on top of the heater, releasing its vapor that would become transformed into a perfumed scent after adding the tea. He sipped it with the first cigarette and perhaps something to eat.

In the early morning, the streets looked different from any other time. They were wet with morning dew, humid, the property of the animals: cats, dogs, weasels, sheep tied in front of houses, and the sounds of birds flying over the rooftops. He inhaled the smell of their dung and milk, these delicate preliminary elements that the city steps on with its first movement, ones that remain secluded for the remainder of the day and a long part of the night.

Only during this time of day. . . .

Certain plants emerge on the scene that he normally doesn't notice: drooping trees shrunken in front of closed shops, trying to grow, besieged by cement—nothing like the old verdant ones on Abu Safeen Street that looked as though they had escaped from another time, a time when the Nile, that he could smell close by, used to flood this area with its water and silt.

Abu Safeen Street was lined with rows of giant sycamore trees, each of which constructed its own bygone rural moment: it covered the ground with leaves and dry withered fruit untrimmed by anyone; the old Indian fig trees dangled their roots from their outstretched branches, reaching the ground despite everything.

In the history books, Fort Babylon was located on the banks of the Nile. Amr ibn al-Aas built Fustat and his mosque nearby. The river continued to retreat to the north. Whenever it deposited silt, the land was flooded with houses like the ones he was walking past right now.

He had to cross over the Helwan railway that had not yet become a metro line and walk through al-Sukkar wa-l-lamun alleyway with its lingering amusing name, passing underneath the Mamluk water barrage at Fumm al-Khalig to finally arrive in front of the angular steel skeleton of the new Tumor Institute.

Translated by Samia Mehrez

Hamdi Abu Golayyel
from *Thieves in Retirement*

So Abu Gamal was basically dense, and I found it painless enough to accept his doings as acts only imaginable coming from a genuinely dim fellow. Dimwit, dope, idiot! Idiots can trash everything we know and we don't get angry about it: we even feel a genuine sense of pity and regret for them.

Even so, he's a person who forces you—the moment you enter his breathing space—to practice a kind of dignity in your dealings with him. So you find yourself transformed into a sort of automaton, though a fervently believing one. You keep your voice at a whisper and consider your words carefully and several times over before you utter them. That's if you say anything in the first place, because his eyes are on the watch for your mistakes, reprimanding you, reminding you constantly of tradition, etiquette, and the irreproachable life. Abu Gamal's face, for all its welts, conveys splendid pride, like the face of a man who is always careful to perform the recognized roles attendant upon right conduct.

He offers expansive morning and evening greetings to his neighbors and receives their responses magnanimously; he is never slow to call on the ill or to smile at weddings, and he is sure to locate a front seat inside the tent at other men's funerals.

Abu Gamal went into retirement recently, ending an employment odyssey of thirty-two years in the Helwan Silk Factory. All he retained of it was a proud memory attached to the hand of the great leader Gamal Abd al-Nasser, which had landed and settled precisely on the nape of his neck, and the irony of his being hired at the age of twenty-two as the very first worker to benefit from the laws on nationalization through which the Leader had consecrated his revolution, followed by his severance and retirement at the age of fifty-four as the first among workers to be let go, owing to the laws of privatization.

Anyway . . . Abu Gamal did not fritter away his time in contemplation of this irony. He adjusted quickly to the whole business of retirement. Indeed, and after some time had passed, naturally, he found it held some advantages over staying on the job. For who knows the unseen? Something grimmer might well have lay in store for him—a person whose talents distinguished him even among those select people who always find opportunity to praise God for everything. Hit by a bicycle, they praise God that it wasn't a car; and if it *was* a car, then—thank the Lord!—it wasn't a train. If one of this select group were to break his arm, he would thank God that his neck was safe, and were he to die—and God forbid *that!*—his family would take up where he left off, praising God that he died a martyr. And so, if such a one is startled to find himself put on pension at an early age, he discovers that this fate came exactly at the right moment for the execution of more important projects.

And so Abu Gamal found it opportune to launch the project he had post-poned all along for the sake of raising his four sons.

For every one of them—praise God—now lay serene and secure in his wife's embrace inside one of the apartments in the building he had erected for them on the foundations of his own sweating flesh.

The gist of Abu Gamal's scheme lay in the search for some sort of approba-tion, for respect befitting his head of gray hair. For someone who would give him the eyeball routinely expected by a man of such weight. It seems, though, that Abu Gamal had become thoroughly convinced—through experience, of course—that it was impossible to carry out this project in his own place of residence or in the workplace, or even in the face of any person with whom he had a nodding acquaintance. That he helped out the silk factory's tennis players, and that he insisted on imitating the Chinese by (and only by) riding a bicycle at his age, were enough to rule this out. So he went about searching out his scheme in the faces of strangers.

Abu Gamal always wakes up on schedule, exactly at seven a.m., eats a quick breakfast, and then extracts the hose, his bamboo chair, and the broom he yanked from one of the palm trees at the Helwan silk factory as if in antici-pation of this day.

The chair he stations smack in front of the building with a care that lends it the aura of an orator's podium. The hose he shoves onto the mouth of the tap in the building's open stairwell, and the broom he leans against the right half of the double-leaf front door with a lackadaisical manner well suited to tedious work. Next, he takes a little 'deducted time' and lights up a cigarette.

And then he repeats the whole sequence without a pause but exactly in reverse. Beginning with the broom, he sweeps a strip of street exactly parallel to the front of his building, annexing two additional meters from his neigh-bors to each side. Next, he takes out the hose to wet down the entire swept expanse, slowly and exactly, after which he adjusts the position of his chair until it is just right and sits down with great self-assurance, Umm Gamal's tea always in his right hand (seeing as it's a good thing) and the cigarette in his left hand (seeing as it's a wicked thing) . . . and awaits whatever has been decreed for him. He is ready to pounce on any unfamiliar face, any face as long as he can establish that he has never set eyes on it before. He's got that hunter's sure instinct that his approaching prey will fall. We are on a street, after all, and the streets, as usual, are hardly lacking in strangers.

The moment this face comes in sight, Abu Gamal throws himself into action, his welcoming phrases coming in bursts, surging, supplicating, strenuous, laced with a deeply felt invitation to a glass of tea or even food, and the stranger can find no way out, faced with this hoveringly anxious face and these heartfelt expressions of welcome. The only way out is to comply, to utter the acknowledgment Abu Gamal is searching for, often repeating it several times, sincerely, faithfully, and in unmistakable deference to the addressee. "Thank you, ya Hagg, thank you, sir." At which point Abu Gamal goes completely quiet. He is as mute as a man who has just lifted himself off a woman he has desired for a very long time. Or as silent as someone who has obtained a valuable thing that he knows perfectly well he does not deserve.

Finally I reached the corner of our street, and with it the Neighborhood Salon. As I turned—putting me directly in front of Sheikh Atuwwa's tiny bread bakery—the miraculous truth revealed itself: Abu Gamal's chair was not planted in front of the house, and likewise the strategic zone had not been hosed down, ready to receive strangers. But this wasn't enough to reassure me of the likelihood of sneaking safely all the way to my apartment without some annoying fracas. The absence of a dais does not mean there's no ceremony in progress. Not to mention that it only increases your anxiety if you aren't sure what the next step will bring—and with my very first step over the threshold, the irksome question took me by surprise.

"The stairs are narrow, so how'm I supposed to get by?"

"The stairs are narrow and about to collapse if I'm not careful, and so how am I going to get by you?"

Of course, repeating the question won't solve the problem. Abu Gamal is massive. With his own body, Gamal had squeezed his father into a corner, and they formed an immovable mass right at the point on the staircase that was just broad enough for me to slide by and get away with it unscathed.

"You said, didn't you, you DID say you killed him, you son of a BITCH?"

I could have slunk away, retreated, retraced my steps to find some café where I could waste a little time until Gamal would have finished pummeling his father for lying. (Sayf had returned in one piece, after Abu Gamal had claimed he'd sucked the kid's blood dry, off in some empty trash lot.) But the novelistic character I've chosen for myself ruled out such a possibility. How could my character take cover now, and in this cowardly manner, and withdraw from such significant events, especially when the two parties to this quarrel held the position of Gamal and his father?

Until recently I believed that a person's life unfolds along a line that shoots straight away from his past. The farther time carries you, I thought, the surer you can be that this past will not repeat itself. I even had an image in my mind's eye that illustrates my conviction perfectly. "The present," as we call it, is a train we've boarded. Our pasts are made up of scenes and personalities that drop from view the moment our train rushes by, abandoning them to each side. From our perspectives, as we sit in that train, everything seems to pass so quickly. The past is for *back there,* for forgetting; and the present is given to the past, which swallows it.

Our life's meaning is its end, marked out from the start. But the repetition of the fights in this house has made me doubt all of that. Indeed, those fights have convinced me from up close that the past may well return. I can see now that anyone's life is nothing but an assemblage of repeated scenes.

When I first moved in, I would rush into those fights unthinkingly, exactly like a son of the village and every bit as naive as a country yokel, shouting, "*Ayb ya gama'a!* For shame! Is this any way to behave?" Because of the age factor, I would always look to Abu Gamal first, and then I would whirl around to face Gamal, sending the blame his way with the usual phrases about fatherhood and the duties of sons, although I was sure that he didn't respect a single word I said. In fact, the fight would end with an impressive number of words flung in my face from both sides. I accepted it all with a graciousness that I considered an occasion for pride, comparing myself to the venerable head of a tribe who has to endure the rage of both adversaries in order to make peace between them.

Now, though, I was afraid, as I paused at the landing halfway up the staircase to watch and wait. I still had a way to go: my apartment was two floors above. Gamal was fully occupied in applying his knife to his father's neck. I estimated each leg of the distance I'd have to go, with a precision acquired from my skill at dashing across streets directly in front of speeding vehicles. I even took into account the extra space I needed if I were to avoid a collision between my face and a fist that might chance to stray from its usual course. I waited for just the right moment, and when Gamal yanked his father close I sped by them with an elegance I mulled over a few minutes later, after I was inside my apartment and breathing easier. It had been an embarrassingly tight fit, with my nose and Abu Gamal's tremendous back sharing the same narrow space on the stairs, so tight that I figured the reason his back was quivering was that my breaths were jetting out quick and hard. Gamal's back had been against the railing, and it was my good luck that he was completely absorbed in the matter at hand. No sooner had I squeezed by behind Abu Gamal's back—with an ordinary, casual hello such as I always offer when they're eating or watching a football match—than they ended the quarrel suddenly to stare after me. . . . Why, I don't know. Were they admiring what I'd just performed as a character from a novel, or were they irritated by what I'd done in my capacity as a new resident in the family building?

Abu Gamal is a decent man, and so is Gamal, and I'm a decent man, too. People are basically decent. But something is simply and fundamentally out of whack here. The two of them are passionate about their daily argument, which never goes beyond swearing, spitting, and waving weapons in the air. The underlying and covert reason for it is a struggle for authority when it comes to the family building. The public rationale is a difference of opinion over how best to treat Sayf's insane behavior, which has dragged the family's honorable reputation into the mud. It's an everyday quarrel that doesn't sever the bonds of affection but in fact, perhaps strengthens them. That seems to be the case, anyway, because after it's over they discover that *we only got each other, and nothing lasts for nobody*. Meanwhile, someone has been putting food on the table for the two of them. And anyway, what's wrong with whetting an appetite with a few verbal slings, the devil and anger and insanity? God's curses on Sayf and the day he was born.

As for me, I'm all in favor of a different quarrel, a bloody fight that brings on a permanent hostility through which I can guarantee my security and my release from a haunting and persistent fear that they'll unite against me—an instinctive phobia that lay behind my flight from the Bedouin hamlets to Cairo, only to find, here, that it's the sole guarantee of my safety among these people.

Translated by Marilyn Booth

Hani Abdel-Mourid

from *Kyrie Eleison*

IT WAS VERY OBVIOUS that the house was illegally built. True, it had been there for more than ten years in one of the nicest spots in the area, where several streets intersect and where there was ample space in front of it and to its right, but it was still illegal. It was built without authorization on a piece of land that was supposed to be part of the street.

Perhaps it was unfortunate that it was built two minutes away on foot from a spacious lot that was suddenly destined to become the seat of an organization under the auspices of the First Lady. That's why special attention and planning descended upon the street.

Before that building was erected, all illegal structures were demolished. It would have been difficult for Abu Amer's house to remain, even if it was one of the landmarks of the area. His free-of-charge repair of police-station trucks as well as police officers' and lieutenants' cars did not help him plead his case.

The house was made up of two floors: the upstairs for living, and the ground floor with two rooms and another inner storage room. One of the rooms was a car-body workshop and the other was Abu Amer's coffee shop.

My father sat there all the time, for he and Abu Amer were great friends with mutual interests. He was also a weak man who had three daughters. The younger two, Shawqiya and Adalat, ran the coffee shop. That's why people called it "the girls' coffee shop," despite the big sign that he had placed on top of the coffee shop entrance and his name that was engraved on the backs of the seats and the aluminum tea trays.

The eldest daughter was married in Upper Egypt and seldom came to visit.

God only gave him one male child, who came into the world with deformed legs and brain development that stopped at the age of four. You always saw him stretched out on a wooden bench and covered with flies, perhaps because he had no control over his bowel movements.

My father was a strong and violent man. He imposed his protection on Abu Amer and his daughters out of alleged decency. In public he benefited from the situation because he was contracted to redo the body paint of the cars that Abu Amer fixed. In private, rumor had it that he slept with one of his daughters, with varying opinions on which one it was.

But everybody confirmed that the only one who escaped him was Damma, the sister-in-law of their sister, who came from Upper Egypt for a change of air. She was innocent and fresh; she was afraid of speaking in front of anyone lest they make fun of her accent. She was amazed at Abu Amer's daughters and their audacity and at all the stories that they told her before they went to bed. During her prolonged stay with them, she gradually started to work in the coffee shop. She learned how to prepare the drinks only, without having to interact with the customers except under the strictest circumstances. They did not rely on her completely except on very specific occasions: when a complaint was sent against Abu Amer and his daughters that they were selling drugs. They were summoned and promptly released, but she stayed alone in the coffee shop for the whole morning. She was able to maintain control over the situation and he was very happy with her, "That's the way to go! I want you to get good at this. You never know what might be in store for you."

Days of important football matches have a special taste. Work at the coffee shop is tight all day. The number of customers increases, and in the evening Abu Amer comes back with grilled chicken, "Eat, everybody! Eat, Damma! We deserve a treat."

On the day of the match between Egypt and Cameroon, Abu Amer's TV died just as the TV anchorwoman was announcing the beginning of the match. If it had been a bigger TV set or even a colored one, he would have given it as a present to my father, but it was an old, locally made, pre-transistor era Telemisr that took ten minutes to kick off the image, which initially looked like moving ghosts.

All the customers transferred to another coffee shop on one of the side streets. Even my father and Abu Amer went with them to watch the match.

Damma remained alone after Sharbat had gone up to the house to watch over her sister, who was sick that day, "Keep an eye on the coffee shop, Damma. I will go see Adalat and rest a little. When things get going, I'll come down to help you."

There were no customers in the coffee shop until he came asking for a cup of coffee. He sat sipping it in silence. One of the passersby greeted him, "How are you, doctor?" He was a drug and sex-pills dealer. That's why they called him "doctor." Rumor has it that he was indeed a student in medical school but that he had been expelled after he was caught stoned in the auditorium.

He seemed sad that he couldn't secure any merchandise on this special occasion of the match, until she approached him, "Are you really a doctor?"

When asked the question, he responded, as usual, "Yes, I am."

"What's your field?"

"Everything. I mean, I'm a doctor of all things."

"I have a problem that is bothering me. Where is your clinic?"

Perhaps he didn't believe that she was that naive. He must have thought that she was trying to seduce him. He may have started this as a joke but he was aroused. So he cast his net.

In the storage room she complained of an irregular period and red pimples below her belly button.

He asked her as he held her breast if she felt pain. She said no. He continued fondling her breast. She felt uneasy and from time to time would say, "Doctor!"

And he would answer reassuringly, "Don't be afraid."

He took her. He didn't ever try to appear before her again. She never found out his name and she may still believe that the man who slept with her was a "doctor of all things."

Translated by Samia Mehrez

On the Move in Cairo

During the twentieth century Cairo witnessed not only massive expansion at the geographic level, reaching 214 square kilometers at the beginning of the new millennium that today constitute one of the most densely populated cities in the world but it also experienced an astounding explosion in the population and major shifts in its distribution. At the beginning of the twentieth century the city counted no more than one million inhabitants; currently Greater Cairo is home to more than seventeen million people whose lives, destinies, and fortunes intersect through an increasingly complex network of transportation that connects the heart and edges of this ever-expanding metropolis.

Indeed, Cairo's century-old transportation network in its different guises, shapes, and forms—from the horse-drawn carriage to the private car, from the public bus system to the empire of privately owned minibuses, from the city cab to the 'tock-tock' (Cairo's local version of the Indian subcontinent's rickshaw), from the tramway to the modern metro system—constitutes part and parcel of the city dwellers' daily lives and histories. In fact, means of transportation in the metropolis determine Cairenes' relationship with and perceptions of their city. No wonder then that so much creative energy has gone into representing everyday life as it unfolds on the move in Cairo.

The selections in this chapter bear testimony to how central Cairo's transportation network is to our understanding and reading of the city and the lives of its inhabitants. Like private spaces, these different means of moving around in the city are self-contained worlds with not only characteristic dynamics and levels of human and social interaction but also distinct ways of seeing Cairo and being in it as well. Class and gender are determining factors in the writers' representations of these moving worlds and the perspectives from which the outside space is reconstructed. In Taha Hussein's *A Man of*

Letters, the blind narrator describes Al-Azhar neighborhood while inside a horse-drawn carriage in such a manner that the outside becomes a spectacle, a theater of the burlesque. As the alleys become narrower, the voices louder, and the density higher, he senses "the intensity of agitation," the "tension and hostility" which, for him as an outsider and spectator, are still "pleasant and charming." In contrast, his friend who lives in the teeming neighborhood cannot wait to get home, to be delivered from the "burden" of the city with its "filth and dirt" to a space where he can "purify" his soul. *Al-Qahira*, the vanquishing city, has the potential of crushing its inhabitants who, when privileged, seek refuge in some of the more private moving worlds that allow them an aesthetic distance from the suffocation outside. Sahar al-Mougy's narrator in *N* is a university professor who watches student demonstrations at Cairo University from the privacy of her car, behind closed windows, as she listens to a cassette tape of the diva, Umm Kulthum. Like the narrator's friend in *A Man of Letters*, who feels aggressed by the city, al-Mougy's university professor feels that she "had to drive through the packed streets and get home quickly to be alone."

These more private and privileged means of being on the move in the city contrast quite sharply with more public, collective transportation vehicles that have the potential to break down class and gender boundaries. Unlike the private spaces of the homes where social order, hierarchy, and decorum are upheld and regulated, the self-contained worlds of public transportation allow for anonymity and impersonality, both potentially liberating and subversive elements. In Ihsan Abdel Quddus's classic *I Am Free*, the tram carriage provides a space for middle-class women to fabulate freely about their domestic lives. Young women, otherwise constrained by the home, can circulate love letters and share details of their private relationships. Women's coaches also offer a golden opportunity for brokering a future engagement or marriage by mother passengers seeking pretty young brides for their sons. In Salwa Bakr's *Rabbits*, the bus is a space for the underprivileged to daydream and construct unrealized lives with affluent futures otherwise impossible in the real, outside world of "haggard faces." Packed with human bodies as they always are, buses also allow for transgression, complicity, and the fulfillment of illicit human desires made possible by the unspoken pact of anonymity which, if broken, as in Raouf Mosad's *Ithaca*, can be the cause for public scandal.

These liberating collective mobile worlds also give occasion to new levels of consciousness: political, social, and economic. In Tharwat Abaza's *Fog*, a ride on a donkey cart during the 1919 national strike in support of the leaders of the Wafd Party transforms the narrator's relationship with his mistress. Likewise, Mona Prince's narrator in "Today I'm Gonna Pamper Myself" suddenly realizes that dress code on the metro is a public display of her religious affiliation; because she is unveiled in an increasingly Islamized society she is taken to be a Christian. Cab drivers are an indispensable source of information and its circulation in the city much of which is political satire of the state and its transparent wheeling and dealing. Their conversations with the passengers constitute the wisdom of the street: "We live a lie and believe it. The government's only role is to check that we believe the lie, don't you think?"

Significantly, these different networks of transportation are also responsible for the invention not just of new urban languages but also of new urban creatures whose behavior is determined by the collective transportation culture itself. Ahmed Alaidy's *Being Abbas el Abd* captures the inherent violence of the highly unregulated, lawless world of the microbus, "a canful of performing animals" where the narrator rhetorically asks: "Under a sky polluted with hatred and smoke, what kind of creatures are these that can breathe and multiply?" Indeed, the potential violence and lawlessness of the empire of microbuses was ruthlessly driven home in September 2009 when a microbus driver who had dented writer Tawfik Abdel Rahman's car deliberately ran him over, in broad daylight, leaving the writer's bleeding, dead body on the street in the midst of one of Cairo's busiest neighborhoods because he threatened to report him to the police.

Just as Cairo's moving worlds represent changes in social behavior and interaction in a city that is increasingly difficult to survive, so do they historicize dominant taste, etiquette, and mores. The vendor of women's dainty hair accessories of the first half of the twentieth century is substituted by the vendor of Quranic verses at the end of the same century; the playfulness of popular songs is replaced by cassette tapes that bellow condemnations against unveiled women and sermons on torture in the grave. In order to survive this burlesque reality, Mona Prince's narrator, who spends her day hopping from bus to cab to metro to microbus, thoroughly understands that she needs to transform it all into one long hilarious joke, the lesson being that if you can't laugh it up in *al-Qahira*, then you have to shut it out, if you can afford to.

Taha Hussein
from *A Man of Letters*

THE CARRIAGE CARRIED US through various neighborhoods with contrasting atmospheres. I sensed this in the people's voices and the sounds of their movements, in the intensity of agitation surrounding us. I sensed it also in the very movement of the carriage itself and in the driver's tone in urging the people in front of him to move out of his way or to beware of his horses and his carriage.

The district was graceful and elegant. The air was sweet and pure. The movements and sounds around me, although not devoid of tension and hostility, were nevertheless pleasant and charming. When we reached Muhammad Ali Street, the road grew narrower, the crowds denser, and the shouting increased. The voices of children and women started to commingle with those of men, laborers, and lorry drivers. Heavy odors permeated the air, most prominent among them those of onions and garlic frying in the fire. The driver's voice grew louder now and more frequent, as did his menaces and warnings and the people's admonishments and reproaches. The air resounded with the familiar sound of the driver's whips lashing to restrain the horses and caution the passersby. Then the road grew wider, the air less dense, and the movements less agitated. The driver breathed more freely and the horses moved more gently.

But this lasts only till the carriage turns right. We are now in a narrow, quiet alley, where the air is heavy and the atmosphere foul. The ground is full of ruts. The carriage is literally bouncing us, the driver is waving his whip in the air, calmly and contentedly cautioning and warning. This invites some windows to open and tempts some children to come out of their homes, or their nests, and tease the driver. Some of them climb onto the carriage then let go. We laugh at all this and at the driver, particularly when he looks before him then behind him, striking the air with his whip and voicing phrases either so gentle they are almost jesting or so coarse they are ugly insults. All this penetrates my soul and beckons different impressions. Yet, in spite of their diversity, they have one thing in common, namely novelty. For I was not accustomed to taking rides in carriages.

Then the driver suddenly comes to a halt and we descend. My friend says, "We are not home yet. But the carriage can go no further. Are you accustomed to climbing to the heights of mountains? I do not like to live on the flat plains and be like other people. I prefer to overlook Cairo and to imagine that I am not entrenched in it, that I enter it when I set out to work in the morning, and leave it when I go home at night. I must admit that I feel much gratification when I enter the city in the daytime, descending upon it from these heights as though invading it, plunging toward it as the vulture plunges toward its prey. I experience another no less gratifying pleasure when I spend the whole day in the city, joining the people in their agitated performance of their tasks, participating in their conversations, sharing in whatever good or evil they do, myself doing good or evil and benefiting or being harmed. When it is evening, I grow weary of them and they of me. I seek asylum in this new university of yours where I find diversion in the interesting and absurd words I hear, words which in either case are of no great import. When I have had my fill of this preliminary relaxation, I go home. Do not ask me about that sweet sensation which gradually seeps into my heart as I come closer to this place. I feel as though I am slipping out of the town, discarding its burden, casting its sins behind me, and purifying my body and soul from its filth and dirt. When I have ascended this mountain and reached this peak, when I have experienced the strain of climbing a high and winding road, I stand as one who has narrowly escaped an ordeal. I let out a deep sigh which I imagine bears the last remnants of such evils of the city as may still cling to me. Then I fill my lungs once, twice. Finally, calm and reassured, I leisurely walk to this door."

Here he stopped and knocked twice on the door. It opened then closed behind us.

We turned right, took a few steps and reached a corridor. We climbed up some more steps. A young maid walked with us carrying in her pretty hands a night lamp, from which a faint light faltered. When we reached the top of the stairs my host paused, feeling for something in his pocket. He took out a key and turned it in the lock before him. When the door opened he loudly instructed me, "Take your shoes off, you have reached the sacred room!"

Immediately, I stooped to remove my sandals. What was strange about that? I was accustomed to removing my sandals many times each day: when I went to classes at al-Azhar, Muhammad Bey mosque, al-Adawi mosque or al-Ashraf mosque. There I listened to lectures on usul, fiqh, nahw, mantiq, and tawhid. I was also accustomed to removing my sandals when I visited some houses, especially the homes of our 'ulama, and in particular the home of that sheikh whom the khedive had categorically banished from al-Azhar and prohibited from teaching there. We followed him to his home and insisted that he continue to lecture us. We did not do so out of fondness for his teachings or enthusiasm for his personality, but in defiance of that sovereign we judged to be despotic and tyrannical. We did not wish to capitulate to this despotism and tyranny. To demonstrate this, we arranged for an item to be published in the newspapers describing our insistent pleading with the professor, his consent, and the fact that we visited his home at noon each day to learn principles of law on some days and logic on others. There, in Darb al-Ahmar, we would reach his home, in our diversity, some shod in sheikh's footwear, others in effendi's. Upon reaching the sitting room, we would all remove our footwear.

Translated by Mona al-Zayyat

Tharwat Abaza

from *Fog*

ZEIN AL-ABEDIN LEFT the hotel and headed for the jewelers' quarter, for he needed to buy a present for the new girlfriend. He stood waiting for a carriage to pass by, to no avail. Zein al-Abedin was fed up with waiting, so he started walking, with the hope that he would come across a carriage—not realizing that it would be difficult to find one, for he had left Cairo before the revolution, when carriage drivers still solicited passengers. When he arrived by train last night he had no problem finding a carriage that remained with him until he was escorted back to the hotel. The driver had asked if he needed him the next day, and he was rather surprised at the question but agreed, thinking that the driver wanted to secure his next day's income and that he didn't want to disappoint him. The carriage remained with him all day until he went back to the hotel. So now he simply didn't understand what had suddenly happened to Cairo transportation. He was now paying the price of his ignorance. He had not asked the carriage driver to come again on this day, for he never imagined that he would not find a carriage when he needed one. A karro, a donkey cart, came by, crowded with people, which he was not used to seeing on a karro. He was somewhat astonished. No sooner had this one gone by than another karro appeared. It was not as crowded, so the driver came to a halt beside him and said, "Welcome, ya bey!"

"What did you say?!"

He was on the brink of anger, but when he looked carefully, he saw that the passengers were no less elegant than himself. One of them, a well-dressed effendi, said:

"Welcome, ya bey! You seem to have just arrived from the countryside!"

Zein al-Abedin responded in amazement, "Yes."

"This is the official means of transportation for the time being. The carriage drivers are on strike."

The driver said, "Would you like to be seated in first class?"

"What? Do you have first class?"

"Yes, here, in front. You will sit on a cushion and you will find the seating comfortable and clean."

"How much are you charging?"

"Two piasters. Where are you going?"

"To the jewelers' quarter."

"Please, get on."

Zein al-Abedin paid the two piasters and hopped on, resuming the conversation. "But yesterday I had a carriage."

The driver replied, "You must have gotten it at the train station."

"Yes. What about the tram?"

"The tram workers are also on strike."

One of the elegant passengers said, "We are finding the karro more pleasant."

And the driver added, "It's a royal ride!"

Zein al-Abedin replied, "But why continue with the strike when the Wafd has been allowed to negotiate and Rushdi's government has been constituted and things have started to settle down?"

The effendi who had addressed him earlier said, "The committee of civil servants is still on strike and has drafted conditions to resume work. That's why the strike continues."

Another passenger said, "The strike is still on, even though they have started collecting donations for the Wafd."

"May God help them! The Wafd must succeed in its mission."

The conversation continued among the passengers until Zein al-Abedin arrived at the jewelers' quarter. He alighted and chose a heavy gold bracelet that cost him twenty pounds. He now knew his way back, so he stopped at the karro parking lot and got himself a first-class seat. A young man in the attire of ordinary people alighted with him, as well as an effendi of modest demeanor. Another elegant passenger in traditional religious garb who looked more like a merchant sat next to him in a first-class seat. The karro took off. The modestly dressed effendi started a conversation with the young man in ordinary attire, "I wish I could give more than what I did."

"No problem. Each one should give what he can. . . . I had nothing, and had it not been for my wife, I would have remained miserable for the rest of my life."

"It's okay, brother. You are one, husband and wife."

"Yes, but we are newly wed and I had just given her the necklace."

"Good for her."

"She saw how stuck I was, so she said, 'Sell it. When you get money, you can buy me another one.'"

"Did you sell it?"

"No, I'm going to give it to the donations committee. I'm afraid to sell it at a loss. I bought it for ten pounds and I have the receipt. I will give both to the committee and they will sell it for the price I paid."

Zein al-Abedin overheard the conversation and was quite astonished. He started thinking about this city of Cairo that had risen in revolt. He could no longer hear anything, only the sound of rushing blood in his veins. This is the rebirth! The karro came to a halt; he did not know where. The effendi and the young man alighted and Zein al-Abedin found himself getting off with them. They started to walk and he followed in their footsteps. They entered an old house and each gave his donation, took a receipt, and left. He moved forward and presented the gold bracelet that he had just bought, along with the receipt for the amount he had paid. The person in charge of the donation collection asked him, "Your name, sir?"

Without thinking, he replied, "Anisa Wil'a (Anisa Fireworks)."

Taken aback, the man replied. "What was that?"

Zein al-Abedin came to and said, "Make out the receipt in the name of Anisa Wil'a." When they met, he gave her the receipt. She gave him a long, meaningful look and embraced him, saying, "This is the most magnificent present I have ever received. In fact, I think it is the best one I will ever receive in my entire life. You have made me a human being with a responsibility toward the nation. God bless you!"

Translated by Samia Mehrez

Ihsan Abdel Quddus

from *I Am Free*

AL-KHALIG TRAMWAY NO. 22 came by. She had seen it come by dozens of times. She hated that tram with only one coach that wobbled on the railway like a street kid who had contracted whooping cough. She hated its dry wooden seats that looked like washboards for the dead lined up side by side in a wholesale funerary shop. She hated al-Khalig Street itself that wound, narrow and dark, like a snake that twisted in the mud of a swamp. She hated the old dilapidated houses that stood on both its sides, leaning against each other after so many years of proximity. She hated those peddlers that sprang from the right and left sides, selling hairpins and combs and hair nets or mahallawi kerchiefs and uya headcovers or harisa and guziya. She hated them all, especially that young peddler who jumped on the tram at the intersection of Muski Street and al-Khalig Street, and who, as soon as he laid eyes on her, started to sing: "Ah, ya smarani l-lun, habibi l-asmarani. Habibi wi 'uyunu sud, hatta al-kuhl da rabbani" (Oh, you tanned one, my beloved tanned one with black eyes whose kohl is God-given). He would then interrupt his singing and call out his merchandise, "Custom-made combs and lice combs, uya kerchiefs, safety pins, hairpins." Then he would extend his hand to her with one of the combs, saying, "Don't you need a comb, lady? I swear I made it out of my own left rib." Without waiting for her refusal, he would turn his head away from her and pretend he was talking to one of his colleagues: "You beautiful tanned one! Have pity on me, you're driving me crazy." He would then put the edge of his gallabiya between his teeth and resume jumping from coach to coach with amazing and frightening audacity.

The passengers in the women's coach preferred this vendor to all others and liked the way he displayed his merchandise. Every time he appeared they would turn to Amina and start giggling as they listened to how he sweet-talked her. But Amina continued to hate him and his daring leaps between coaches. One day she screamed when she thought he had fallen under the wheels of the tram coming in the opposite direction as he leaped from the left side. But the tram went by and he suddenly reappeared behind it, standing on his two feet, looking at her and singing: "Asmar malak ruhi. Ya habibi ta'ala bi l-'agal!" (A tanned one possessed my heart. Come quickly, my beloved!)

Even though she hated him, she still waited for him every time the tram approached the intersection of Muski Street and al-Khalig Street. When he was late leaping into the coach she would secretly look for him. His intuitive and innocent sweet talk used to alleviate some of the boredom of the long ride from Abbasiya to Sayeda Zaynab Square where Saniya School stood. His sweet talk was gratifying to her in front of all the other women passengers. If he were to sweet-talk any of them, she would have been envious, and would have hated her ride to school and all the passengers in the women's coach even more than she already did.

She hated them and their strange conversations in the coach: conversations between her schoolmates as they told stories about the romantic letter that was found in their classmate Zaynab's copybook and confiscated by Miss Saniya, the natural-history teacher. They would then bring their heads together and whisper the story of Miss Saniya's own romance with Fahmi effendi, the English teacher, and they would giggle and tell jokes about Sheikh Gabr, the religion and calligraphy teacher. She never partook of these conversations. She used to choose her place at the far end of the coach and sit silently, holding her head up high, as if she were a queen listening to her subjects. She would not utter a word except to redirect the conversation or respond monosyllabically to a question. . . .

It was not just her schoolmates who took the women's coach in al-Khalig tramway no. 22. There were always some other women from Abbasiya with black coats that covered their dresses, wearing turbans or hairpins, or women from the Bab al-Sha'riya and al-Husayn neighborhoods with wrap-around cloaks. She used to marvel at the intimacy that developed between them as soon as they laid eyes on each other without previous acquaintance. They would start an endless conversation about shopping, their husbands, and the most private details of their lives, "what they were cooking for the day" or "the wretched maid who ate two loaves of bread per meal without it ever showing on her—she was still pale and dirty and unattractive, never thankful, like cats."

She used to follow these conversations from a distance and she knew that they were all fibbing about everything they said or told about their shopping and their homes. Even her aunt would fib like this when she took the tram with her and would participate in these conversations. She lied when she said, "It's just that my husband is a bit strict," when she knew that her uncle was not "strict" at all except when ordered by his wife to be so.

She would only become upset with these women when one of them would stretch out her arm and place it on her shoulder and then begin to feel her body, pretending that it was unintentional, as if she were feeling the cloth of a dress to identify its kind, and would then say unassumingly, "God bless you.

A tanned complexion is half the beauty. How are you, my dear? And how's your mother?"

She would grudgingly reply, "She's fine."

"And what's your name, dear?"

"Amina."

"What a beautiful name! Do you go to school, pretty one?"

"Yes."

"Why the trouble, sweetheart? As the saying goes, it's ripe for the picking. You should stay home and await your future husband. I have just the one for you: my son Muhammad, God bless him. He's a respectable civil servant. Young and pleasing, from a good respectable family. Have you heard of Sheikh Ashur, the imam of Sidi al-Sha'rani mosque? He is my brother's immediate brother-in-law!"

The conversation would continue and she would grow increasingly upset until she arrived at school or the woman left the tram coach before her.

Translated by Samia Mehrez

Salwa Bakr

from *Rabbits*

USAMA PROFOUNDLY BELIEVED THAT his future would be brighter with the rabbits, and that those quiet, sweet creatures with soft, straight fur were the solution to all the problems in his life and the happy ending to his daily ordeals that he had for long shouldered alone after the death of his father, his marriage, and his kids. He was almost without family, his social relations with most of his maternal and paternal relatives having shrunk because he was a civil servant with a modest income who could not keep up with their affluent lifestyle, since they were well established in the latest economic business activities recently introduced into the country, namely, real estate and land speculation. Since Usama married and had his two daughters, his salary had been on a steady decrease, given the increase in prices and the never-ending family expenses—so much so that he had forgotten the taste of small bygone pleasures that consisted in his sitting at the coffee shop every evening to play his favorite domino game. Actually, Usama gave up spending half a pound on the drinks he would have daily at the coffee shop, after he made calculations and found that it would be better to save the fifteen pounds every month to buy one kilogram of seedless grapes, or dates or soft drinks to accompany dinner on summer nights, or to buy the navel oranges and bananas that his youngest daughter loved during winter.

He kept daydreaming as he rode the bus, watching out of the window all those who waited at every stop. He contemplated their pale, haggard faces and their dead, dim, meaningless gaze. He felt that they were creatures living like the dead, creatures who came into life and departed from it as if they had never happened. He realized that he was somewhat like them: a being without meaning who came into the world and would leave it one day as if he had never been. He was a being without color, without taste, but with a smell, like all those he saw standing at the bus stops waiting as if they were waiting for death itself. All he had accomplished in his life was that he got married and had children; nothing more, nothing less. Nothing more than any insignificant insect or small worm or strange animal from among God's many creatures would accomplish. He sighed heavily as he bewailed his situation, for he had always dreamed of doing something meaningful in life. How he had hoped to be exceptional and to be able to distinguish himself at some level, just as he dreamed of falling so madly in love that people would never stop telling his unusual story. In any event, he never really had the guts to be a Qays, for he realized that he was not handsome. He dreamed of becoming a famous singer who would break young maidens' hearts, but he never tried singing out loud, perhaps because of the negative reactions he received every time he started singing as he scrubbed his body in the shower. A deep sense of misfortune had settled within him to this day. . . .

He remembered the rabbits with their round, twinkling, intent eyes, as if in a permanent state of discovery and astonishment. He remembered the collective birth they gave, with which he greeted the morning, and he was overtaken by a sense of appreciation and gratitude to such kind and giving creatures who were also calm and quiet, never loud or disturbing like hens, roosters, ducks, and geese. True, their gaze seemed meaningless, but they still looked cute and funny when they devoured the green, moist clover in the morning or the carrot leaves at noon. How delightful they looked when the color of the greens mixed with the white, black, and brown color of their fur! A truly beautiful sight!

At the moment, he was dreaming of planning his future based on a project that would develop and grow beyond the boundaries of the balcony and the apartment; to join the world of distinguished businessmen—a project with the rabbits that would enable him to realize what he had not been able to before. He got off the bus and started walking toward the ministry, holding a cloth bag in his hand with two big rabbits inside.

Translated by Samia Mehrez

Raouf Mosad

from *Ithaca*

I DON'T KNOW HOW I found myself on a bus when I had boycotted buses for ages, ages, among which was the age of brushing up against women, an experience peculiar to crowded Cairene buses and trams. The pleasure of successful brushing up (there is, of course, unsuccessful brushing up, during which the woman would refuse or scandalize you) is when silent complicity is achieved between you and her, so much so that she would allow you her body: her expertise in avoiding the envious eyes of the other males and your expertise in not allowing your body and desire to give you away. This complicity frequently ended on the bus, except for a few cases when you established contact after getting off at the bus stop, her bus stop, for it is preordained and I have no free choice. The best and strangest brush-up was during my university days on board tram no. 15 from Mahattat Misr Square to Giza. Usually, in the morning, the tram is crowded with students who do not want to miss their first lecture. I was around eighteen or nineteen at the time. My body was teeming with ear-splitting hormones. A certain girl. I spotted her once getting off the tram at the university bus stop. He was brushing up against her from behind: a monster, with wild hair, wearing a gallabiya with his hand in its pocket, most probably to help him savor the pleasure. The girl looked as though she were oblivious to what was happening. Her face was clean and quiet, angelically innocent, or at least that's how I imagined angelic faces. I followed her and was astounded by her buttocks, which seemed to have no relation to her face. I followed her and found out from the number of the lecture hall that she was studying law. I copied her schedule and considered it my own until, God willing, I could pull it off. I waited for her discreetly after she finished her class, and followed her to the tram, which was overflooded by the rush of students the minute it arrived. I fought my way through the crowd until I got to a satisfactory position behind her. But I was too shy, so at first I didn't press against her, but the pushing crowd forced me to do what my shyness would not allow. I found her receptive, welcoming, and interactive, moving her buttocks in a silent dialogue as she looked intently out of the window, stooped over slightly to enable me. I trembled with surprise, for I was an excellent robber but I had never encountered such a reception before. I remained in her company until we reached Shubra, where I lived on the other side of town. After more than one encounter and more than one chase, she noticed I was following her again. That was when I, naive as I was, got the first lesson in breaking the silent complicity. When I alighted in Shubra behind her, after she had deliberately avoided me on the tram, she turned around and threatened in a rather high voice that she would hit me in the face with her shoe. I started running in fear of the scandal, not the shoe. That was why I felt strange being on a bus after such a long time. Perhaps I had been waiting for a cab that never came, so when the bus arrived, I hopped on. After a while it got crowded and I found myself next to a young woman with her small children. The satanic within me was awakened: why don't I try to play the game of complicity, especially now that my old age protected me and gave me security? I tried starting with the classic feeling up: lightly interlocking the thighs and pretending to look intently out of the window. If she were to turn around in protest or move away disapprovingly, I would look at her and apologize. She will probably accept your apology. At that point, you would have two options: to continue to press against her, as if under pressure to do so because of the crowd, or to pretend that you are protecting her from rascals (like yourself) and to offer that she stand in front of you in order to protect her respectable buttocks. She would probably accept that complicity in gratitude, for there are no female bus passengers who do not know the rules of the bus game. She looked at me from the corner of her eye and I reciprocated. I smiled and commented on the pressing crowd and pretended to make room for her, calling her 'madame' instead of the more frequently used title of 'hagga.' Madame smiled, excusing me, and said that the world had become narrower than the hole of a needle. I liked the metaphor of the hole. I shuffled into the small spot that I had vacated in front of me. She enabled me without further ado. We played together nicely during the bumps on the road and the crazy, reckless driving. She would play me up with her buttocks when there were no bumps but, of course, I knew my limits from painful, scandalous past experiences.

Translated by Samia Mehrez

Sahar al-Mougy

from *N*

I HAVE CHOSEN TO begin the story by telling you how the story chose me to become its narrator.

It was at the end of a long teaching day at the university that Sara's mind thickened with ominous clouds. She started her car and drove slowly inside the university campus, circling around student demonstrators who held banners that read, "La ilaha illa Allah . . . Sharon 'adu Allah" (There is no god but God . . . Sharon is the enemy of God) and "Khaybar Khaybar ya Yahud . . . al-Quds labudd ti'ud" (Khaybar, Khaybar, oh, you Jews . . . Jerusalem must return).

Several hundred veiled and face-covered women students, along with bearded men students, were chanting in solidarity with the Palestinian intifada, while other groups of students scattered on wooden benches and along the university walls were watching the scene in amusement.

Sara turned to a particular group of students that she always saw in the university gardens and said to herself: When do they ever go to class? Are you going to be stupid forever? They're at the university to fall in love, not to study.

She smiled as she watched the girls' bodies stuck in jeans with faded patches. The tight tops revealed their full, inviting breasts; their faces were smudged with heavy makeup in the stifling heat. She stopped the car to allow the demonstrators to pass, and looked back at the young crowd standing by with Pepsi-Cola cans and cigarettes in their hands. She smiled even wider as she scrutinized their shining gelled hair.

No sooner had she left the university than many thoughts rushed to her head, squeezing it like a pair of heavy metal forceps. She did not resist. She thought only of procrastination. She had to drive through the packed streets and get home quickly to be alone. Congested Cairo traffic at seven o'clock in the evening was no different from that at two in the afternoon. The car twisted and turned among the other cars like a weary serpent as she organized the schedule in her mind: she would take a hot shower after turning on Debussy; a mug of hot Nescafé without sugar and a cigarette would breathe new life into her. Then she would turn on her computer and organize her weary head to work on the research paper that had preoccupied her

for the past months, the colors of the details of her days, and perhaps . . .
she was a bit muddled.

On al-Bahr al-Aazam Street, cars were packed side by side. Had Sara not
been a Cairene, she would have thought that something had gone wrong or
that there was another demonstration taking place. Of course not! It's just
a microbus letting off passengers in the middle of the street. Her voice rose
in subdued anger, "Just normal!" She tried to swerve around it but she almost
bumped into a Peugeot that was coming in the opposite direction. She took a
deep breath that she then held in for a few seconds and then released slowly.
She turned up her cassette player as she shut the windows:

> *Then I remembered how happy I was with you.*
> *I also remembered, my love, why we separated . . . why we separated . . . why we
> separated,*
>   *After I had finally . . .*

She was suddenly overtaken by nostalgia for Padstow, where she used to
spend her summer vacations with her grandmother when she was a child. Sara
could walk to the small village in south Wales on the ocean in no more than an
hour. It would take longer if she decided to go to Gaff Woods or Under Town,
where she could be completely alone with the whispering black elder trees
and wild red flowers. She would only go home after she had gathered some
wild herbs with an intoxicating smell. She would often come across wild rabbits and would enjoy their sudden appearance and disappearance. When she
came to from this dazzling experience, she would realize that several hours
had gone by with the silence of the place and the fog that covered the face
of the sun even on summer days. The memory brought forth a damp breeze
in her hands laden with dew, and the smell of fresh grass that swept away the
dust of Cairo and the black exhaust fumes that filled her lungs despite the
closed window.

She took a deep breath and smiled. As she continued her daydream she
looked around her to the right and then to the left. Her eyes fell on the
shocked gaze of a man in a nearby car. She kept herself from cracking up so
that the man would not misunderstand her behavior. It was enough that she
might appear crazy to him. It was not necessary for him also to think that she
was a loose woman trying to seduce him.

Translated by Samia Mehrez

Khaled Al Khamissi

from *Taxi*

WE DROVE INTO TAHRIR Square and found it transformed into a military barracks with the arrival of giant riot police trucks and large numbers of officers and policemen. This was about a month after the suicide operation, or the terrorist attack, or the stupid, retarded, desperate attack which led to the death of the attacker and injured some tourists including an Israeli, and which had helped create even more intolerable traffic jams in Cairo.

We turned into Ramses Street and I was surprised to see an endless line of riot police trucks parked on the right-hand side of the street. I looked with sympathy at those wretched policemen, stunted from poor nutrition, their bodies apparently consumed by bilharzia. One of them gave me an imploring look through a small opening like the window of a prison cell. The taxi driver looked at me sarcastically and asked, "Pasha, did you hear the horrible story of what happened to the officer yesterday?"

I said no and he began the story: "They say one of the officers went in to see his troops in one of these trucks (he gestured to the riot police vehicles) and died from the smell." Then the driver burst out laughing. I didn't laugh myself and he carried on, "Can you imagine, sir, the smell of the wretches in this heat when they're packed into the truck like sardines? They keep sweating and farting. The officer, no God, just dropped down dead, he died of asphyxia."

I looked incredulous and asked him: "Did that really happen?"

"Wakey, wakey, it's a joke," said the driver. "You looked grumpy so I thought I'd give you something to laugh about."

"I am a little depressed," I said. "But I hadn't thought it was so obvious."

"Well you don't take anything with you when you go," said the driver. "Well then, listen to this one. A guy was walking through the desert when he found Aladdin's lamp. He rubbed it and a genie appeared and said, 'Hey presto, at your service, your wish is my command.' The guy didn't believe his eyes but went and asked for a million pounds. The genie went and gave him half a million. The guy asked him, 'Okay, so where's the other half? You're going to fleece me from the start?' 'All the government's got a 50-50 stake in the lamp,' the genie replied." The driver burst out laughing again and his laugh made me laugh more than the joke did.

"You know, the government really does take about half our earnings," the driver said.

"How's that?" I asked.

"Various tricks," he said. "Every now and then they dream up a new story. But the best one of all is the seatbelt story."

"What's with the seatbelts?" I asked.

"The seatbelt's a joke," said the driver. "A bad joke and can only be a trick, a seatbelt for the driver and for the person sitting next to him, like in foreign countries, the bastards. And most people in this country don't drive faster than 30 kilometers an hour, but you know what, business is business.

"Suddenly, just like that, sir, they told you you have to fit in the seatbelt and the fine is fifty pounds. Really expensive seatbelt then appeared, you can't find one for less than two hundred pounds. It's obviously a racket big people are involved in, very big people. Imagine, sir, how many taxis there are in Egypt and how many cars are driving around Egypt without seatbelts. Count it up, that's a job worth millions, the perfect scam."

"Seatbelts are compulsory throughout the world," I said. "You have to fit seatbelts."

"Whadyamean, throughout the world? This is a son-of-a-bitch government. You know, right, that previously the seatbelt counted as a luxury, in other words you had to pay extra customs duty on it. I was importing a Toyota from Saudi Arabia and I had to cut off the seatbelts myself and take out the air-conditioning so that I wouldn't have to pay the luxury customs duty. Then, no more than a few months later, the seatbelt was compulsory. I mean, straight from luxury and extra duty to compulsory. So we ran out and bought seatbelts and they did some good business at our expense.

"The whole story was business on business. The big guys imported seatbelts and sold them and made millions. The Interior Ministry worked on giving out loads of tickets and collected millions. The wretched cops on the street would stop you and say, 'Where's your seatbelt, you bastard?' and you'd have to slip him a fiver, and if he stopped you when an officer was there, it would be twenty pounds. I mean, everyone benefited.

"And there's something else I want to tell you. I'm sure you know the seatbelt's a lie through and through in the first place. Everyone knows it's for decoration, we fit it just for show." The driver lifted up his seatbelt to show me it wasn't fastened.

"If the police officer stops you, he looks at the belt and he knows very well that it's for decoration. That seatbelt, you have to slam on the brakes to make it grip. But with our cars, when you hit the brakes, the seatbelt comes undone." He laughed aloud. "We live a lie and believe it. The government's only role is to check that we believe the lie, don't you think?"

Translated by Jonathan Wright

Ahmed Alaidy
from *Being Abbas el Abd*

DON'T BELIEVE HER.

She will tell you of crimes I never committed and will weep in your arms in the hope that your heart will soften or relent.

She will give you of herself things that will alter your being, and you know very well how much a woman who is good at giving can take.

This is the truth in all its cruelty, so do as you damn well please.

I wake up, late as usual, to the foul-mouthed yelling of the neighbors. Today's lesson is a painful one and goes: Nothing can teach you better how to bawl someone out than a wife who's hot for it and loses all sense of proportion on catching sight of a bed. I call Abbas on the phone in the apartment of his elderly neighbor, a lady afflicted with Alzheimer's, and then I explain to her—as usual—who I am and who he is and ask her, with a show of good manners:

"Could you possibly call him over?"

"Certainly, sonny, certainly."

The old lady puts down the receiver and comes back after a reasonable length of time and says that he'll talk to me "when he's finished something he has in hand."

She asks me how I am.

"Same old stuff," and "Not too bad," and "Thanks for asking."

The usual clichés you say if you can't find anything else to vomit down the receiver. I read the morning paper in the bathroom, have breakfast, drink my tea. I crack my knuckles in front of the television and when the morning movie finishes I try him again. Abbas won't answer, but I pick up the receiver anyway.

"Hello."

I know Abbas won't answer, and so does Abbas. "Yes. Who is it?"

"Abbas's friend from work, ma'am."

"Abbas who?"

God bless the absentminded and make their curse a joy to them forever!

"Abbas. Abbas el Abd, the one you rented the flat opposite to. I was just wondering if he's finished what he had in hand yet."

"Hang on a tick, sonny, and I'll go and see."

Saying this she disappears. I wait. I drum my fingers. I scratch the usual 'area of low pressure,' if you know what I mean and I think you do. And I wait. Someone knocks on my door and I yell—*God save just me and send the rest to the usual hell*—that I'm busy. I do not wish to be disturbed. Something like that. I put the receiver to my ear again waiting for the 'dear old lady,' who picks up after three seconds and says, "Sorry, sonny, I can hear him talking to someone. One of your friends must be with him."

When you think about things it feels, sometimes, like the things that are happening aren't really happening. "And how are you, ma'am?"

"Crappy, son."

"Never mind. God help you."

"That's it, sonny, pray for me to the Lord!"

"O Lord!"

"That He take me."

Cough, splutter. "'Bye now!"

I swear I'll never understand the older generation.

I go and take a refreshing shower that helps me forget all the things I can't remember because I've forgotten them.

I shove on the usual dumb blue jeans with a shirt and pullover.

Watch on wrist, wallet in the proper pocket. Cell phone in case on belt. Cigarettes, matches. And slam the door behind me.

I walk to the end of the street, where the minibus drivers have come up with a new unofficial stop.

"Ramses! Ramses! Ramses!"

As the tout shouts he waves at me and says: "Heh, *mizter*! Going to Ramses?"

I shake my head and make my way to the big minibus that some call "The Phantom."

The tout pulls me in by the shoulder like someone dragging his drawers off the line. Then he goes off again looking for more underwear, drumming on the paneling the while to pass the time as he shouts: "This way and watch your step! (Bam bam bam!)

Ramses! (Bam bam bam!) Coming with us, miss?"

In gets a petticoat.

(Bam bam bam!)

In gets an undershirt.

(Bam bam bam!)

"You, sonny?"

In gets a pair of boxers.

"All Helpful All Wise All Giving All Gener . . . ! Something wrong, *mizter*?!"

"What do you think you're doing, buddy? Whacking cockroaches with a slipper? Enough with the bang, bang, bang. Give your hand a nice dangle for a bit."

"What's it to you, buddy? Someone bang *you*?"

Have a horrible day!

"'Someone bang you?' Whoa! You want to try out your smartass cracks on me? Wise up. I've been around since before your mommy peeled your daddy's banana."

"Uh . . . what's that mean?"

That's right. Back off and try and pretend to be at least semihuman.

A giant materializes out of nowhere and gives the tout a telling off, then turns to me and says:

"Apologies. Your rights are as dear to me as the hairs on my head" (of which Mendel's laws have left precisely five).

"Aren't you ashamed, boy, talking dirty to the customers in front of me? Isn't my mustache" (which is big enough to make anyone else's a goatee) "big enough to get a little respect around here??"

I settle back in the uncomfortable foam seat ignoring the curious looks of my fellow passengers and reward my lips, capable of tossing off abuse in all weather, by lobbing a cigarette in their direction and immediately lighting its end; soon I'm comfortably dragging on its contaminated air.

I don't know how much time passes before this canful of performing animals fills up but I come to when the giant himself leaps behind the steering wheel and shoves a tape into the cassette player.

He turns the key.

"Teet ta-teet taata!" go the horns of the cars, mimicking a well-known obscenity, as he cuts in front of them without warning to enter the stream of traffic.

A driver shouts from his window: "Hey, you! First day behind the wheel?"

The driver delivers a melodious snort of disgust and says:

"Me?? I've driven further in reverse, sonny, than you've driven forward. Go to hell and God speed!"

More teet ta-teet taata back and forth and everyone goes his own way.

The tout pokes his finger in the faces of the pedestrians and yells: "Ramseeeeeeeeeeeees?"

I hand my fare to the person sitting next to me: "Pass it along."

My face is in the open window. With my thumb and middle finger I flick what's left of my cigarette out of the window.

A passenger sitting in front of me spits out of his window and the post office rejects it as "Unknown at this Address." The gob, God bless it, reenters the car, the air stream taking it upon itself to deliver it directly to my face.

And the result?

I wipe off the adherent filth and reward my lips with a whole cartonful of cigarettes.

This time I'm careful to close the window and content myself with just looking at what's going on outside.

On my right I can see the driver of an American luxury car rubbing his hand over an unresisting white knee.

I envy the equitable way in which he apportions his finger time—a bit for the knee, then a bit for the gear stick. Knee, gear stick, knee, gear stick . . . (waiting perhaps for the gear stick to calm down).

Lords of the World, inventors of AIDS and CNN,

Lords of the World, who discovered the ozone layer and then put a hole in it—

When will the Americans come up with a knee you can caress and shift gears with at the same time?

The minibus stops at a traffic signal and a small barefoot girl goes by.

True, her face is dirty, but it's an innocent dirt. She goes up to a red car with a well-off-looking guy at the wheel and tries to interest him in buying a packet of paper hankies, *God increase your wealth!*

He pushes her, this well-off-looking guy. He pushes the little girl with a hand sporting a gold ring on the fourth finger. He pushes her so roughly that the fragile little girl can't stand up and falls to the ground, and the packets of hankies propagate around her on the grungy pavement.

This is where the ladies of the night are born . . . in plain daylight.

Soon the little girl's body will be converted into circles that will accept the geometrical abuse of any miserable oblong.

May the hormonal conscience of our 'brother Arabs' guard her well!

God bless the property rights that turn people into things that can be priced and given 'use by' dates!

God bless the charity of the credit card!

We like to say that we hold our "little innocents" "dear." So TEAR AT HER, so long as you're gonna pay!

Let our tourist slogan in the future be Altruism, Not Egotism!

The little girl cries.

The light changes and the minibus takes off, while the voice of Abd al-Wahhab wafts from somewhere singing:

Do you know why?

Don't ask why.

Do you know why?

Under a sky polluted with hatred and smoke, what kind of creatures are these that can breathe and multiply?

Are we seeing the survival of the most corrupt or the corruption of the best survivors?

"Ramses and the end of the line, ladies and gentlemen."

Abbas says I'm suffering from heavy-duty depression.

To hell with good old Abbas.

Translated by Humphrey Davies

Mona Prince

from *Today I'm Gonna Pamper Myself*

PROFESSOR M FINISHED HER day's work at Suez Canal University earlier than she had expected. She got on the East Delta bus to Cairo feeling grateful that the AC was working and that the VCR was not. Her joy was short-lived, however, for the driver turned on the cassette player and one of those voices started bellowing condemnations against unveiled women. "What luck! Whose face did I wake up to today?! During the morning ride it was a sermon on torture in the grave and now it's the devils in hell. God help us!" She put in her earplugs that she always carried in her bag in preparation for such occasions. She looked around her and felt that the driver had deliberately chosen this particular cassette tape for her alone, for she was the only unveiled woman and the only one wearing a sleeveless top and a short skirt. She tried to think of something uplifting. Tonight there will be a full moon. She checked her watch and decided that she would go back to Fayoum that evening. But will she watch the full moon while drinking tea? She thought of her boyfriend. She discreetly opened her wallet and counted what remained of her salary: about one hundred pounds and the month was not over yet. She felt depressed as she calculated the expenses of the remaining week. The one hundred pounds wouldn't do. But she decided with determination, "Today, I'm gonna pamper myself."

On the way home she started craving fish. She got off the bus at Fangari Bridge on Salah Salim highway and took a cab. "Malek Street, please." Professor M insisted on using the old names of streets that have been changed since the 1952 revolution. At the fish restaurant on the ground floor of what used to be a villa owned by one of the old-time pashas — now an ugly residential high-rise — she signaled to the driver to stop. She sat at a table overlooking the street and ordered fish. The clamor of the street that ended with Qubba Palace flooded her ears. All kinds of noise: bad loud music, rattling voices of unknown Qur'an reciters, different cusses. The culture of 'ashwa'iyyat has taken over the not-so-long-ago aristocratic street. She put the plugs in her ears again and looked at the passersby. The shapes of men and women were depressing: disproportionate bodies, dangling bellies, dark and faded colors, frowning faces, veils, and the zibiba-stamped foreheads from frequent prayer. She suddenly discovered that it was only the Egyptians, among all the Muslims in the world, who had the zibiba mark on their foreheads, as if, during prayer, they prostrated on stone and not on Chinese-made velvet prayer rugs that pilgrims brought back as presents for their families. She also reflected that only Egyptian Copts tattooed a cross on their wrists. She concluded that Egyptians, whether Muslim or Copt, were obsessed with showing off their religiosity, which frequently did not go beyond the zibiba and the tattooed cross.

Three girls came into the restaurant and ordered sandwiches. They noticed Professor M and they started to giggle exaggeratedly: "Look, look what she's done to herself!" Professor M looked at them in amazement, for their clothing, or rather their veiling attire, was arguably more ridiculous than her own normal clothes. Their garments looked more like nightgowns glued to their bodies, worn on top of tight jeans, with several layers of bright-colored head covers and cheap accessories and very heavy makeup. Professor M ignored them, following the wise proverb, "No answer is the best answer." She finished her meal, paid her check, and left the restaurant with a full stomach. She remembered the full moon and her boyfriend. She must buy a phone card for twenty-five pounds so she could make an international call, and she must buy a bottle of Old Stag whiskey for seventy pounds. She would buy the small one, then. She bought the card and then went to Orphanidis's store, but found it closed. She was surprised. She took the bus and went to another store at the end of the street. The young man beside her tried to move closer to her. She gave him a stern silent look; he ignored her and pretended that he was looking out of the window. The other store was closed. "What's wrong today?!" She tried to remember which Muslim month it was or whether there was a special religious occasion that may have mandated that liquor stores be closed. But she still insisted on buying the bottle of whiskey, even if she had to go downtown in the heat and in the midst of all these crowds. For she had decided: "Today, I'm gonna pamper myself."

She made the mistake of getting onto the women's car in the metro. She almost fell between the rails amid the pressing crowds of overweight women as they got on and off the car. She damned herself and the day some government official conceded to the demands of these savages and assigned two coaches for women only. No sooner did she get on than the women and girls begin to eye her with suspicion, displeasure, and disapproval. One of the veiled women hurled a nasty comment at her before she got off: "God forgive us! Why don't you just take off all your clothes?!" Professor M was taken aback, but when she looked around her, she understood: the Muslim veiled women thought that she was Christian, and the Christian women disapproved of the fact that another Christian woman would be wearing a short skirt and a sleeveless top. This generation had never seen legs and arms before. Professor M sighed as she remembered her university days at Ain Shams almost twenty years ago, when girls used to show off their legs. Those who used to cover their hair were labeled "fallaha" and considered baladi. The girls used to consult with each other about tailors and fashion magazines. . . . Aaah! What a pity! Cairo had now unfortunately been ruralized. She quickly reminded herself: "Today, I'm gonna pamper myself," before she started lapsing into nostalgia for the good old days, and the girls of the good old days, and Cairo of the good old days.

At Mubarak metro station—better known as Ramses station, even after the state officials had dethroned the king from his central position in the square among his subjects and dragged him alone in chains and dumped him on the Cairo–Alexandria desert road—a girl with complete body veiling, known as isdal, got on the metro and asked the women passengers to repeat the prayer of travel after her, which some of them did. This was something Professor M had not heard before, even though it had started spreading a few months back: "Subhan al-lazi sakhar lana haza . . . wa inna li rabbina lamunqalibun" (Thanks be to God who provided us with this . . . unto him we shall return). You would hear these words in everything that you got into or mounted, from the elevator to the bicycle to the motorbike to the car to EgyptAir flights. Professor

M smiled as she wondered whether couples recited the same verse before having sex, since that also was a case of mounting! She imagined how the husband would be turned over after he had finished mounting his wife, who had been provided for him, and she let off an almost impudent laugh. Professor M repeated in a loud voice: "Please, God, don't let the metro be turned over," and she got off the women's car and hopped into the mixed compartment at Orabi station. A bearded man was preaching aloud to the passengers, urging them to perform their prayers and avoid sinful acts. Professor M found herself saying in a loud sarcastic voice, "Is this a new job on the metro that you get paid for? Does anyone who knows a couple of verses from the Qur'an get on the metro and start preaching to people?" The bearded man gave her a wicked look as he yelled at her, "How dare you say this when you are not covering your body? God damn you!" Professor M replied angrily: "God damn you! Is this your life problem? Have you solved all the problems in the world except for my uncovered hair and arms? How petty!" The passengers intervened, some to calm them down and others to egg them on; some made room for Professor M and asked her to sit next to them; while others told her to go to the women's coach. The one closest to her asked, "Are you Muslim or Christian?" She replied with disgust, "What business is it of yours? I'm Egyptian." The man mumbled: "Mmm, I see. . . ." The metro stopped at Isaaf station, and she got off with the crowds. She walked mechanically toward the Twenty-sixth of July exit. Suddenly she stopped and asked herself why she had gotten off at this station. What was it that she wanted to do? Those miserable creatures had interrupted her chain of thought. Oh yes! She was going to the liquor store to buy a small bottle of whiskey. She reminded herself of the day's motto, "Today, I'm gonna pamper myself." Her determination not to allow anything to ruin her decision for the day increased. She walked toward the store and found it open and bought the bottle. She started craving a piece of gateau. She crossed the street and went to al-Abd pastry shop on Talaat Harb Street. She bought a fruit-topped gateau and enjoyed savoring it. The cake apparently improved Professor M's mood, to the extent that she caught herself relaxed, walking lazily, almost coquettishly, when she was known for her military-like stride. She smiled to herself and the passersby. Now, should she take the metro again to Munib or take a cab directly to the Upper Egypt bus terminal? She decided to spend the ten pounds and take a cab even though she knew it would be difficult to get a cab driver to accept this sum. She tried her luck. No one wanted the ten pounds. She walked toward the Tahrir metro station. A cab stopped in front of her at the traffic light. She looked at the driver and asked, "Munib for ten pounds?"

"Make it fifteen."

"Ten."

"Thirteen."

"Ten."

"Ok, eleven."

"I said ten."

"Get in."

Professor M got into the cab and told him to drop her off inside the bus terminal.

"No, I'll drop you off outside."

"No, inside, otherwise why do you think I took you? I could've taken the metro."

The driver eyed her through his rear mirror and said, "Lady, you took a cab, you didn't take me."

Professor M suddenly realized the connotation of what she had just said, so she added, trying to mend things, "I'm sorry, I meant took a cab." He went round Talaat Harb Square and headed toward the Corniche.

"Driver, aren't you going to take Salah Salim Road?"

"No, the Corniche is nicer, and I might pick up another passenger on the way."

"Are you gonna take me all around Cairo so that you can pick up another passenger?"

"Lady, nobody goes where you want to go for ten pounds."

"I never twisted your arm! You're the one who stopped."

"The road is clear ahead of us."

She looked at her watch. It was four-thirty and she knew that it would take her another four hours to get to Fayoum by public transportation. The full moon would be out before she could watch it rising and she would not be able to call her boyfriend after eight. She prayed to God that the remainder of the journey would be easy. The young driver turned on an Umm Kulthum cassette tape. Professor M enjoyed listening and lit a cigarette and offered one to the driver.

"Is it a Marlboro?"

"No, it's a local Boston. Had I bought Marlboros I would not have been able to afford taking you."

"Are you gonna start with 'taking you' again?"

"I mean taking the cab. You know what I mean. Cut it out!"

"Lady, you look like you're really broke. Its only ten pounds! No problem, if you don't have it."

"Are you trying to butter me up?"

The cab finally arrived at Munib Terminal. Professor M told him to drive in. "Give me a pound for the toll."

"No, just drive in."

He stopped in front of a security guard, who signaled him to enter, but the driver asked him whether he should pay the toll.

The security guard answered in the negative. So the driver asked him, "Don't you want your tea?" Then, turning around, he added, "Give him a pound, lady."

"Are you gonna dish out tips out of my pocket?!"

The driver and the security guard laughed. At the terminal, she got off in front of the row of service cabs to Ibshaway. She handed the driver the ten-pound note. He unfolded it, saying, "Brand new! I'm gonna keep it for good luck!" Professor M laughed and bid him goodbye.

She got on the first microbus scheduled to leave, but she found that some passengers were getting off in exasperation as the driver calmly repeated that it would be his turn to leave even if the next car were full. Professor M did not understand what was happening and looked anxiously at her watch. It was almost five o'clock. If things continued this way, she would never make it home until after sunset. "God help me!"

The driver loaded one passenger's luggage on top of the car but he didn't have a rope to tie it. No one knew where he got some nylon stockings and, drenched in sweat, started tying the boxes without responding to the passengers' sarcastic comments: "Come on, man, hurry up. Are we gonna spend the night here in the terminal?" "For God's sake, driver, we want to get going." "Whose face did we wake up to today? Someone's bad luck in this car." The sarcastic comments continued as the driver grew increasingly muddled. The other driver filled up his minibus with passengers so he could get going as well. Finally, the vehicle was full while the driver was still trying to tie the boxes. The nylon stocking tore when the driver pulled hard at it and bounced in the face of the passenger who owned the box, so he started to insult the driver and damn his inadequacy. The car rolled out very slowly onto the Ring Road. "Is this the speed you drive at? It will be ten hours before we get there."

Professor M surrendered to her fate. The moon would be full the next day as well, and she would be able to call up her boyfriend at an appropriate time and have a drink. But she still hoped deep inside that fate would be on her side so that she could make her wish of pampering herself that day and not the next come true. She overheard the driver speaking on his mobile phone: "Umm Muhammad, find me a long rope, I'm on my way right now. Yes, I'm coming home." The passengers—men and women, peasant and urban—started making fun of the thick-skinned driver again: "What?! Umm Muhammad!" "Are we still going to go to your place?" "Have pity on us! Don't you have any feelings at all? You're so inconsiderate!" "Buy us dinner, then." "We won't leave the vehicle until you take each and every one of us to his house." The driver did not respond. "If it were another driver, he would have thrown us all off." They all started laughing. After the Mariutiya Canal the driver headed toward Faysal Street and then came to a halt at the end of the street. He got off quickly and crossed the street. Umm Muhammad in her peasant dress was waiting for him on the other side with the coil of plastic rope. The driver grabbed it and crossed the street without really paying attention to the speeding cars. He was almost run over. The passengers yelled, "Be careful! You're the only one we've got." The driver returned to the minibus that he had left in the middle of the street, got on the top of the car, and tied on the boxes with the rope. Finally he returned to his seat and the car dashed off. On the way, Professor M sent an SMS to her boyfriend, telling him that she would be home by eight-thirty. Her boyfriend called her after receiving her message. She told him to hang up and that she would call him later. He asked her to explain why. She told him she would explain later. She got off with another passenger on the new highway, after Shakshuk. They took another collective cab going to the Lake Qarun intersection. At the foot of the village of Tunis to the west she pressed the bell inside the car. The driver stopped. She paid the fee and got off. She had barely started walking up toward the village when she met her neighbor coming down on his motorbike. She couldn't believe her luck! She got on behind him and he gave her a ride home. "Today, I'm gonna pamper myself," hummed Professor M to herself. She quickly took a shower. She recharged her mobile phone with the prepaid card. She prepared a drink and went up to the rooftop to watch the moon rising and call her boyfriend and pamper herself.

Translated by Samia Mehrez

About the Authors

AHMED ALAIDY (b. 1974) studied marketing at Cairo University. He has worked as a scriptwriter for quiz shows and the cinema, and is also a book designer. He has written satirical stories for younger readers and participated in international writers' programs at Iowa University and Hong Kong Baptist University. He has previously published a long short story. *Being Abbas el Abd* is his first novel.

AHMED KHALED TAWFIK (b. 1962) is a medical doctor and writer who specializes in horror fiction and youth literature, of which he has published several series. He has also written poetry and has translated numerous western classics into Arabic, including *Fight Club*. He is a columnist with the Egyptian weekly *Al-Dustur* and is a regular contributor to *Buss wa tull* website. He has published several short stories and novels as well as a number of articles and essays that can be found online.

AHMED MOURAD was born in Cairo in 1978. He started working at his father's photography studio when he was only fifteen years old. He graduated from the Higher Institute of Cinema and made photography his profession. His varied life experiences motivated him to begin writing and his photographic background adds significant value to his writing style.

ALAA AL ASWANY was born in Cairo in 1957. Educated in Cairo and Chicago, he is currently a dentist by profession. He is a columnist with several Egyptian newspapers where he writes about literature, politics, and social issues. He has become an internationally bestselling author after the publication of his much-acclaimed novel *The Yacoubian Building*, which has been translated into twenty languages and adapted as a major film production. His other works include *Chicago* and a story collection titled *Friendly Fire.*

317

ALBERT COSSERY (1913–2008) is a French-speaking writer of Egyptian origin who was born in Cairo but settled in France since 1945. He published eight novels set in Egypt and other Arab countries that portray the contrast between poverty and wealth, the powerful and the powerless, in a witty although dramatic style. In 1990 Cossery was awarded the Grand Prix de La Francophonie de l'Academie Française and in 2005 the Grand Prix Poncetton de la SGDL.

AMINA AL-SAID (1910–95) was born in Asyut and brought up in Cairo. A leading feminist, journalist, and activist, in the 1940s she became the first paid female journalist to work for a mainstream publishing house, Dar al-Hilal, and was elected vice president of the Board of the Press Syndicate in 1956. She wrote for al-*Musawwar* and founded and edited the pan-Arab journal *Hawa*.

ANDRÉE CHEDID was born in Cairo in 1920. She grew up in a family of mixed Lebanese and Egyptian ancestry and in 1946 moved with her physician husband to Paris. She is a prolific poet and fiction writer, her fiction writing grounded in images and emotions of the Middle East. Her poetry is, as she describes it, "free of time and place." She writes in French and her work has been widely translated.

ANNE-MARIE DROSSO was born in Cairo in 1951 and raised in the heart of downtown. She left Egypt to pursue graduate studies in British Columbia, Canada. Her studies led to teaching positions in economics, a law degree, and work for an administrative tribunal. She is of Syrian/Italian descent and writes in English about Cairo from her perspective as a member of a minority in Egypt. She lives in Monterey, California.

BAHAA TAHER was born in Cairo in 1935. He studied history and published his first short story in 1964. He was active in the left-wing and avant-garde literary circles of the 1960s, and his views cost him his job at the Radio & TV Broadcasting Union and he was prevented from publishing in the mid-1970s during the Sadat era . In 1981 he chose to leave for Geneva to work as a translator for the United Nations. After many years of exile in Switzerland, he has returned to Egypt and is very active in all cultural circles. He received Egypt's highest national award for literature twice during the 1990s and was awarded the first Arabic Booker Prize for his novel *Sunset Oasis*.

CHAFIKA HAMAMSY grew up in Zamalek. She received an MA in English literature from the American University in Cairo and for many years headed the

Catalog Department of the AUC Library, where she later became a consultant. Hamamsy started publishing after her retirement. She is the widow of the leading Egyptian journalist Galal al-Din al-Hamamsy.

GAMAL AL-GHITANI was born in 1945 in Sohag, Upper Egypt. He wrote his first story in 1959 at the age of fourteen. His work is infused with history, and his fascination with medieval Arabic writing, especially the work of the Egyptian historian Ibn Iyas, is reflected in his great historical novel *Zayni Barakat*. He is a novelist, short story writer, and journalist. Al-Ghitani is editor-in-chief of the influential literary weekly *Akhbar al-adab*. He worked closely with Naguib Mahfouz and has received numerous national, regional, and international awards for his literary works.

HALA EL BADRY was born in 1954 in Cairo. She worked as a correspondent for *Ruz al-Yusuf* and *Sabah al-kheir* in Baghdad. She is deputy editor-in-chief of Egypt's *Radio and TV Magazine* and the author of several novels, including *A Certain Woman* which was awarded Best Novel of the year at the Cairo International Book Fair in 2001.

HAMDI ABU GOLAYYEL was born in 1967 in Fayoum. Of Bedouin origin, he later moved to Cairo. He is the author of three short story collections and two novels, the first of which is *Thieves in Retirement*. He is editor-in-chief of the Popular Studies series, which specializes in folklore research, and writes for the Emirates newspaper *al-Ittihad*. He was awarded the Naguib Mahfouz Medal for Literature in 2008 for his *al-Fa'il* which was translated in 2009 by the American University in Cairo Press as *A Dog with No Tail*.

HAMDY AL-GAZZAR was born in 1970 in Cairo, and has a degree in philosophy from Cairo University. Since 1990 he has published several short stories and articles in the Arabic press, as well as writing and directing three plays. *Black Magic*, his debut novel, was awarded the Sawiris Foundation Prize in Egyptian Literature in 2006.

HANI ABDEL-MOURID was born in 1972 and is an information systems specialist at one of Cairo's public libraries. He was awarded reader's choice awards in 2002 and 2008 for his novels *Ighma'a dakhil tabut* (Passing out in a coffin) and *Kyrie Eleison* respectively.

HASSAN HASSAN (1924–2000) was born in San Remo, Italy, the son of Prince Aziz, the nephew of King Fuad I, and thereby a great-grandson of Khedive Ismail. He was a painter and a pianist and died shortly before his book *In the House of Muhammad Ali* was published.

IBRAHIM ASLAN was born in 1937 in Tanta. He published his first collection of short stories in 1971. *The Heron* is his first novel and was listed among the best 100 novels in Arabic literature and also made into a popular film *Kit Kat*. He worked as the culture editor in the Cairo bureau of the London-based daily newspaper *al-Hayat*. He has a weekly column in *al-Ahram* daily newspaper.

IBRAHIM FARGHALI was born in 1967 in Mansura in the Nile Delta and grew up in Oman and the United Arab Emirates. He has a regular column in the Cairo daily newspaper *al-Ahram* and is author of several short story collections and novels, the last of which, *Awlad al-Gabalawi,* published in 2009, has won great acclaim.

IBRAHIM ISSA was born in 1965 and is one of the most outspoken journalists against the current political regime in Egypt. Editor-in-chief of the daily newspaper *Al-Dostur,* he has been prosecuted for slander and had his works banned several times. He was awarded the Goubran Tweeny (WAN) journalistic award in 2008. Issa also hosts a regular TV show.

IHAB ABDEL HAMID was born in 1977. He has a degree in English literature from Cairo University as well as a ceritificate in translation from the American University in Cairo. He works as a journalist and translator. He was awarded second prize at the Sawiris Literary award competition for Egyptian Literature in 2007.

IHSAN ABDEL QUDDUS (1919–90) graduated from the Faculty of Law in 1942 and while a law trainee joined *Ruz al-Yusuf* magazine as a journalist. In 1944 he began writing filmscripts, followed by two collections of short stories featuring memories of a young man on a visit to Europe. He was inclined toward the sentimental novel. He received many state awards for his prolific writings, and many of his works have been adapted into films and TV series.

ISMAIL WALI AL-DIN was born in 1939 and studied architecture at Cairo University and worked for the Armed Forces until his retirement. A prolific writer, he has published more than twenty novels. Between 1975 and 1995, many of Wali al-Din's novels were turned into films such as *Hammam al-Malatili, al-Batneya,* and *Beit al-Qadi.*

KHAIRY SHALABY was born in 1938 in Kafr al-Sheikh in Egypt's Nile Delta, and has written seventy books, including novels, short stories, historical tales, and critical studies. His works are heavily influenced by his love for *sira* (traditional oral epic poetry) and his pride in the local heritage. He was awarded the Naguib Mahfouz Medal for Literature in 2003 for his novel *The Lodging House* and has received several other distinguished national and regional awards. His novel *The Time-Travels of the Man who Sold Pickles and Sweets* is published by the AUC Press (2010).

KHALED AL KHAMISSI was born in 1962 and is a writer, film director, and producer. He received an MA in political science from the Sorbonne University. He is a journalist who contributes weekly articles to numerous Egyptian newspapers. *Taxi* is his first book and has been a bestseller since its release in January 2007. *Noah's Arc* is his second and most recent work.

MAHMOUD AL-WARDANI was born in 1950 in Cairo. He began writing shortly after leaving university and is the author of three volumes of short stories, six novels, and three works of nonfiction. His stories have appeared in translation in English, German, Italian, and French. Al-Wardani has served as deputy editor-in-chief of the weekly Cairo newspaper *Akhbar al-yawm* and editor of the opinion page of the daily *al-Badil.*

MAY KHALED was born in 1985 and is a graduate of the American University in Cairo, which she used as the setting for her novel *The Last Seat in Ewart Hall* in which she recounts her days at university. She has several artistic interests including choir singing along with writing. Her first work was published in 1998.

MAY AL-TELMISSANY was born in 1965 in Egypt, and is a writer and film critic. She moved to Paris in 1990, completing an MA in French literature in 1995 and translating a number of academic works from French into Arabic. She has written extensively about Egyptian cinema, following a PhD from the University of Montréal focusing on the concept of the *hara* (alley) in Egyptian cinema. She is an assistant professor in modern languages at the University of Ottawa. She has published two collections of short stories and her novel *Dunyazad* has been translated into English.

MEKKAWI SAID was born in 1955 and began his career by writing scripts for documentaries. He published his first selection of short stories in 1981 and in 1991 was awarded the Suad al-Sabbah Award for his novel *Ship Rats*. His novel *Cairo Swan Song* was short-listed for the Arabic Booker Prize in 2007.

MIDHAT GAZALÉ was born in Alexandria, Egypt in 1930(?). Formerly the president of AT&T France, he is currently a special science and technology adviser to the Egyptian prime minister . He is the author of works on mathematics in both French and English. He was made Chevalier dans l'Ordre national du Mérite in 1981.

MIRAL AL-TAHAWY was born in 1968 into the Bedouin al-Hanadi tribe in Egypt. As an adult she left for Cairo University where she studied Hebrew, Persian, Urdu, and English. She writes short stories and novels in classical Arabic, and credits her liberal-minded father with the fact that she obtained an education despite living in traditional seclusion. She is the author of *The Tent*, *Blue Aubergine*, and *Gazelle Tracks*, all of which have been translated into English by the American University in Cairo Press. Her work has also appeared in the UK's *Banipal* magazine.

M.M. TAWFIK was born in 1956 in Cairo. He earned degrees in civil engineering (Cairo University), international law (University of Paris), and international relations (International Institute of Public Administration in Paris) and has pursued careers in engineering, diplomacy, and writing. He conducts an online writers' workshop and is literary editor of an online magazine. He is the author of two novels and three volumes of short stories in Arabic, a selection from which was published in English under the title *The Day the Moon Fell*. His novel *Tifl shaqi ismuhu antar* has been translated into English by the author under the title *Murder in the Tower of Happiness*.

MONA PRINCE was born in 1970. She received a PhD in English literature from Ain Shams University and is currently assistant professor at Suez Canal University. She is an essayist, a translator, a short story writer, and a novelist. She has published one collection of short stories and two novels, in addition to uncollected short stories and essays in different local and regional magazines and newspapers. Her short story collection and her first novel *Three Suitcases for Departure* have earned her distinguished national and regional literary awards.

MUHAMMAD AL-FAKHARANI was born in 1975. His work as a geologist enabled him to visit many remote areas in Egypt. He authored three short story collections prior to the publication of his first novel *An Interval for Bewilderment* which addresses the marginalized in society and created a stir in the literary community due to its daring language and subject matter. His collection titled *Hayat* was awarded the Dubai Literary Award.

MUHAMMAD GALAL was born in 1924. He graduated from law school and pursued a career in journalism. He eventually became editor-in-chief of *Radio & TV Magazine*. Beginning in 1961, he published over 20 novels and authored several plays. Many of his works have been adapted into films. He received several national awards.

MUHAMMAD AL-MUWAILIHI (1868–1930) worked with his journalist father Ibrahim al-Muwailihi on introducing several newspapers in Egypt. He was briefly exiled following his participation in the Urabi uprising in 1882. His famous work *A Period of Time: A Study and Translation of Hadith 'Isa ibn Hisham* is a celebrated work that critiques the era of colonialism in Egypt.

MUHAMMAD SALAH AL-AZAB was born in 1981 in Cairo. He published several short story collections and three novels. He won the Supreme Council for Culture Award for the short story twice, in 1999 and 2003 respectively, as well as the award for best novel in 2003 along with several other awards from Kuwait, the Emirates, and Libya.

MUSTAFA ZIKRI was born in 1966 in Helwan near Cairo. He started studying philosophy at Alexandria University then decided to attend the Film Academy in Cairo, from which he graduated in 1992 to become an author and scriptwriter. Zikri belongs to the so-called "Nineties generation" of Egyptian writers; his first novel, *Drivel about a Gothic Labyrinth*, like *'Afarit al-asfalt* (Asphalt Goblins), drew on his experience of lowlife Helwan. His novel *Mir'at 2002* (Mirror 2002) won him the Sawiris Literary Award for Egyptian literature in 2006.

NABIL NAOUM GORGY was born in 1944 in Cairo. He studied engineering at Cairo University then moved to the United States to work as an engineer in New York. His first novel, *The Door* was published in Egypt 1977. In 1979 he returned to Cairo, where he opened a gallery for modern art. In the 1980s he published a series of short story collections, twenty stories came out in English translation under the title *The Slave's Dream and Other Stories* in 1991. He now lives in Paris.

NAGUIB MAHFOUZ (1911–2006) is probably the best-known Arabic writer of the twentieth century. He studied philosophy at Cairo University, graduating in 1934. Throughout his career he held many governamental positions within the Ministry of Culture until his retirement in 1973. Mahfouz has written over 30 novels and short stories, many of them about the Cairo neighborhood of Gamaliya that he knew intimately. He was awarded the 1988 Nobel prize for literature. His most noted works include *Children of the Alley* and *The Cairo Trilogy*.

NAIM SABRI was born in 1946 and graduated from the Faculty of Engineering, Cairo University in 1968. He started his literary career as a poet and published two collections of poems and authored two plays. Since 1995, he has become a full-time writer and has published several novels.

OMAR TAHER was born in 1973 in Sohag. He started work in journalism upon graduation from Helwan University. He is a regular contributor to several newspapers and magazines. He is also a scriptwriter and songwriter, and participates in TV shows. He is known for his comical satiric style of writing.

RADWA ASHOUR was born in 1946 in Cairo. She graduated from the Faculty of Arts, Cairo University, and has an MA in comparative literature from Cairo University and a PhD in African–American Literature from the University of Massachusetts at Amherst. She is currently professor of English and comparative literature at Ain Shams University and is co-editor of the *Encyclopaedia of Arab Women Writers*. Her works include five volumes in literary criticism, several collections of short stories, and novels. As a translator Ashour co-translated, supervised, and edited the Arabic translation of Vol. 9 of *The Cambridge History of Literary Criticism*, 2005. She has also translated Mourid Barghouti's *Midnight and Other Poems*, 2008. Her novel *Granada* won the Cairo International Book Fair Book of the Year award in 1994. She was awarded the Constantine Cavafy Prize for Literature in 2007.

RAOUF MOSAD was born in 1937(?). He was raised in Egypt as a Protestant but later renounced his faith. He was imprisoned during the 1950s along with many of Egypt's leftist intellectuals. After his release, he left Egypt, finally settling in Holland. His writings reflect concern for minority rights and discrimination and are noted for their audacious representation of many taboo subjects. He is the author of several noted novels including *Ostrich Egg*, *The Temper of Crocodiles*, and *Ithaca*.

ROBERT SOLÉ was born in 1946 in Cairo. He moved to France at the age of eighteen and studied journalism at Lille University. He writes in French and works for *Le Monde* where he has been a correspondent in several locations including Washington and Rome. He is the author of more than ten novels, all of which revolve around Egypt and Egyptian history. Several have been translated into English.

SAHAR AL-MOUGY was born in 1963 in Cairo. She studied English literature and is currently a professor of English literature at Cairo University. She has published a collection of short stories and three novels, the most recent of which is *N*, named after the Arabic letter. She is an active participant in the Women and Memory Forum, a regular contributor to the Egyptian independent press, as well as a radio announcer. She was awarded the Constantine Cavafy Prize in 2007 for her novel *N*.

SALWA BAKR was born in 1949 and has become one of Egypt's most respected novelists and short story writers. She graduated with a degree in business management and another in literary criticism. A leftist and activist since her university years, she was imprisoned in 1989 for her support of the Egyptian labor movement. She is the author of several short story collections and novels that have been translated into English as well as many other languages. She won the German national radio award for literature in 1993.

SAMIA SERAGELDIN was born and raised in Egypt, educated in Europe, and emigrated to the United States with her family in 1980. She holds an M.S. in politics from the University of London, and is a writer, political essayist, editor and literary critic. She is also a part-time instructor at Duke University.

SHEHATA AL-ERIAN was born in 1961. He started his career as a poet, writing in both classical and colloquial Arabic. His first novel *Dikka khashabiya tasaʻ ithnayn bi l-kad* (A Wooden Bench Hardly Big Enough for Two) received the Egyptian National Merit award in 2000.

SONALLAH IBRAHIM was born in 1937. After studying law and drama at Cairo University, he became a journalist until his imprisonment in 1959 as an advocate for the Left. Upon his release in 1964, he briefly returned to journalism in Egypt before moving to Berlin to work for a news agency and to Moscow where he studied cinematography. He returned to Egypt in 1974 and since then has dedicated his time to writing. Ibrahim is well known for his documentary novels that employ a literary style unique in Arabic writing. He is the author of several novels and short stories, as well as a dozen children's books. In 1998 his novel *Sharaf* received the award for best Egyptian novel at the Cairo International Book Fair.

TAHA HUSSEIN (1889–1973) was one of the most influential Egyptian writers and intellectuals. He was the first graduate to receive a Ph.D. and become a professor of Arabic literature in the newly established Fuad al-Awwal Univerity (now Cairo University). Perceived as the figurehead of the modernist movement in Egypt, he earned the title of Dean of Arabic letters. He was an encyclopedic figure: a translator, poet, and essayist. He also wrote many novels, though in the west he is best known for his autobiography, *al-Ayyam* which was published in English as *An Egyptian Childhood* (1932) and *The Stream of Days* (1943).

THARWAT ABAZA (1927–2002) graduated from the Faculty of Law, Cairo University in 1950. He was appointed editor-in-chief of the *Radio and TV Magazine* in 1974. He wrote scores of novels and short stories about life in the city and the countryside, and the kind of connections and clashes governing relations among different social strata. He was one of the founders of the Writers' Union and later its president. In recognition of his outstanding works, Abaza received numerous honors and awards including the Medal of Science and Arts of the first degree and the state Appreciation Award in literature.

WAGUIH GHALI (1920?–1968) studied medicine and was known for his leftist views. As a journalist he visited Israel and reported news from a different perspective. He left Egypt during the 1950s and later committed suicide in London. *Beer in the Snooker Club* is his only novel. It has recently been translated into Arabic by Iman Mersal.

YAHYA HAKKI (1905–90) started his career as a lawyer and then served in different parts of the world as a diplomat. After resigning from the diplomatic corps he devoted himself wholly to writing and became one of a small group of intellectuals who laid the foundations for the literary renaissance in Egypt. He published four collections of short stories, one novel, and a novella, *The Lamp of Umm Hashim,* which was twice translated into English. He was editor of the literary magazine *al-Majalla* from 1961 to 1971, when it was banned in Egypt. During that period, and even before, Hakki championed budding Egyptian authors whose works he admired and believed in.

YASSER ABDEL LATIF was born in 1969. He graduated from Cairo University with a degree in philosophy in 1994. He has published two collections of poetry and is also a screenwriter for several documentaries. He volunteers his time conducting writing workshops to assist aspiring writers. In 2005 he received the Sawiris Literary Award for his first novel *The Law of Inheritance*.

YUSUF IDRIS (1927–92) graduated from medical school in 1951 and practiced medicine for several years. His first collection of stories was published in 1954. In 1960 he gave up medicine to become editor of the Cairo daily newspaper *al-Gumhuriya* and continued to write and publish prolifically until his death in 1992. He is deemed one of the great figures of twentieth-century Arabic literature. Many of his works are in the Egyptian vernacular, and he was considered a master of the short story. He sought to lay the foundations of a modern Egyptian theater based on popular traditions and folklore. He was nominated several times for the Nobel prize in literature.

YUSUF AL-SIBAIE (1917–78) was an army officer who had a passion for literature. He headed the Al-Ahram organization and was appointed minister of culture in 1973. He was assassinated in Cyprus in 1978 due to his support of Sadat's peace treaty with Israel. He was known as the Knight of Romance of Egyptian literature, and many of his works have been been adapted into films.

Bibliography

Ahmed Alaidy, *Being Abbas el Abd*. Translated by Humphrey Davies. Cairo: AUC Press, 2006.

Ahmed Khaled Tawfik, *Yutubiya*. Cairo: Merit, 2008.

Ahmed Mourad, *Vertigo*. Cairo: Merit, 2007.

Alaa Al Aswany, *The Yacoubian Building*. Translated by Humphrey Davies. Cairo: AUC Press, 2004.

Albert Cossery, *Proud Beggars*. Translated by Thomas W. Cushing. Boston: Black Sparrow Books, 1981.

Amina al-Said, *Akhir al-tariq: Ma'sa min samim al-haya*. Cairo: Dar al-Hilal, 1972.

Andrée Chedid, *From Sleep Unbound*. Translated by Bettina L. Knapp and Sharon Spencer. Ohio: Swallow Press, 1983.

Anne-Marie Drosso, *Cairo Stories*. London: Telegram Books, 2007.

Bahaa Taher, *Nuqtat al-nur*. Cairo: Dar al-Hilal, 2001.

Chafika Hamamsy, *Zamalek: The Changing Life of a Cairo Elite 1850–1945*. Cairo: AUC Press, 2005.

Gamal al-Ghitani, "Harith al-athar" in *Risalat al-Basa'ir fi l-masa'ir*. Cairo: Dar al-Hilal, 1989.

_____, *Pyramid Texts*. Translated by Humphrey Davies. Cairo: AUC Press, 2007.

Hala El Badry, *al-Sibaha fi qumqum*. Cairo: Dar al-Ghadd, 1988.

Hamdi Abu Golayyel, *Thieves in Retirement*. Translated by Marilyn Booth. Cairo: AUC Press, 2007.

Hamdy al-Gazzar, *Black Magic*. Translated by Humphrey Davies. Cairo: AUC Press, 2007.

Hani Abdel-Mourid, *Kyrie Eleison*. Cairo: al-Dar, 2008.

Hassan Hassan, *In the House of Muhammad Ali*. Cairo: AUC Press, 2000.

Ibrahim Aslan, *The Heron*. Translated by Elliott Colla. Cairo: AUC Press, 2005.

Ibrahim Farghali, *The Smiles of Saints*. Translated by Andy Smart and Nadia Fouda-Smart. Cairo: AUC Press, 2007.

Ibrahim Issa, *Ashbah wataniya*. Cairo: Merit, 2005.

Ihab Abdel Hamid, *'Ushaq kha'ibun*. Cairo: Merit, 2005.

Ihsan Abdel Quddus, *La tutfi' al-shams*. Cairo: Dar al-Hilal, 1959.

———, *Ana Hurra*. Cairo: Dar al-Ma'arif, 1958.

Ismail Wali al-Din, *Hammam al-Malatili*. Cairo: Dar Gharib, 1976.

Khairy Shalaby, *The Time-Travels of the Man Who Sold Pickles and Sweets*. Translated by Michael Cooperson. Cairo: AUC Press, 2010.

———, *Sariq al-farah*. Cairo: Dar al-Fikr, 1991.

Khaled Al Khamissi, *Taxi*. Translated by Jonathan Wright. London: Aflame Books, 2008.

Mahmoud Al-Wardani, *Heads Ripe for Plucking*. Translated by Hala Halim. Cairo: AUC Press, 2008.

———, *Musiqa al-mol*. Cairo: Merit, 2005.

May Khaled, *Miq'ad akhir fi qa'at Iwart*. Cairo: Sharqiyyat, 2005.

May al-Telmissany, *Heliopolis*, Cairo: Sharqiyyat, 2000.

Mekkawi Said, *Cairo Swan Song*. Translated by Adam Talib. Cairo: AUC Press, 2009.

Midhat Gazalé, *Pyramids Road*. Cairo: AUC Press, 2004.

Miral al-Tahawy, *Blue Aubergine*. Translated by Anthony Calderbank. Cairo: AUC Press, 2002.

M.M. Tawfik, *Murder in the Tower of Happiness*. Translated by M.M. Tawfik. Cairo: AUC Press, 2008.

Mona Prince, "Innaharda hadalla' nafsi," *www.kikah.com*.

Muhammad al-Fakharani, *Fasil li-l-Dahsha*. Cairo: al-Dar, 2007.

Muhammad Galal, *Ayyam al-Mounira*. Cairo: Dar Suad al-Sabbah, 1993.

Muhammad al-Muwailihi, *A Period of Time: A Study and Translation of Hadith 'Isa ibn Hisham*. Translated by Roger Allen. Reading: Ithaca Press, 1992.

Muhammad Salah al-Azab, *Wuquf mutakarrir*. Cairo: Merit, 2006.

Mustafa Zikri, "Ma la ya'rifuhu Amin," in *Hura' mataha qutiya*. Cairo: Sharqiyyat, 1997.

Nabil Naoum Gorgy, "Al-Qahira madina saghira," in *al-Qahira Madina Saghira*. Cairo: al-Markaz al-Firinsi li l-Tarjama, 1985.

Naguib Mahfouz, *Children of the Alley*. Translated by Peter Theroux. Cairo: AUC Press, 2001.

———, *Khan al-Khalili*. Translated by Roger Allen. Cairo: AUC Press, 2008.

———, *Midaq Alley*. Translated by Trevor Le Gassick. Cairo: AUC Press, 1975.

_____, *Palace of Desire*. Translated by William Maynard Hutchins and Olive E. Kenny. Cairo: AUC Press, 1991.

_____, *Palace Walk*. Translated by William Maynard Hutchins and Olive E. Kenny. Cairo: AUC Press, 1989.

_____, *The Day the Leader was Killed*. Translated by Malak Hashem. Cairo: AUC Press, 1997.

Naim Sabri, *al-Hayy al-sabiʿ*. Cairo: al-Hadara li-l-Nashr, 2001.

Omar Taher, *Shaklaha bazit*. Cairo: Atlas li-l-Nashr, 2005.

Radwa Ashour, *Qitʿa min Urubba*. Cairo: Dar al-Shorouk, 2003.

Raouf Mosad, *Ithaka*. Cairo: Merit, 2007.

Robert Solé, *Birds of Passage*. Translated by John Brownjohn. London: Harvill Press, 2000.

Sahar al-Mougy, *Nun*, Cairo: Dar al-Hilal, 2007.

Salwa Bakr, *Aranib*, Cairo: Dar Sina, 1994.

_____, "Thirty-one Beautiful Green Trees," in *The Wiles of Men*. Translated by Denys Johnson-Davies. London: Quartet Books, 1992.

Samia Serageldin, *The Cairo House*. Syracuse University Press, 2000.

Shehata al-Erian, *Sahibat al-akharin*. Cairo: Merit, 2005.

Sonallah Ibrahim, *Sharaf*. Cairo: Dar al-Hilal, 2000.

_____, *Zaat*. Translated by Anthony Calderbank. Cairo: AUC Press, 2001.

Sonallah Ibrahim and Jean Pierre Ribière, *Cairo from Edge to Edge*. Translated by Samia Mehrez. Cairo: AUC Press, 1998.

Taha Hussein, *A Man of Letters*. Translated by Mona El-Zayyat. Cairo: AUC Press, 1994.

Tharwat Abaza, *al-Dabab*. Cairo: Dar al-Maʿaraif, 1965.

Waguih Ghali, *Beer in the Snooker Club*. London: Serpent's Tail, 1987.

Yahya Hakki, *The Lamp of Umm Hashim*. Translated by Denys Johnson-Davies, Cairo: AUC Press 2004.

Yasser Abdel Latif, *Qanun al-wiratha*. Cairo: Merit, 2002.

Yusuf Idris, "The Siren," in *Rings of Burnished Brass*. Translated by Catherine Cobham. Cairo: AUC Press, 1990.

_____, "The Dregs of the City," in *The Cheapest Nights*. Translated by Wadida Wassef. London: Three Continents Press, 1989.

Yusuf al-Sibaie, *Nahnu la nazraʿ al-shawk*. Cairo: Maktabat al-Khanji, 1968.

Glossary

Allah hayy God is alive.

Amm title of respect for an elderly person; literally 'uncle.'

'ashwa'iyyat informal urban settlements.

baladi literally 'of the country;' popular, but also low-class.

baladi bread brown, flat, round loaves of bread.

balah al-sham literally 'the dates of Syria,' a finger-like honeyed pastry originating in Greater Syria.

basbousa a sweet cake made of semolina soaked in syrup.

bashkateb chief clerk.

bawwab doorman; concierge.

Bek Turkish title that denotes distinction at the social or economic level.

Burda/Burdat al-Busayri a Sufi poem extolling the Prophet Muhammad.

busara mashed fava beans with parsley.

colla glue.

dallala a woman peddler who provides door to door cosmetics, clothing, services, including matchmaking if needed.

Effendi Turkish title for civil servants and educated individuals.

fallaha peasant girl; may be used as a derogatory reference to denote low class.

Fatiha the opening verse of the Qura'n.

feddan around 80 hectares.

fiqh Islamic Jurisprudence.

fitir pastry usually eaten with cheese or honey.

ful fava beans.

ful nabit fava bean sprouts.

futuwwa thug.

gallabiya a loose fitting, long garment for comfort and ease of wear.

ghorza coffee shop or space for smoking hashish.

goza waterpipe for smoking hashish.

guziya pastry made with walnuts.

habara a shawl or wrap worn across the face starting under the eyes.

Hagg(a) title that denotes a person who has been on pilgrimage but also a title of social respect that came into wider circulation with the increasing Islamization of the public sphere.

haggala dance a folk dance in Marsa Matruh.

hammam traditional Arab bath.

Hanim title to denote the lady of the house. Also a title for social status.

hara alleyway.

haramlik women's quarters in traditional homes.

harisa a pastry made with semolina.

hashiya postscript; commentary; marginal notes

iftar (Ramadan) the break of fasting at sunset.

imam spiritual and religious leader in Islam.

Infitah the "open door" liberal economic policies of the Sadat era (1971–1981).

insha'allah God willing.

Jarkasi of Circassian origin.

karro donkey-drawn wooden cart.

khan marketplace.

Ka'ba a holy structure located in the Mosque of Mecca that holds the ancient black stone around which Muslim pilgrims circumambulate.

kabab cubes of grilled meat.

kilim Persian word for rug or carpet.

kofta grilled minced meat.

kohl black eyeliner.

kushari a popular dish made of rice, macaroni, and lentils served with fried onion, garlic, and vinegar topped with a hot sauce.

kuskusi couscous with sugar.

la ilaha illa Allah There is no god but God.

luqmat al-qadi a puffy, deep-fried pastry.

maalesh colloquial Egyptian expression that means 'no problem.'

ma'allim boss, owner of a business.

mahallabiya milk and rice pudding.

Mahallawi from Mahalla, a town in the Nile Delta.

mantiq logic.

mashrabiya wood latticed window where clay water containers were placed and through which the women of the household could view the street without being seen.

metahir the person who circumcises children.

mi'assil honeyed tobacco that is used for smoking waterpipes.

mihrab a niche in the wall of a mosque that indicates the *qibla*; that is, the direction of the Ka'ba in Mecca and hence the direction that Muslims should face when praying.

mihzim towels used in a traditional *hammam*.

milaya traditional Egyptian wraparound for women.

mish aged white cheese.

miswak toothpick.

mizmar reed wind instrument.

muezzin the person who calls for prayer at a mosque.

mughat is a prepackaged spice drink, sold in a dark powder form in most Egyptian spice shops. It is prepared with milk and is usually used by pregnant women because of its nutritious value.

mulid birthday of a revered or saintly figure.

mulukhiya green leafy soup with fried coriander and garlic.

munshid singer of religious songs.

nahw grammar.

Naksa literally 'calamity;' is used to refer to the Arab defeat by Israel in 1967.

Pasha title that denotes superior social, political and economic status.

qulqas a variety of taro cultivated in tropical regions for its edible startchy tubers, cooked in a green leafy sauce.

rib'a fourfold; four cycle.

riqq tambourine.

rumi literally 'Byzantine' but used in this text to refer to the new foreign elements of architectural design in Khedive Ismail's modern Cairo.

sabil drinking fountain.

sahlab a pre-packaged spice drink, sold in a white powder form in spice shops. It is prepared with hot milk.

salamlik guesthouse.

shawerma strips of meat grilled on an upright rotating grill.

shawish policeman.

shisha waterpipe.

Sitt literally 'woman;' used as a title of respect to indicate age or class.

subia a sweet drink made of ground rice, coconut, sugar, and milk mixed with water.

subu' celebration of the seventh day of a child's birth.

surra pastry rolled like a small bundle.

taamiya basic and popular flat cakes of minced fava bean with parsley and coriander fried in oil.

tabla drum.

takbeer to say "Allahu Akbar" (God is Great).

takiyis peeling of dead skin after a hot bath in a traditional hammam.

tarawih a long prayer that is performed during the holy month of Ramadan.

tarboush felt, red headcover for men.

tawhid unity.

tikkiya A Sufi hospice consisting of an open courtyard surrounded by arcades on its four sides. Ringing the arcades were the Sufi cells, which were usually small vaulted rooms. Also included were a small mosque and a graveyard.

'ulama religious scholars.

umm mother; mother of someone; also used as a title for respect.

Umm al-Awagiz mother of the destitute.

Usta title used to address various professional workers such as cab drivers, carriage drivers, and so on.

Usul Islamic jurisprudence.

uya traditional handmade frills for women's kerchiefs and shawls.

zaar spirit appeasement ceremony.

zibiba mark on the forehead that attests to regular prayer caused by pressing the forehead against the ground.

zikr remembrance or invocation of God. An Islamic devotional act, it typically involves the repetition of the names of God, supplications or formulas taken from hadith texts, and verses of the Qur'an. In some Sufi orders it is instituted as a ceremonial activity.

Index of Authors